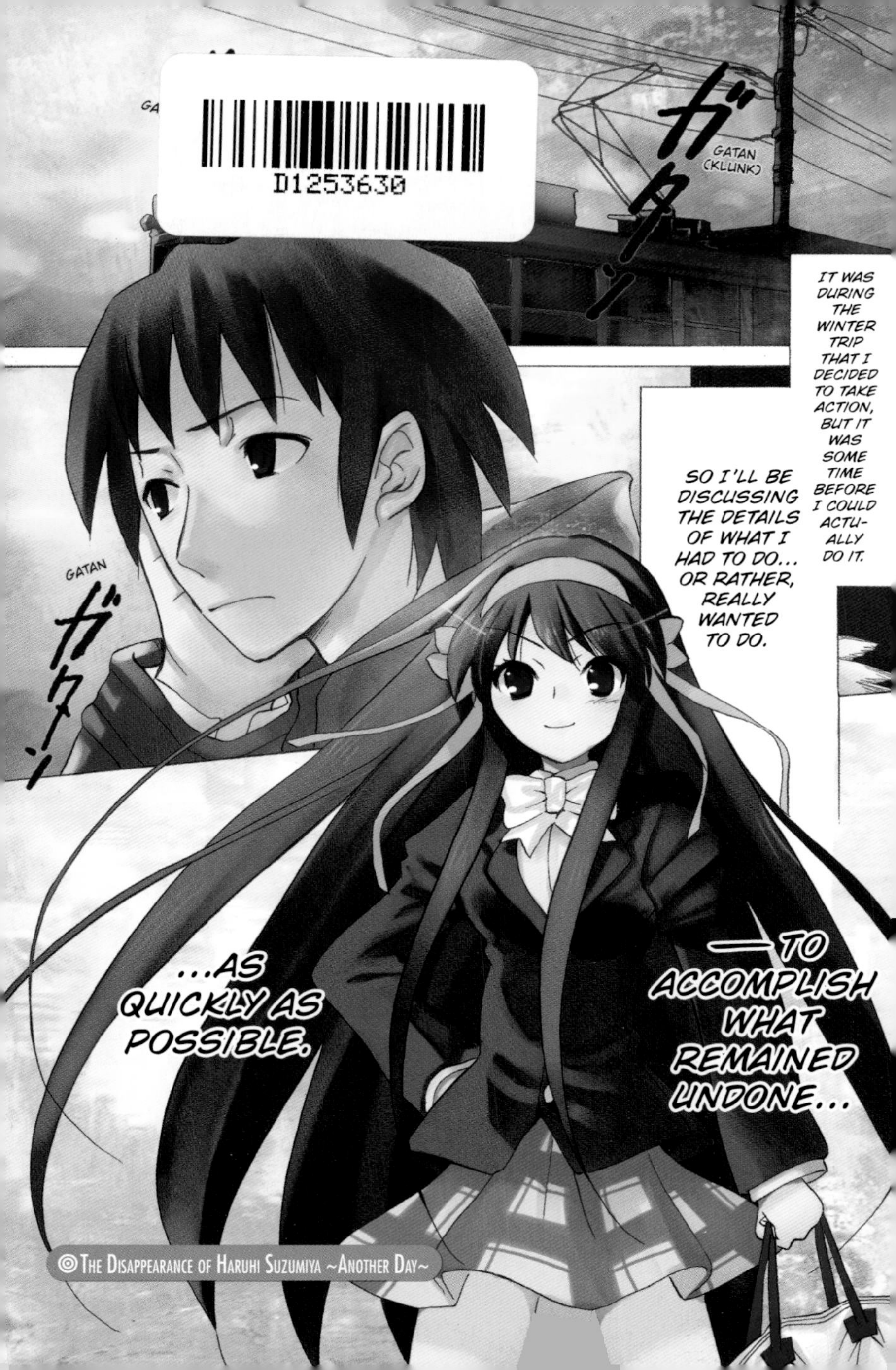
ガタン
GATAN (KLUNK)
IT WAS DURING THE WINTER TRIP THAT I DECIDED TO TAKE ACTION, BUT IT WAS SOME TIME BEFORE I COULD ACTUALLY DO IT.
SO I'LL BE DISCUSSING THE DETAILS OF WHAT I HAD TO DO... OR RATHER, REALLY WANTED TO DO.
GATAN
ガタン
——TO ACCOMPLISH WHAT REMAINED UNDONE...
...AS QUICKLY AS POSSIBLE.
◎The Disappearance of Haruhi Suzumiya ~Another Day~

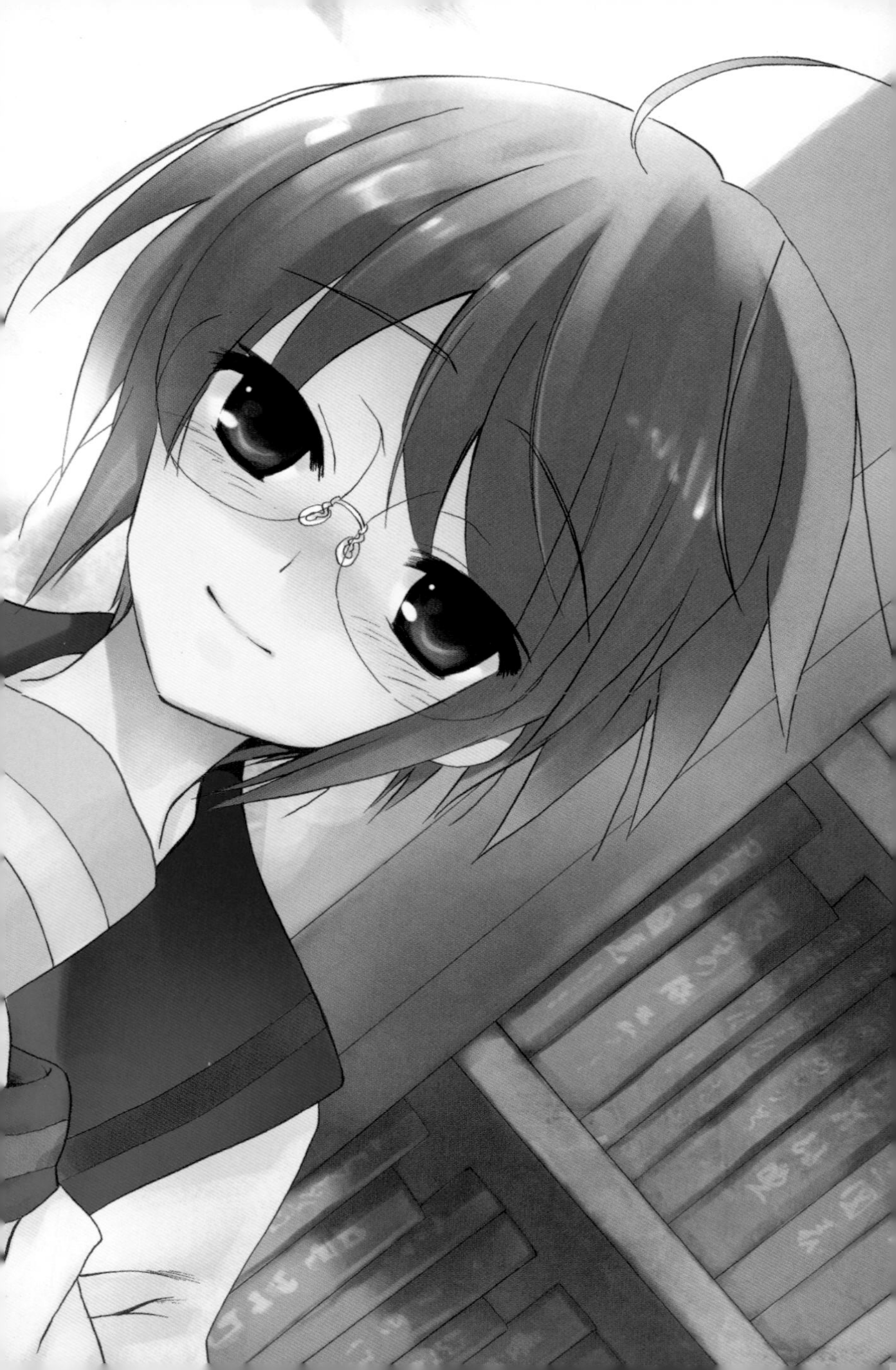

THE MELANCHOLY of HARUHI SUZUMIYA

ORIGINAL STORY **NAGARU TANIGAWA**

MANGA **GAKU TSUGANO**

12

CHARACTER DESIGN:
NOIZI ITO

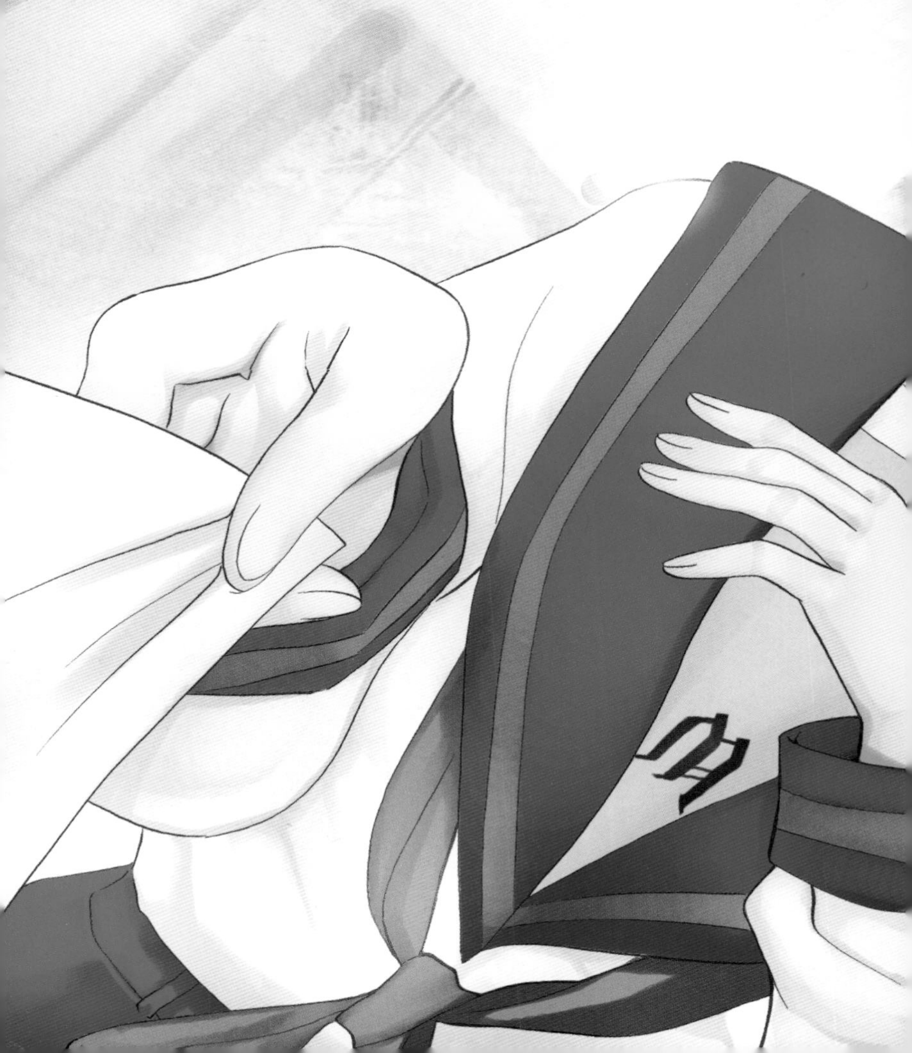

CONTENTS

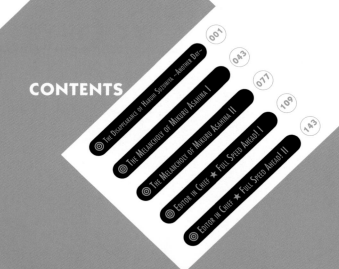

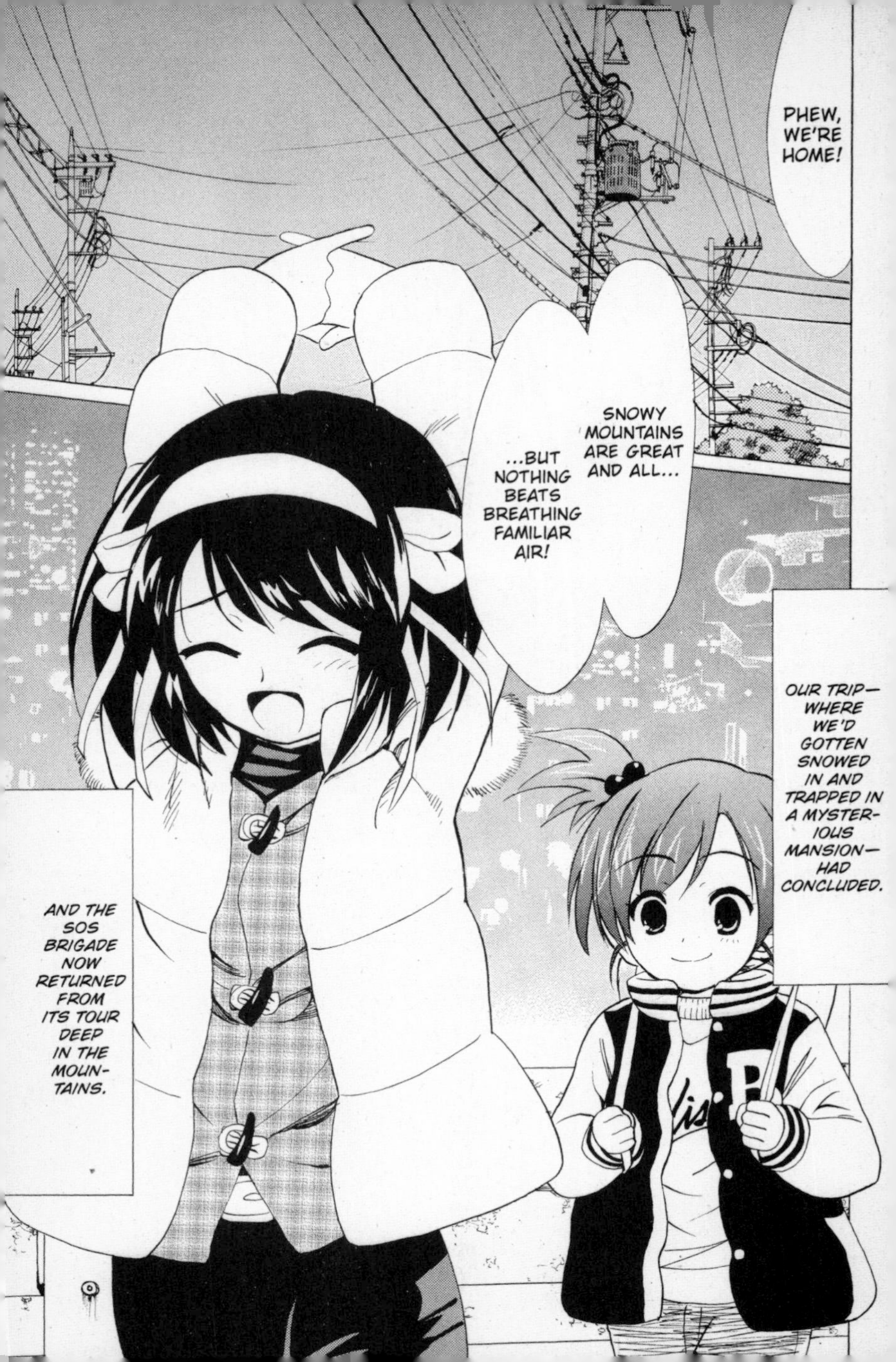
PHEW, WE'RE HOME!
SNOWY MOUNTAINS ARE GREAT AND ALL...
...BUT NOTHING BEATS BREATHING FAMILIAR AIR!
OUR TRIP—WHERE WE'D GOTTEN SNOWED IN AND TRAPPED IN A MYSTER-IOUS MANSION—HAD CONCLUDED.
AND THE SOS BRIGADE NOW RETURNED FROM ITS TOUR DEEP IN THE MOUN-TAINS.

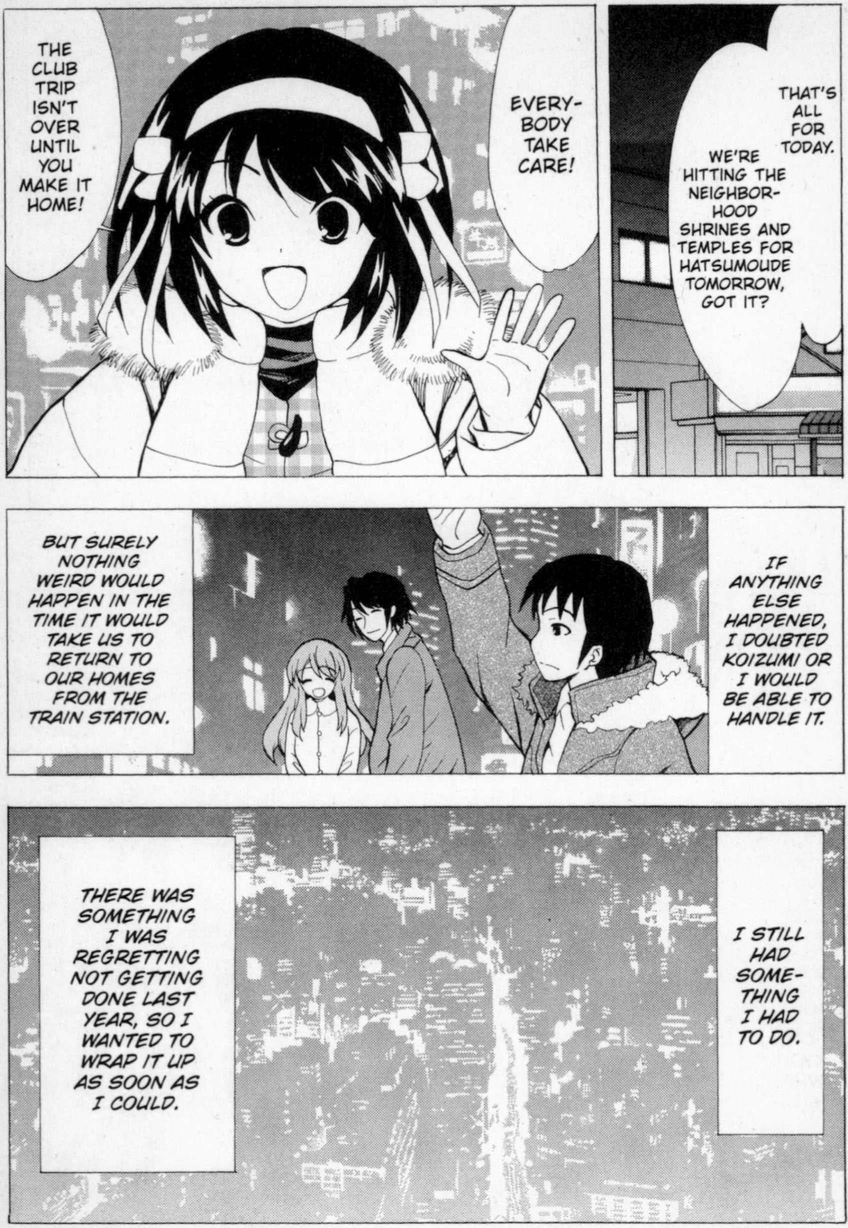
THAT'S ALL FOR TODAY.
WE'RE HITTING THE NEIGHBOR-HOOD SHRINES AND TEMPLES FOR HATSUMOUDE TOMORROW, GOT IT?
EVERY-BODY TAKE CARE!
THE CLUB TRIP ISN'T OVER UNTIL YOU MAKE IT HOME!
IF ANYTHING ELSE HAPPENED, I DOUBTED KOIZUMI OR I WOULD BE ABLE TO HANDLE IT.
BUT SURELY NOTHING WEIRD WOULD HAPPEN IN THE TIME IT WOULD TAKE US TO RETURN TO OUR HOMES FROM THE TRAIN STATION.
I STILL HAD SOME-THING I HAD TO DO.
THERE WAS SOMETHING I WAS REGRETTING NOT GETTING DONE LAST YEAR, SO I WANTED TO WRAP IT UP AS SOON AS I COULD.

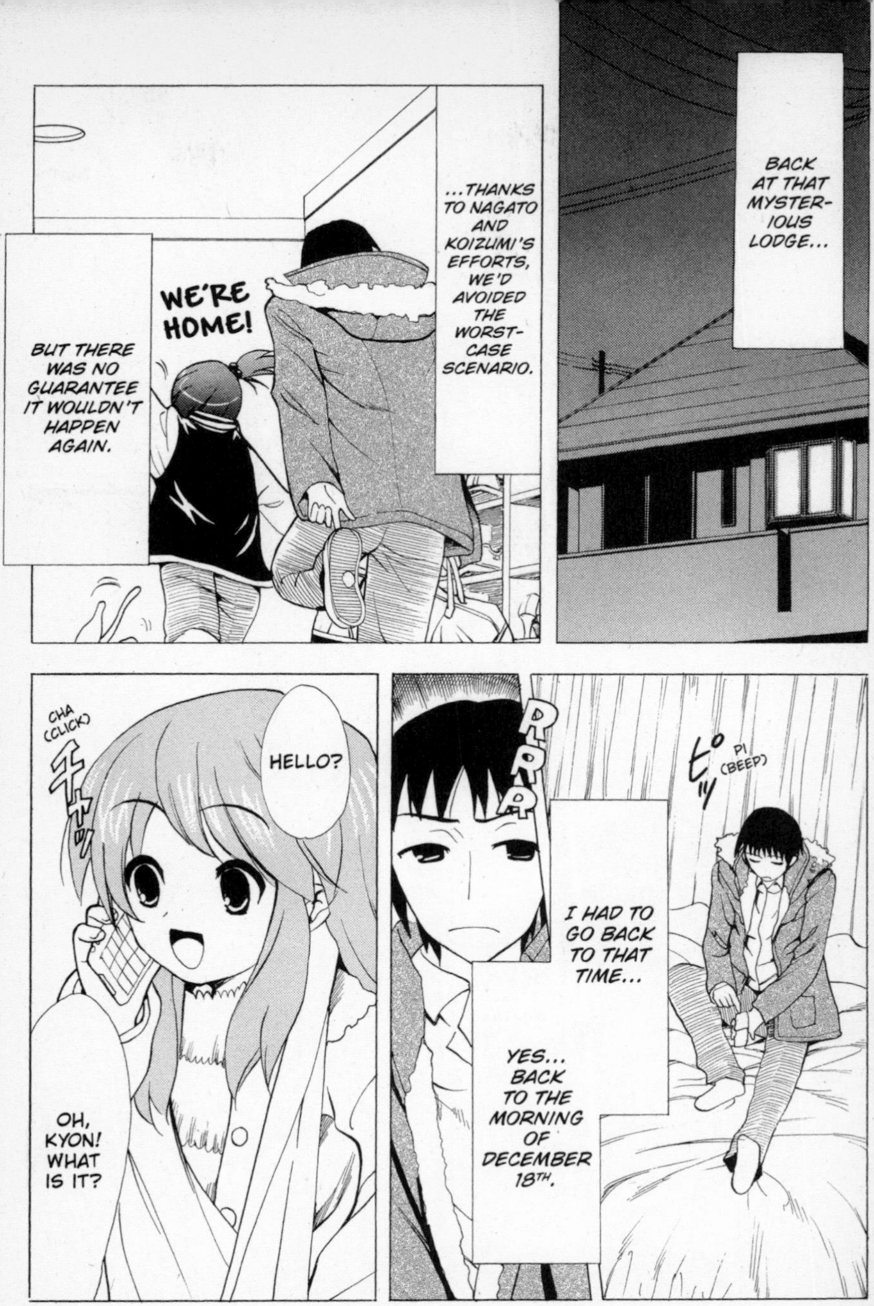
BACK AT THAT MYSTERIOUS LODGE...
...THANKS TO NAGATO AND KOIZUMI'S EFFORTS, WE'D AVOIDED THE WORST-CASE SCENARIO.
WE'RE HOME!
BUT THERE WAS NO GUARANTEE IT WOULDN'T HAPPEN AGAIN.
PI (BEEP)
RRR
I HAD TO GO BACK TO THAT TIME...
YES... BACK TO THE MORNING OF DECEMBER 18TH.
CHA (CLICK)
HELLO?
OH, KYON! WHAT IS IT?

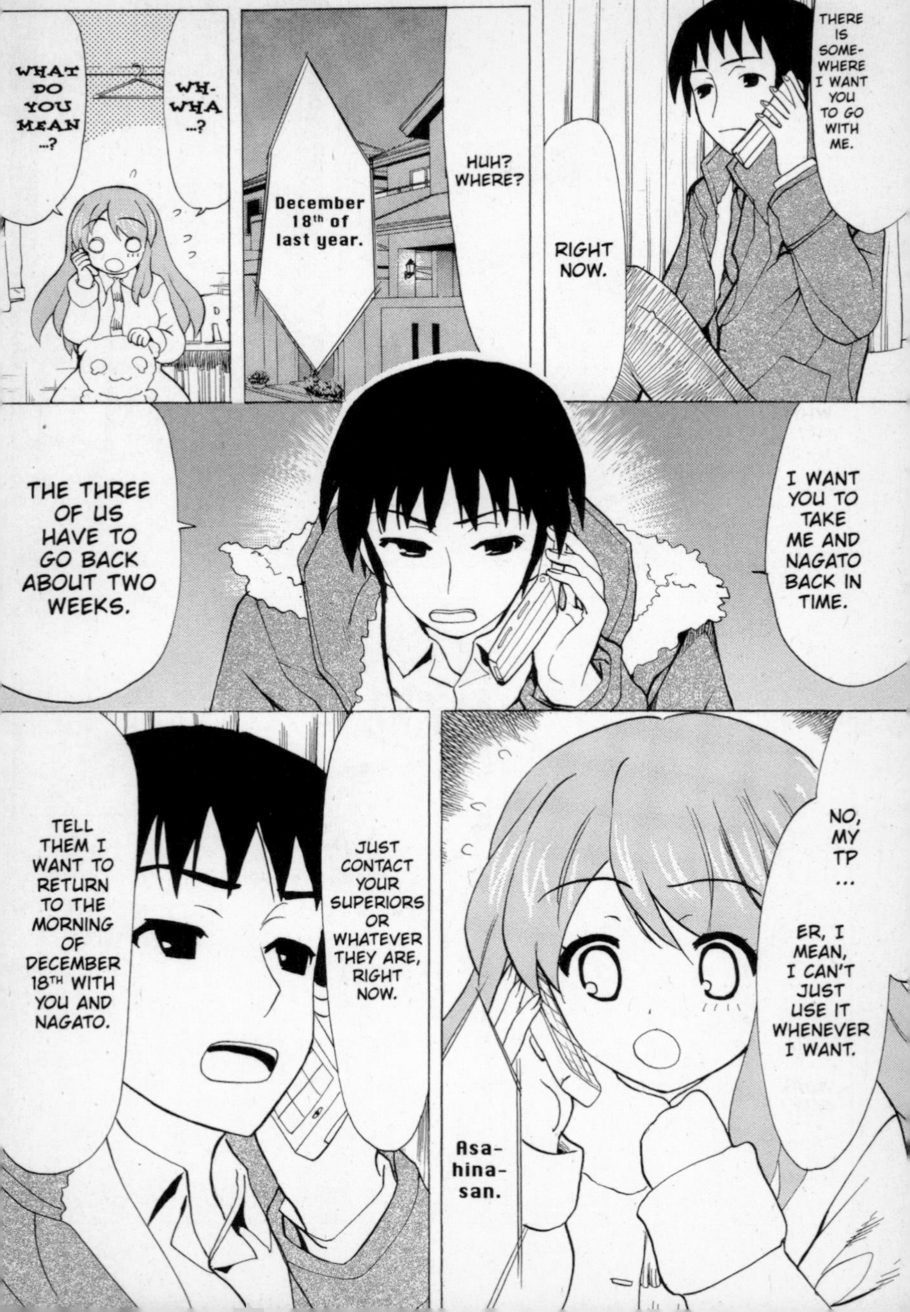
THERE IS SOME-WHERE I WANT YOU TO GO WITH ME.
RIGHT NOW.
HUH? WHERE?
December 18th of last year.
WH-WHA ...?
WHAT DO YOU MEAN ...?
I WANT YOU TO TAKE ME AND NAGATO BACK IN TIME.
THE THREE OF US HAVE TO GO BACK ABOUT TWO WEEKS.
NO, MY TP ...
ER, I MEAN, I CAN'T JUST USE IT WHENEVER I WANT.
Asa-hina-san.
JUST CONTACT YOUR SUPERIORS OR WHATEVER THEY ARE, RIGHT NOW.
TELL THEM I WANT TO RETURN TO THE MORNING OF DECEMBER 18TH WITH YOU AND NAGATO.

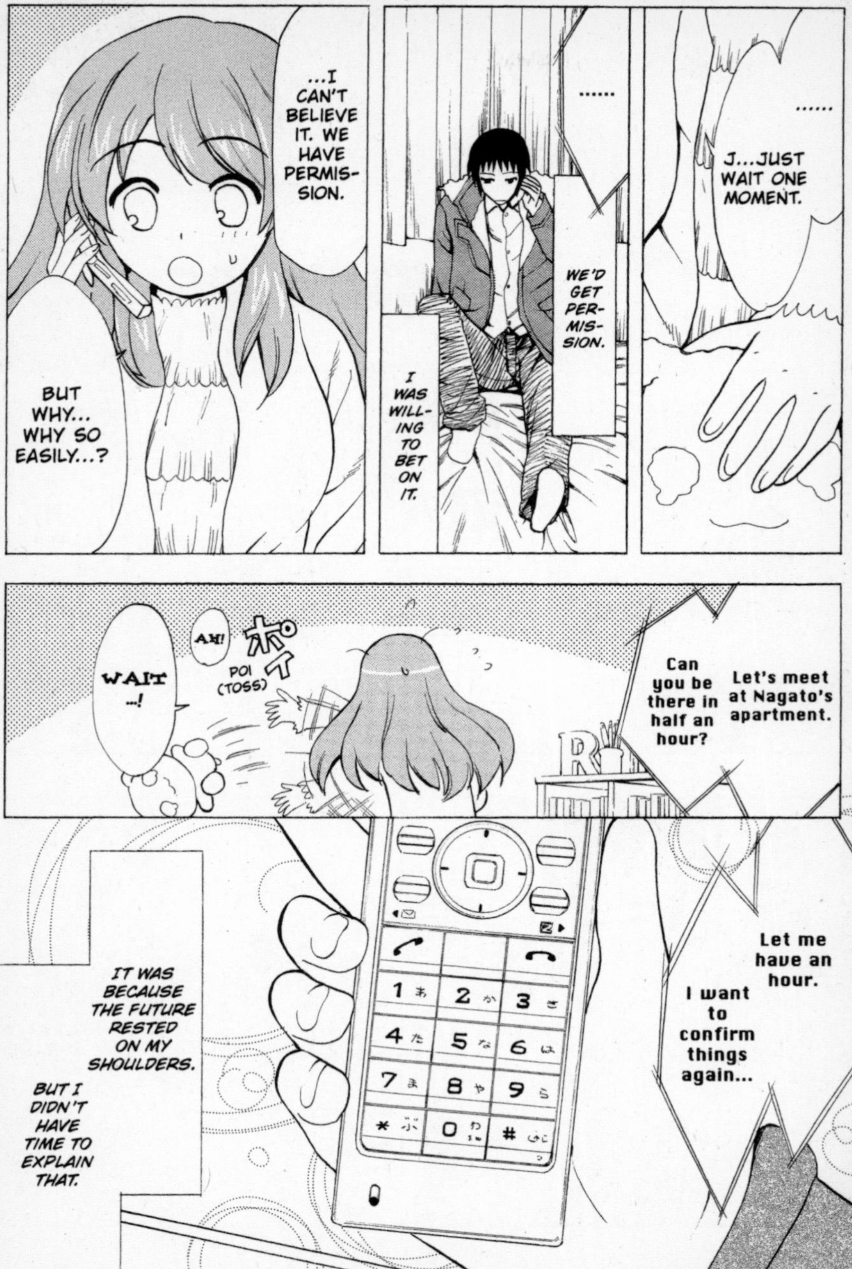
......
J...JUST WAIT ONE MOMENT.
......
WE'D GET PERMISSION.
I WAS WILLING TO BET ON IT.
...I CAN'T BELIEVE IT. WE HAVE PERMISSION.
BUT WHY... WHY SO EASILY...?
Let's meet at Nagato's apartment.
Can you be there in half an hour?
ポイ
POI (TOSS)
AH!
WAIT ...!
Let me have an hour.
I want to confirm things again...
IT WAS BECAUSE THE FUTURE RESTED ON MY SHOULDERS.
BUT I DIDN'T HAVE TIME TO EXPLAIN THAT.

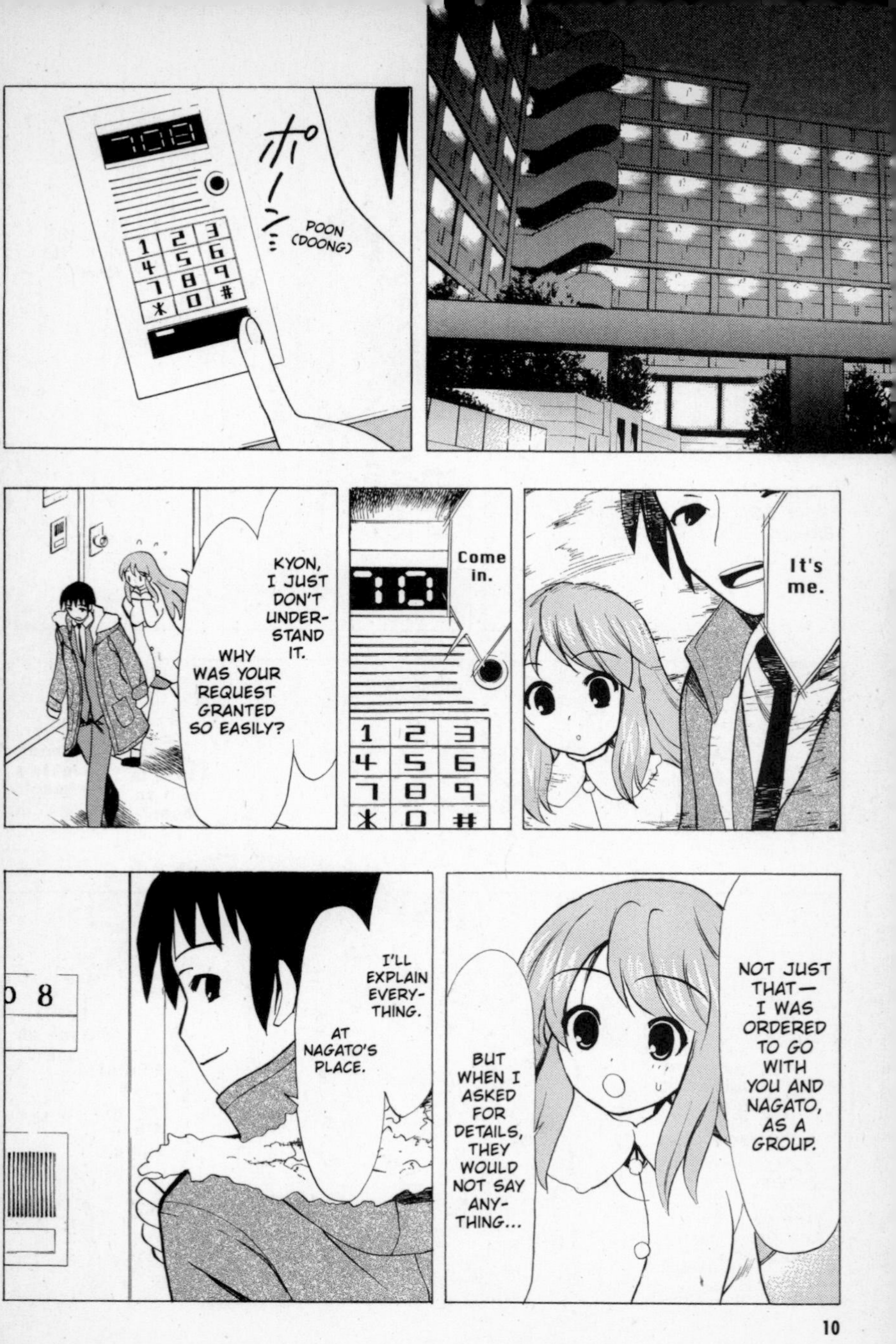
ポーン
POON (DOONG)
It's me.
Come in.
KYON, I JUST DON'T UNDERSTAND IT.
WHY WAS YOUR REQUEST GRANTED SO EASILY?
NOT JUST THAT— I WAS ORDERED TO GO WITH YOU AND NAGATO, AS A GROUP.
BUT WHEN I ASKED FOR DETAILS, THEY WOULD NOT SAY ANYTHING...
I'LL EXPLAIN EVERYTHING.
AT NAGATO'S PLACE.

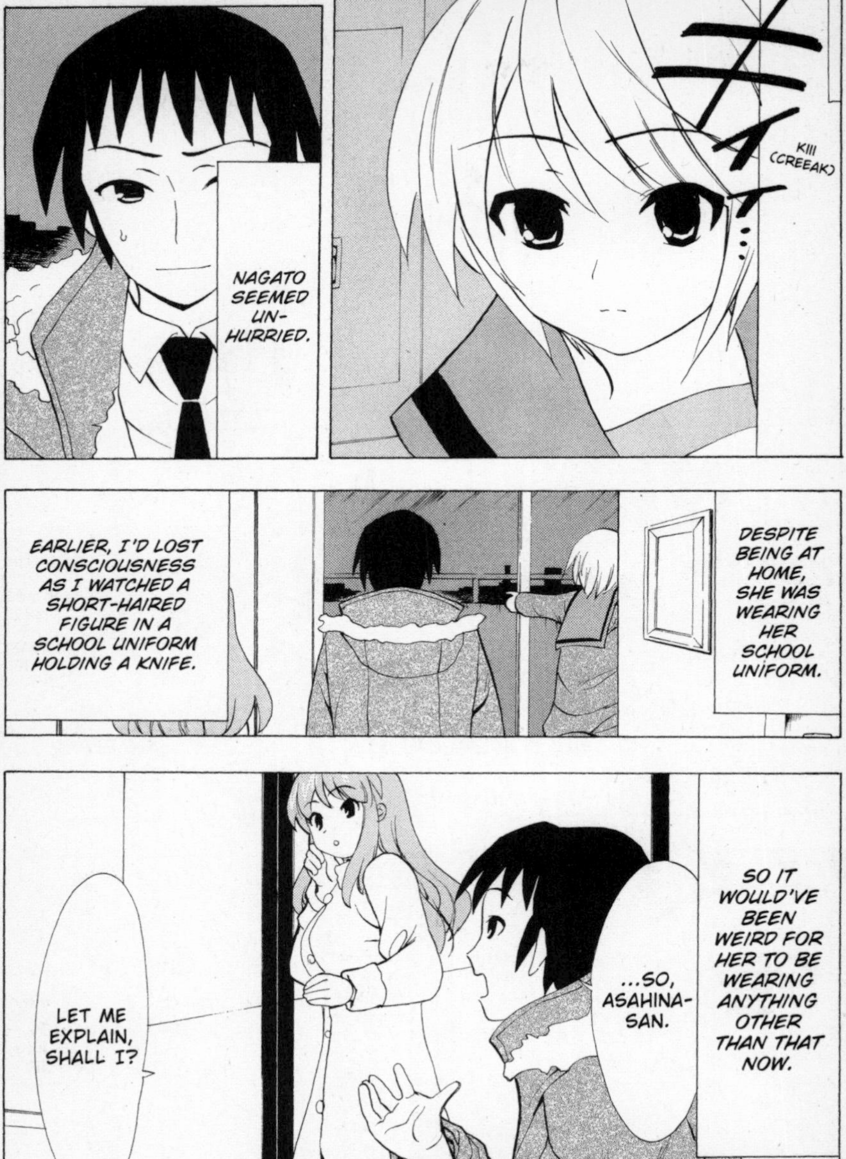
KIII
(CREEAK)
NAGATO SEEMED UN-HURRIED.
DESPITE BEING AT HOME, SHE WAS WEARING HER SCHOOL UNIFORM.
EARLIER, I'D LOST CONSCIOUSNESS AS I WATCHED A SHORT-HAIRED FIGURE IN A SCHOOL UNIFORM HOLDING A KNIFE.
SO IT WOULD'VE BEEN WEIRD FOR HER TO BE WEARING ANYTHING OTHER THAN THAT NOW.
...SO, ASAHINA-SAN.
LET ME EXPLAIN, SHALL I?

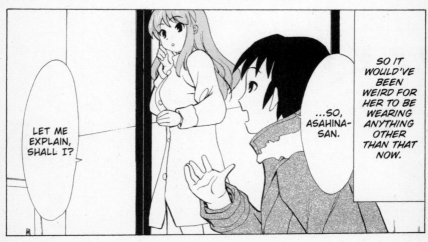

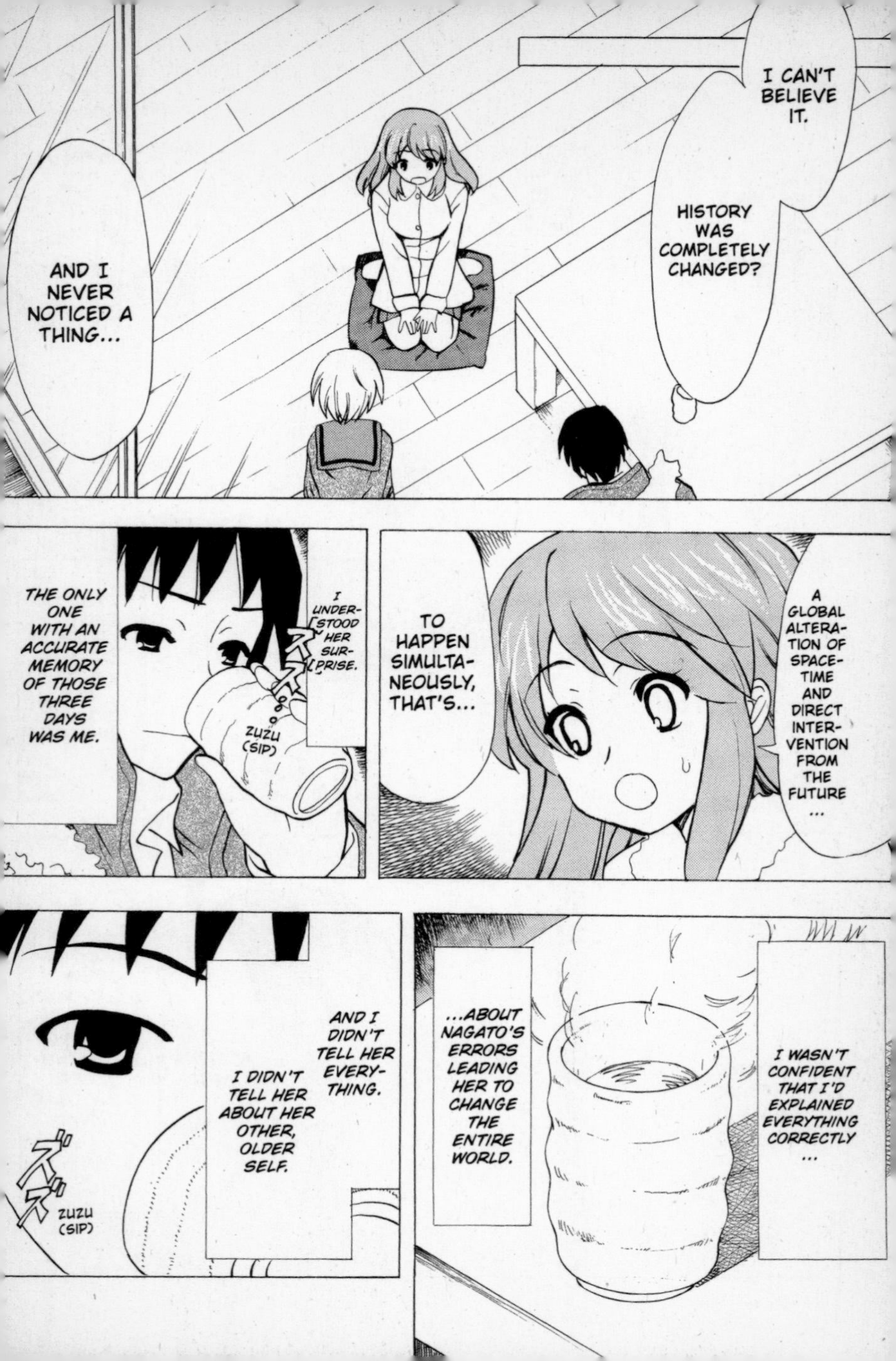

I CAN'T BELIEVE IT.
HISTORY WAS COMPLETELY CHANGED?
AND I NEVER NOTICED A THING...
A GLOBAL ALTERATION OF SPACE-TIME AND DIRECT INTERVENTION FROM THE FUTURE...
TO HAPPEN SIMULTANEOUSLY, THAT'S...
I UNDERSTOOD HER SURPRISE.
ZUZU (SIP)
THE ONLY ONE WITH AN ACCURATE MEMORY OF THOSE THREE DAYS WAS ME.
I WASN'T CONFIDENT THAT I'D EXPLAINED EVERYTHING CORRECTLY...
...ABOUT NAGATO'S ERRORS LEADING HER TO CHANGE THE ENTIRE WORLD.
AND I DIDN'T TELL HER EVERYTHING.
I DIDN'T TELL HER ABOUT HER OTHER, OLDER SELF.
ZUZU (SIP)

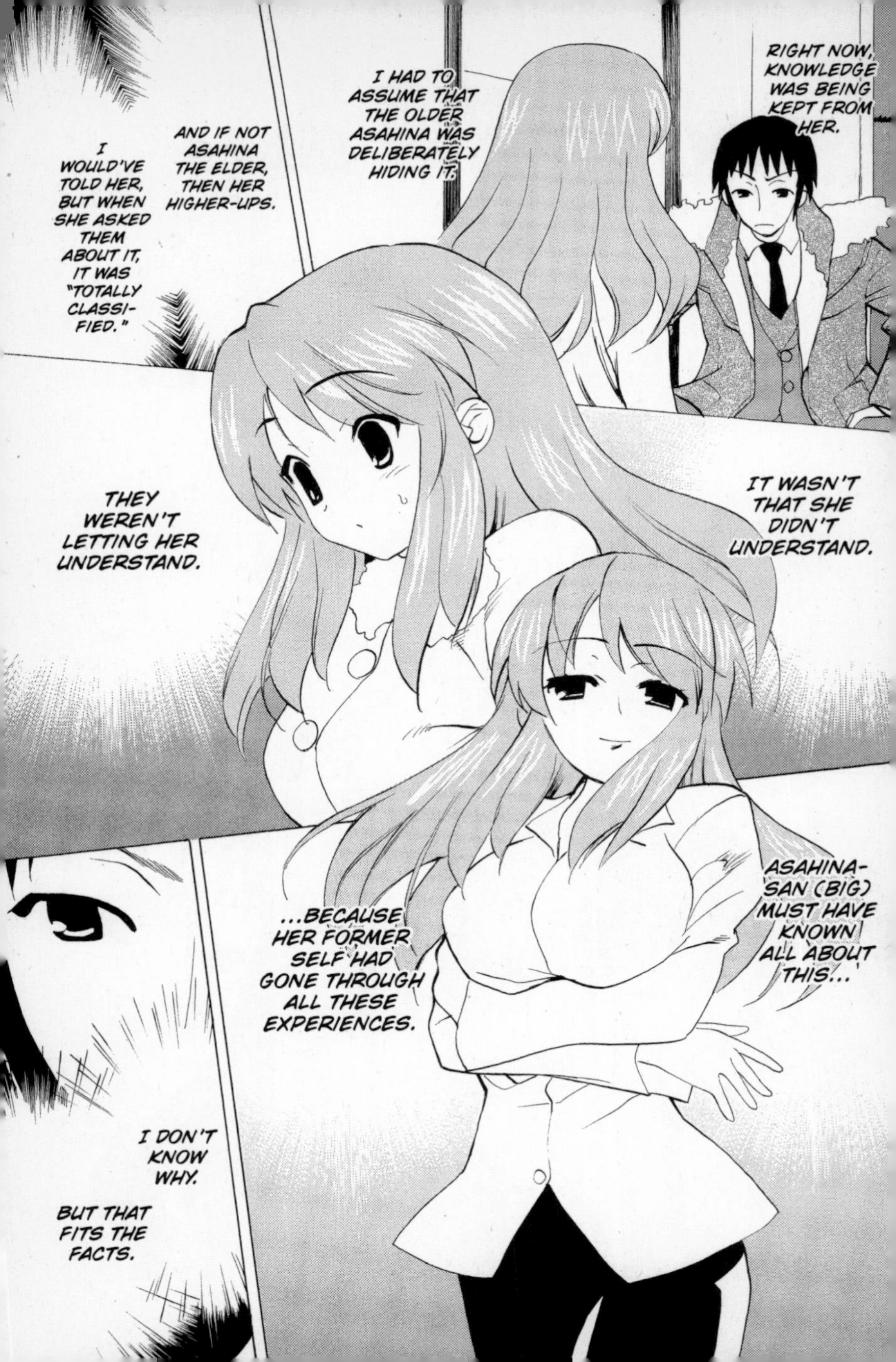
RIGHT NOW, KNOWLEDGE WAS BEING KEPT FROM HER.
I HAD TO ASSUME THAT THE OLDER ASAHINA WAS DELIBERATELY HIDING IT.
AND IF NOT ASAHINA THE ELDER, THEN HER HIGHER-UPS.
I WOULD'VE TOLD HER, BUT WHEN SHE ASKED THEM ABOUT IT, IT WAS "TOTALLY CLASSI-FIED."
IT WASN'T THAT SHE DIDN'T UNDERSTAND.
THEY WEREN'T LETTING HER UNDERSTAND.
ASAHINA-SAN (BIG) MUST HAVE KNOWN ALL ABOUT THIS...
...BECAUSE HER FORMER SELF HAD GONE THROUGH ALL THESE EXPERIENCES.
I DON'T KNOW WHY.
BUT THAT FITS THE FACTS.

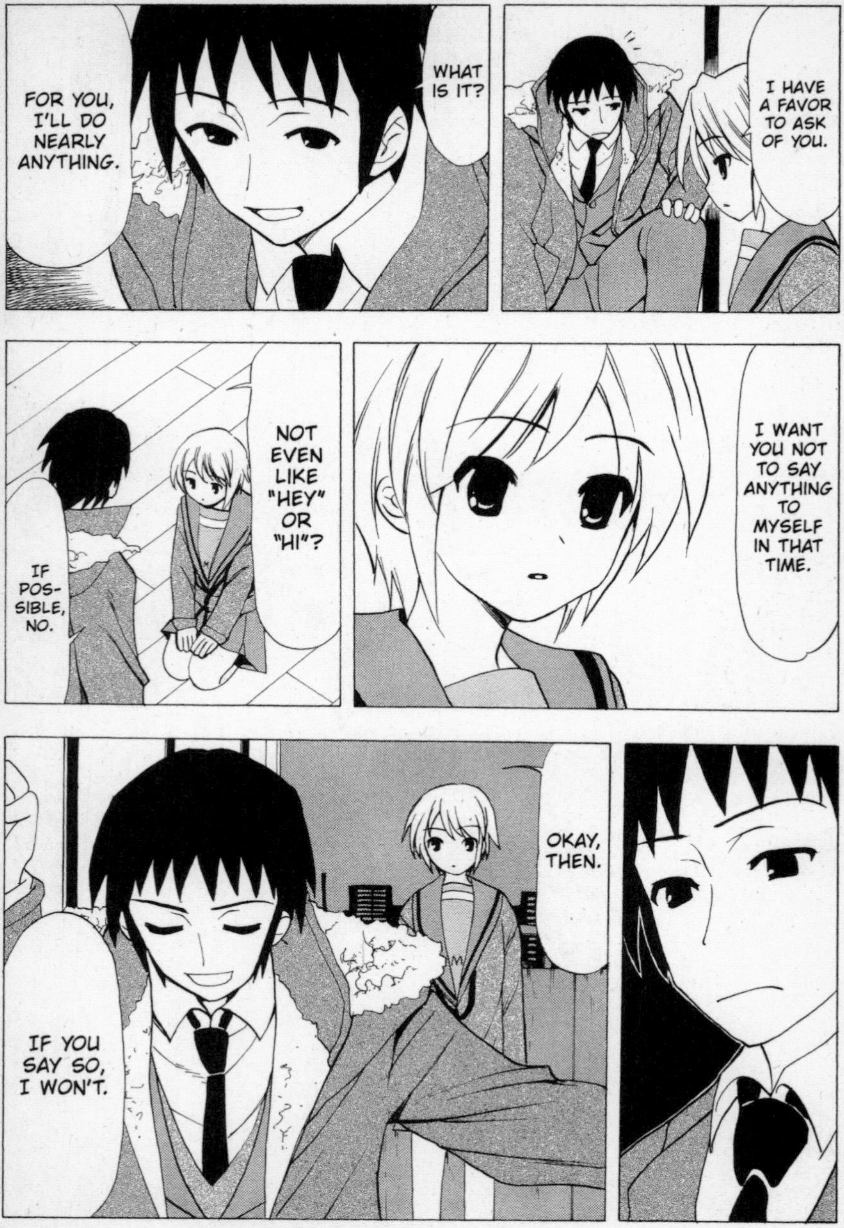
I HAVE A FAVOR TO ASK OF YOU.
WHAT IS IT?
FOR YOU, I'LL DO NEARLY ANYTHING.
I WANT YOU NOT TO SAY ANYTHING TO MYSELF IN THAT TIME.
NOT EVEN LIKE "HEY" OR "HI"?
IF POS-SIBLE, NO.
OKAY, THEN.
IF YOU SAY SO, I WON'T.

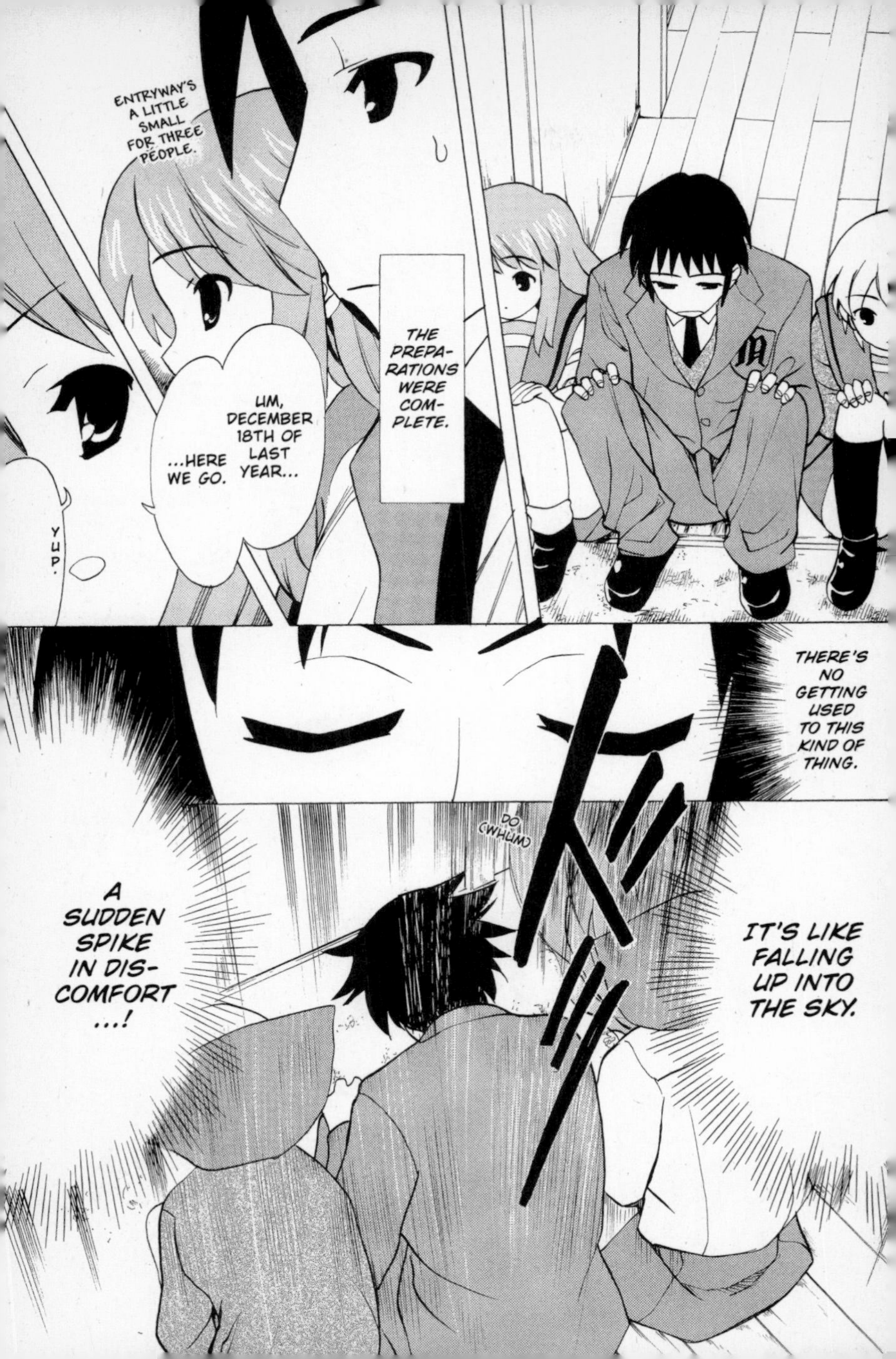
THE PREPARATIONS WERE COMPLETE.
ENTRYWAY'S A LITTLE SMALL FOR THREE PEOPLE.
UM, DECEMBER 18TH OF LAST YEAR...
...HERE WE GO.
YUP.
THERE'S NO GETTING USED TO THIS KIND OF THING.
IT'S LIKE FALLING UP INTO THE SKY.
DO (WHUM)
A SUDDEN SPIKE IN DISCOMFORT...!

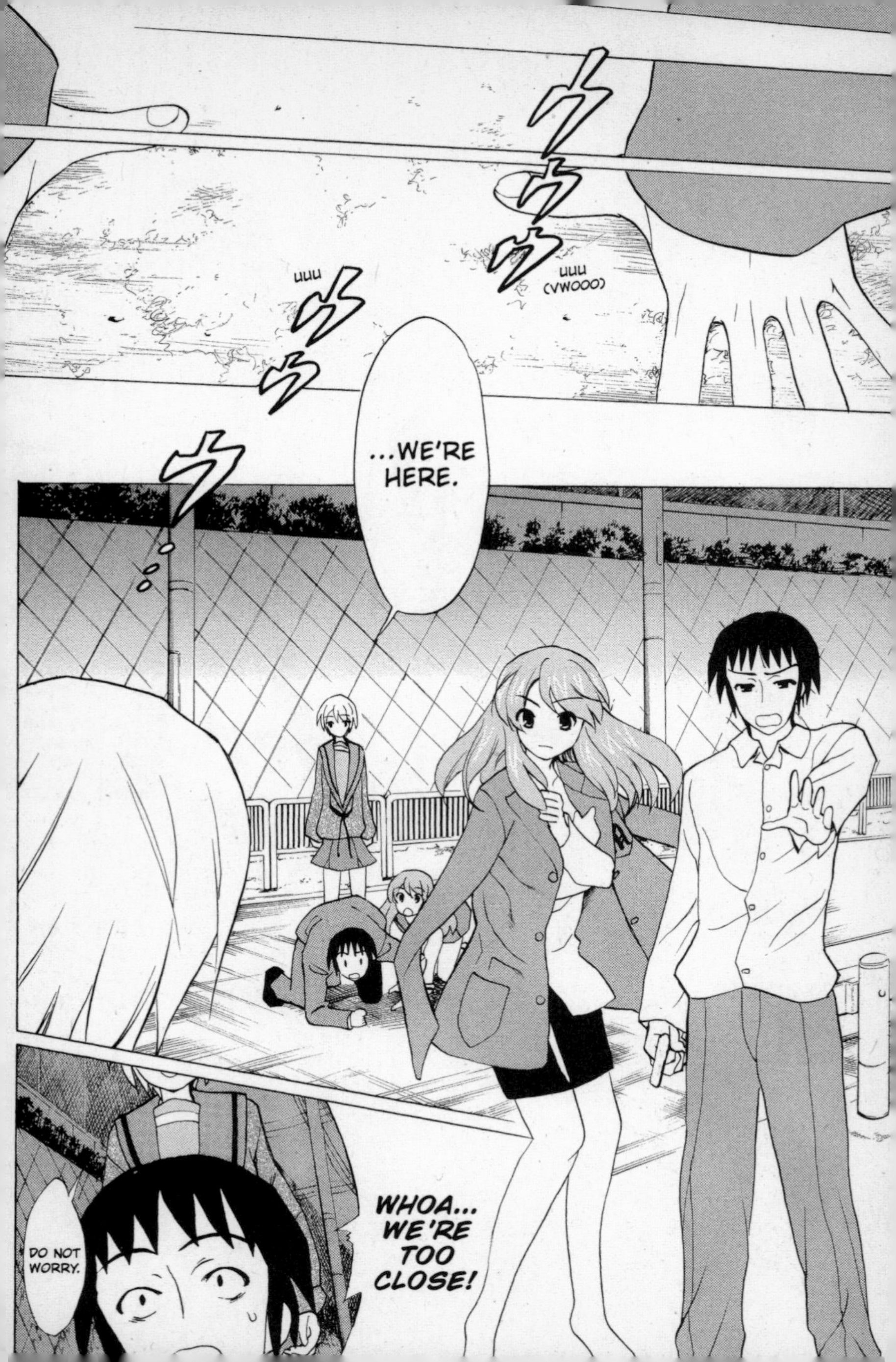
ウウウ
uuu
(VWOOO)
ウウウ
uuu
...WE'RE HERE.
WHOA... WE'RE TOO CLOSE!
DO NOT WORRY.

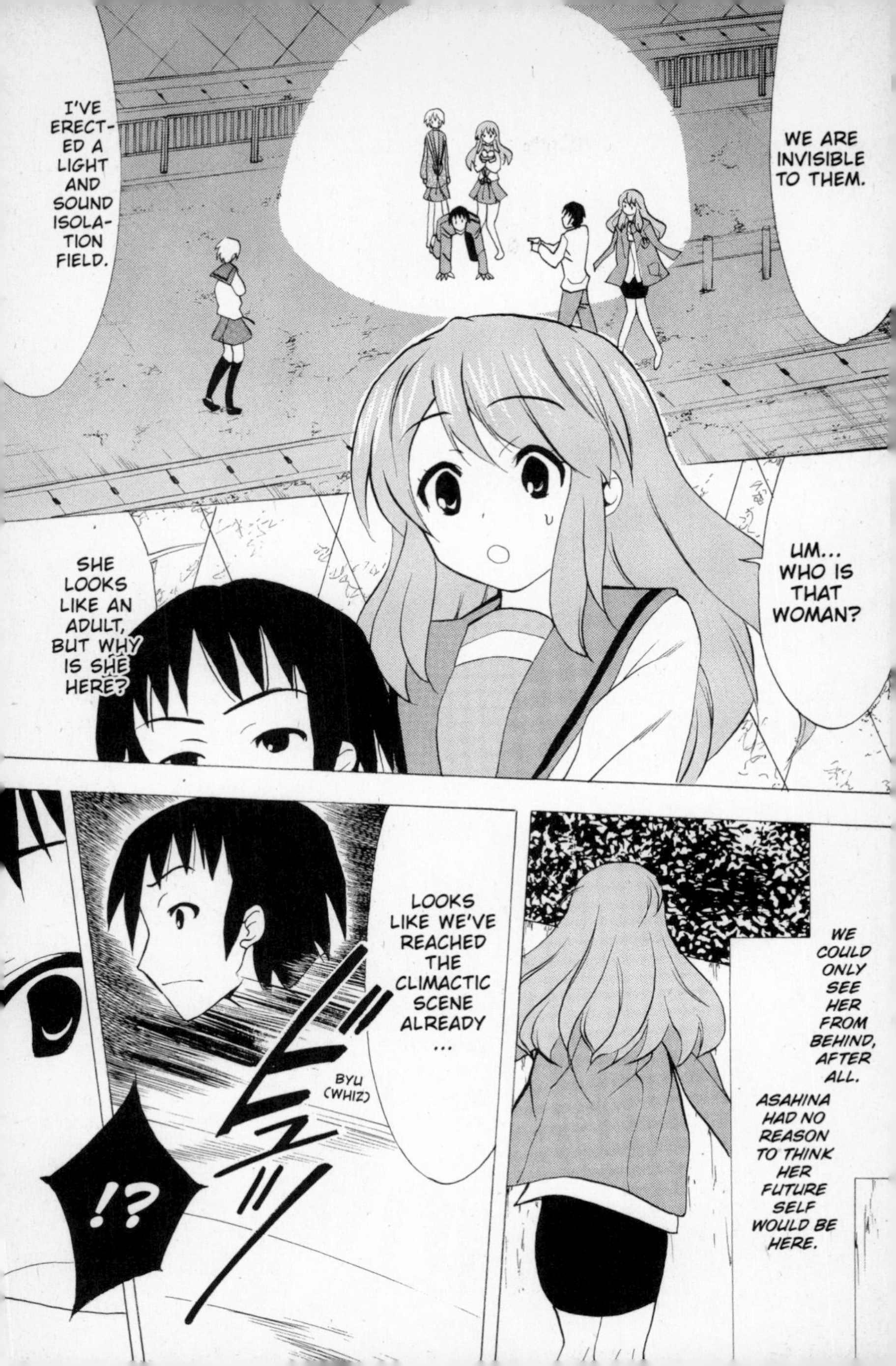
WE ARE INVISIBLE TO THEM.
I'VE ERECTED A LIGHT AND SOUND ISOLATION FIELD.
UM... WHO IS THAT WOMAN?
SHE LOOKS LIKE AN ADULT, BUT WHY IS SHE HERE?
WE COULD ONLY SEE HER FROM BEHIND, AFTER ALL.
ASAHINA HAD NO REASON TO THINK HER FUTURE SELF WOULD BE HERE.
LOOKS LIKE WE'VE REACHED THE CLIMACTIC SCENE ALREADY...
BYU (WHIZ)
!?

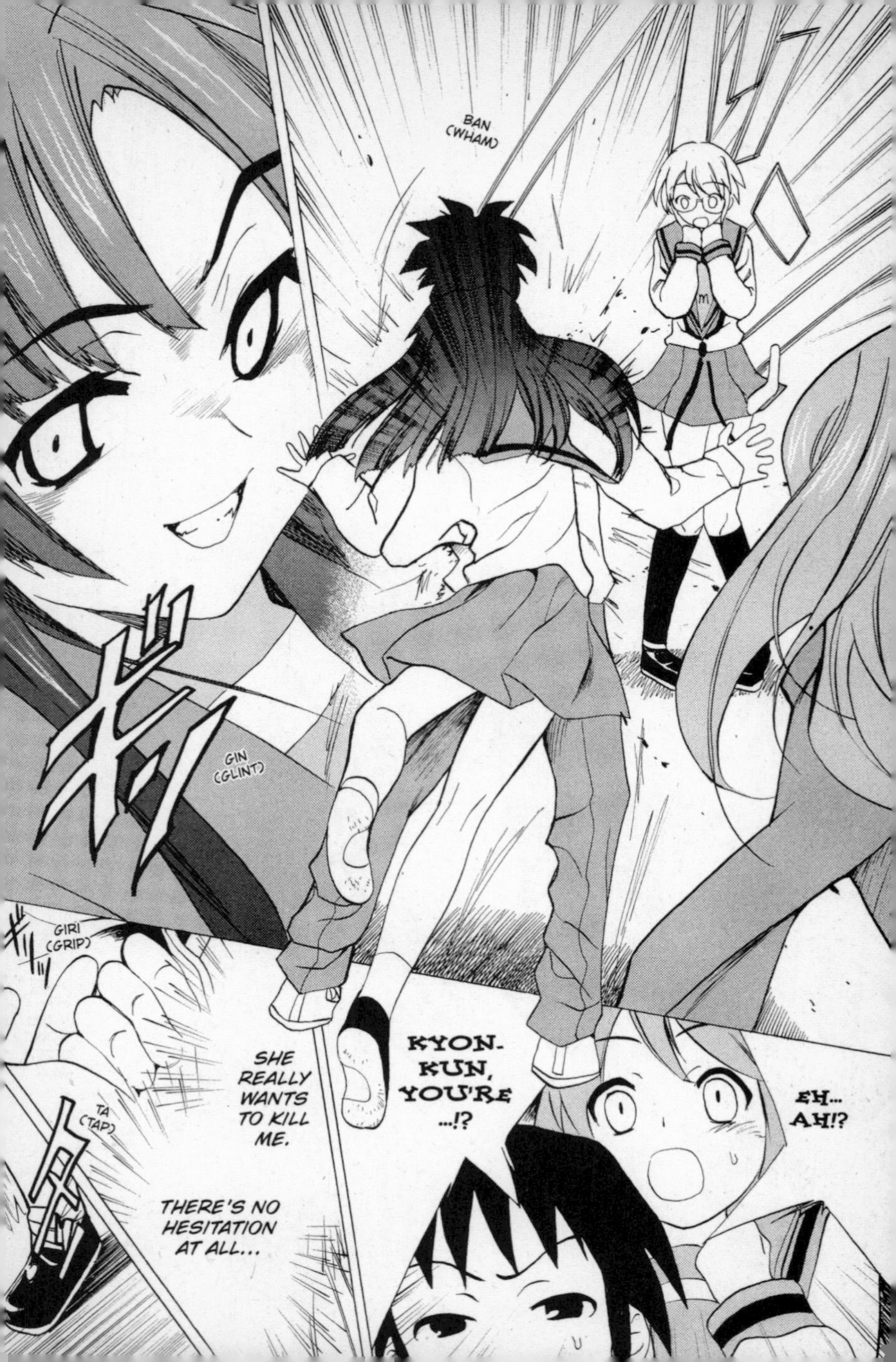
BAN
(WHAM)
GIN
(GLINT)
EH... AH!?
KYON-KUN, YOU'RE ...!?
SHE REALLY WANTS TO KILL ME.
GIRI
(GRIP)
TA
(TAP)
THERE'S NO HESITATION AT ALL...

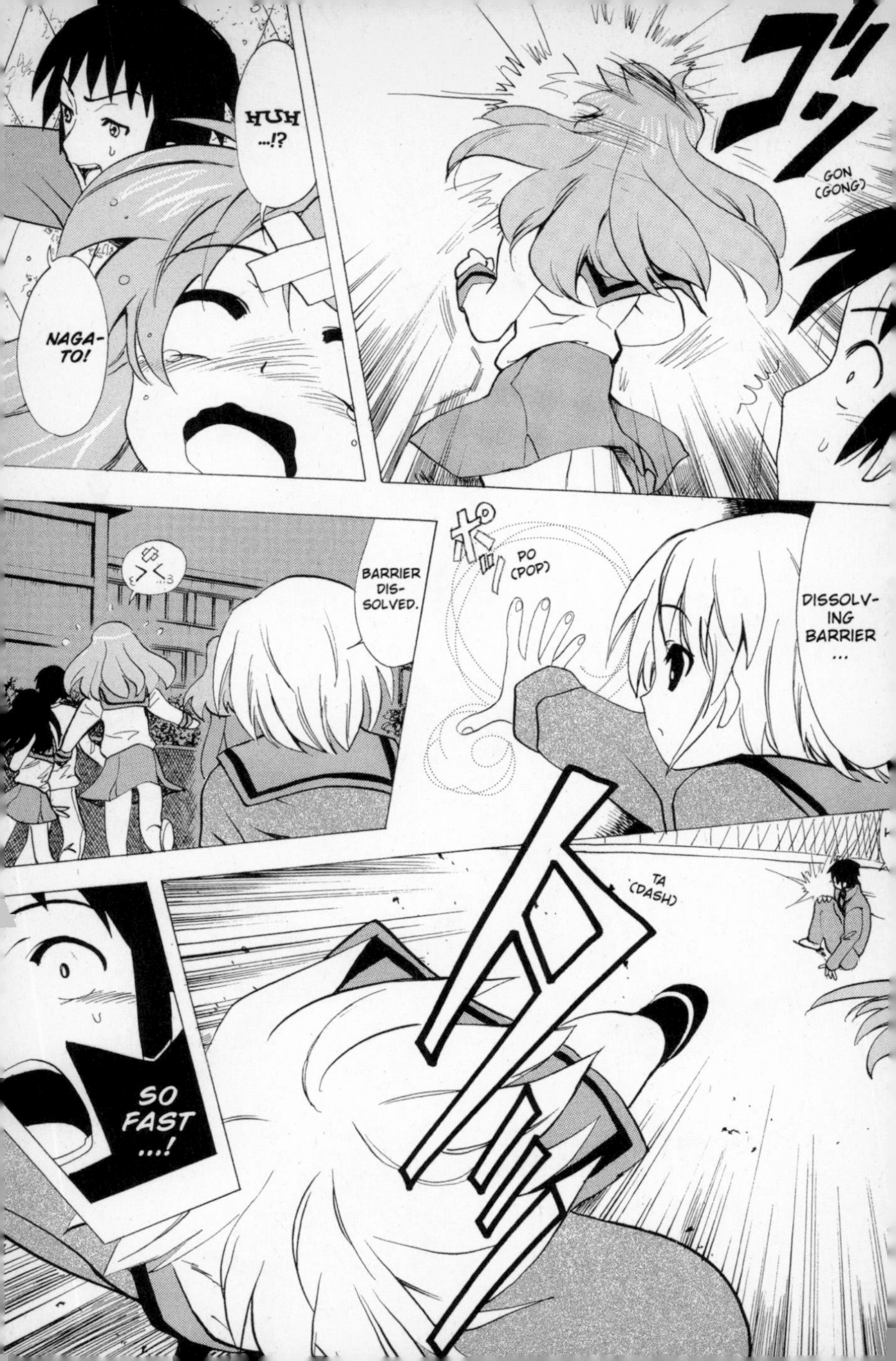
GON (GONG)
HUH ...!?
NAGA-TO!
DISSOLV-ING BARRIER ...
PO (POP)
BARRIER DIS-SOLVED.
TA (DASH)
SO FAST ...!

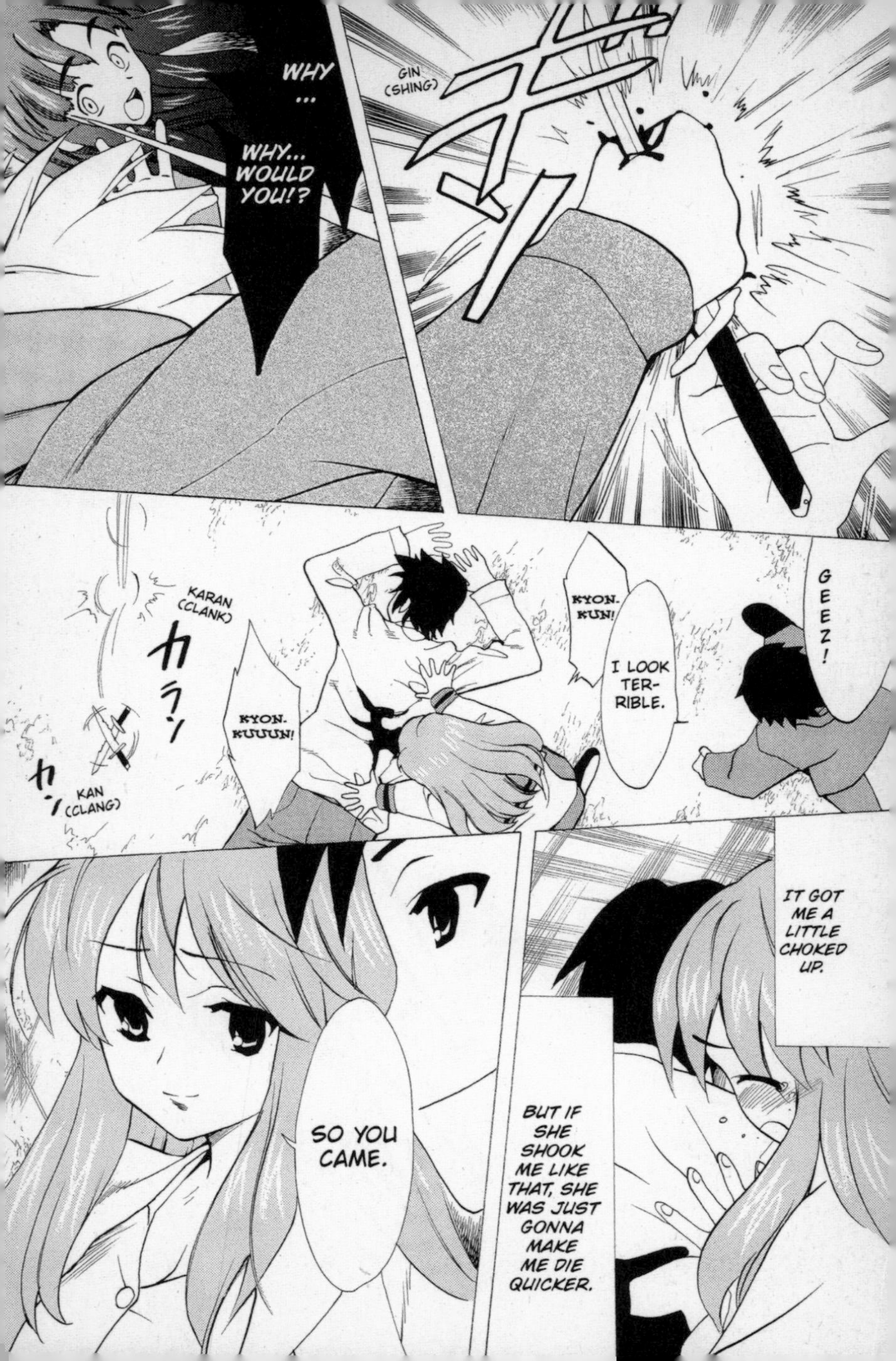

ギン
GIN (SHING)
WHY ...
WHY... WOULD YOU!?
GEEZ!
KYON-KUN!
I LOOK TERRIBLE.
KYON-KUUUN!
KARAN (CLANK)
カラン
カン
KAN (CLANG)
IT GOT ME A LITTLE CHOKED UP.
BUT IF SHE SHOOK ME LIKE THAT, SHE WAS JUST GONNA MAKE ME DIE QUICKER.
SO YOU CAME.

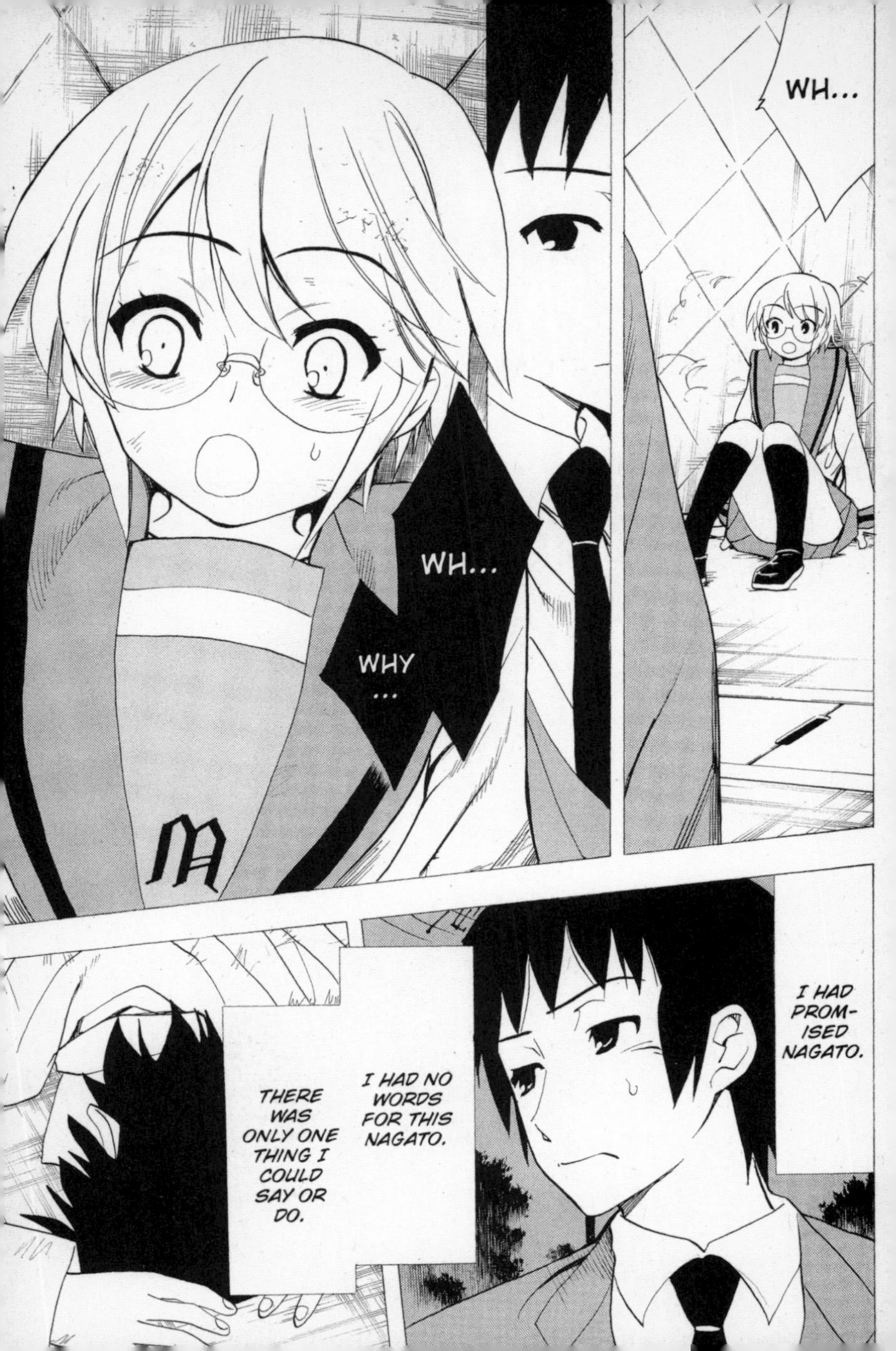
WH...
WH...
WHY ...
I HAD PROM-ISED NAGATO.
I HAD NO WORDS FOR THIS NAGATO.
THERE WAS ONLY ONE THING I COULD SAY OR DO.

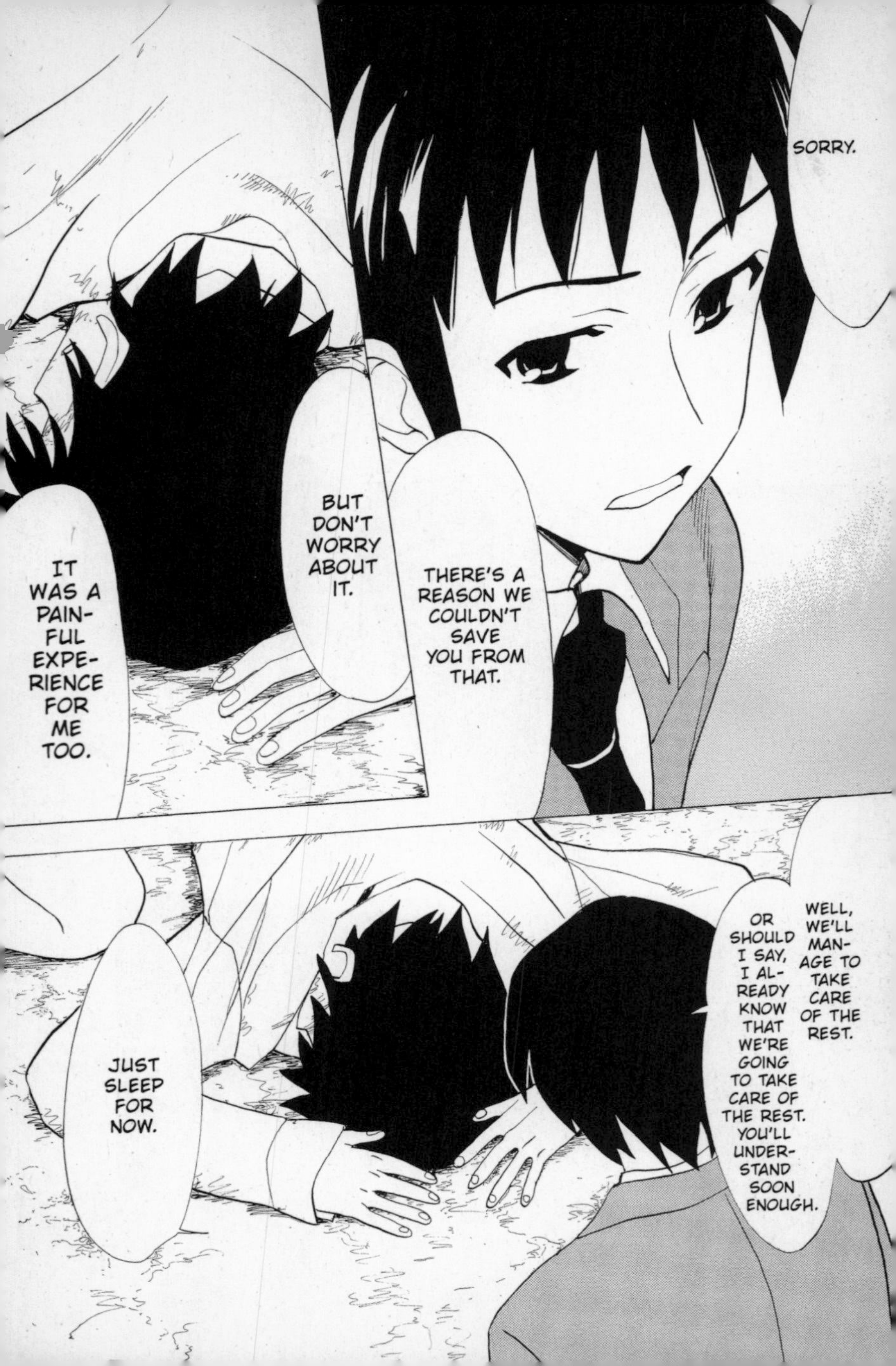
SORRY.
THERE'S A REASON WE COULDN'T SAVE YOU FROM THAT.
BUT DON'T WORRY ABOUT IT.
IT WAS A PAIN-FUL EXPE-RIENCE FOR ME TOO.
WELL, WE'LL MAN-AGE TO TAKE CARE OF THE REST.
OR SHOULD I SAY, I AL-READY KNOW THAT WE'RE GOING TO TAKE CARE OF THE REST. YOU'LL UNDER-STAND SOON ENOUGH.
JUST SLEEP FOR NOW.

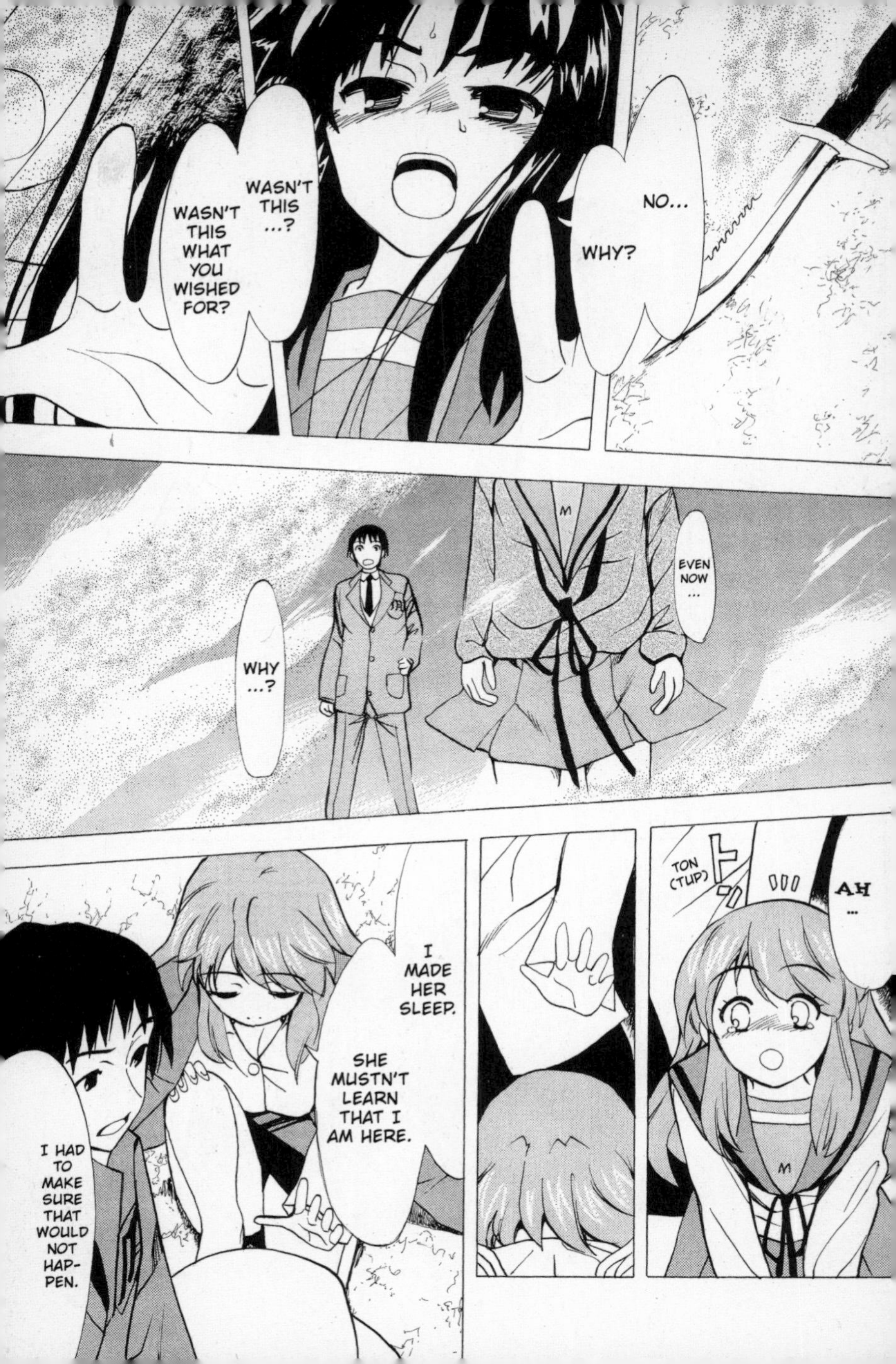
NO...
WHY?
WASN'T THIS ...?
WASN'T THIS WHAT YOU WISHED FOR?
EVEN NOW ...
WHY ...?
AH ...
TON (TUP)
I MADE HER SLEEP.
SHE MUSTN'T LEARN THAT I AM HERE.
I HAD TO MAKE SURE THAT WOULD NOT HAP-PEN.

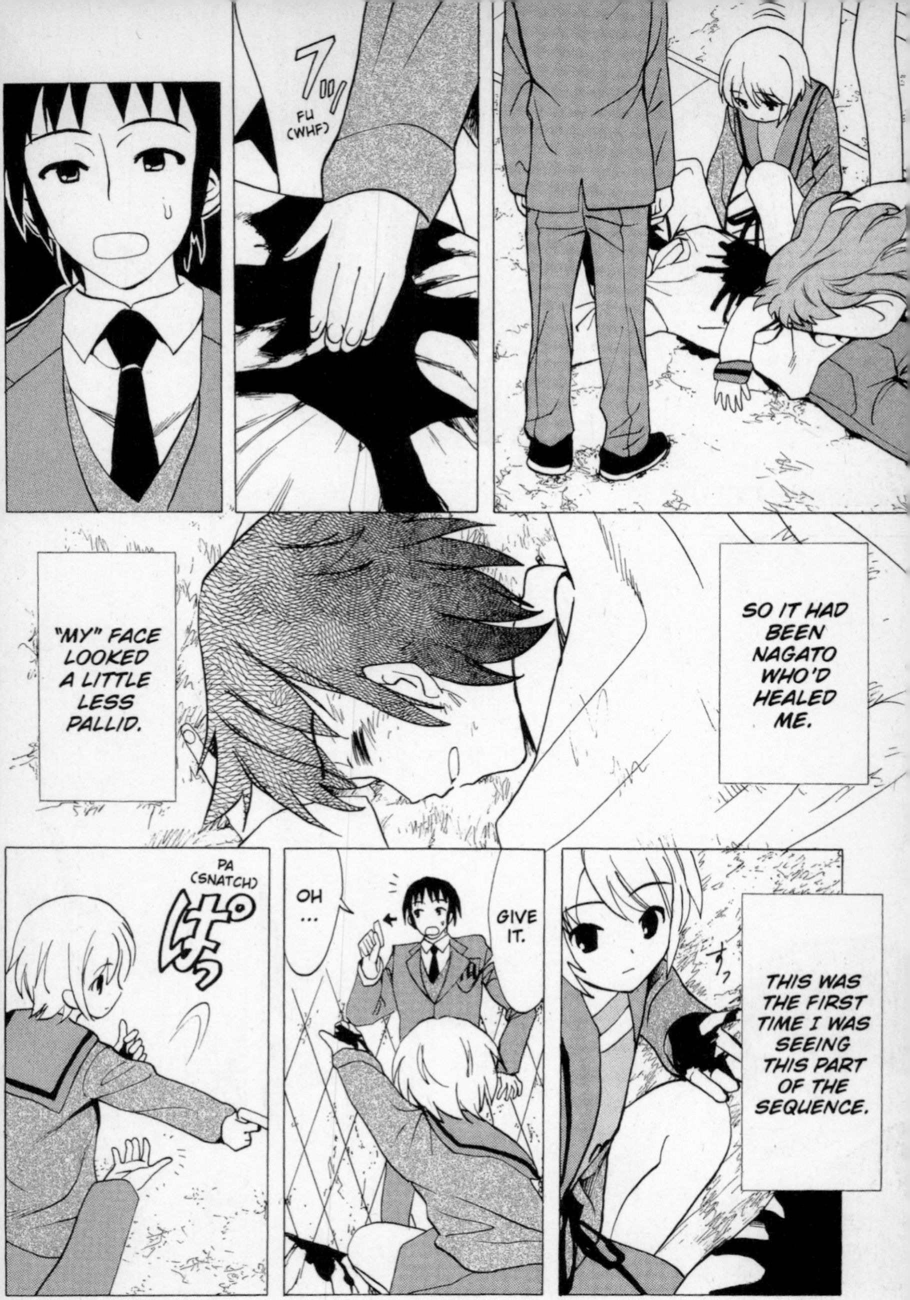

FU
(WHF)
SO IT HAD BEEN NAGATO WHO'D HEALED ME.
"MY" FACE LOOKED A LITTLE LESS PALLID.
THIS WAS THE FIRST TIME I WAS SEEING THIS PART OF THE SEQUENCE.
GIVE IT.
OH ...
PA
(SNATCH)

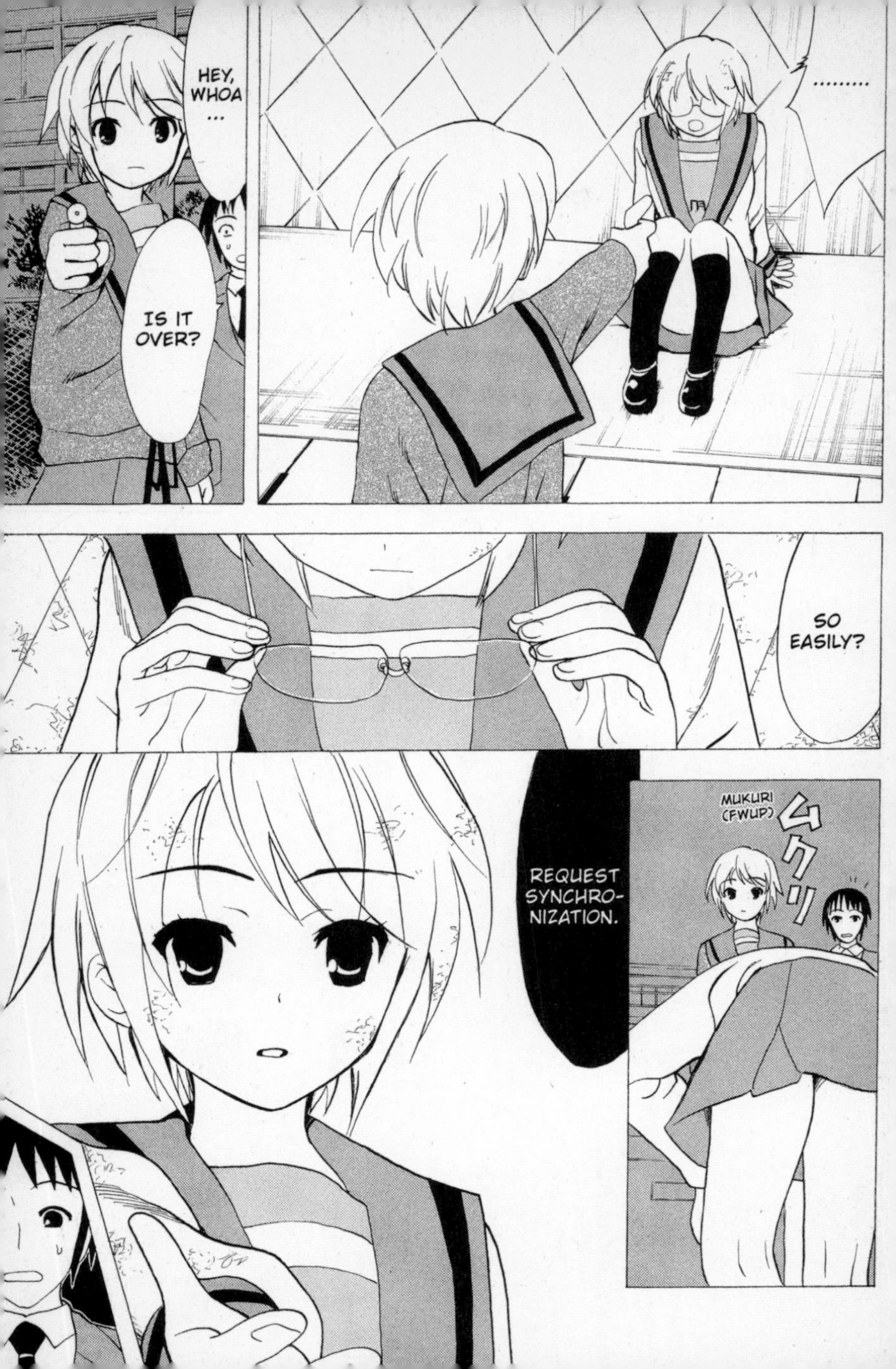
....
HEY, WHOA ...
IS IT OVER?
SO EASILY?
MUKURI (FWUP)
ムクリ
REQUEST SYNCHRO-NIZATION.

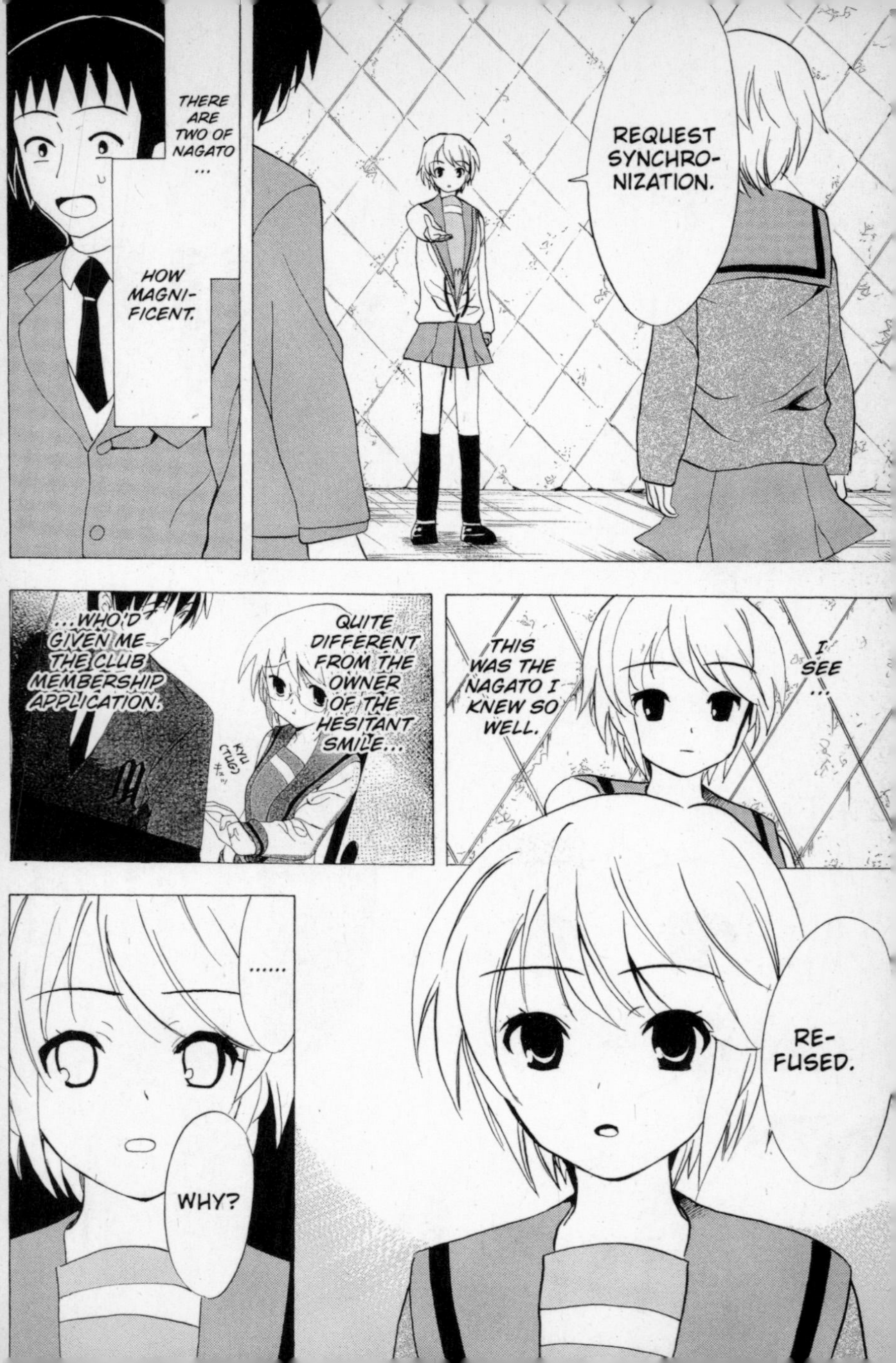
REQUEST SYNCHRO-NIZATION.
THERE ARE TWO OF NAGATO ...
HOW MAGNI-FICENT.
I SEE ...
THIS WAS THE NAGATO I KNEW SO WELL.
QUITE DIFFERENT FROM THE OWNER OF THE HESITANT SMILE...
...WHO'D GIVEN ME THE CLUB MEMBERSHIP APPLICATION.
KYU (TUG)
RE-FUSED.
......
WHY?

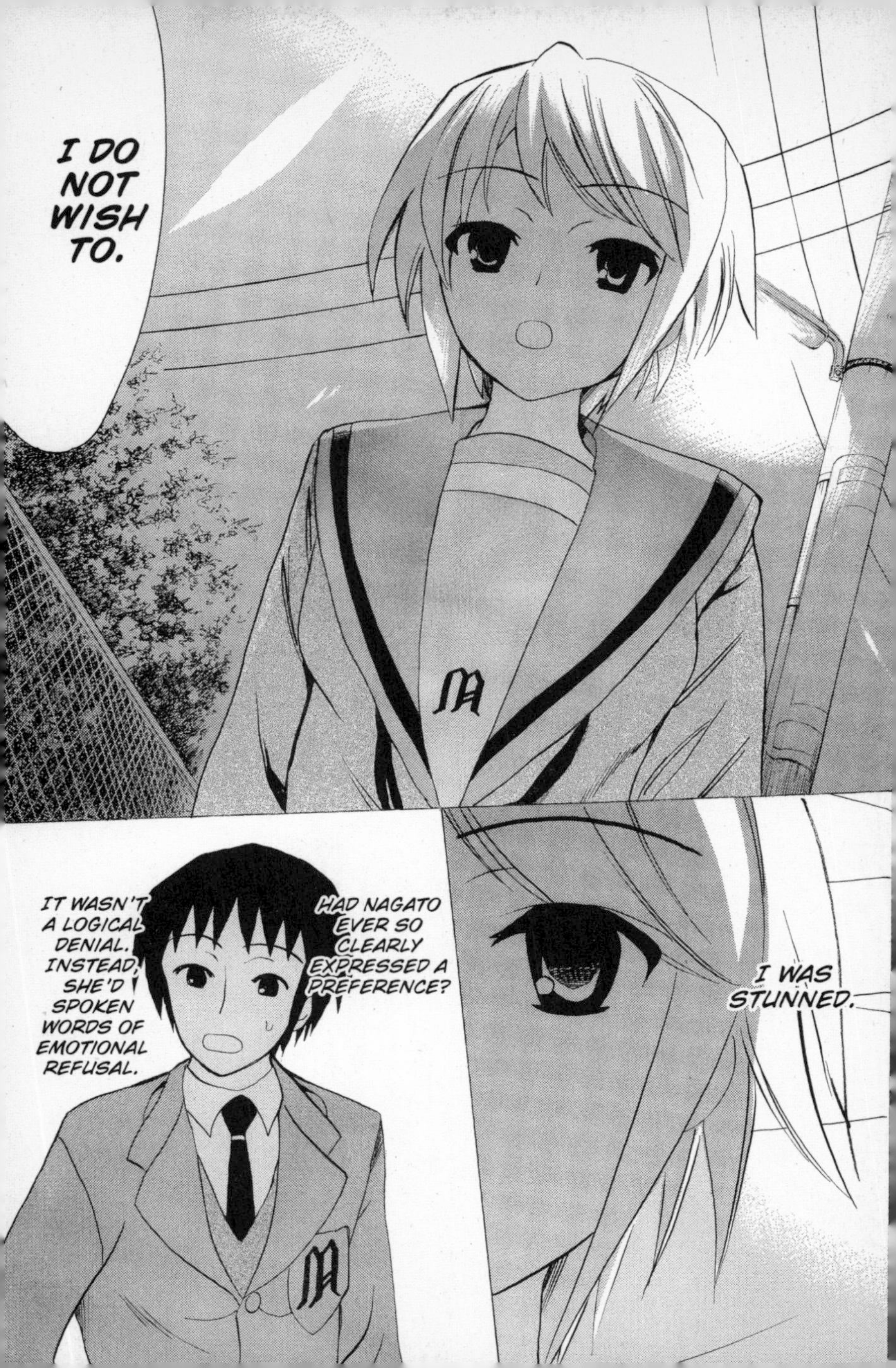
I DO NOT WISH TO.
I WAS STUNNED.
HAD NAGATO EVER SO CLEARLY EXPRESSED A PREFERENCE?
IT WASN'T A LOGICAL DENIAL. INSTEAD, SHE'D SPOKEN WORDS OF EMOTIONAL REFUSAL.

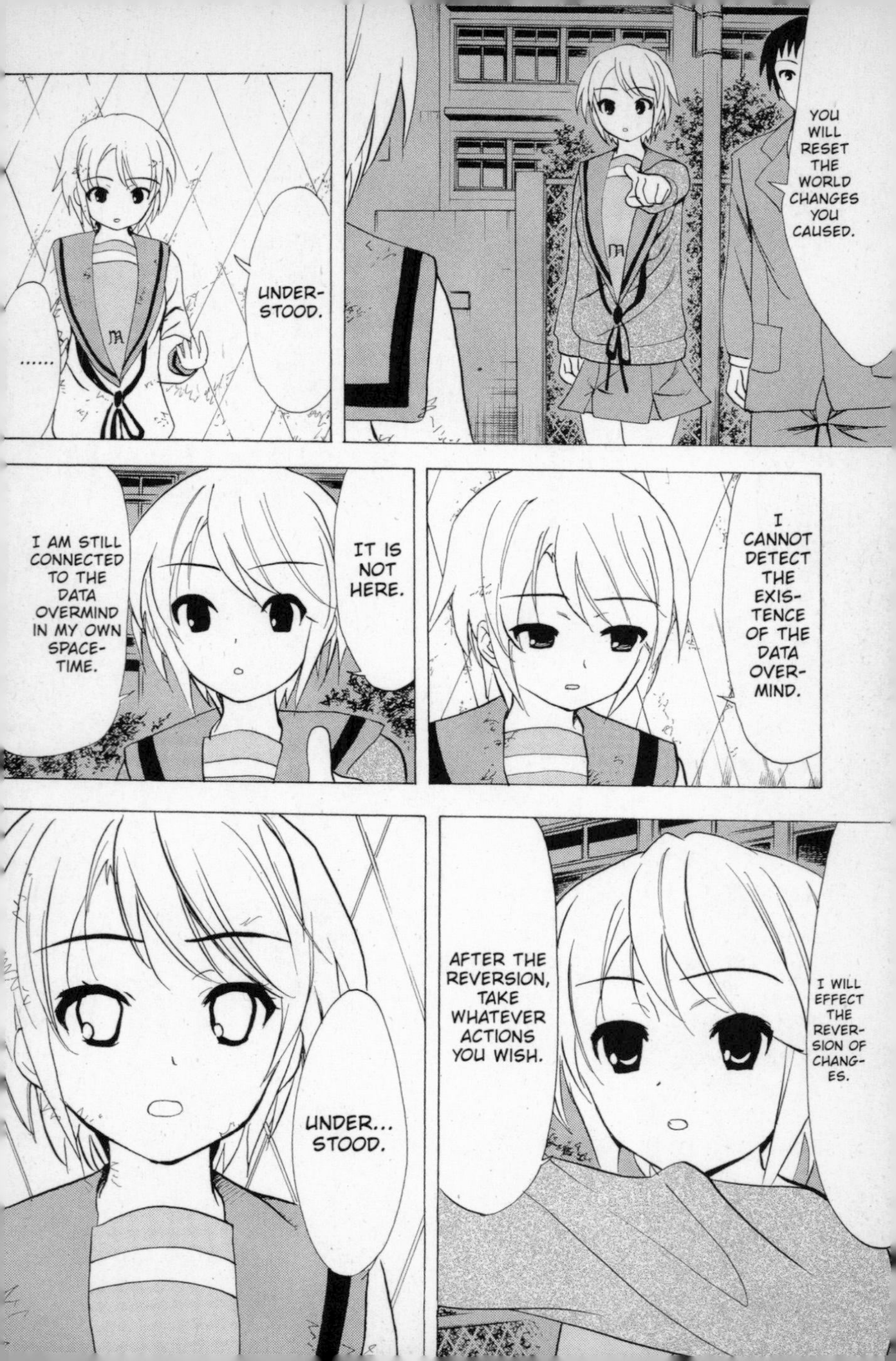
YOU WILL RESET THE WORLD CHANGES YOU CAUSED.
UNDER-STOOD.
......
I CANNOT DETECT THE EXISTENCE OF THE DATA OVERMIND.
IT IS NOT HERE.
I AM STILL CONNECTED TO THE DATA OVERMIND IN MY OWN SPACE-TIME.
I WILL EFFECT THE REVERSION OF CHANGES.
AFTER THE REVERSION, TAKE WHATEVER ACTIONS YOU WISH.
UNDER... STOOD.

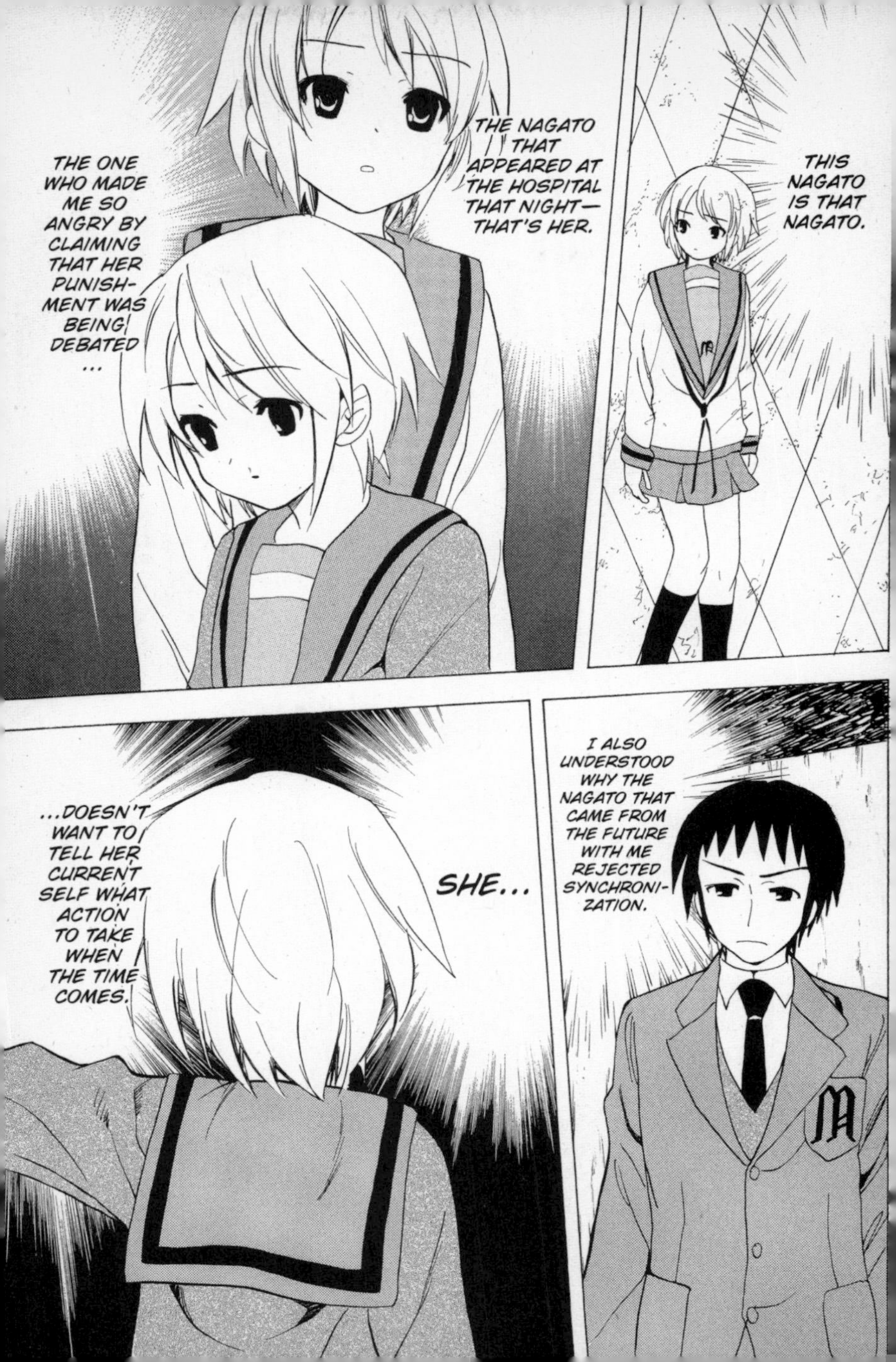
THIS NAGATO IS THAT NAGATO.
THE NAGATO THAT APPEARED AT THE HOSPITAL THAT NIGHT— THAT'S HER.
THE ONE WHO MADE ME SO ANGRY BY CLAIMING THAT HER PUNISH-MENT WAS BEING DEBATED ...
I ALSO UNDERSTOOD WHY THE NAGATO THAT CAME FROM THE FUTURE WITH ME REJECTED SYNCHRONI-ZATION.
SHE...
...DOESN'T WANT TO TELL HER CURRENT SELF WHAT ACTION TO TAKE WHEN THE TIME COMES.

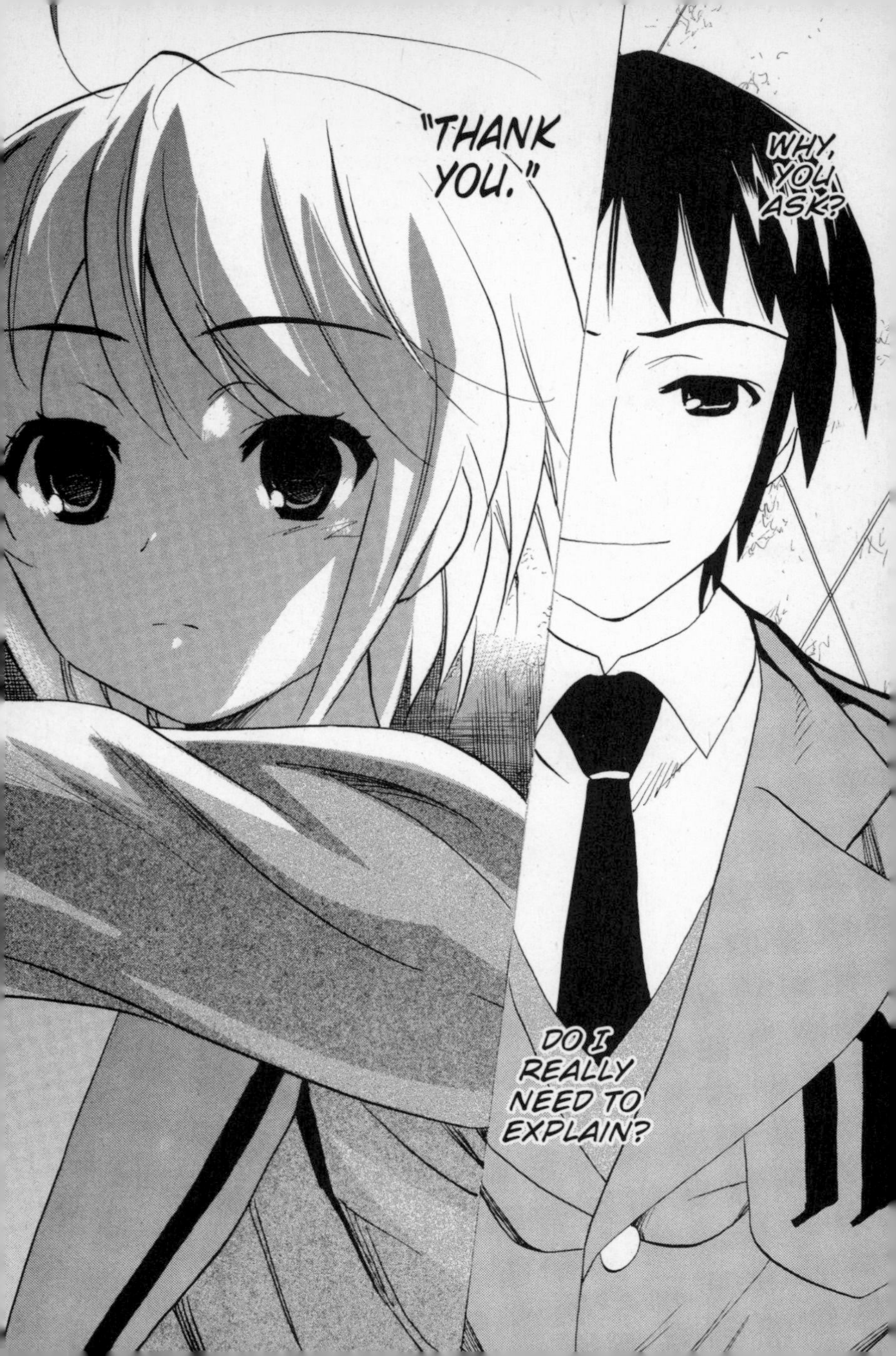
WHY, YOU ASK?
DO I REALLY NEED TO EXPLAIN?
"THANK YOU."

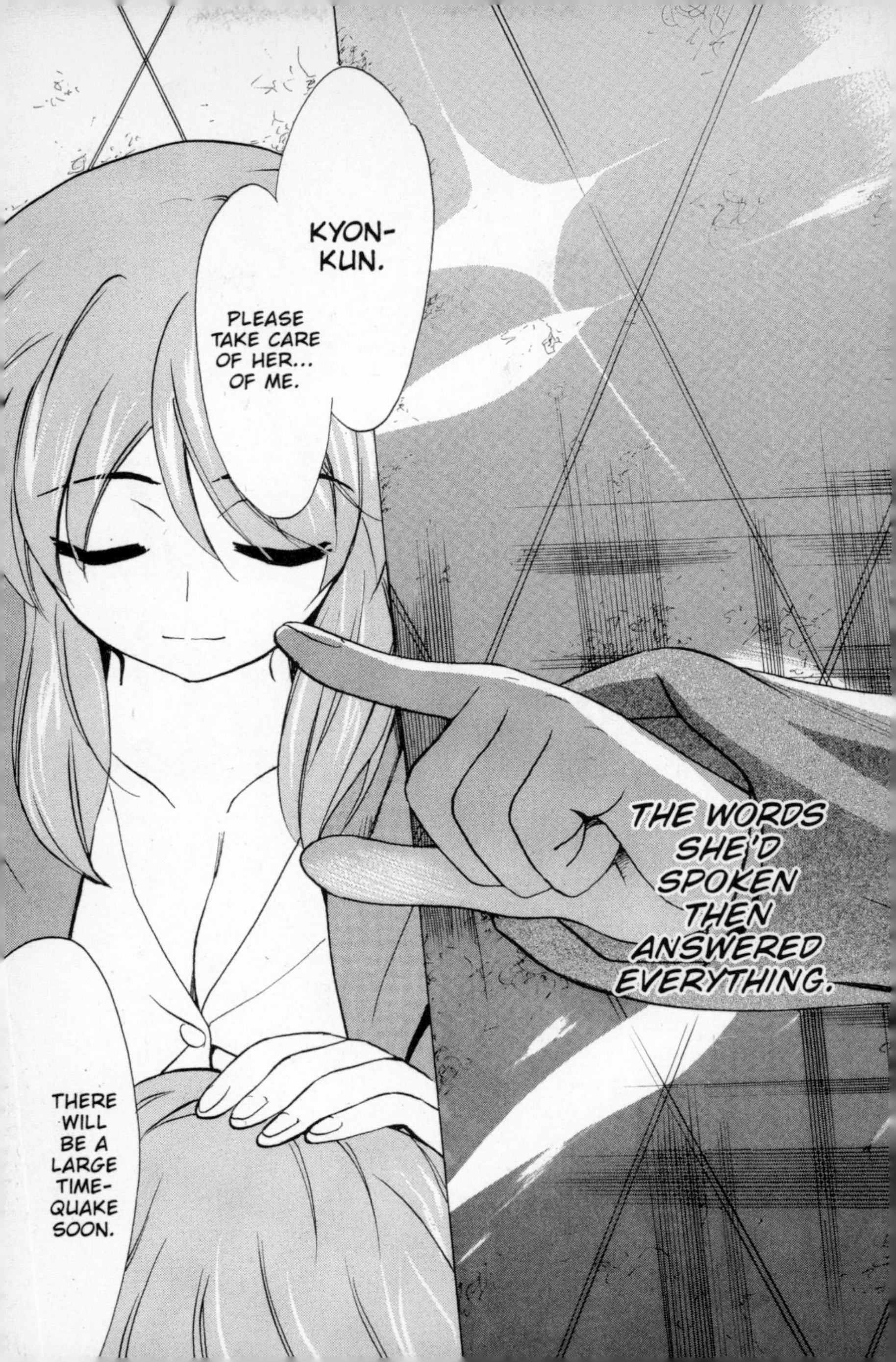
KYON-KUN.
PLEASE TAKE CARE OF HER... OF ME.
THE WORDS SHE'D SPOKEN THEN ANSWERED EVERYTHING.
THERE WILL BE A LARGE TIME-QUAKE SOON.

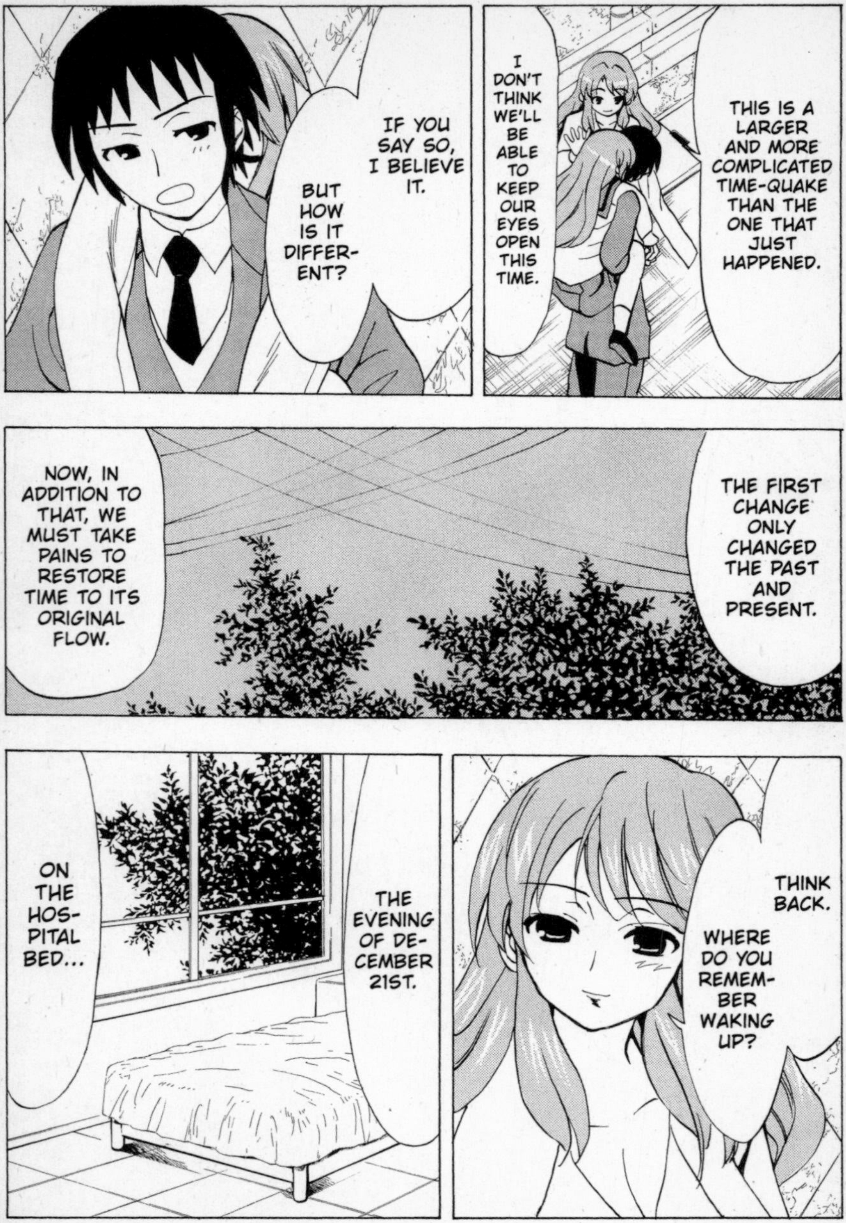
THIS IS A LARGER AND MORE COMPLICATED TIME-QUAKE THAN THE ONE THAT JUST HAPPENED.
I DON'T THINK WE'LL BE ABLE TO KEEP OUR EYES OPEN THIS TIME.
IF YOU SAY SO, I BELIEVE IT.
BUT HOW IS IT DIFFERENT?
THE FIRST CHANGE ONLY CHANGED THE PAST AND PRESENT.
NOW, IN ADDITION TO THAT, WE MUST TAKE PAINS TO RESTORE TIME TO ITS ORIGINAL FLOW.
THINK BACK.
WHERE DO YOU REMEMBER WAKING UP?
THE EVENING OF DECEMBER 21ST.
ON THE HOSPITAL BED...

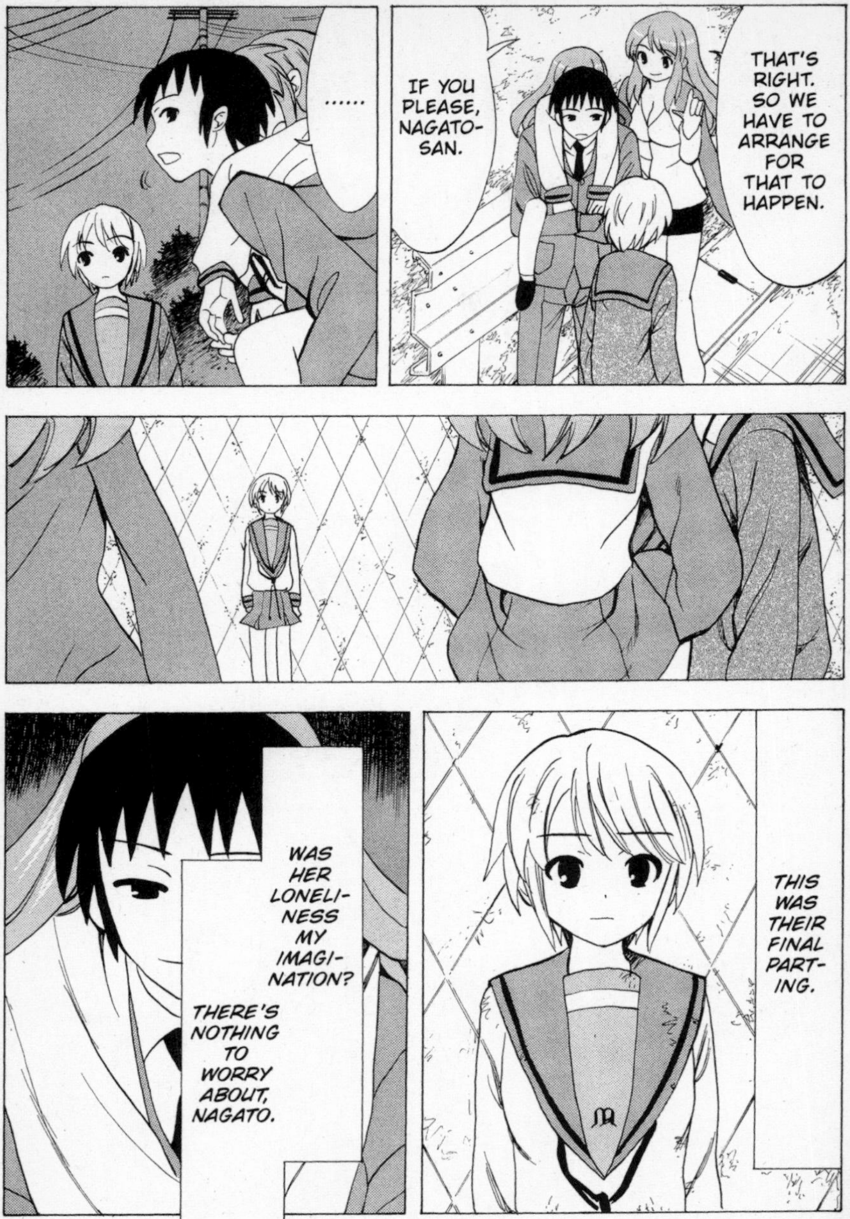
THAT'S RIGHT. SO WE HAVE TO ARRANGE FOR THAT TO HAPPEN.
IF YOU PLEASE, NAGATO-SAN.
......
THIS WAS THEIR FINAL PARTING.
WAS HER LONELINESS MY IMAGINATION?
THERE'S NOTHING TO WORRY ABOUT, NAGATO.

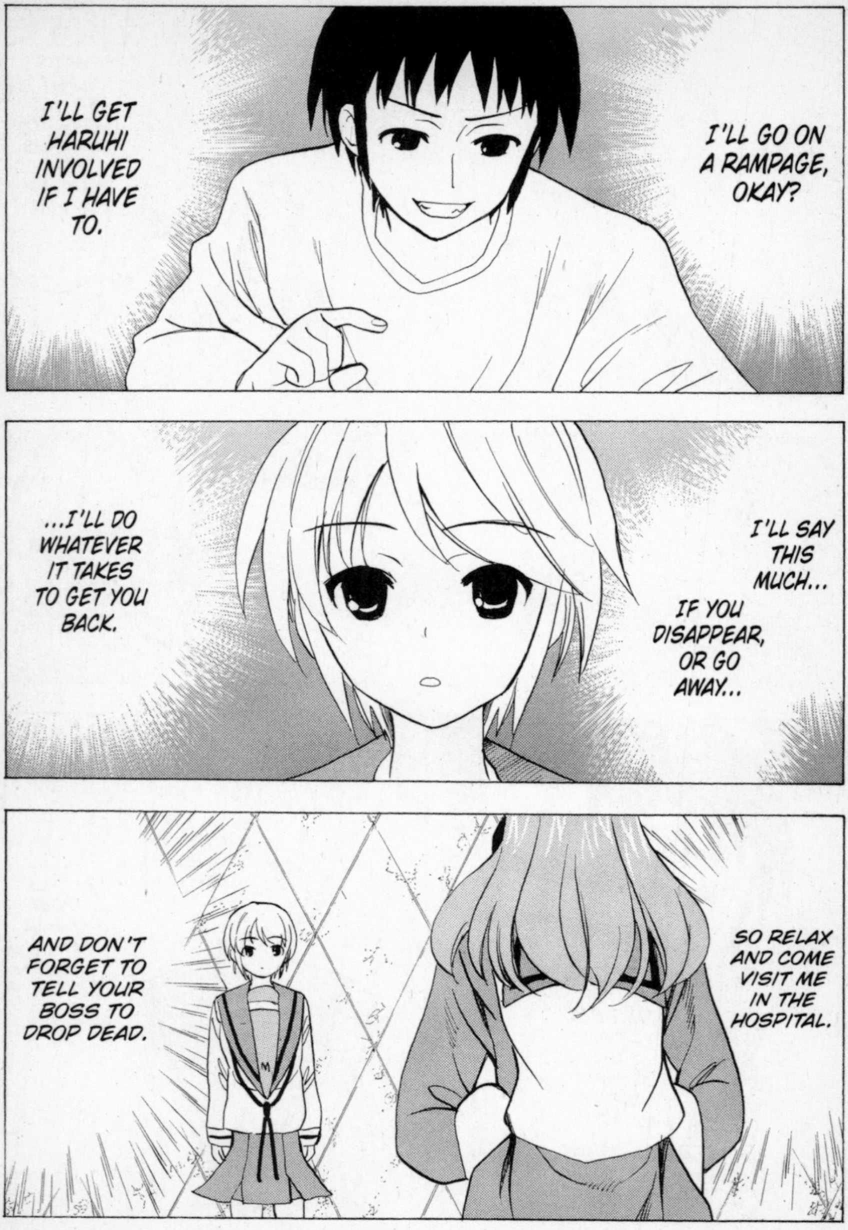
I'LL GO ON A RAMPAGE, OKAY?
I'LL GET HARUHI INVOLVED IF I HAVE TO.
I'LL SAY THIS MUCH...
IF YOU DISAPPEAR, OR GO AWAY...
...I'LL DO WHATEVER IT TAKES TO GET YOU BACK.
SO RELAX AND COME VISIT ME IN THE HOSPITAL.
AND DON'T FORGET TO TELL YOUR BOSS TO DROP DEAD.

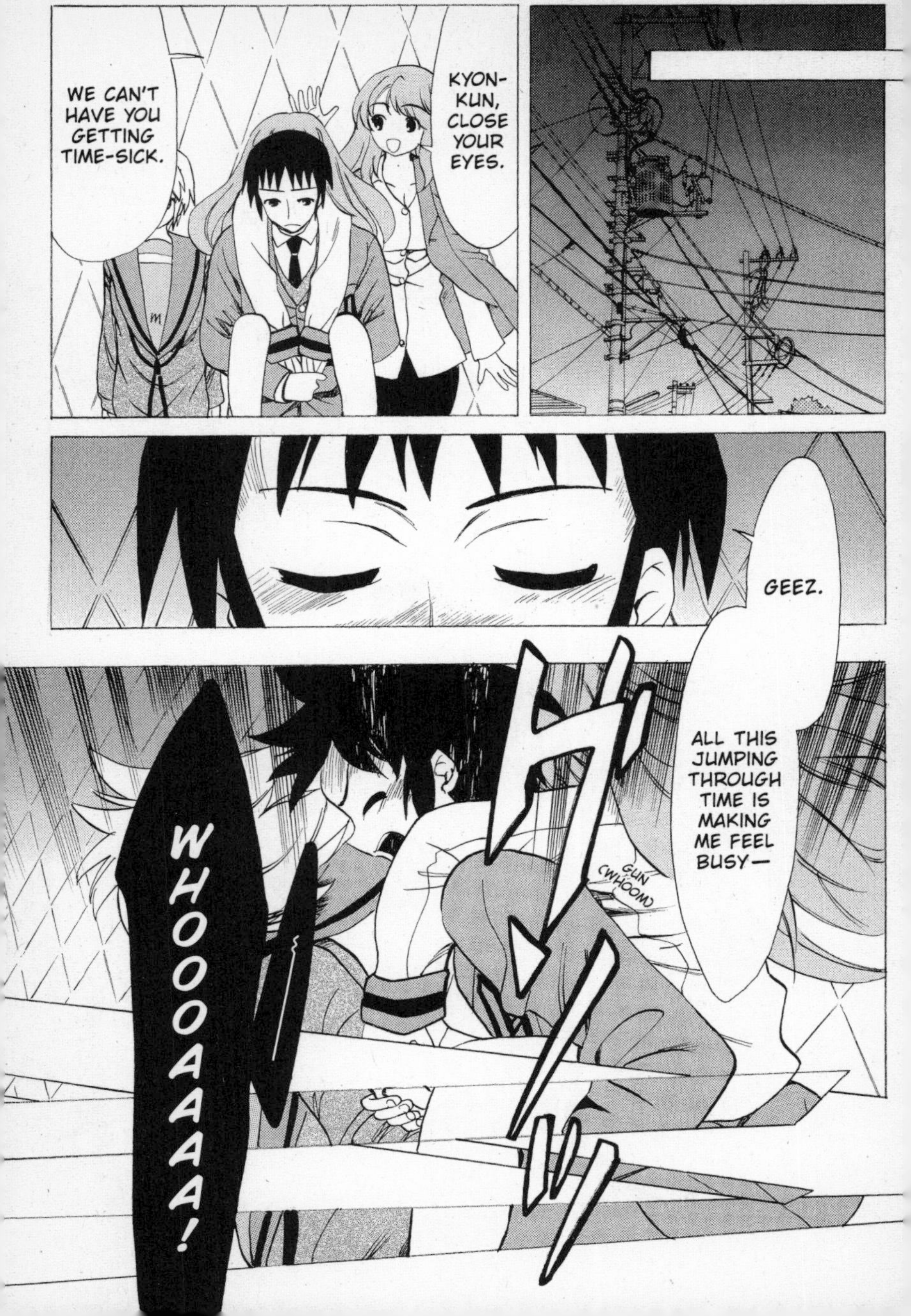
KYON-KUN, CLOSE YOUR EYES.
WE CAN'T HAVE YOU GETTING TIME-SICK.
GEEZ.
ALL THIS JUMPING THROUGH TIME IS MAKING ME FEEL BUSY—
GUN (WHOOM)
WHOOOAAAA!

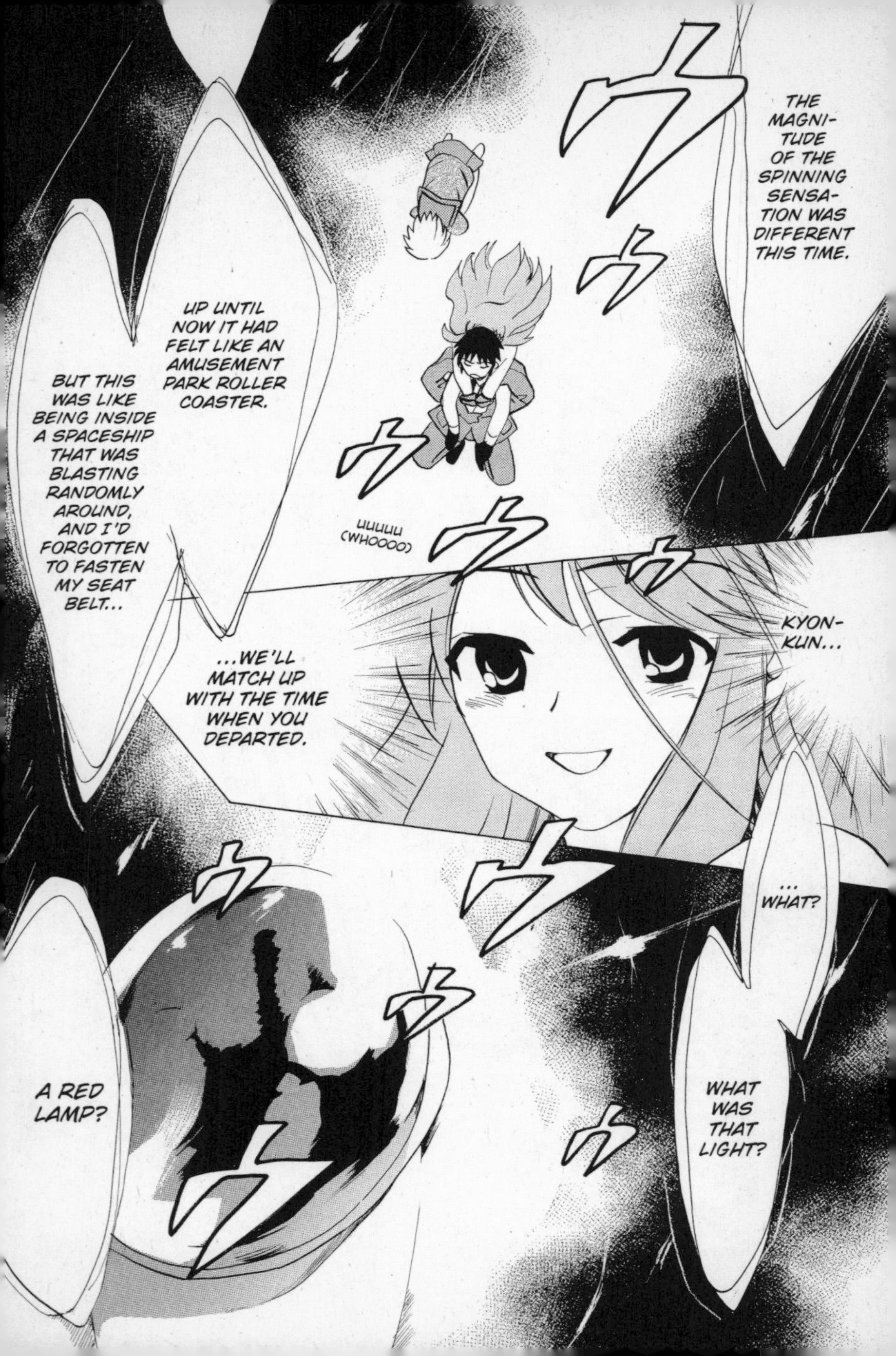
THE MAGNITUDE OF THE SPINNING SENSATION WAS DIFFERENT THIS TIME.
UP UNTIL NOW IT HAD FELT LIKE AN AMUSEMENT PARK ROLLER COASTER.
BUT THIS WAS LIKE BEING INSIDE A SPACESHIP THAT WAS BLASTING RANDOMLY AROUND, AND I'D FORGOTTEN TO FASTEN MY SEAT BELT...
uuuuu (WHOOOO)
KYON-KUN...
...WE'LL MATCH UP WITH THE TIME WHEN YOU DEPARTED.
...WHAT?
WHAT WAS THAT LIGHT?
A RED LAMP?

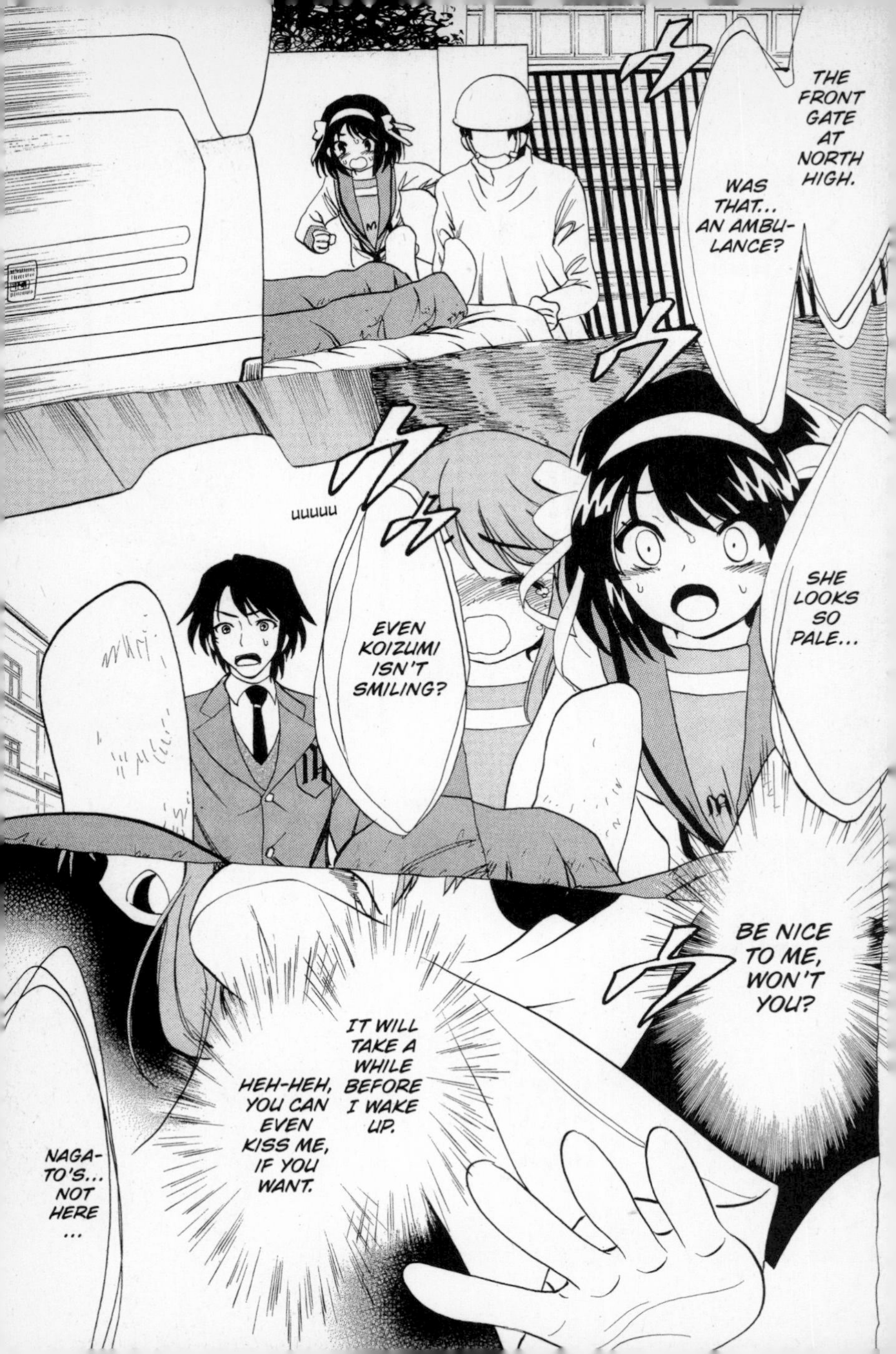
THE FRONT GATE AT NORTH HIGH.
WAS THAT... AN AMBULANCE?
SHE LOOKS SO PALE...
EVEN KOIZUMI ISN'T SMILING?
uuuuu
BE NICE TO ME, WON'T YOU?
IT WILL TAKE A WHILE BEFORE I WAKE UP.
HEH-HEH, YOU CAN EVEN KISS ME, IF YOU WANT.
NAGATO'S... NOT HERE ...

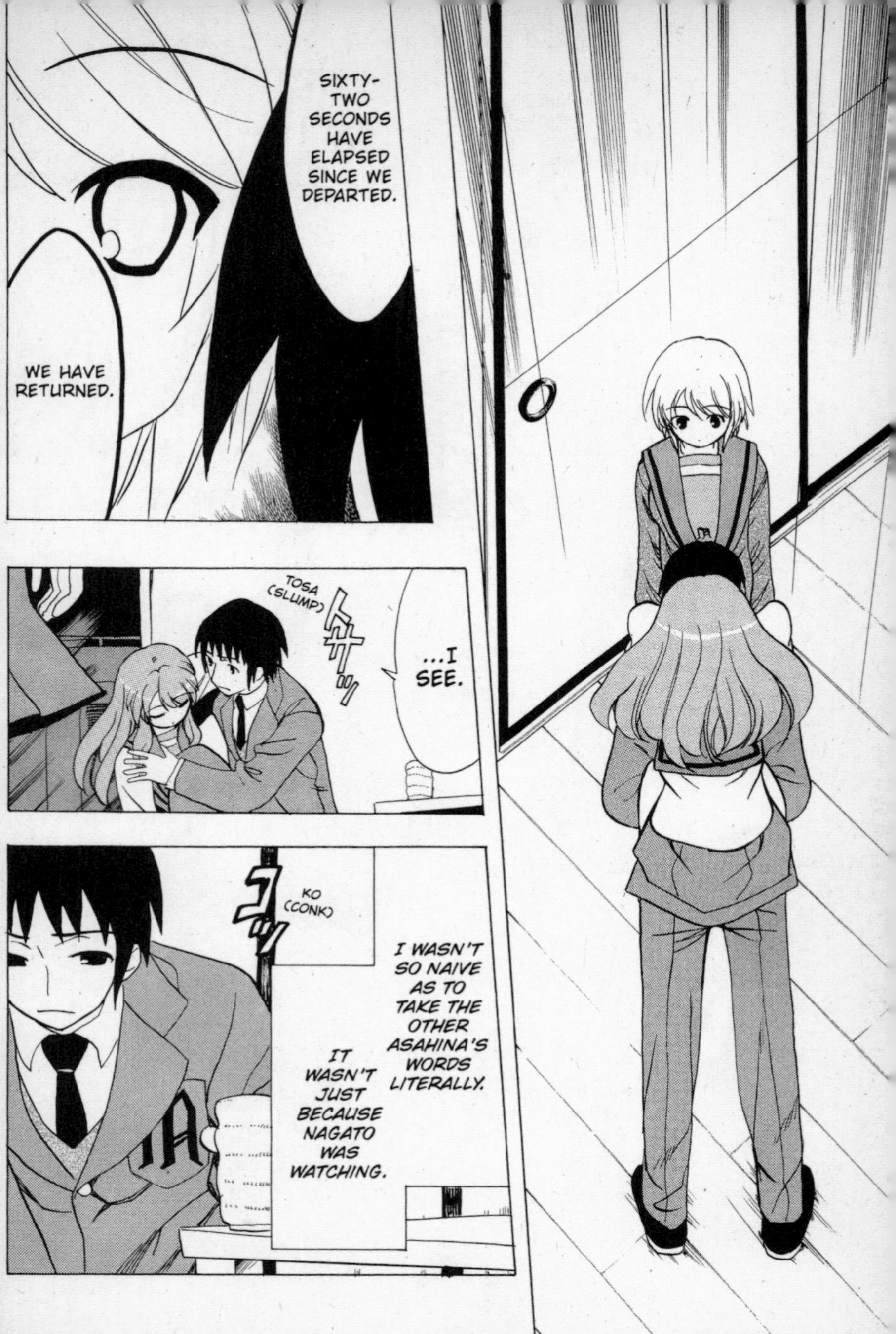
SIXTY-TWO SECONDS HAVE ELAPSED SINCE WE DEPARTED.
WE HAVE RETURNED.
...I SEE.
TOSA (SLUMP)
KO (CONK)
I WASN'T SO NAIVE AS TO TAKE THE OTHER ASAHINA'S WORDS LITERALLY.
IT WASN'T JUST BECAUSE NAGATO WAS WATCHING.

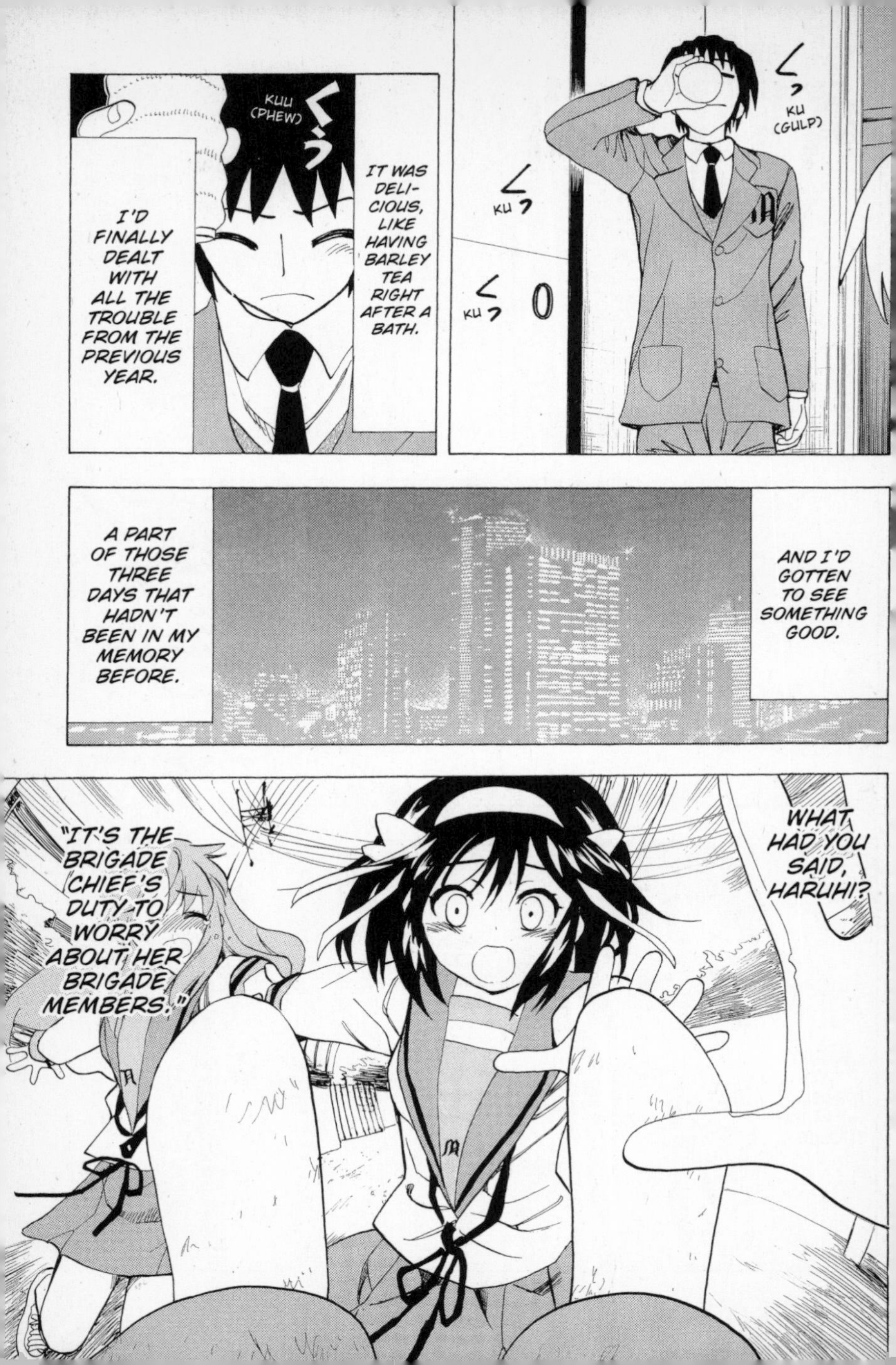
く
KU (GULP)
く
KU
く
KU
くう
KUU (PHEW)
IT WAS DELICIOUS, LIKE HAVING BARLEY TEA RIGHT AFTER A BATH.
I'D FINALLY DEALT WITH ALL THE TROUBLE FROM THE PREVIOUS YEAR.
A PART OF THOSE THREE DAYS THAT HADN'T BEEN IN MY MEMORY BEFORE.
AND I'D GOTTEN TO SEE SOMETHING GOOD.
WHAT HAD YOU SAID, HARUHI?
"IT'S THE BRIGADE CHIEF'S DUTY TO WORRY ABOUT HER BRIGADE MEMBERS."

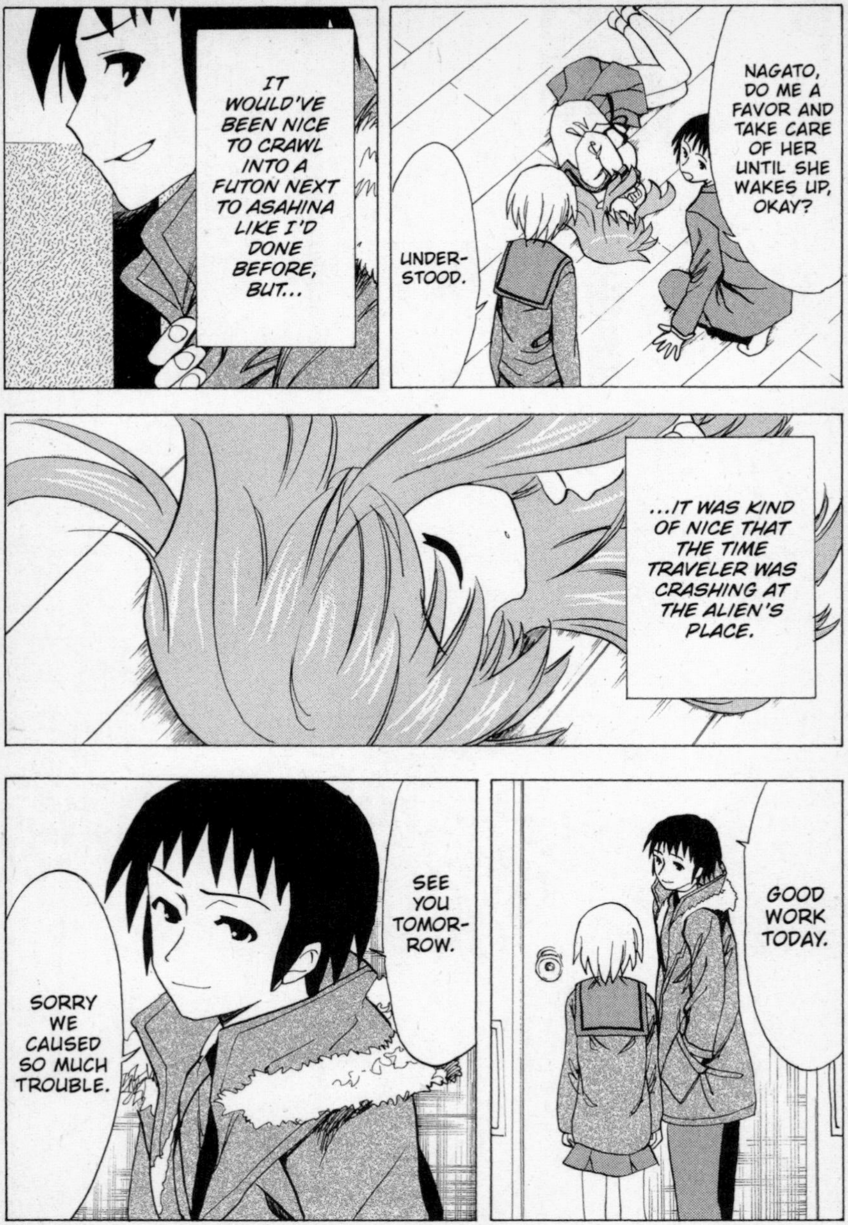
NAGATO, DO ME A FAVOR AND TAKE CARE OF HER UNTIL SHE WAKES UP, OKAY?
UNDER-STOOD.
IT WOULD'VE BEEN NICE TO CRAWL INTO A FUTON NEXT TO ASAHINA LIKE I'D DONE BEFORE, BUT...
...IT WAS KIND OF NICE THAT THE TIME TRAVELER WAS CRASHING AT THE ALIEN'S PLACE.
GOOD WORK TODAY.
SEE YOU TOMOR-ROW.
SORRY WE CAUSED SO MUCH TROUBLE.

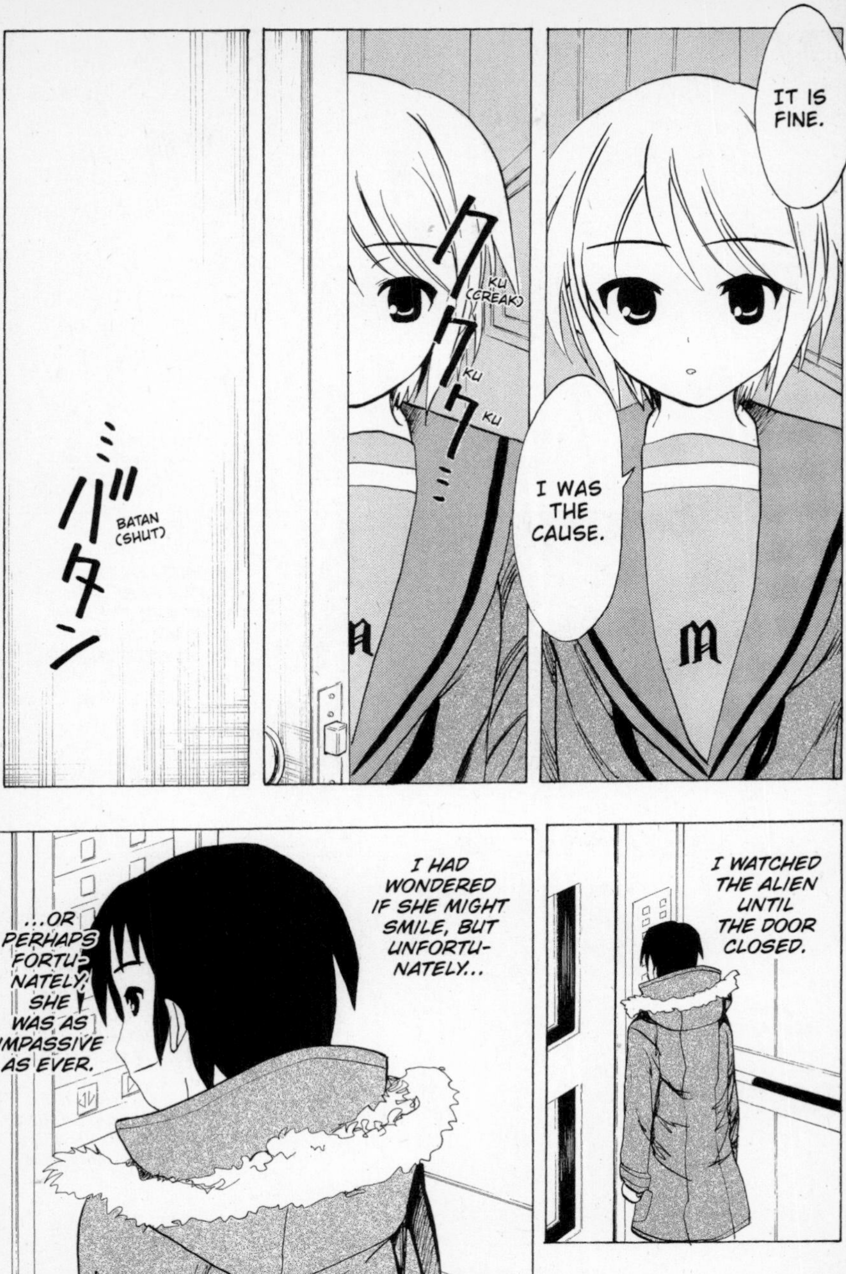
IT IS FINE.
I WAS THE CAUSE.
ククク
KU (CREAK)
KU
KU
バタン
BATAN (SHUT)
I WATCHED THE ALIEN UNTIL THE DOOR CLOSED.
I HAD WONDERED IF SHE MIGHT SMILE, BUT UNFORTUNATELY...
...OR PERHAPS FORTUNATELY, SHE WAS AS IMPASSIVE AS EVER.

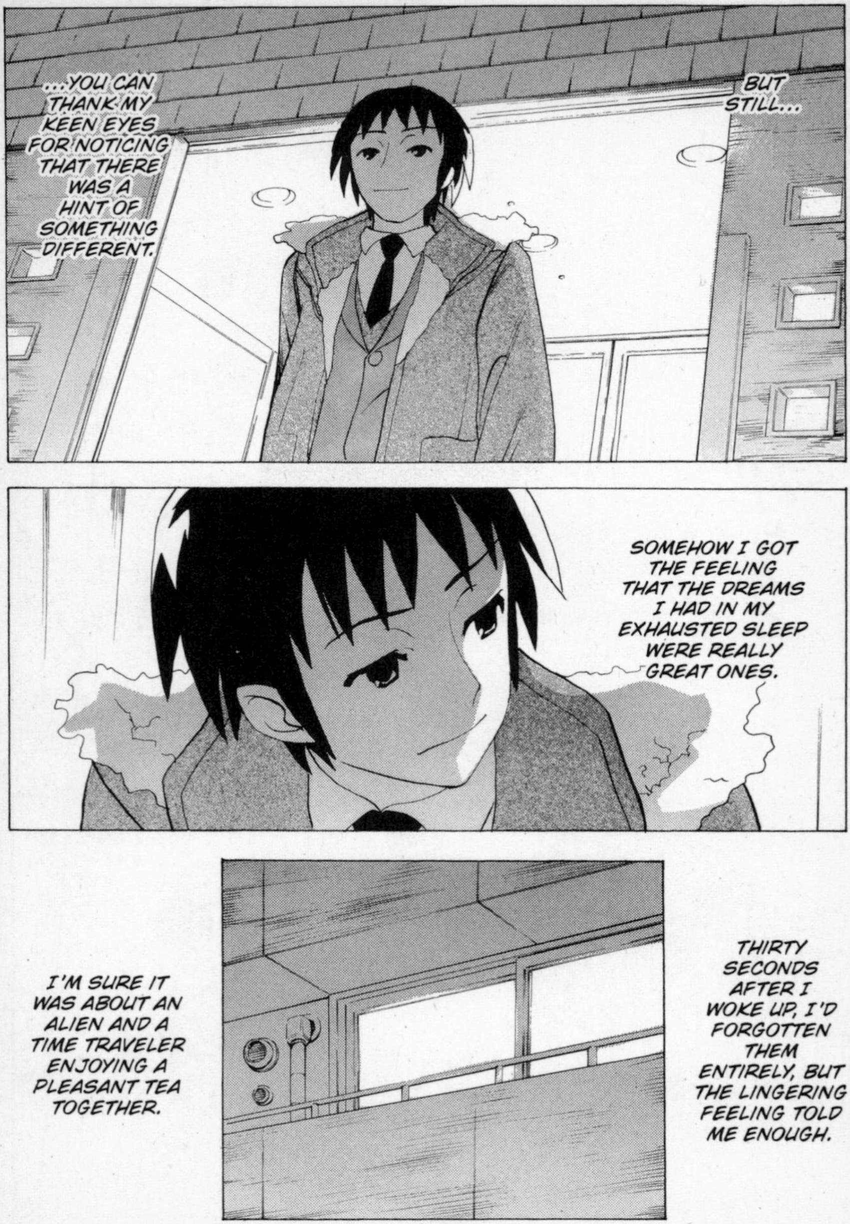
BUT STILL...
...YOU CAN THANK MY KEEN EYES FOR NOTICING THAT THERE WAS A HINT OF SOMETHING DIFFERENT.
SOMEHOW I GOT THE FEELING THAT THE DREAMS I HAD IN MY EXHAUSTED SLEEP WERE REALLY GREAT ONES.
THIRTY SECONDS AFTER I WOKE UP, I'D FORGOTTEN THEM ENTIRELY, BUT THE LINGERING FEELING TOLD ME ENOUGH.
I'M SURE IT WAS ABOUT AN ALIEN AND A TIME TRAVELER ENJOYING A PLEASANT TEA TOGETHER.

The Disappearance of Haruhi Suzumiya—Another Day : END

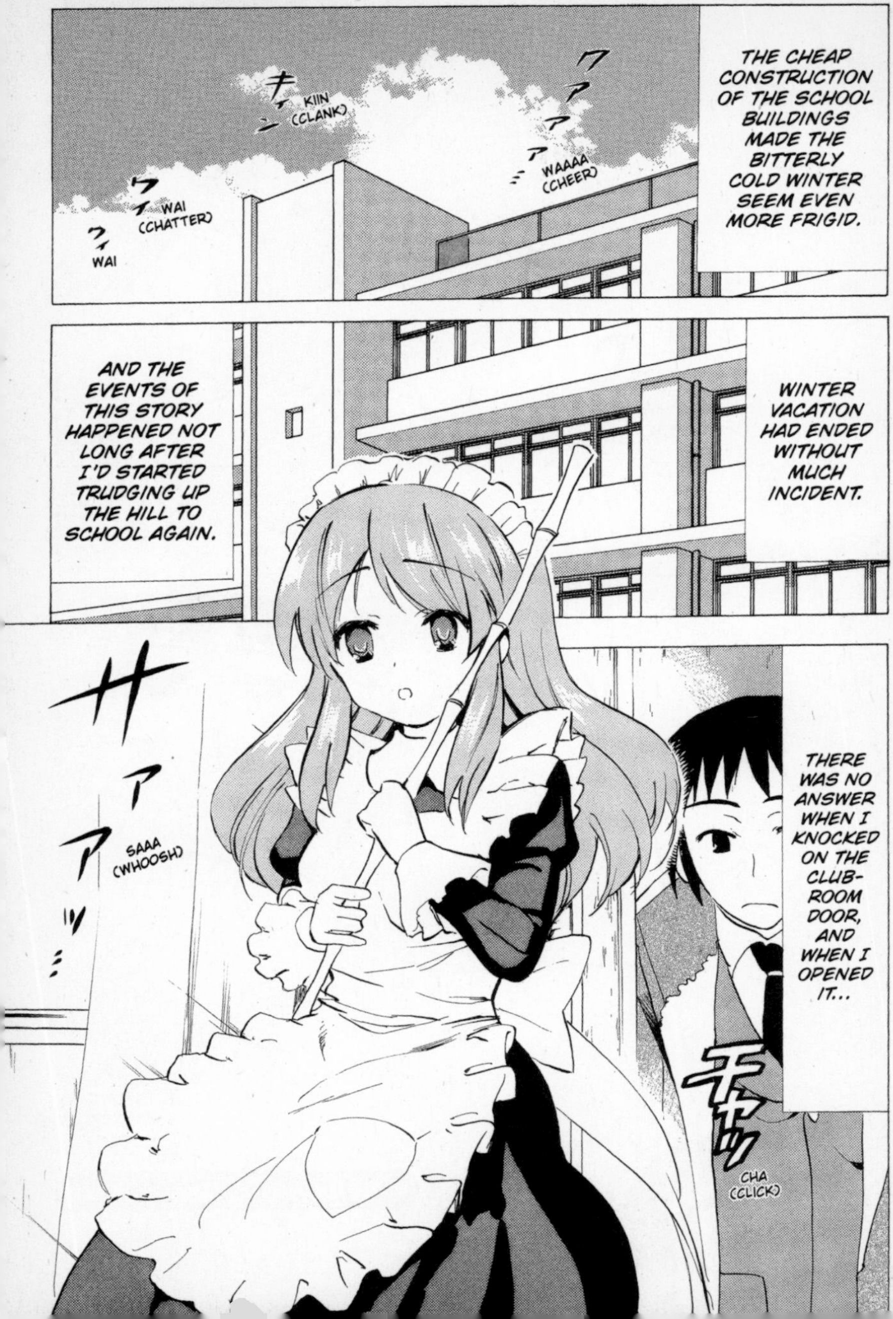
THE CHEAP CONSTRUCTION OF THE SCHOOL BUILDINGS MADE THE BITTERLY COLD WINTER SEEM EVEN MORE FRIGID.
WAAAA (CHEER)
KIIN (CLANK)
WAI (CHATTER)
WAI
WINTER VACATION HAD ENDED WITHOUT MUCH INCIDENT.
AND THE EVENTS OF THIS STORY HAPPENED NOT LONG AFTER I'D STARTED TRUDGING UP THE HILL TO SCHOOL AGAIN.
THERE WAS NO ANSWER WHEN I KNOCKED ON THE CLUB-ROOM DOOR, AND WHEN I OPENED IT...
CHA (CLICK)
SAAA (WHOOSH)

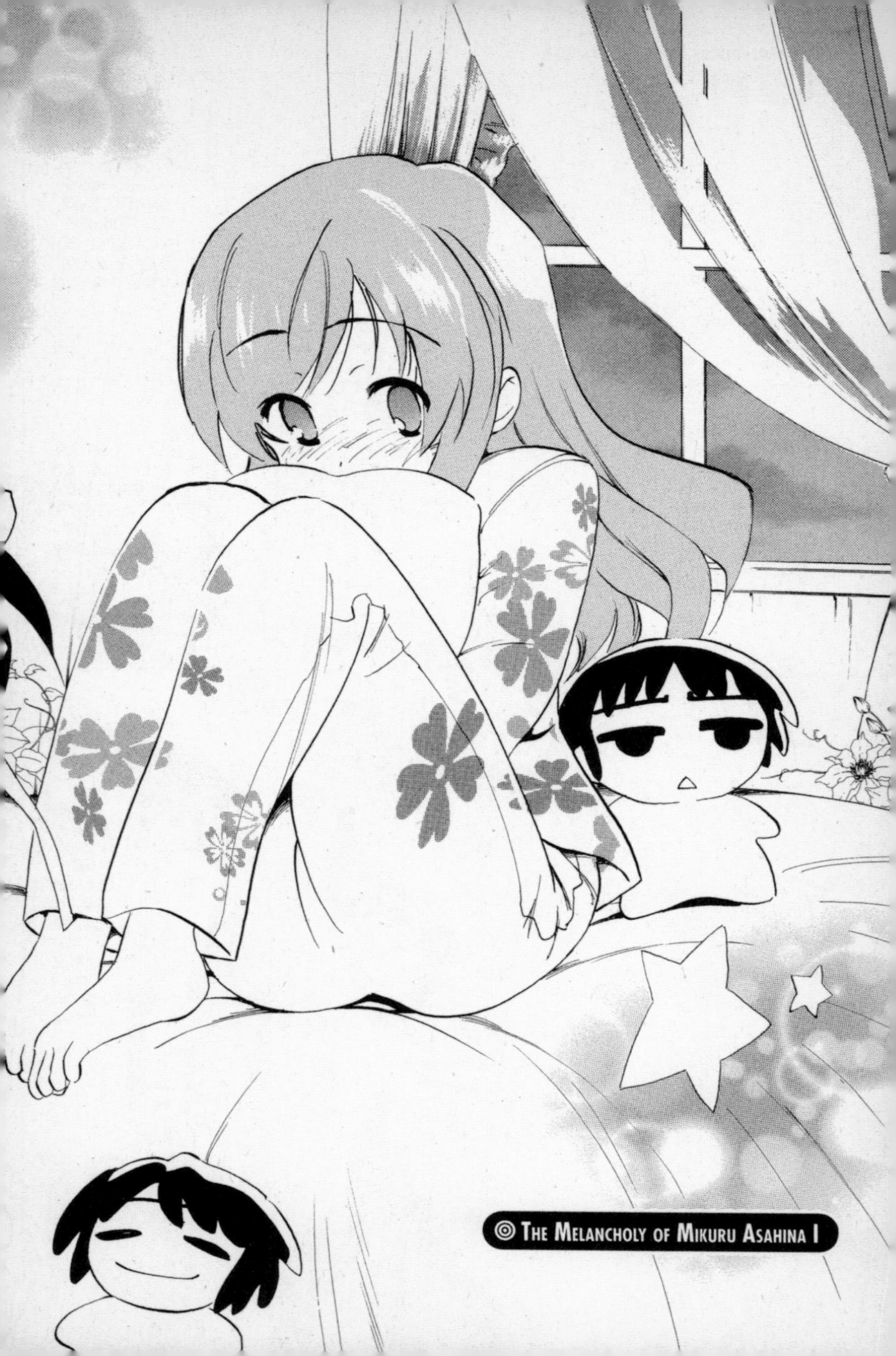
THE MELANCHOLY OF MIKURU ASAHINA I

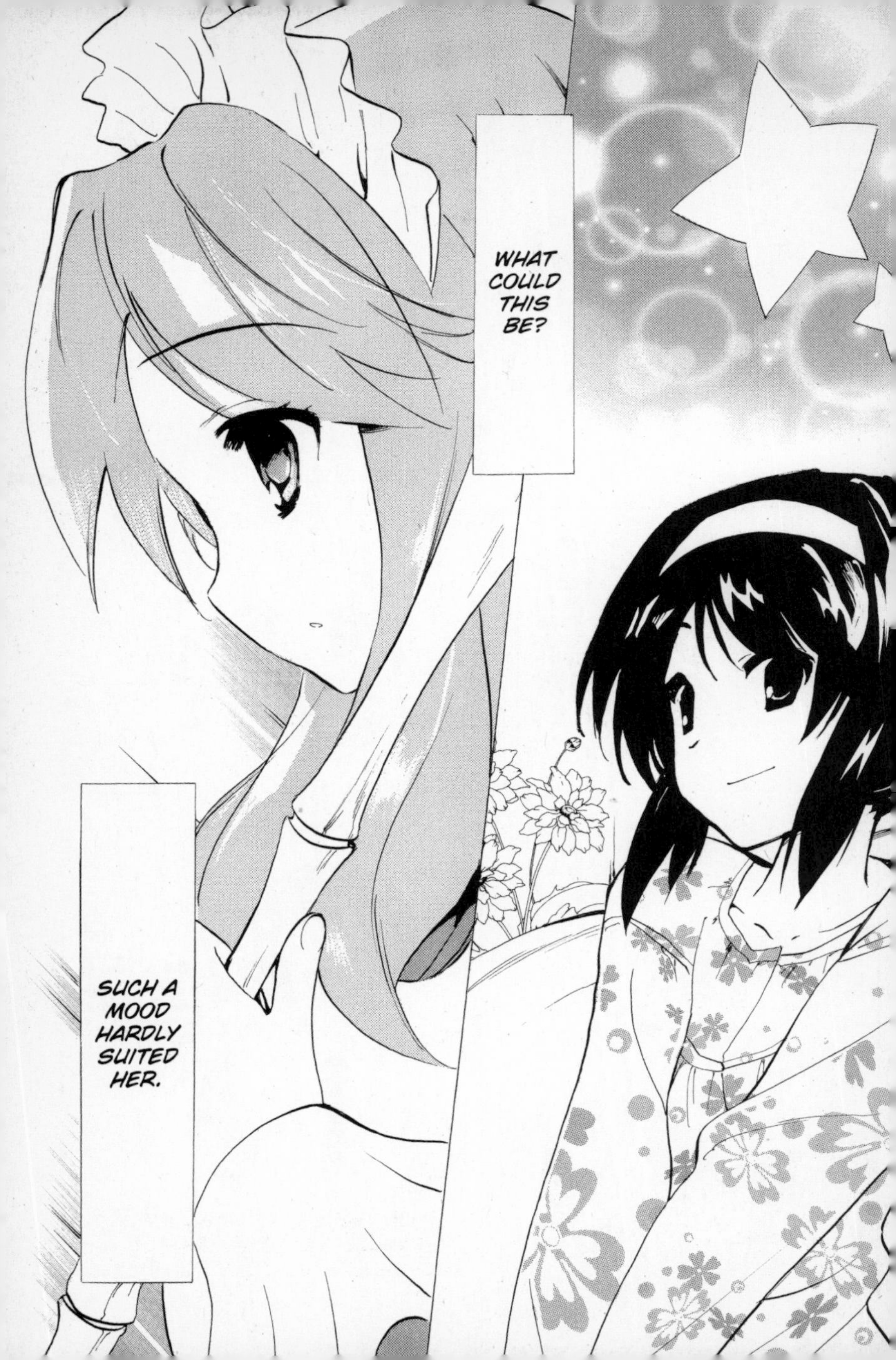
WHAT COULD THIS BE?
SUCH A MOOD HARDLY SUITED HER.

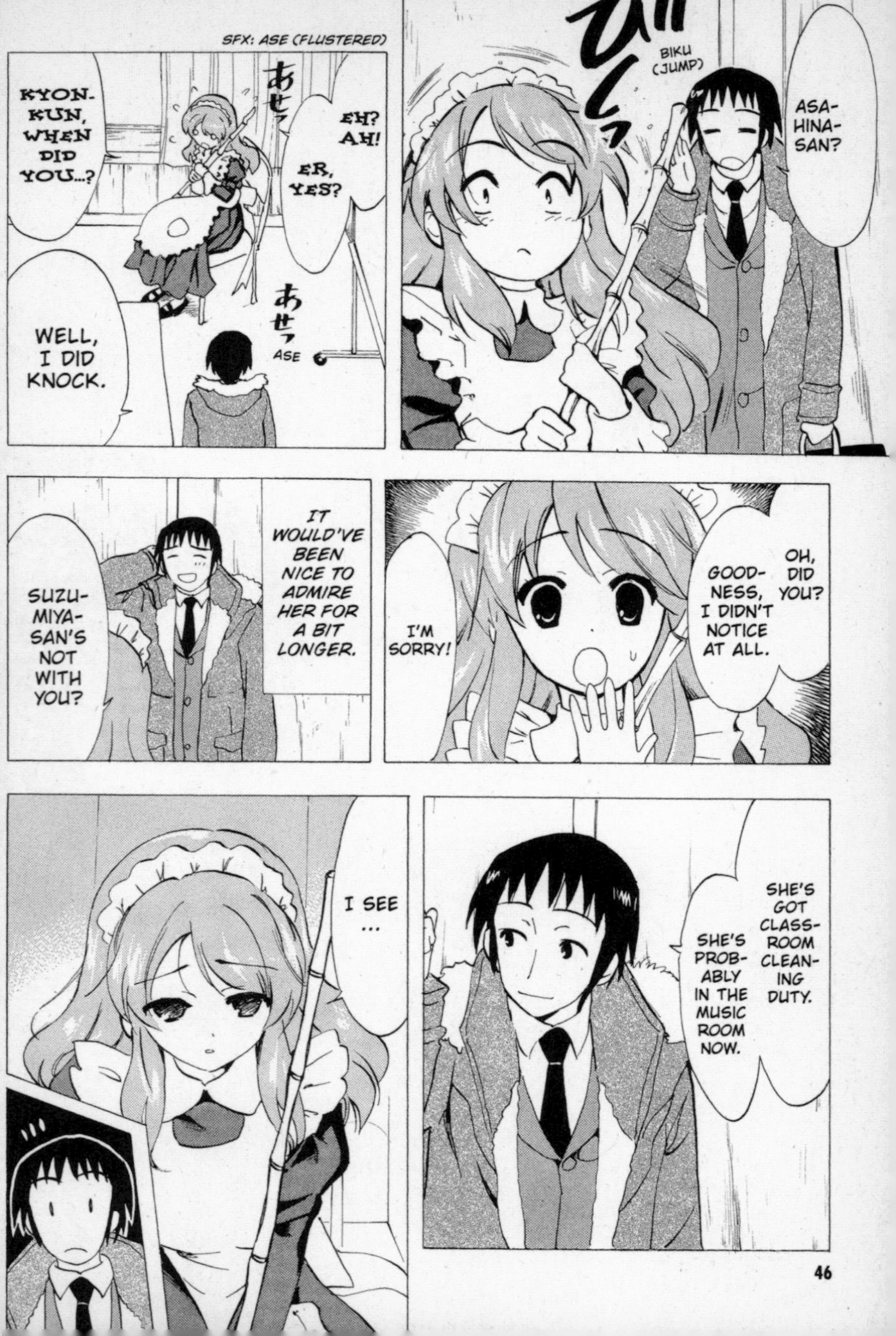
ASA-HINA-SAN?
BIKU (JUMP)
ひくっ
ひ
SFX: ASE (FLUSTERED)
あせっ
EH? AH! ER, YES?
KYON-KUN, WHEN DID YOU...?
あせっ ASE
WELL, I DID KNOCK.
OH, DID YOU?
GOODNESS, I DIDN'T NOTICE AT ALL.
I'M SORRY!
IT WOULD'VE BEEN NICE TO ADMIRE HER FOR A BIT LONGER.
SUZUMIYA-SAN'S NOT WITH YOU?
SHE'S GOT CLASSROOM CLEANING DUTY.
SHE'S PROBABLY IN THE MUSIC ROOM NOW.
I SEE ...

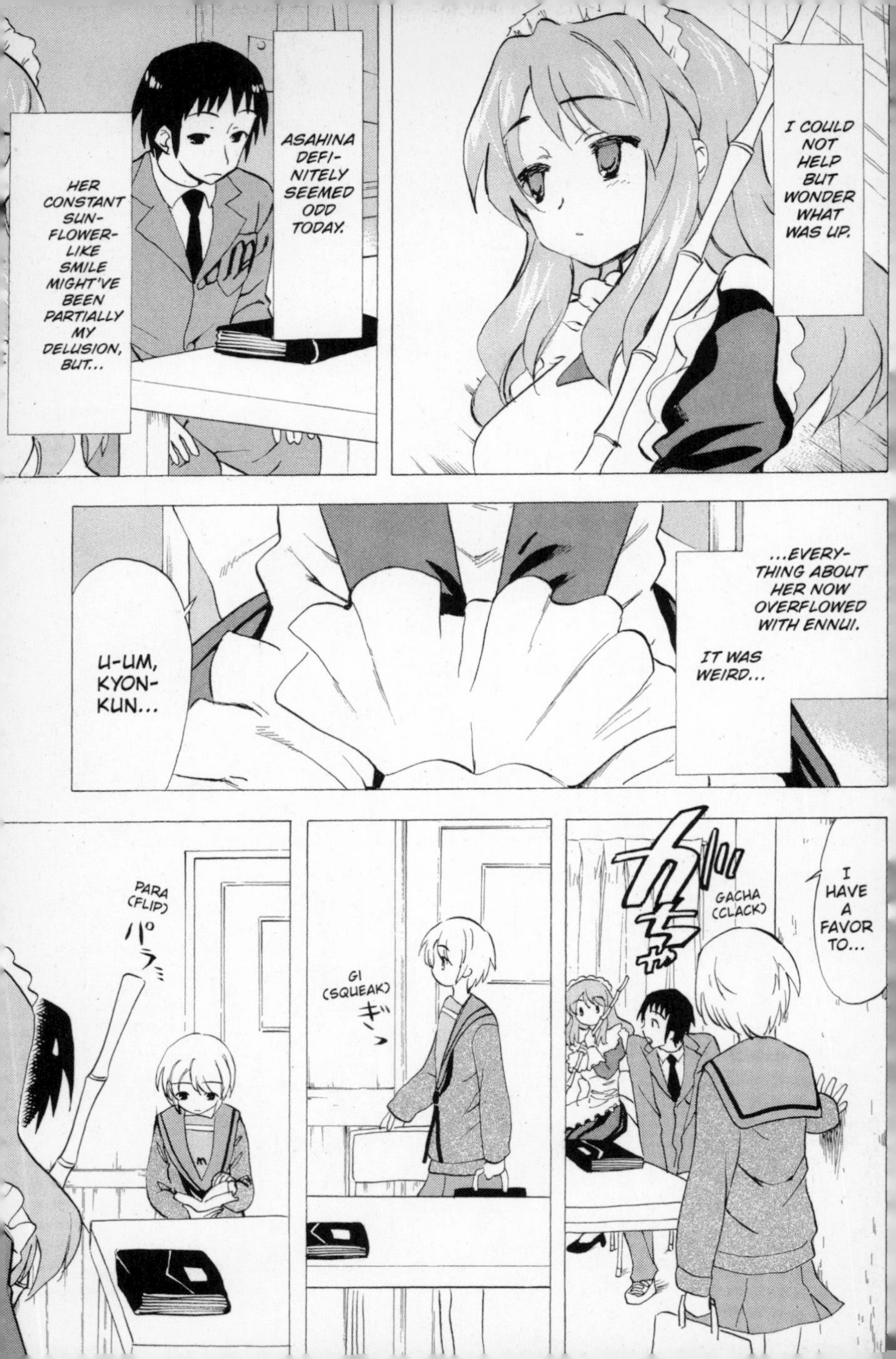
I COULD NOT HELP BUT WONDER WHAT WAS UP.
ASAHINA DEFINITELY SEEMED ODD TODAY.
HER CONSTANT SUNFLOWER-LIKE SMILE MIGHT'VE BEEN PARTIALLY MY DELUSION, BUT...
...EVERYTHING ABOUT HER NOW OVERFLOWED WITH ENNUI.
IT WAS WEIRD...
U-UM, KYON-KUN...
I HAVE A FAVOR TO...
ガチャ
GACHA (CLACK)
GI (SQUEAK)
ギッ
PARA (FLIP)
パラ

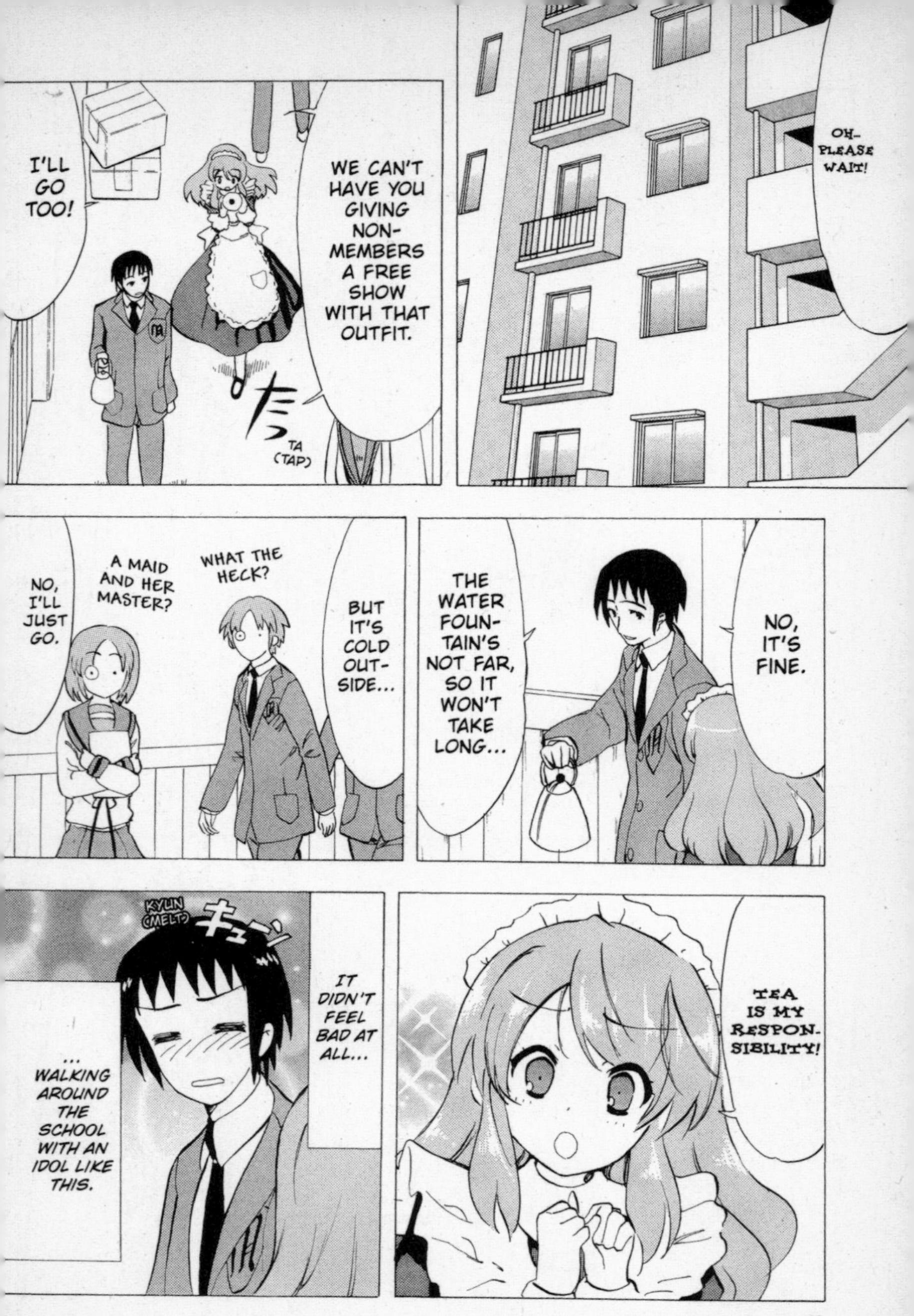
OH- PLEASE WAIT!
WE CAN'T HAVE YOU GIVING NON-MEMBERS A FREE SHOW WITH THAT OUTFIT.
I'LL GO TOO!
TA (TAP)
NO, IT'S FINE.
THE WATER FOUNTAIN'S NOT FAR, SO IT WON'T TAKE LONG...
BUT IT'S COLD OUTSIDE...
WHAT THE HECK?
A MAID AND HER MASTER?
NO, I'LL JUST GO.
TEA IS MY RESPONSIBILITY!
IT DIDN'T FEEL BAD AT ALL...
KYUN (MELT)
...WALKING AROUND THE SCHOOL WITH AN IDOL LIKE THIS.

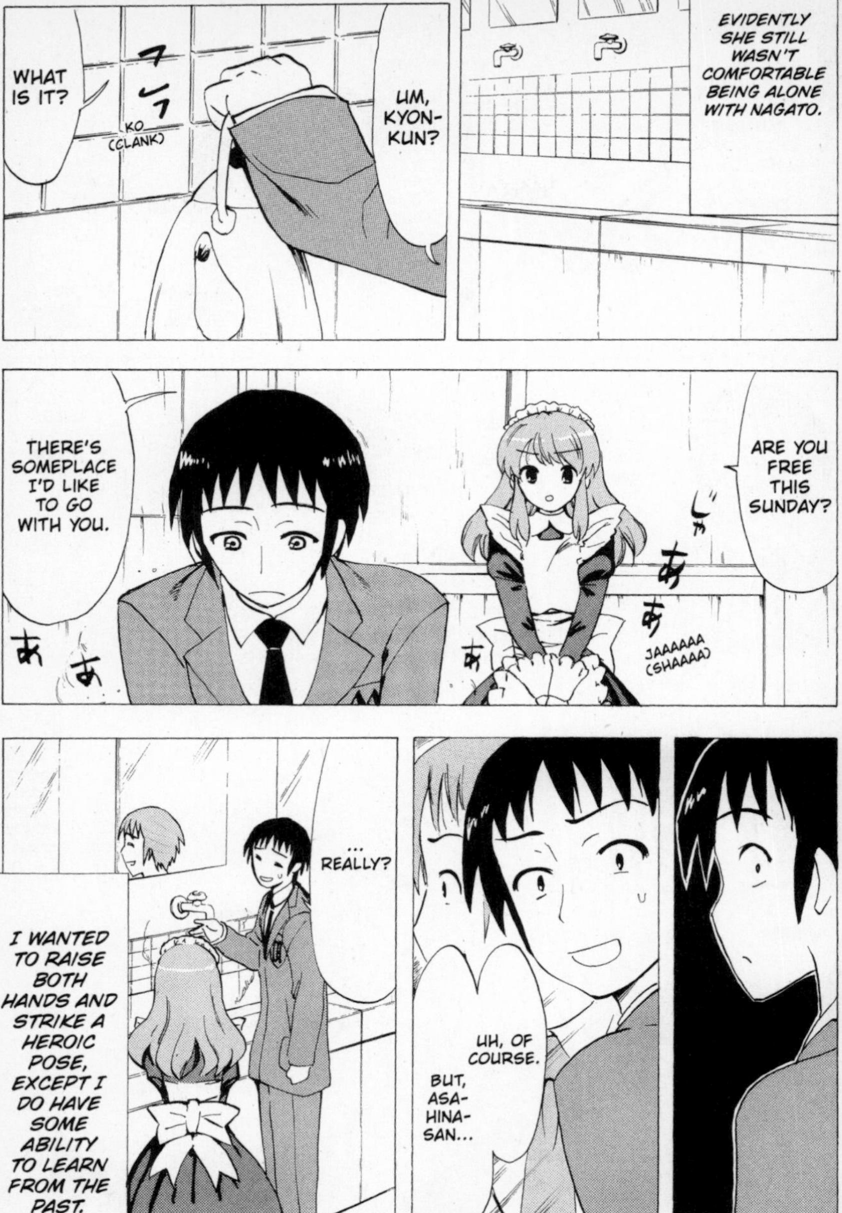
EVIDENTLY SHE STILL WASN'T COMFORTABLE BEING ALONE WITH NAGATO.
UM, KYON-KUN?
KO (CLANK)
WHAT IS IT?
ARE YOU FREE THIS SUNDAY?
じゃあああ
JAAAAAA (SHAAAA)
THERE'S SOMEPLACE I'D LIKE TO GO WITH YOU.
UH, OF COURSE.
BUT, ASA-HINA-SAN...
... REALLY?
I WANTED TO RAISE BOTH HANDS AND STRIKE A HEROIC POSE, EXCEPT I DO HAVE SOME ABILITY TO LEARN FROM THE PAST.

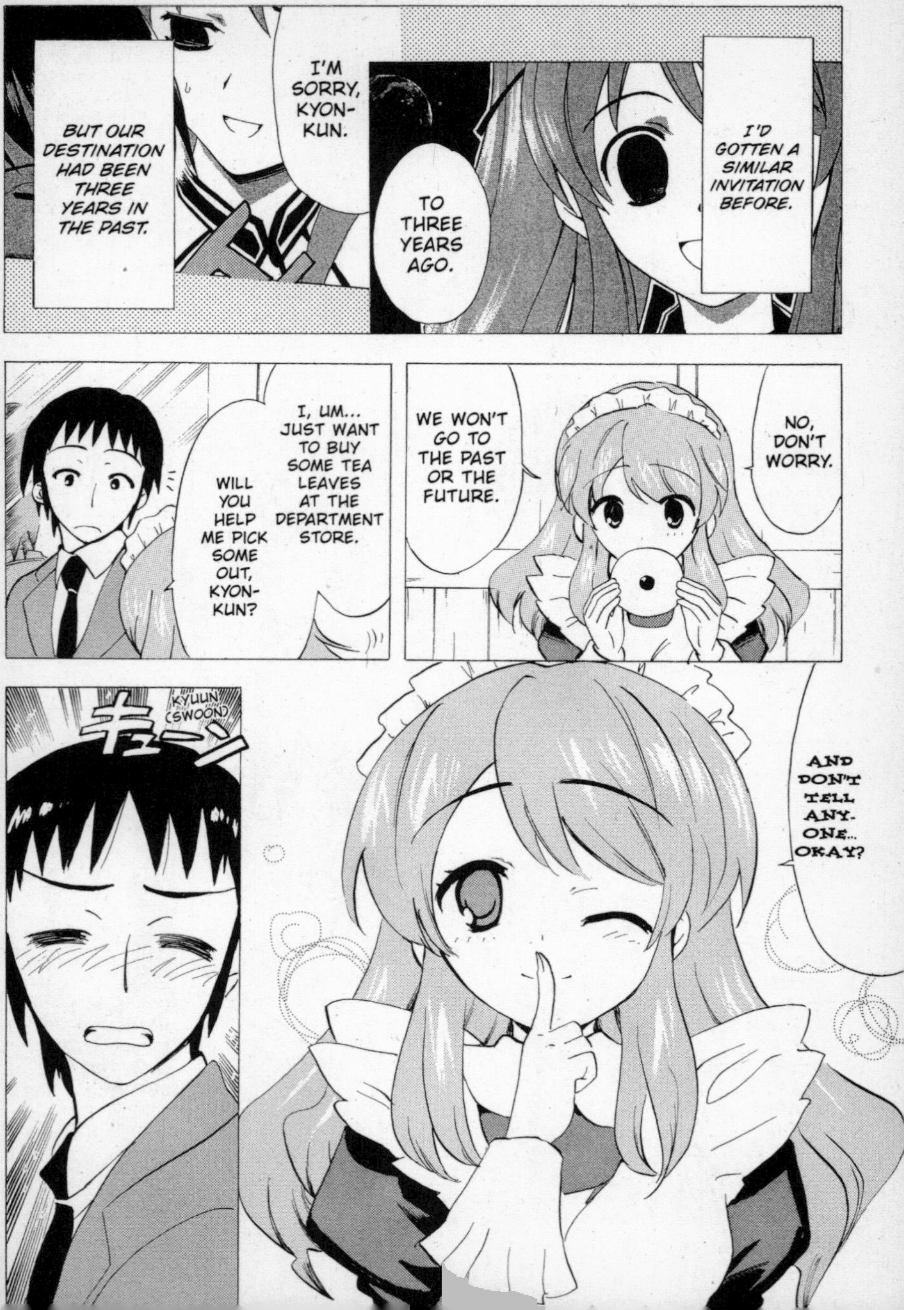
I'D GOTTEN A SIMILAR INVITATION BEFORE.
TO THREE YEARS AGO.
I'M SORRY, KYON-KUN.
BUT OUR DESTINATION HAD BEEN THREE YEARS IN THE PAST.
NO, DON'T WORRY.
WE WON'T GO TO THE PAST OR THE FUTURE.
I, UM... JUST WANT TO BUY SOME TEA LEAVES AT THE DEPARTMENT STORE.
WILL YOU HELP ME PICK SOME OUT, KYON-KUN?
AND DON'T TELL ANY-ONE... OKAY?
KYUUN (SWOON)

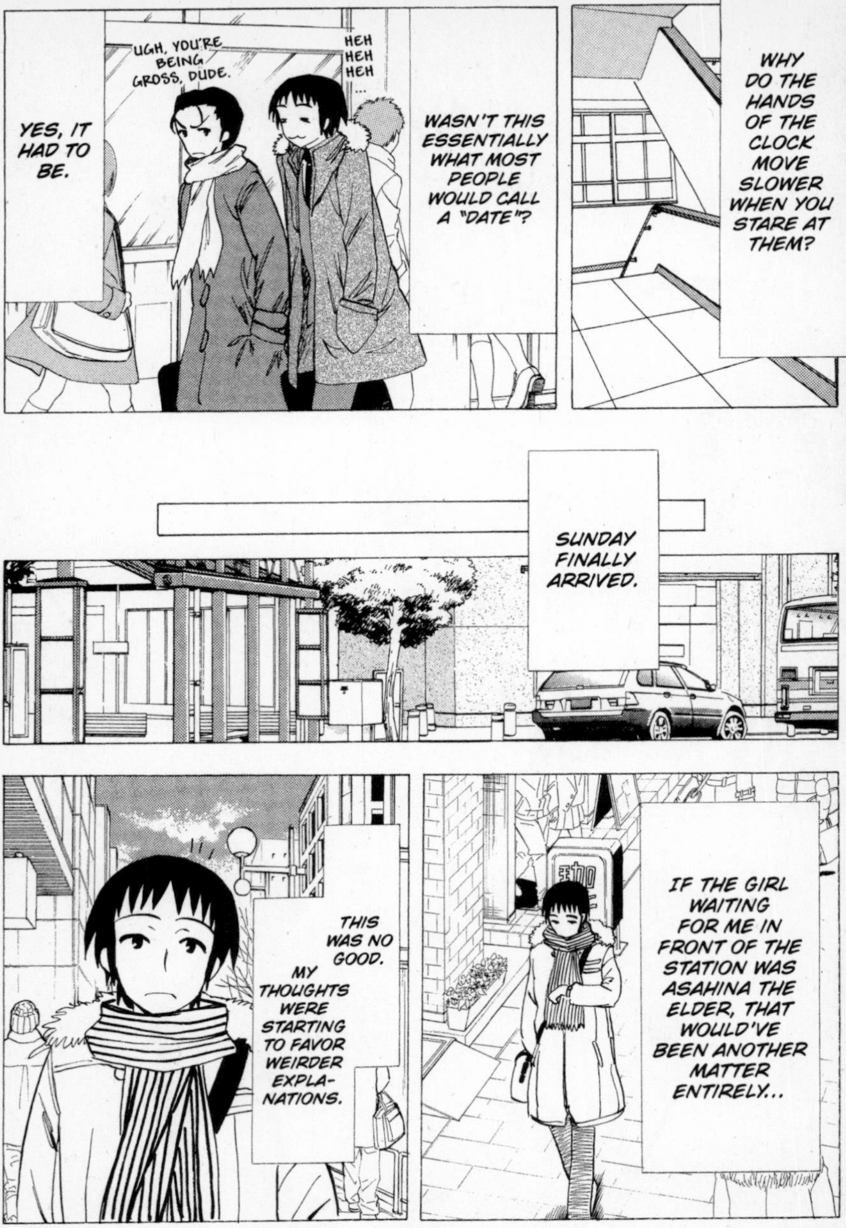
WHY DO THE HANDS OF THE CLOCK MOVE SLOWER WHEN YOU STARE AT THEM?
WASN'T THIS ESSENTIALLY WHAT MOST PEOPLE WOULD CALL A "DATE"?
HEH HEH HEH ...
UGH, YOU'RE BEING GROSS, DUDE.
YES, IT HAD TO BE.
SUNDAY FINALLY ARRIVED.
IF THE GIRL WAITING FOR ME IN FRONT OF THE STATION WAS ASAHINA THE ELDER, THAT WOULD'VE BEEN ANOTHER MATTER ENTIRELY...
THIS WAS NO GOOD.
MY THOUGHTS WERE STARTING TO FAVOR WEIRDER EXPLA-NATIONS.

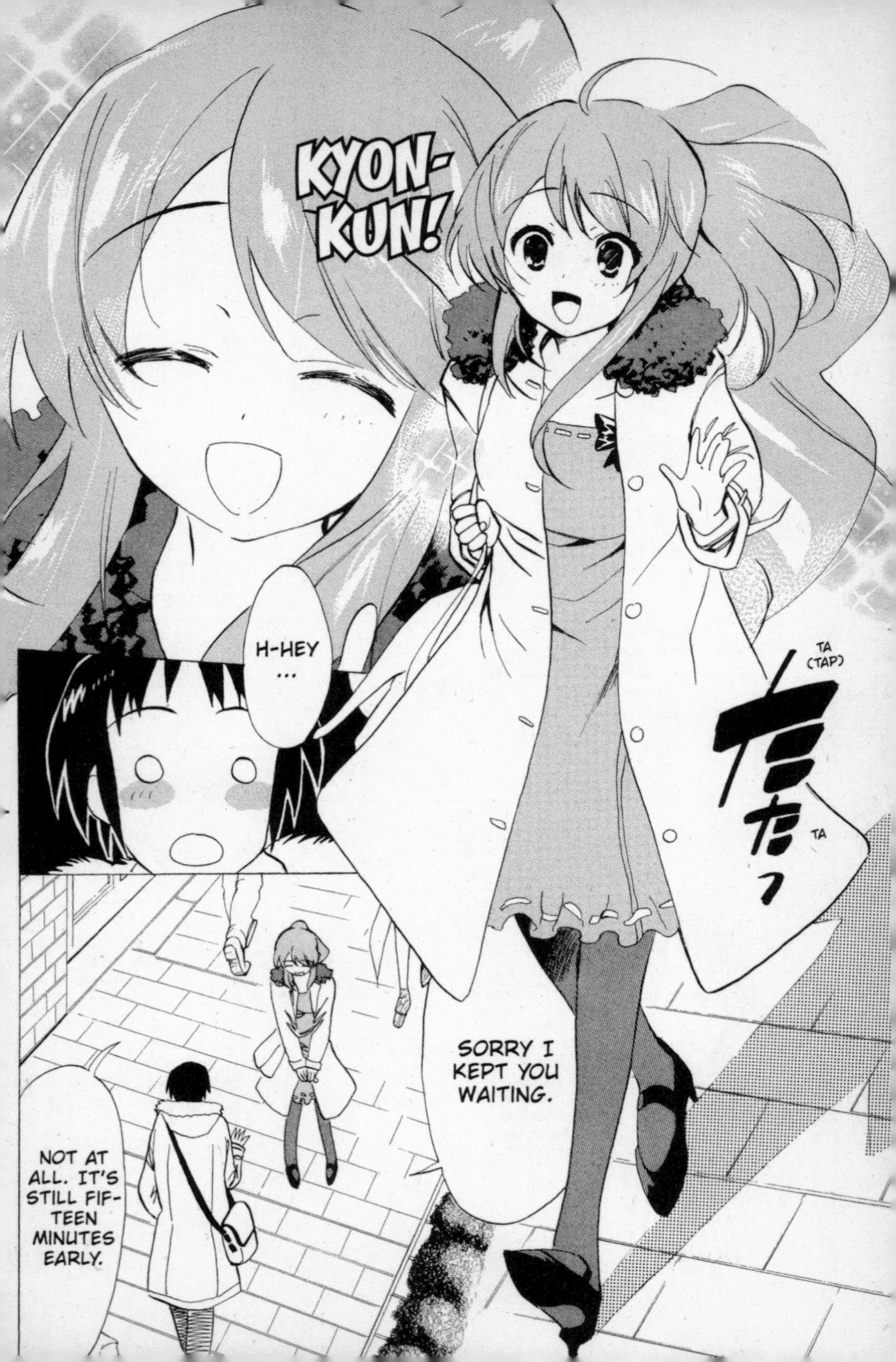
KYON-KUN!
TA (TAP) TA
H-HEY ...
SORRY I KEPT YOU WAITING.
NOT AT ALL. IT'S STILL FIF-TEEN MINUTES EARLY.

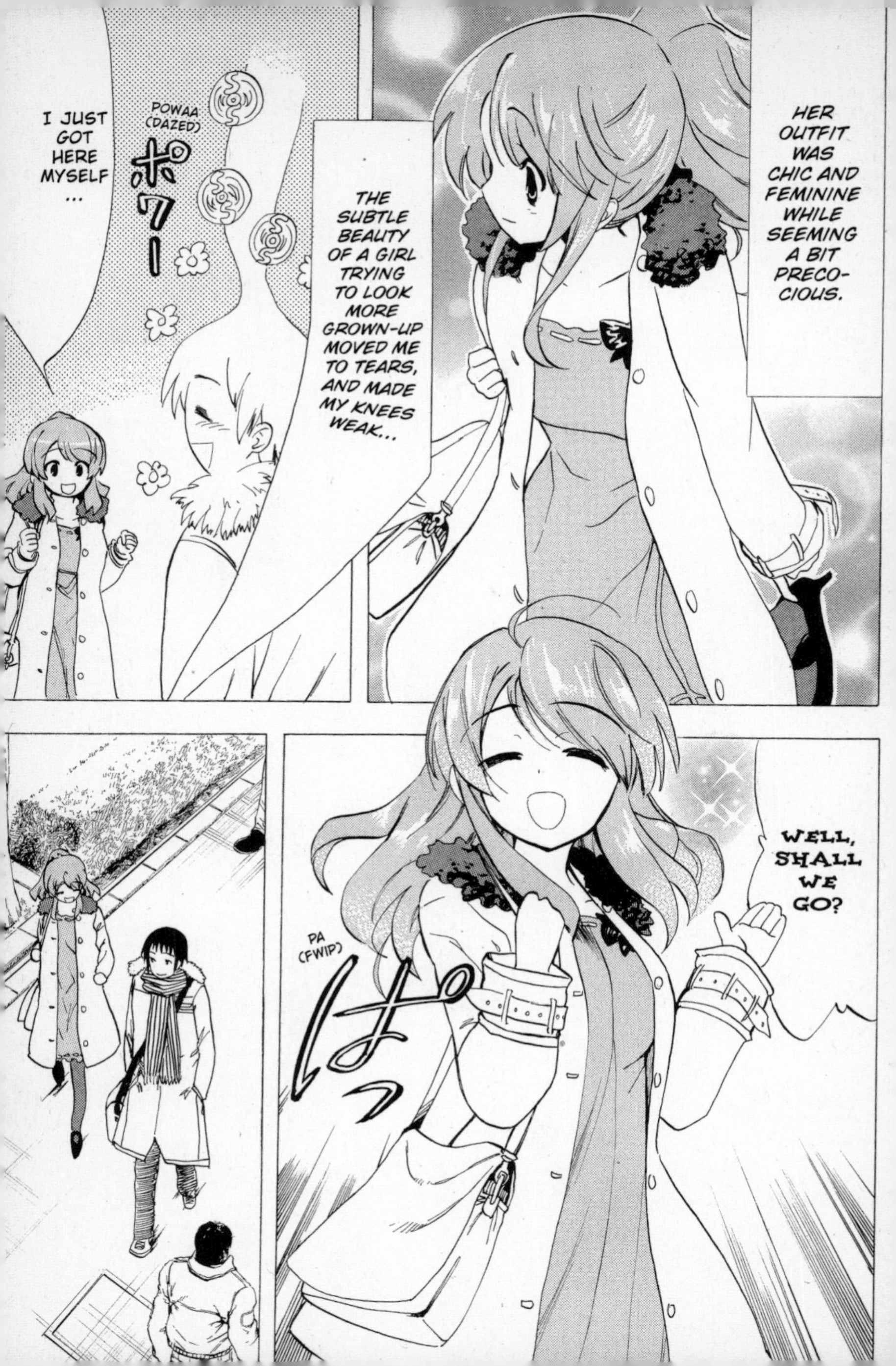
HER OUTFIT WAS CHIC AND FEMININE WHILE SEEMING A BIT PRECOCIOUS.
THE SUBTLE BEAUTY OF A GIRL TRYING TO LOOK MORE GROWN-UP MOVED ME TO TEARS, AND MADE MY KNEES WEAK...
I JUST GOT HERE MYSELF...
POWAA (DAZED)
ポワー
WELL, SHALL WE GO?
PA (FWIP)
ぱっ

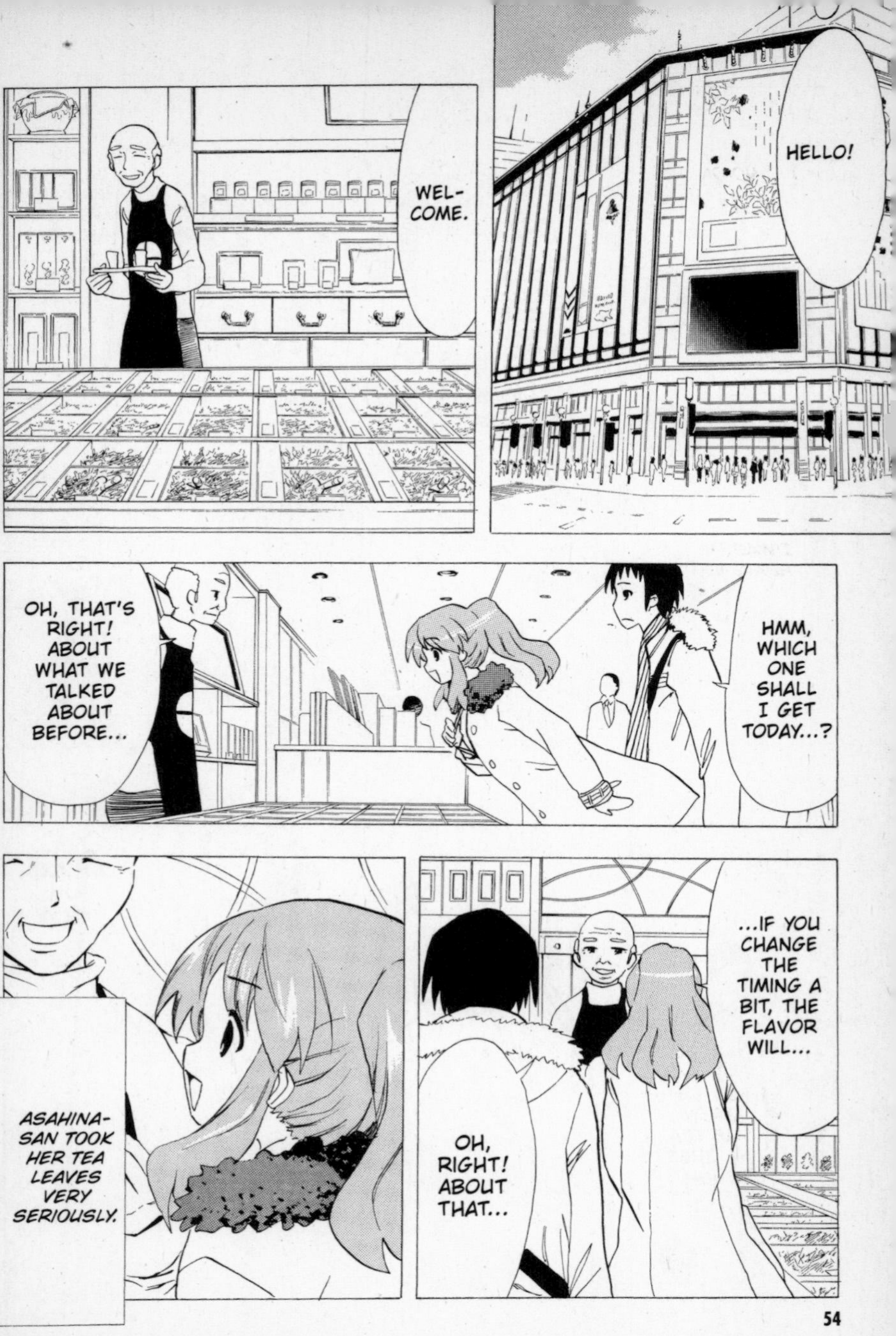
HELLO!
WEL-COME.
HMM, WHICH ONE SHALL I GET TODAY...?
OH, THAT'S RIGHT! ABOUT WHAT WE TALKED ABOUT BEFORE...
...IF YOU CHANGE THE TIMING A BIT, THE FLAVOR WILL...
OH, RIGHT! ABOUT THAT...
ASAHINA-SAN TOOK HER TEA LEAVES VERY SERIOUSLY.

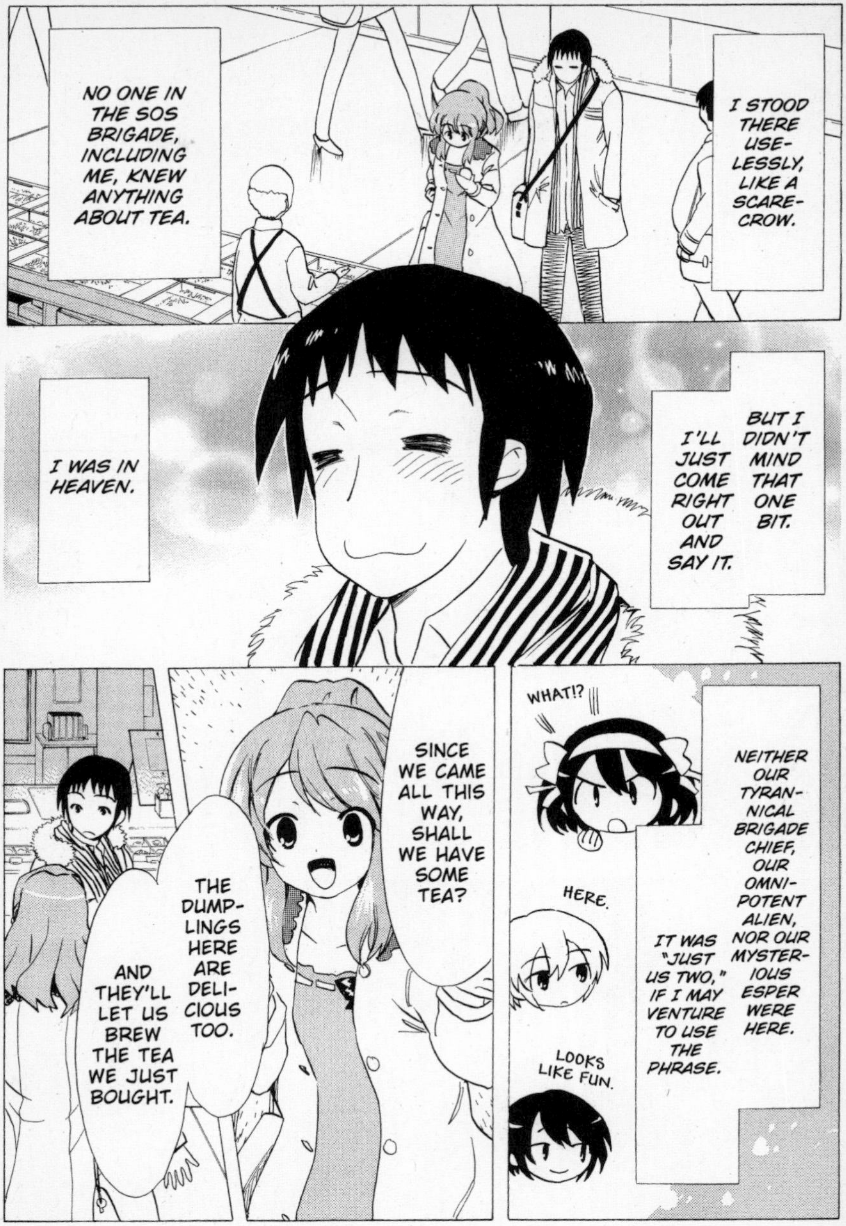
I STOOD THERE USELESSLY, LIKE A SCARECROW.
NO ONE IN THE SOS BRIGADE, INCLUDING ME, KNEW ANYTHING ABOUT TEA.
BUT I DIDN'T MIND THAT ONE BIT.
I'LL JUST COME RIGHT OUT AND SAY IT.
I WAS IN HEAVEN.
NEITHER OUR TYRANNICAL BRIGADE CHIEF, OUR OMNIPOTENT ALIEN, NOR OUR MYSTERIOUS ESPER WERE HERE.
WHAT!?
IT WAS "JUST US TWO," IF I MAY VENTURE TO USE THE PHRASE.
HERE.
LOOKS LIKE FUN.
SINCE WE CAME ALL THIS WAY, SHALL WE HAVE SOME TEA?
THE DUMPLINGS HERE ARE DELICIOUS TOO.
AND THEY'LL LET US BREW THE TEA WE JUST BOUGHT.

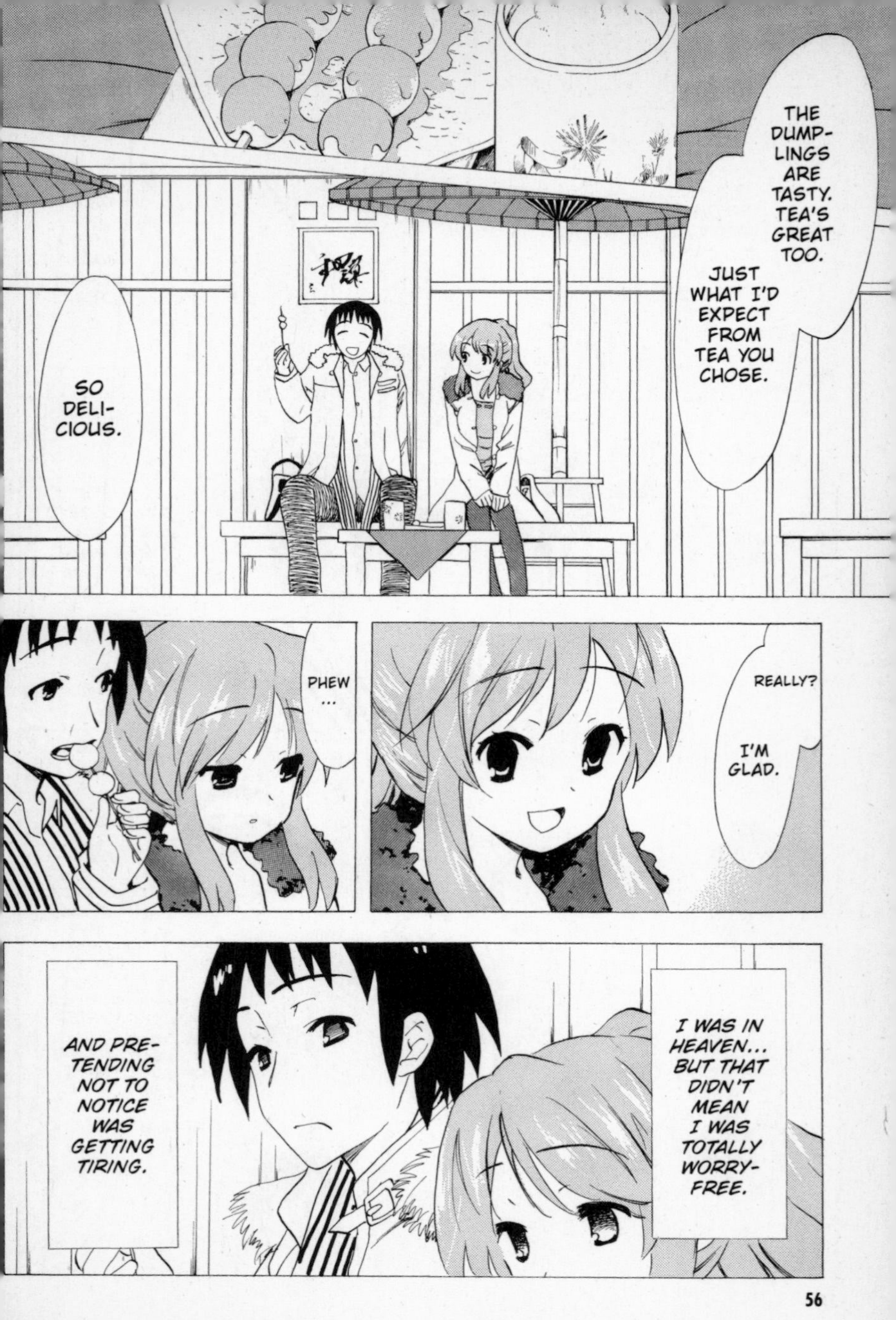
THE DUMP-LINGS ARE TASTY. TEA'S GREAT TOO.
JUST WHAT I'D EXPECT FROM TEA YOU CHOSE.
SO DELI-CIOUS.
REALLY?
I'M GLAD.
PHEW ...
I WAS IN HEAVEN... BUT THAT DIDN'T MEAN I WAS TOTALLY WORRY-FREE.
AND PRE-TENDING NOT TO NOTICE WAS GETTING TIRING.

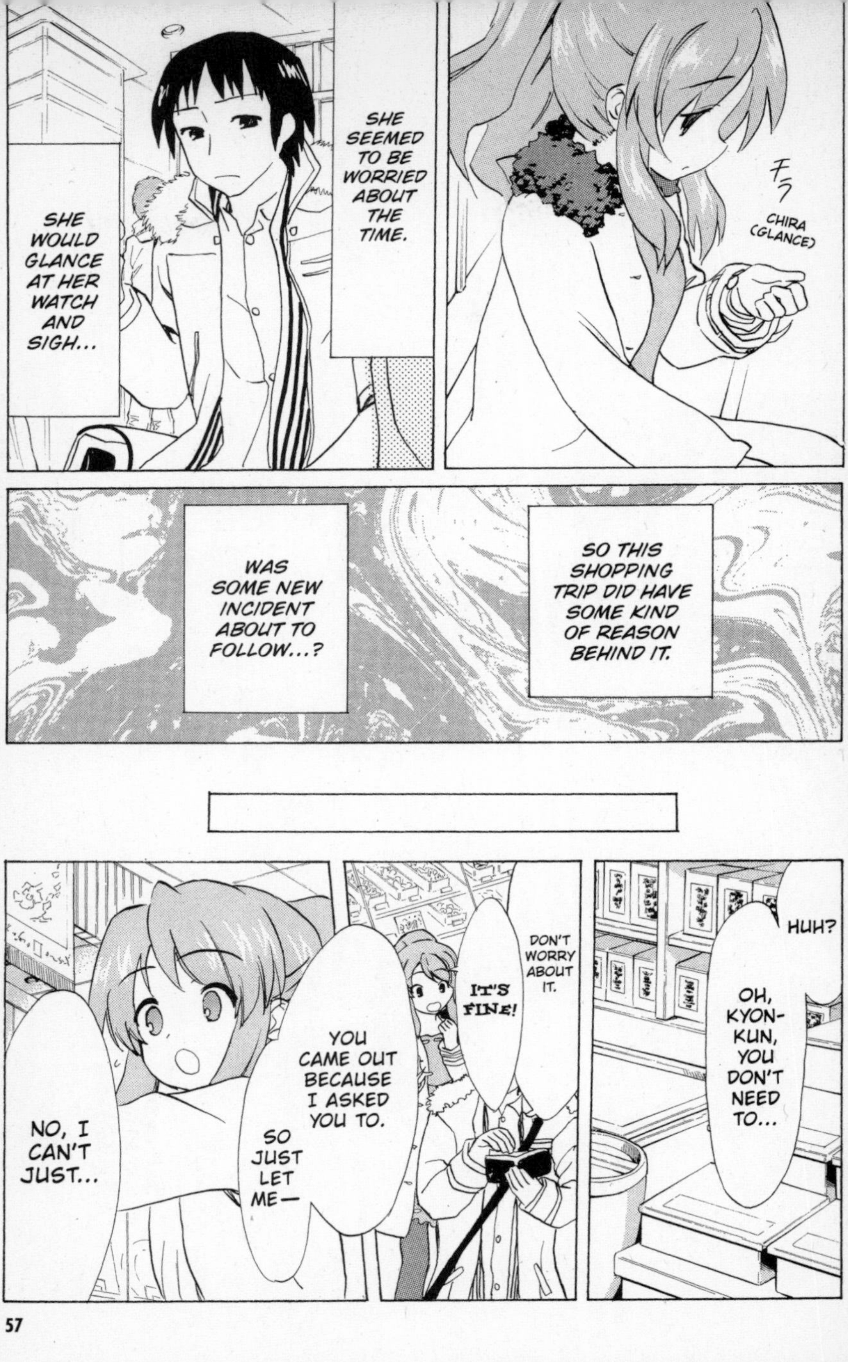
チラ
CHIRA (GLANCE)
SHE SEEMED TO BE WORRIED ABOUT THE TIME.
SHE WOULD GLANCE AT HER WATCH AND SIGH...
SO THIS SHOPPING TRIP DID HAVE SOME KIND OF REASON BEHIND IT.
WAS SOME NEW INCIDENT ABOUT TO FOLLOW...?
HUH?
OH, KYON-KUN, YOU DON'T NEED TO...
DON'T WORRY ABOUT IT.
IT'S FINE!
YOU CAME OUT BECAUSE I ASKED YOU TO.
SO JUST LET ME—
NO, I CAN'T JUST...

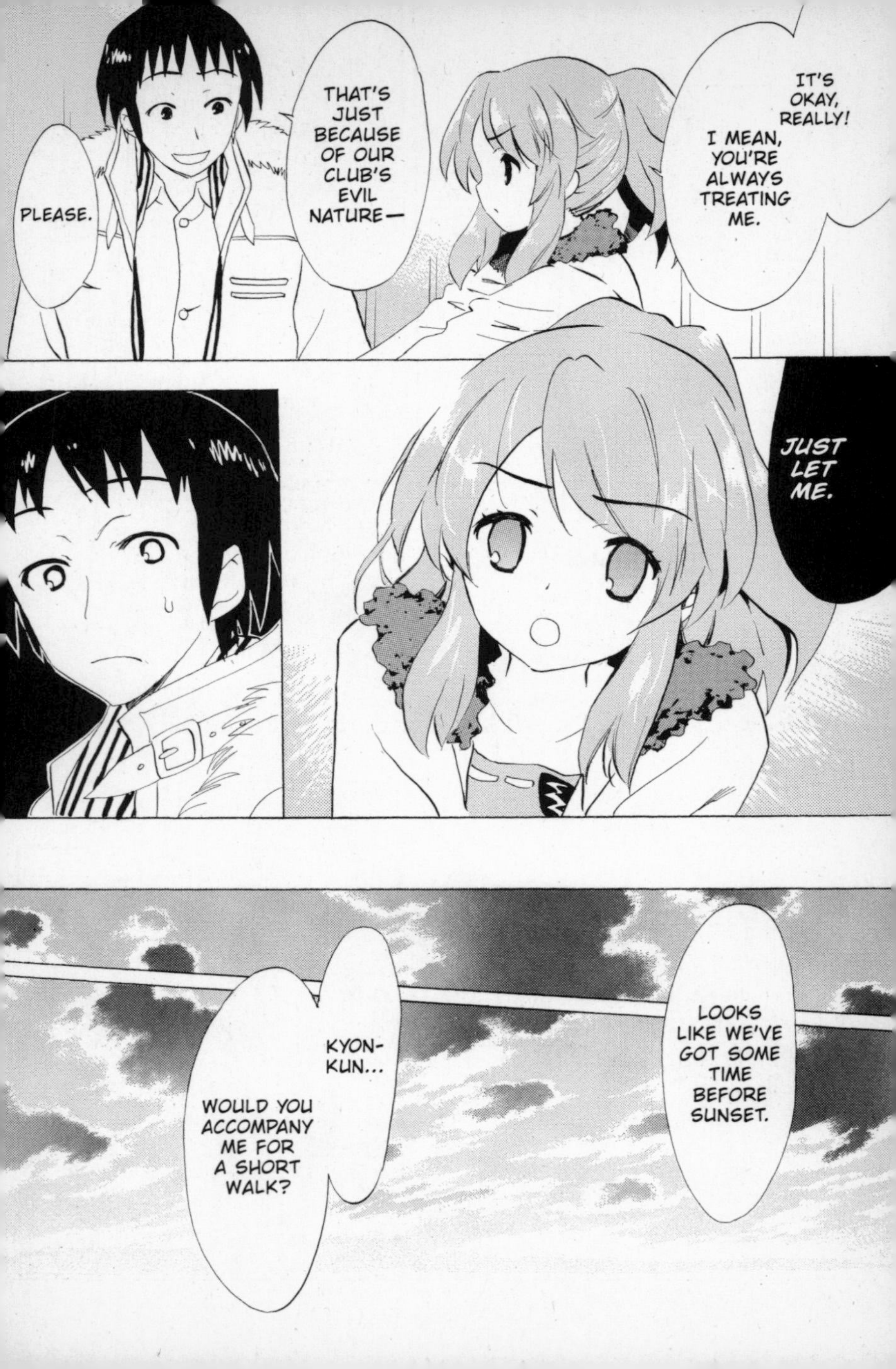
IT'S OKAY, REALLY!
I MEAN, YOU'RE ALWAYS TREATING ME.
THAT'S JUST BECAUSE OF OUR CLUB'S EVIL NATURE—
PLEASE.
JUST LET ME.
LOOKS LIKE WE'VE GOT SOME TIME BEFORE SUNSET.
KYON-KUN...
WOULD YOU ACCOMPANY ME FOR A SHORT WALK?

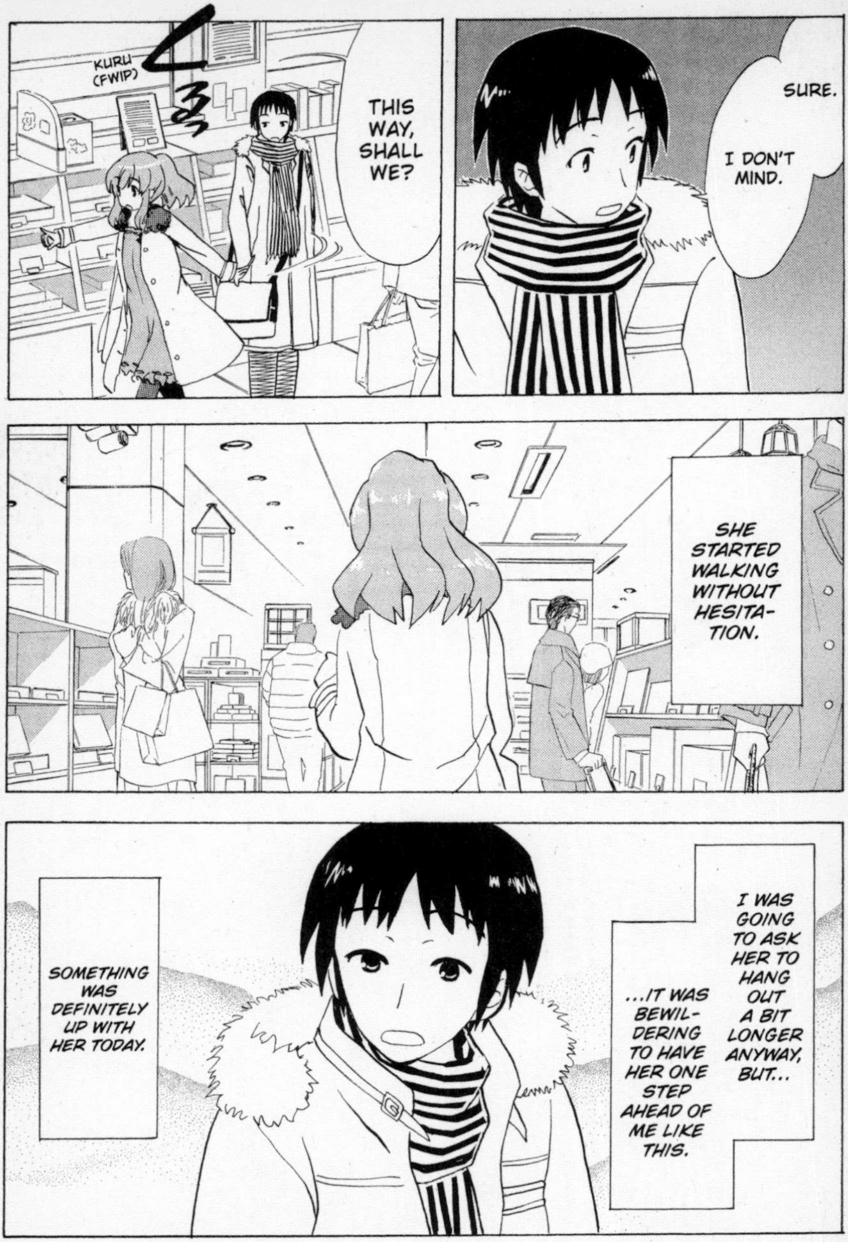
SURE.
I DON'T MIND.
KURU (FWIP)
THIS WAY, SHALL WE?
SHE STARTED WALKING WITHOUT HESITATION.
I WAS GOING TO ASK HER TO HANG OUT A BIT LONGER ANYWAY, BUT...
...IT WAS BEWILDERING TO HAVE HER ONE STEP AHEAD OF ME LIKE THIS.
SOMETHING WAS DEFINITELY UP WITH HER TODAY.

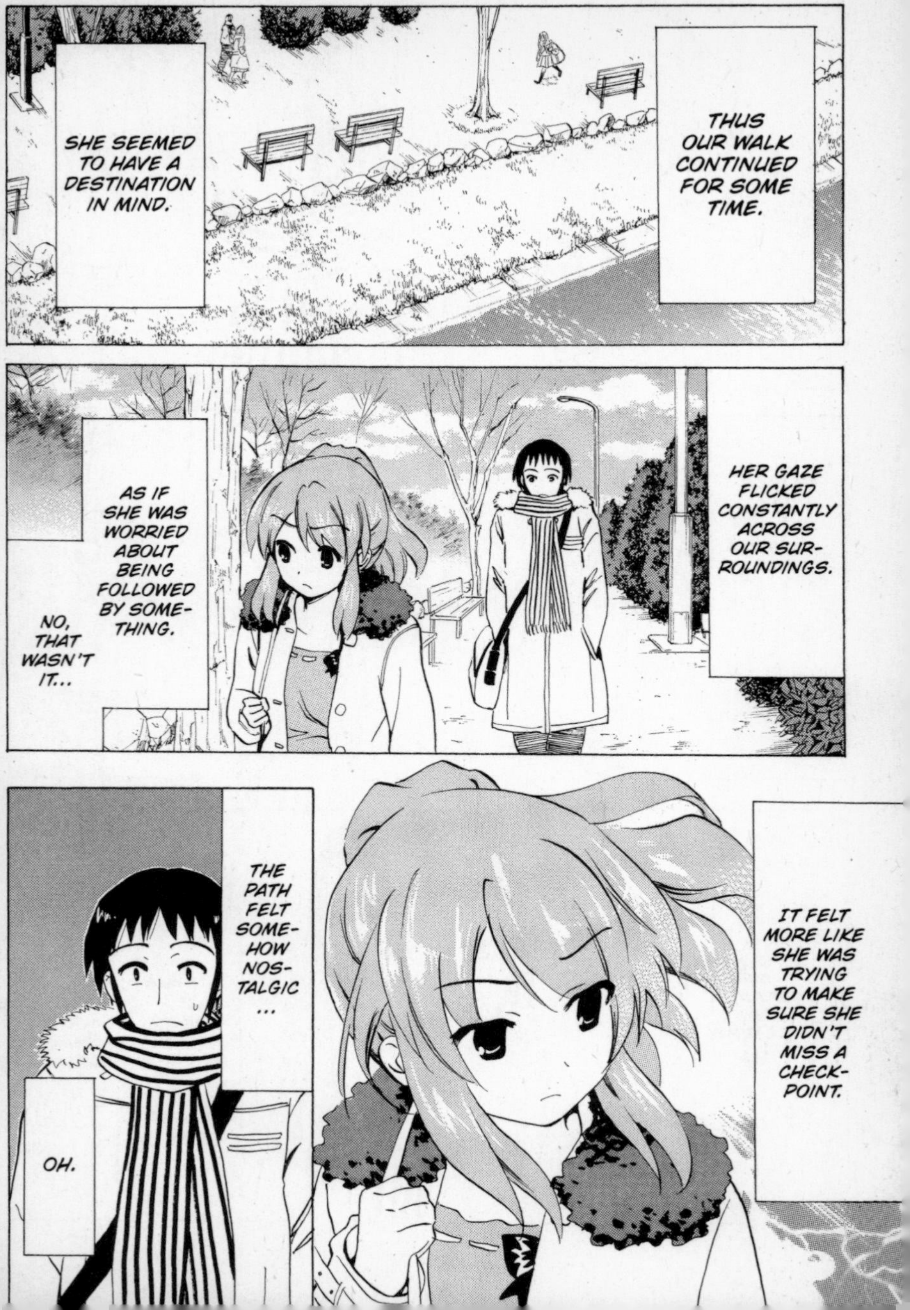
THUS OUR WALK CONTINUED FOR SOME TIME.
SHE SEEMED TO HAVE A DESTINATION IN MIND.
HER GAZE FLICKED CONSTANTLY ACROSS OUR SUR-ROUNDINGS.
AS IF SHE WAS WORRIED ABOUT BEING FOLLOWED BY SOME-THING.
NO, THAT WASN'T IT...
IT FELT MORE LIKE SHE WAS TRYING TO MAKE SURE SHE DIDN'T MISS A CHECK-POINT.
THE PATH FELT SOME-HOW NOS-TALGIC ...
OH.

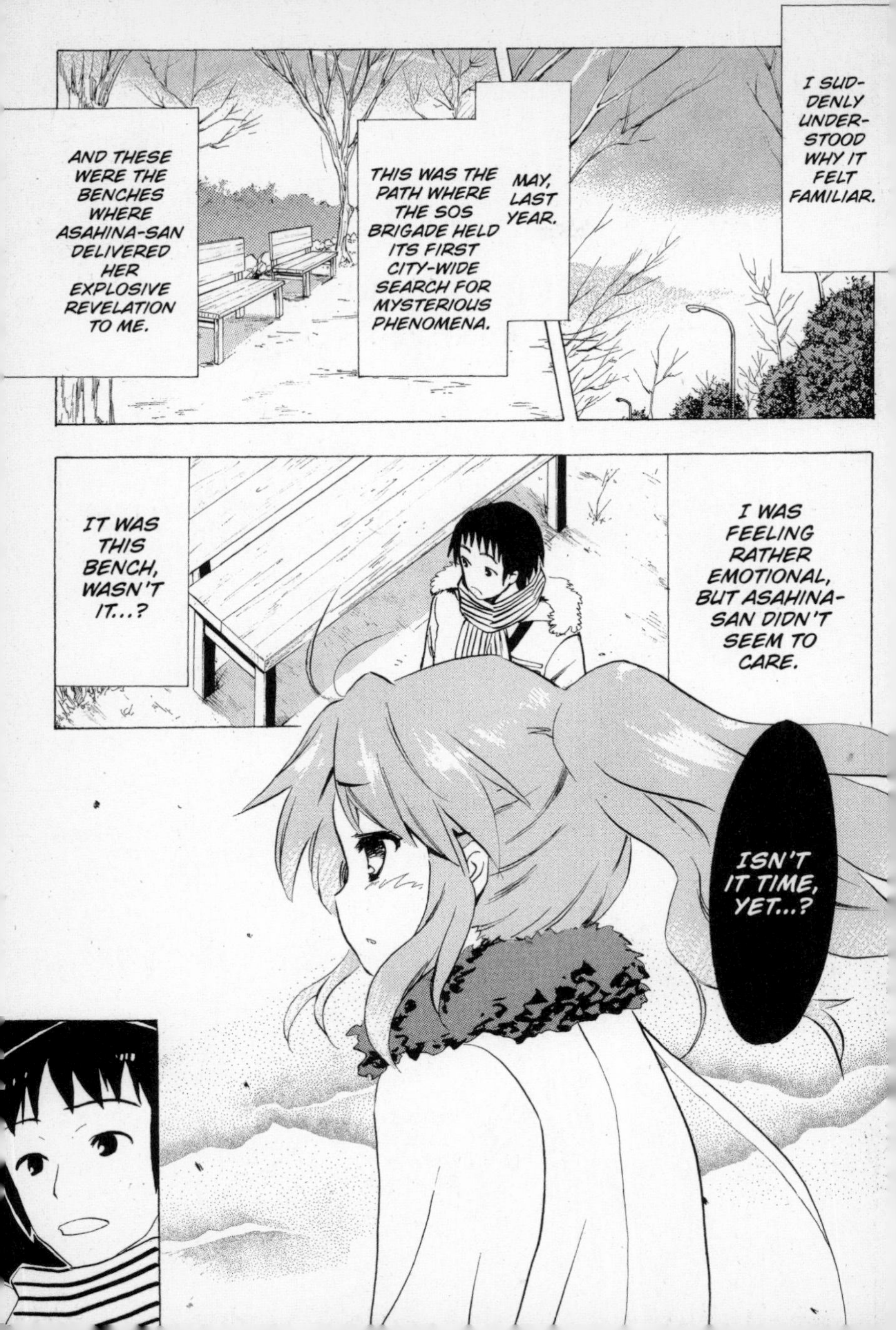
I SUDDENLY UNDERSTOOD WHY IT FELT FAMILIAR.
MAY, LAST YEAR.
THIS WAS THE PATH WHERE THE SOS BRIGADE HELD ITS FIRST CITY-WIDE SEARCH FOR MYSTERIOUS PHENOMENA.
AND THESE WERE THE BENCHES WHERE ASAHINA-SAN DELIVERED HER EXPLOSIVE REVELATION TO ME.
I WAS FEELING RATHER EMOTIONAL, BUT ASAHINA-SAN DIDN'T SEEM TO CARE.
IT WAS THIS BENCH, WASN'T IT...?
ISN'T IT TIME, YET...?

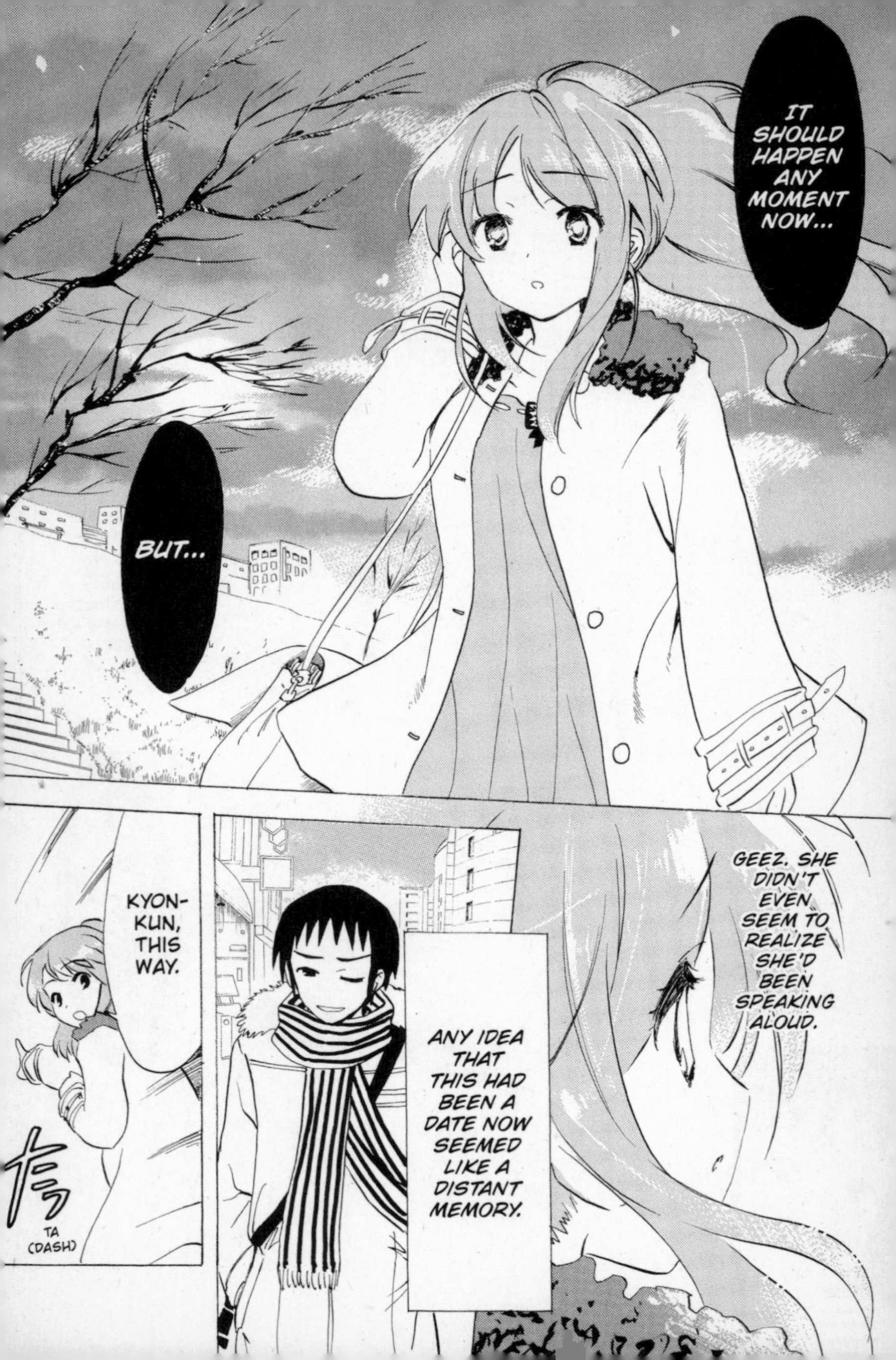
IT SHOULD HAPPEN ANY MOMENT NOW...
BUT...
GEEZ. SHE DIDN'T EVEN SEEM TO REALIZE SHE'D BEEN SPEAKING ALOUD.
ANY IDEA THAT THIS HAD BEEN A DATE NOW SEEMED LIKE A DISTANT MEMORY.
KYON-KUN, THIS WAY.
TA (DASH)

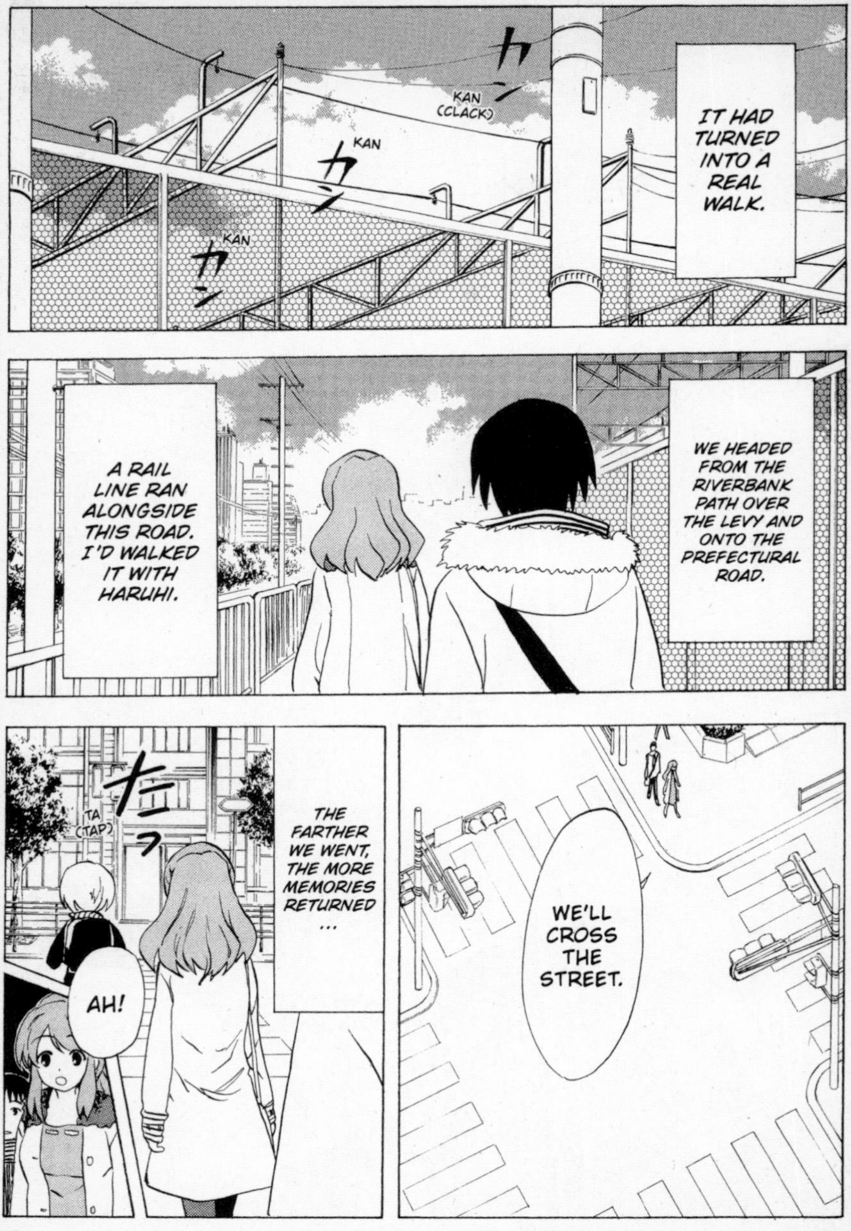
IT HAD TURNED INTO A REAL WALK.
KAN (CLACK)
KAN
KAN
WE HEADED FROM THE RIVERBANK PATH OVER THE LEVY AND ONTO THE PREFECTURAL ROAD.
A RAIL LINE RAN ALONGSIDE THIS ROAD. I'D WALKED IT WITH HARUHI.
WE'LL CROSS THE STREET.
THE FARTHER WE WENT, THE MORE MEMORIES RETURNED ...
TA (TAP)
AH!

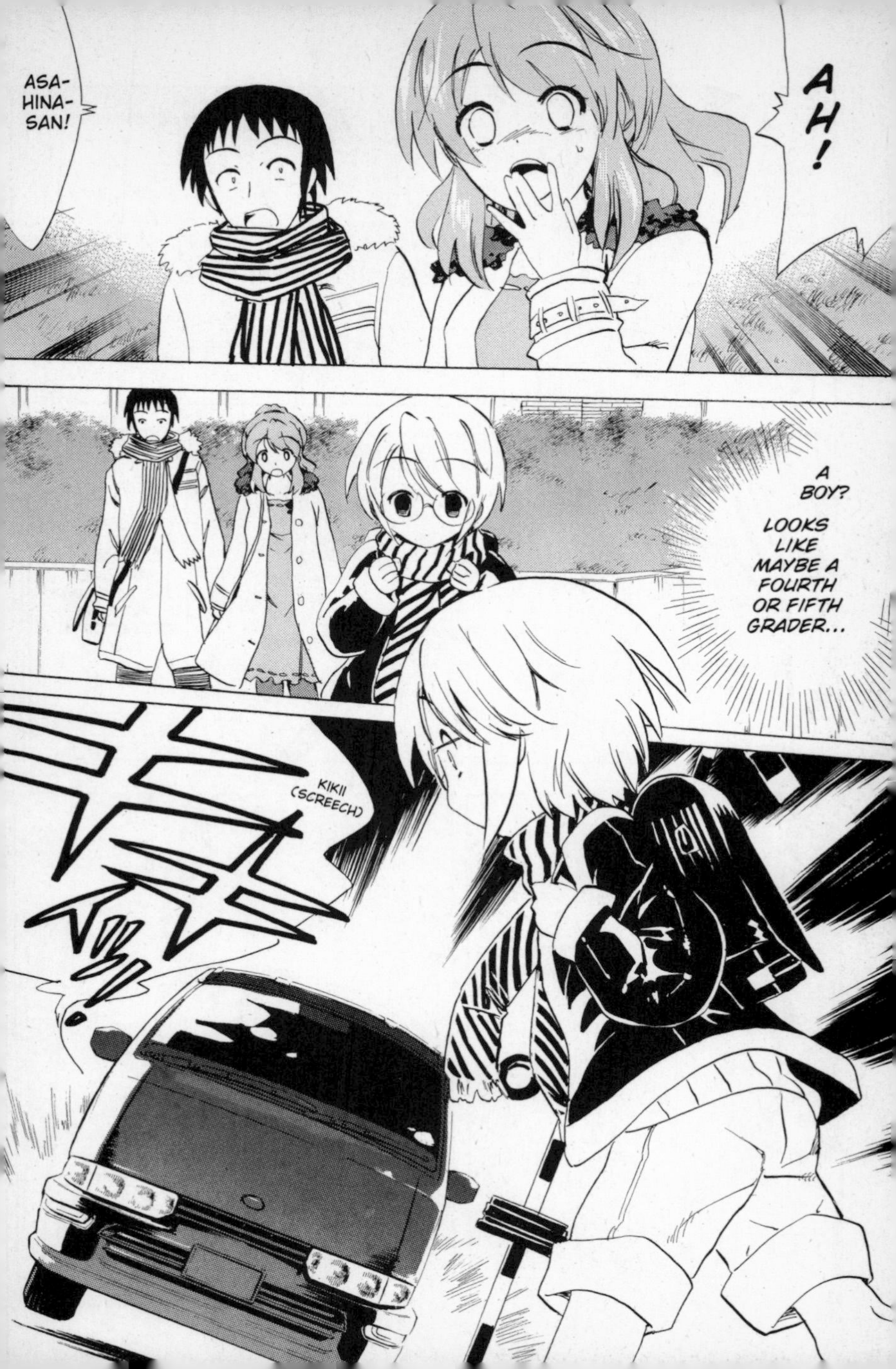
AH!
ASA-HINA-SAN!
A BOY?
LOOKS LIKE MAYBE A FOURTH OR FIFTH GRADER...
KIKII (SCREECH)

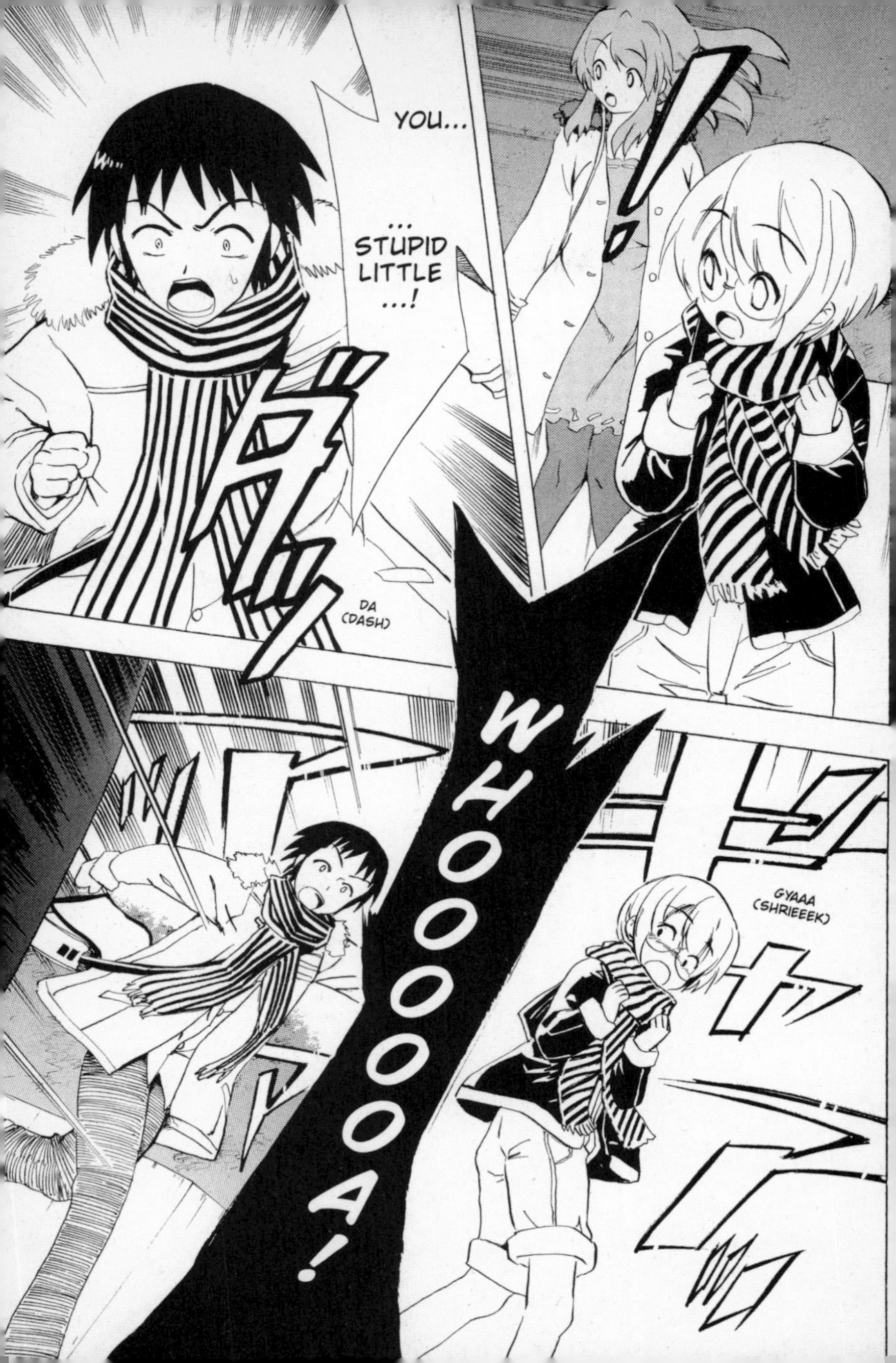

YOU...
... STUPID LITTLE ...!
DA (DASH)
GYAAA (SHRIEEEK)
WHOOOOOA!

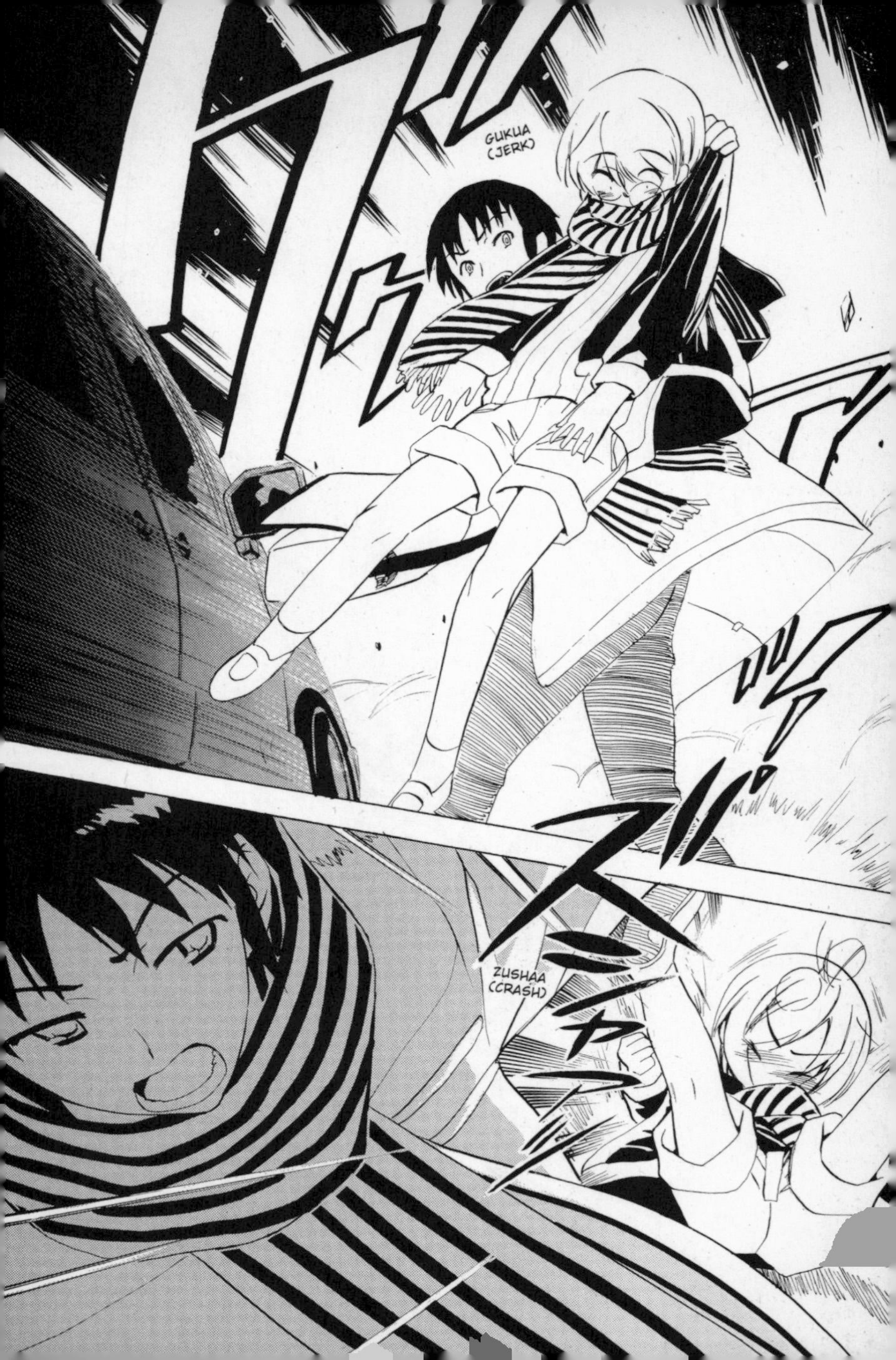
GUKUA
(JERK)
ZUSHAA
(CRASH)

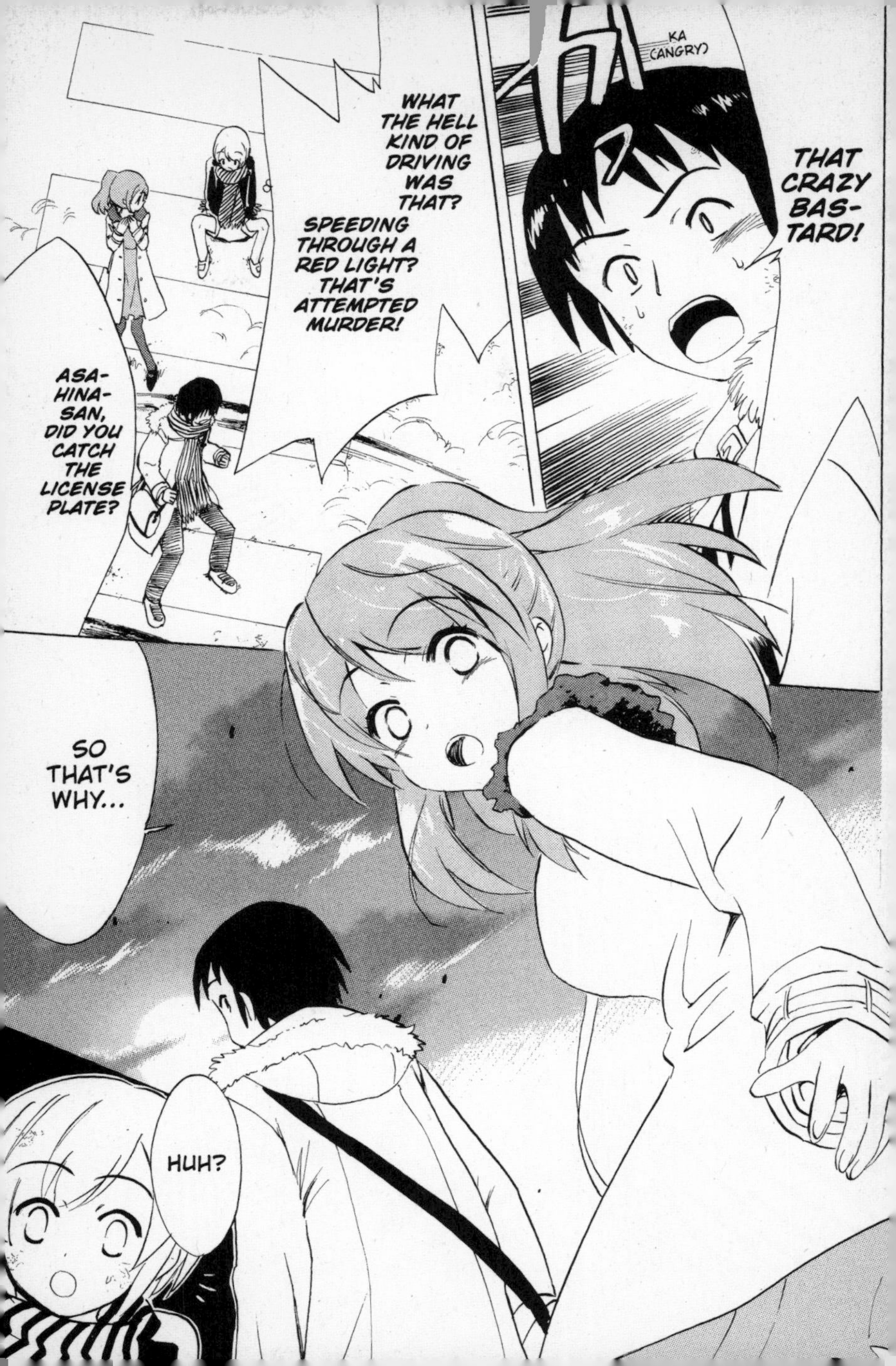
KA (ANGRY)
THAT CRAZY BAS-TARD!
WHAT THE HELL KIND OF DRIVING WAS THAT?
SPEEDING THROUGH A RED LIGHT? THAT'S ATTEMPTED MURDER!
ASA-HINA-SAN, DID YOU CATCH THE LICENSE PLATE?
SO THAT'S WHY...
HUH?

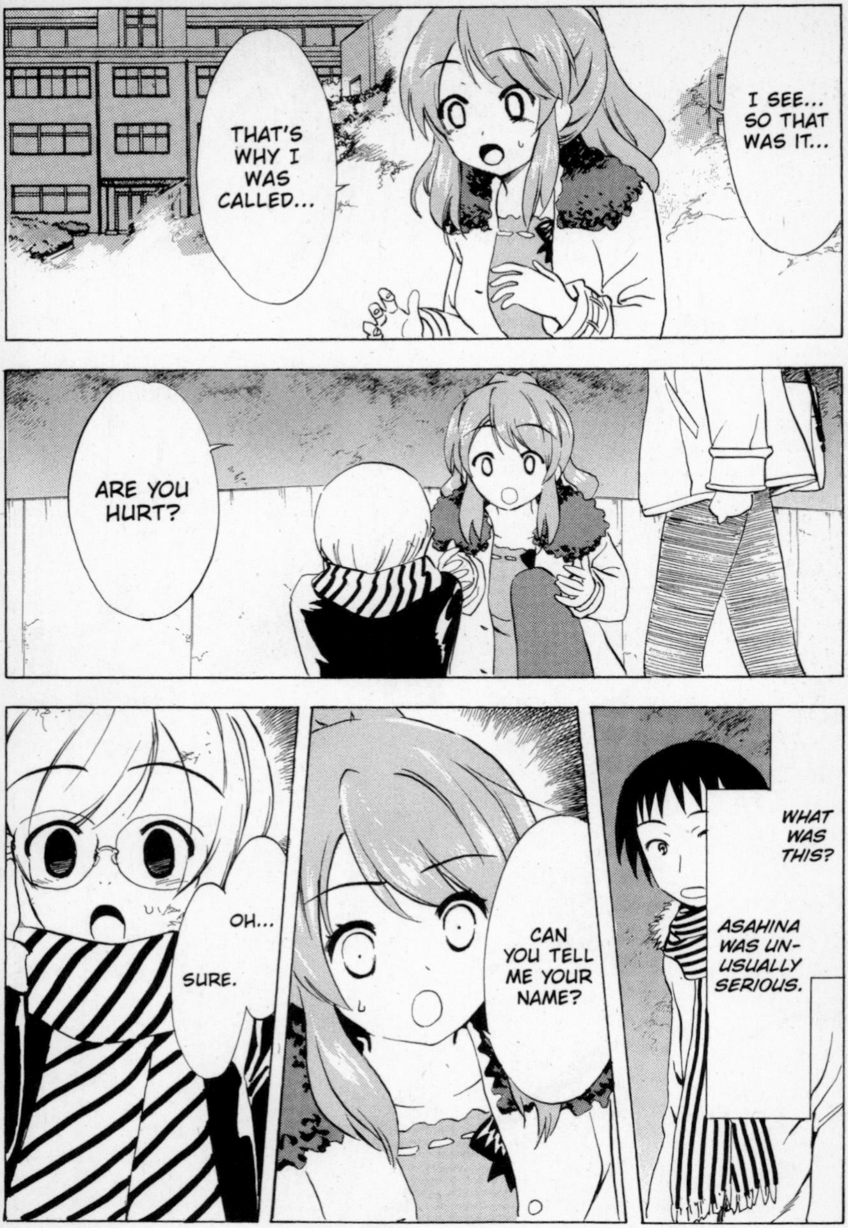
I SEE... SO THAT WAS IT...
THAT'S WHY I WAS CALLED...
ARE YOU HURT?
WHAT WAS THIS?
ASAHINA WAS UN-USUALLY SERIOUS.
CAN YOU TELL ME YOUR NAME?
OH...
SURE.

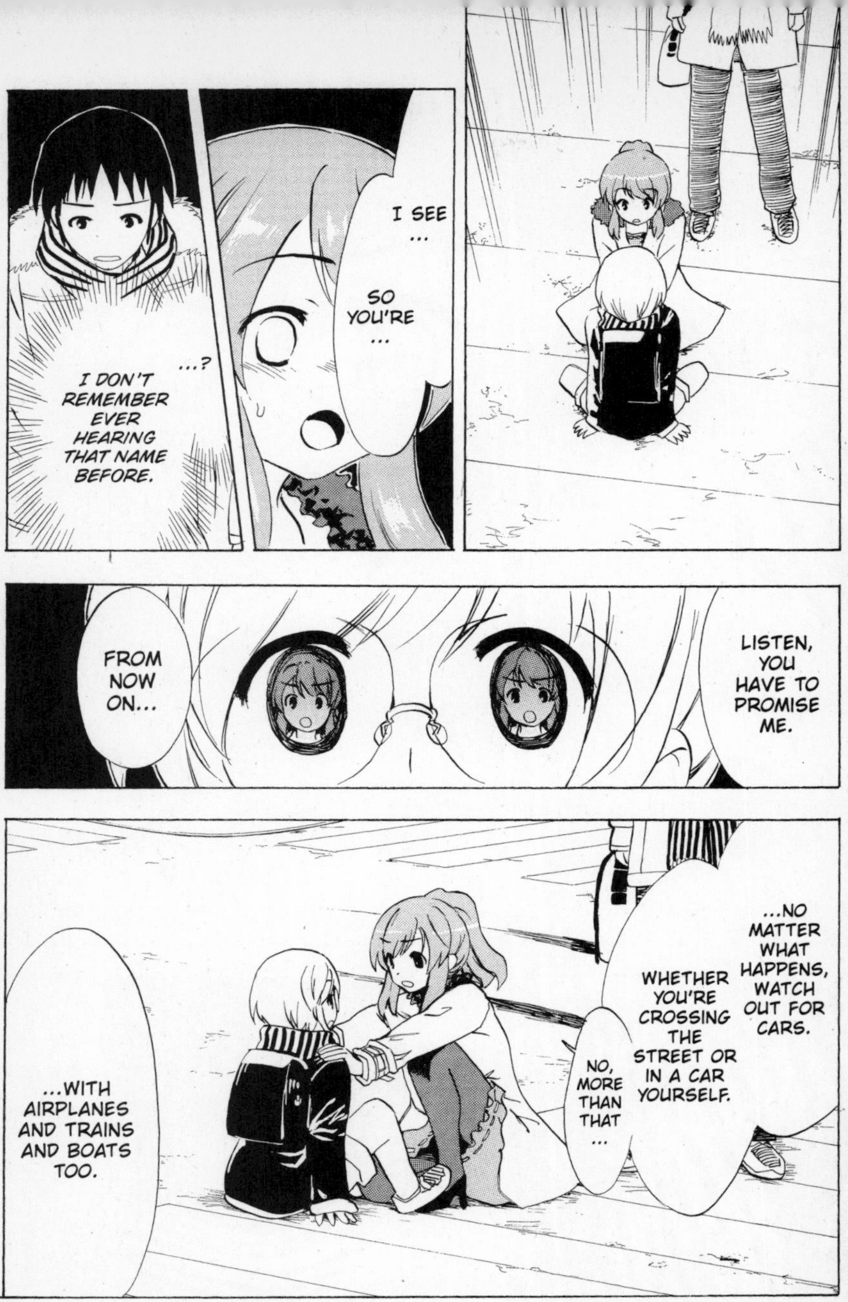
I SEE ...
SO YOU'RE ...
...?
I DON'T REMEMBER EVER HEARING THAT NAME BEFORE.
LISTEN, YOU HAVE TO PROMISE ME.
FROM NOW ON...
...NO MATTER WHAT HAPPENS, WATCH OUT FOR CARS.
WHETHER YOU'RE CROSSING THE STREET OR IN A CAR YOURSELF.
NO, MORE THAN THAT ...
...WITH AIRPLANES AND TRAINS AND BOATS TOO.

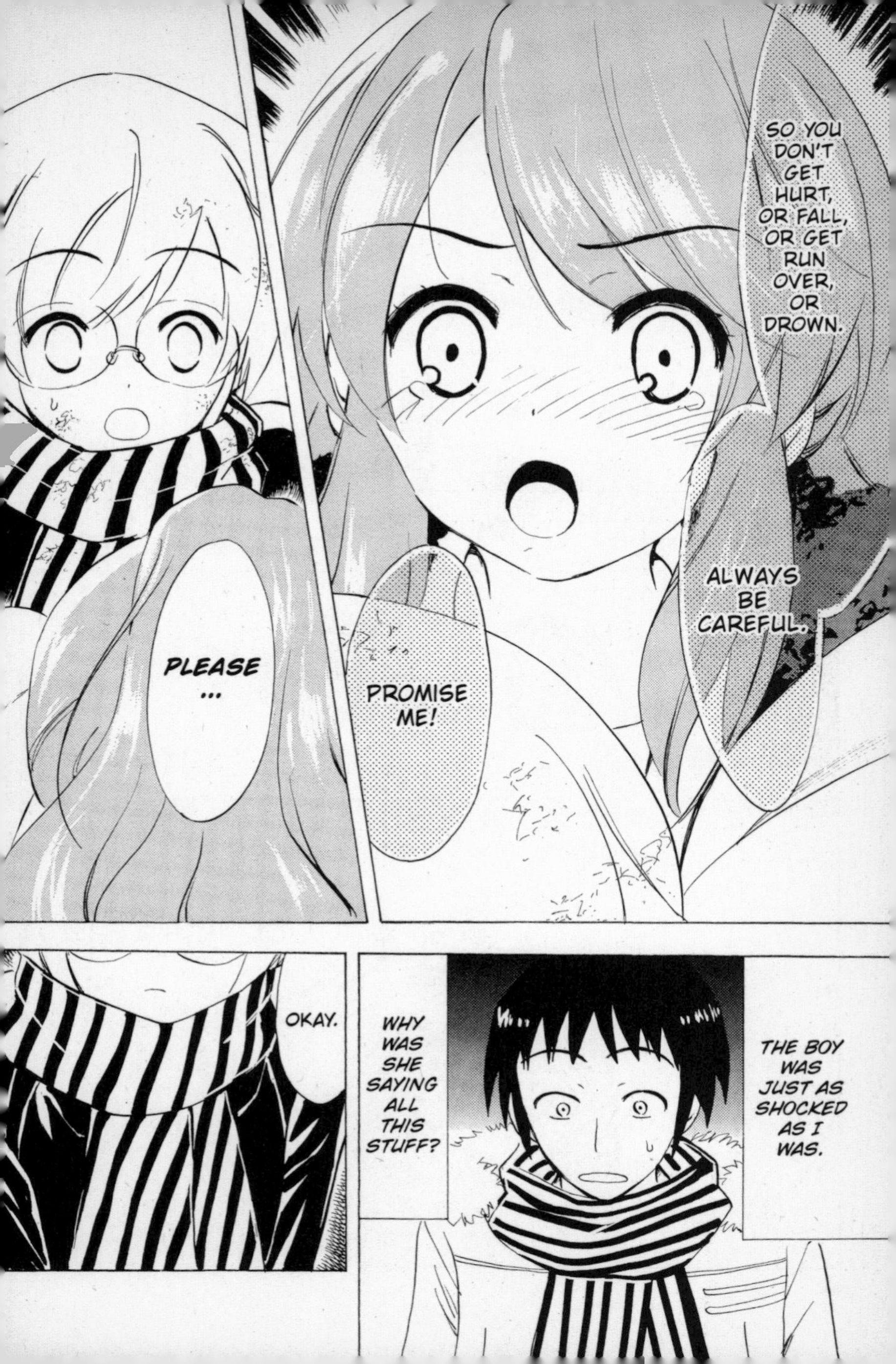
SO YOU DON'T GET HURT, OR FALL, OR GET RUN OVER, OR DROWN.
ALWAYS BE CAREFUL.
PROMISE ME!
PLEASE ...
THE BOY WAS JUST AS SHOCKED AS I WAS.
WHY WAS SHE SAYING ALL THIS STUFF?
OKAY.

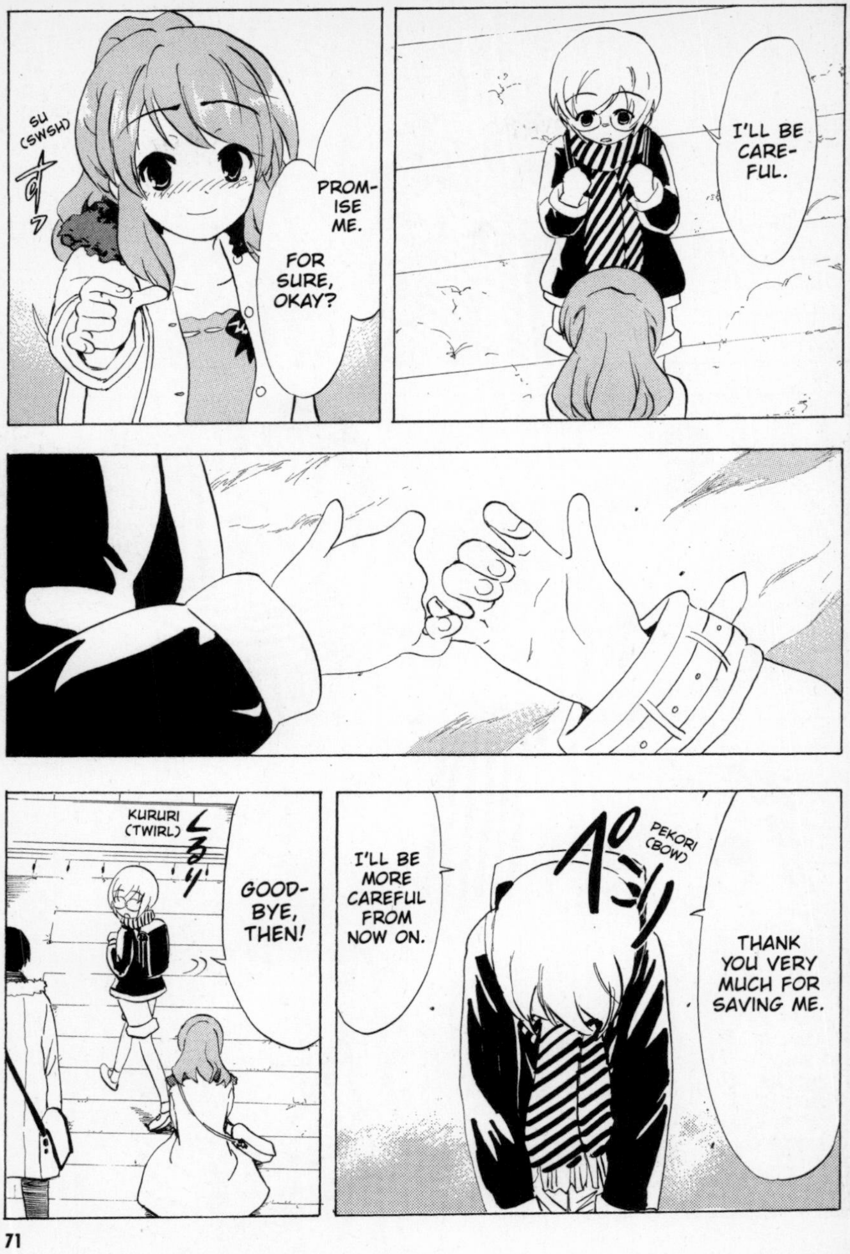
I'LL BE CAREFUL.
PROMISE ME.
FOR SURE, OKAY?
SU (SWSH)
PEKORI (BOW)
THANK YOU VERY MUCH FOR SAVING ME.
I'LL BE MORE CAREFUL FROM NOW ON.
KURURI (TWIRL)
GOOD-BYE, THEN!

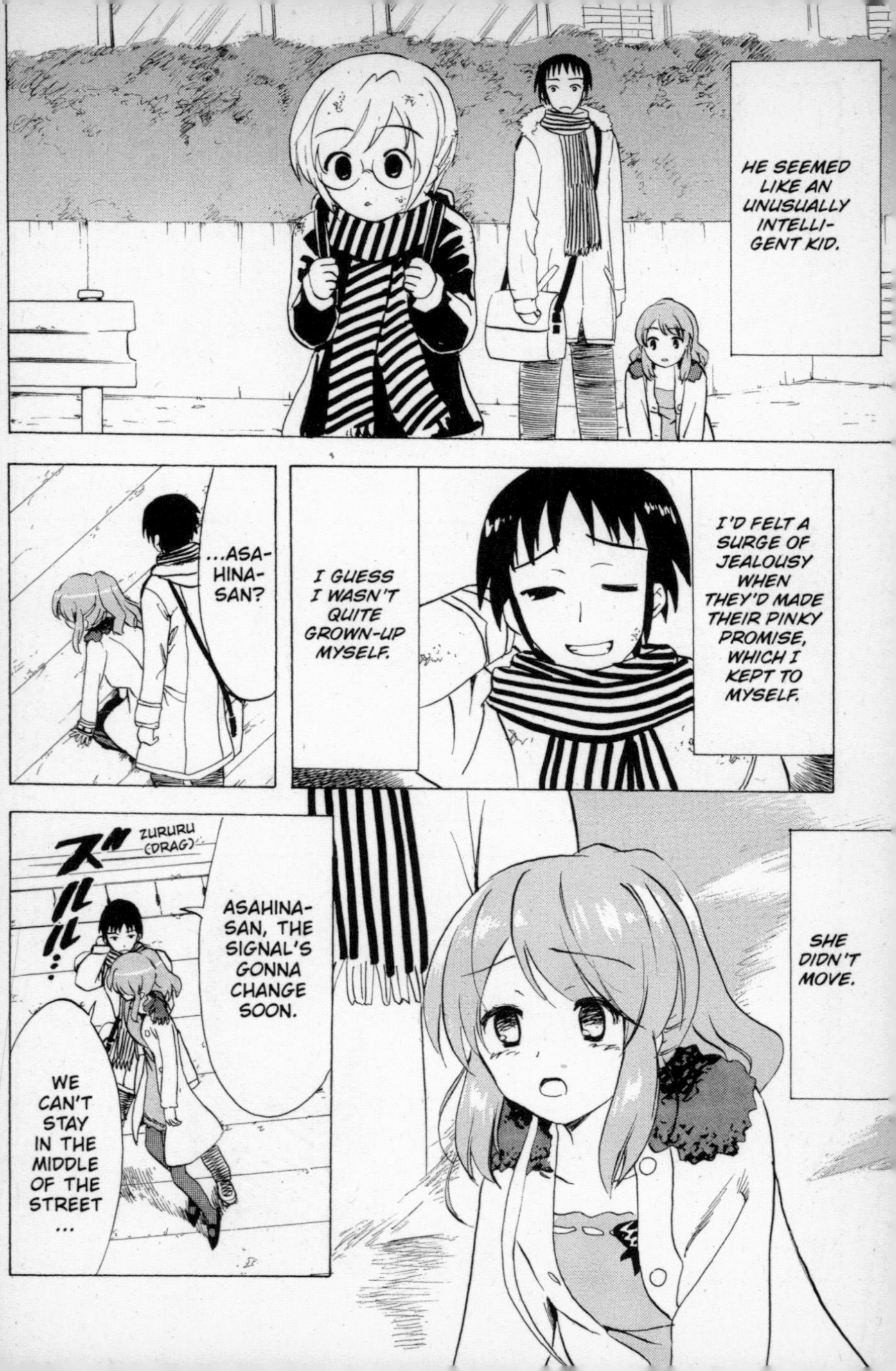
HE SEEMED LIKE AN UNUSUALLY INTELLI-GENT KID.
I'D FELT A SURGE OF JEALOUSY WHEN THEY'D MADE THEIR PINKY PROMISE, WHICH I KEPT TO MYSELF.
I GUESS I WASN'T QUITE GROWN-UP MYSELF.
...ASA-HINA-SAN?
SHE DIDN'T MOVE.
ズルル…
ZURURU (DRAG)
ASAHINA-SAN, THE SIGNAL'S GONNA CHANGE SOON.
WE CAN'T STAY IN THE MIDDLE OF THE STREET ...

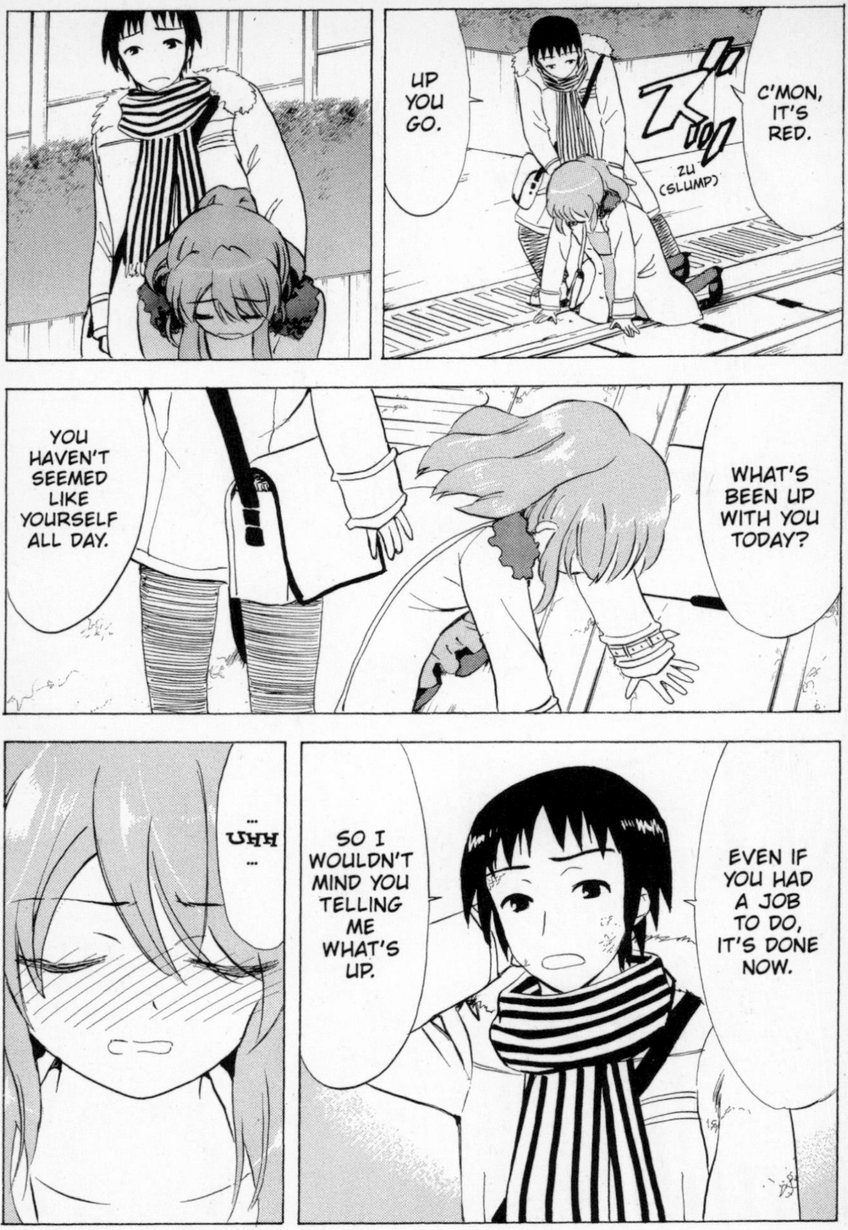
C'MON, IT'S RED.
ZU (SLUMP)
UP YOU GO.
WHAT'S BEEN UP WITH YOU TODAY?
YOU HAVEN'T SEEMED LIKE YOURSELF ALL DAY.
EVEN IF YOU HAD A JOB TO DO, IT'S DONE NOW.
SO I WOULDN'T MIND YOU TELLING ME WHAT'S UP.
...UHH...

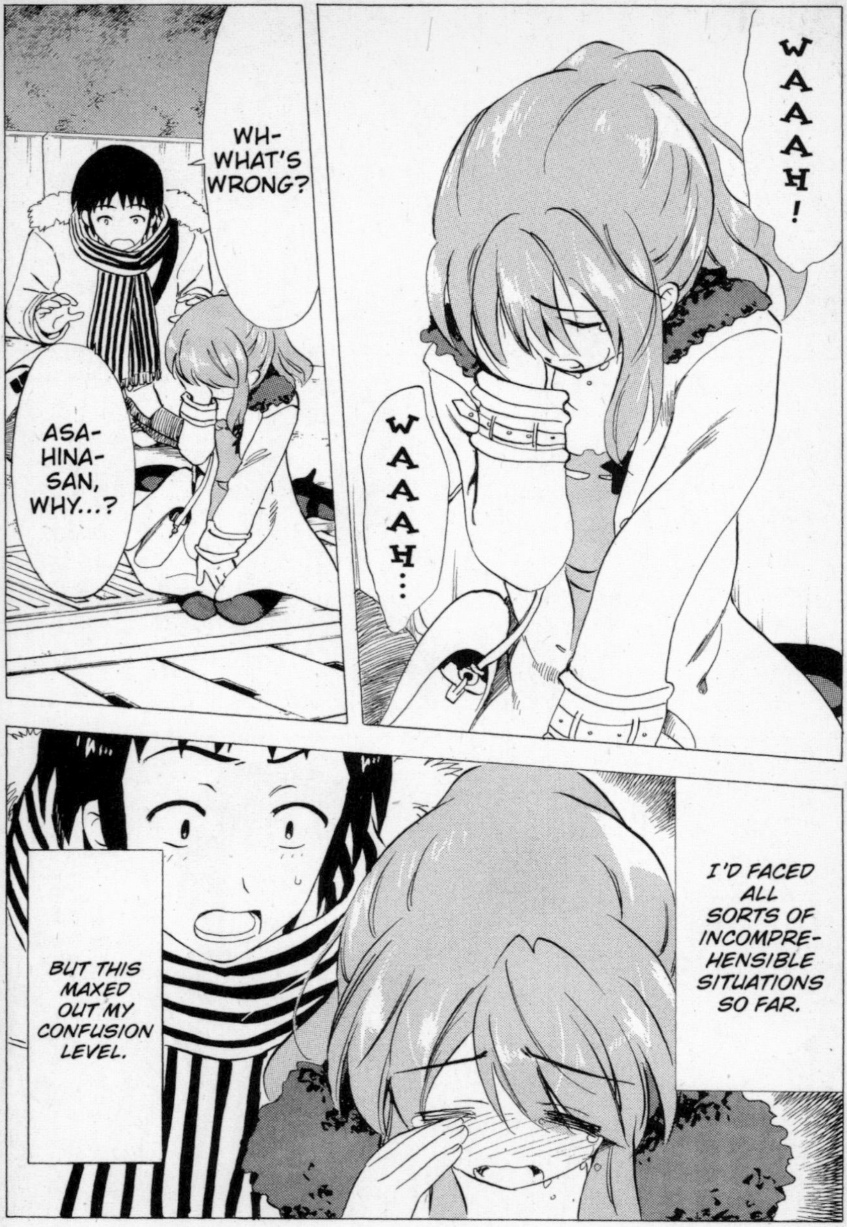
WAAAH!
WAAAH...
WH-WHAT'S WRONG?
ASA-HINA-SAN, WHY...?
I'D FACED ALL SORTS OF INCOMPRE-HENSIBLE SITUATIONS SO FAR.
BUT THIS MAXED OUT MY CONFUSION LEVEL.

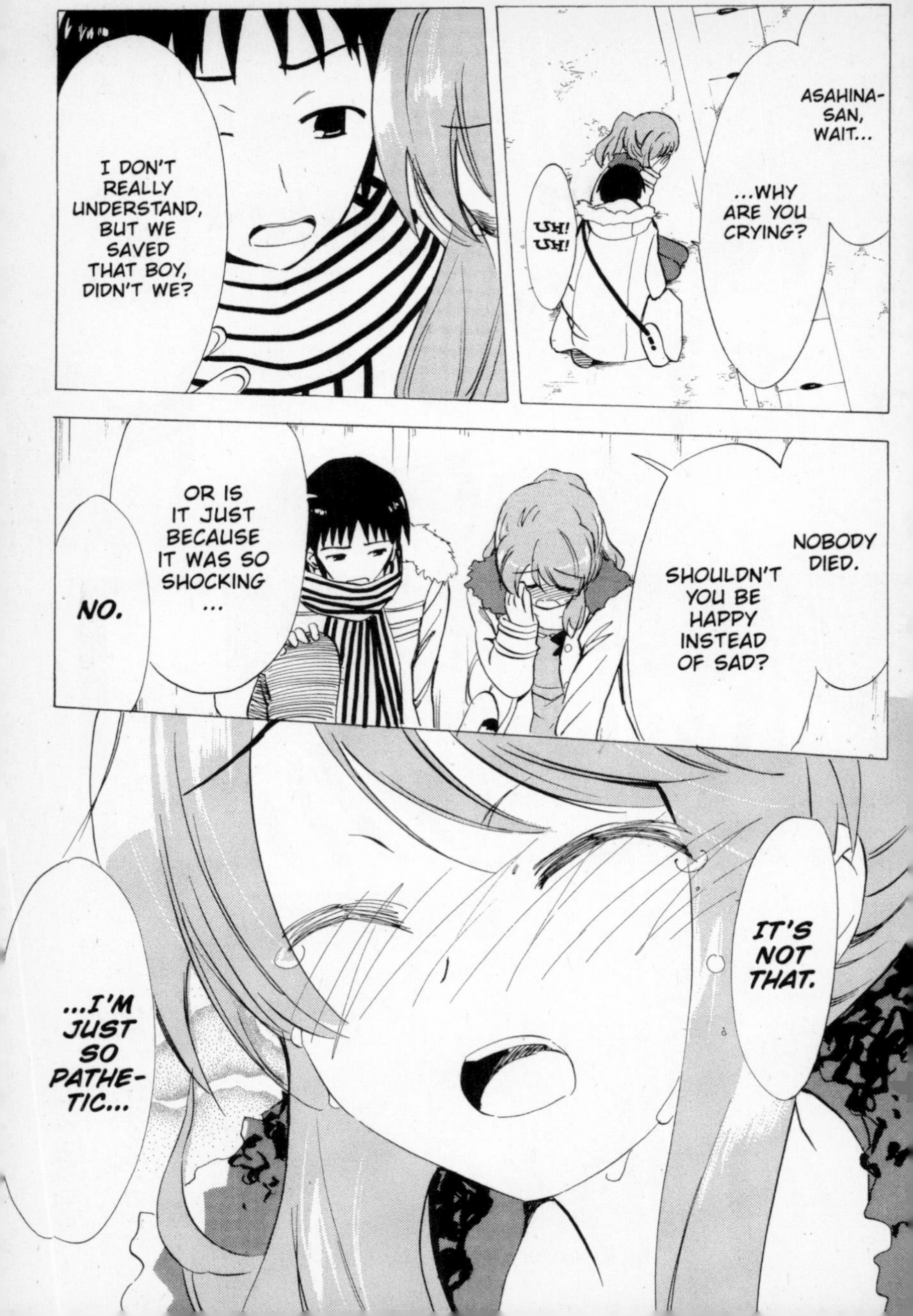
ASAHINA-SAN, WAIT...
...WHY ARE YOU CRYING?
UH! UH!
I DON'T REALLY UNDERSTAND, BUT WE SAVED THAT BOY, DIDN'T WE?
NOBODY DIED.
SHOULDN'T YOU BE HAPPY INSTEAD OF SAD?
OR IS IT JUST BECAUSE IT WAS SO SHOCKING...
NO.
IT'S NOT THAT.
...I'M JUST SO PATHETIC...

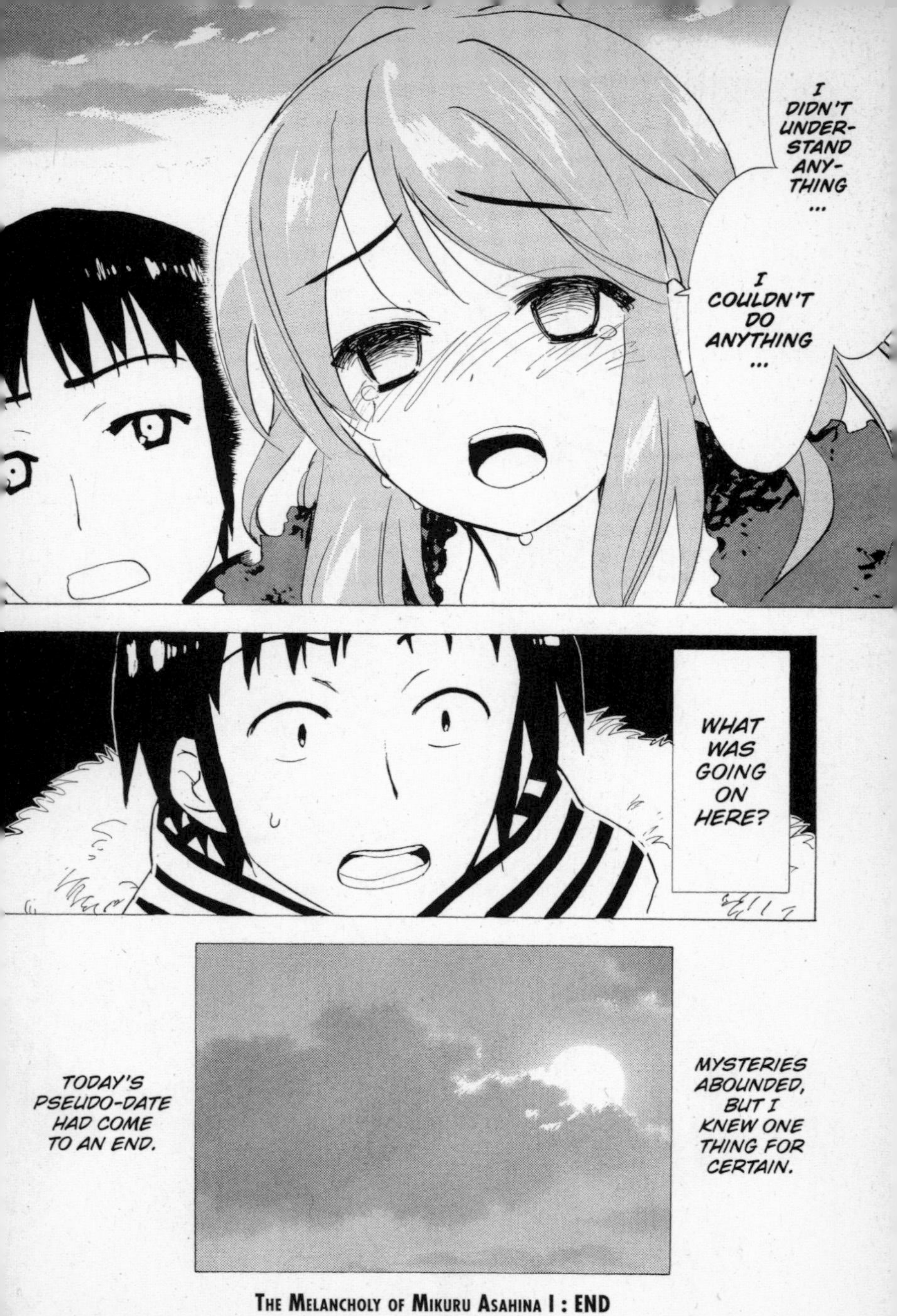
I DIDN'T UNDERSTAND ANYTHING...
I COULDN'T DO ANYTHING...
WHAT WAS GOING ON HERE?
MYSTERIES ABOUNDED, BUT I KNEW ONE THING FOR CERTAIN.
TODAY'S PSEUDO-DATE HAD COME TO AN END.

THE MELANCHOLY OF MIKURU ASAHINA I : END

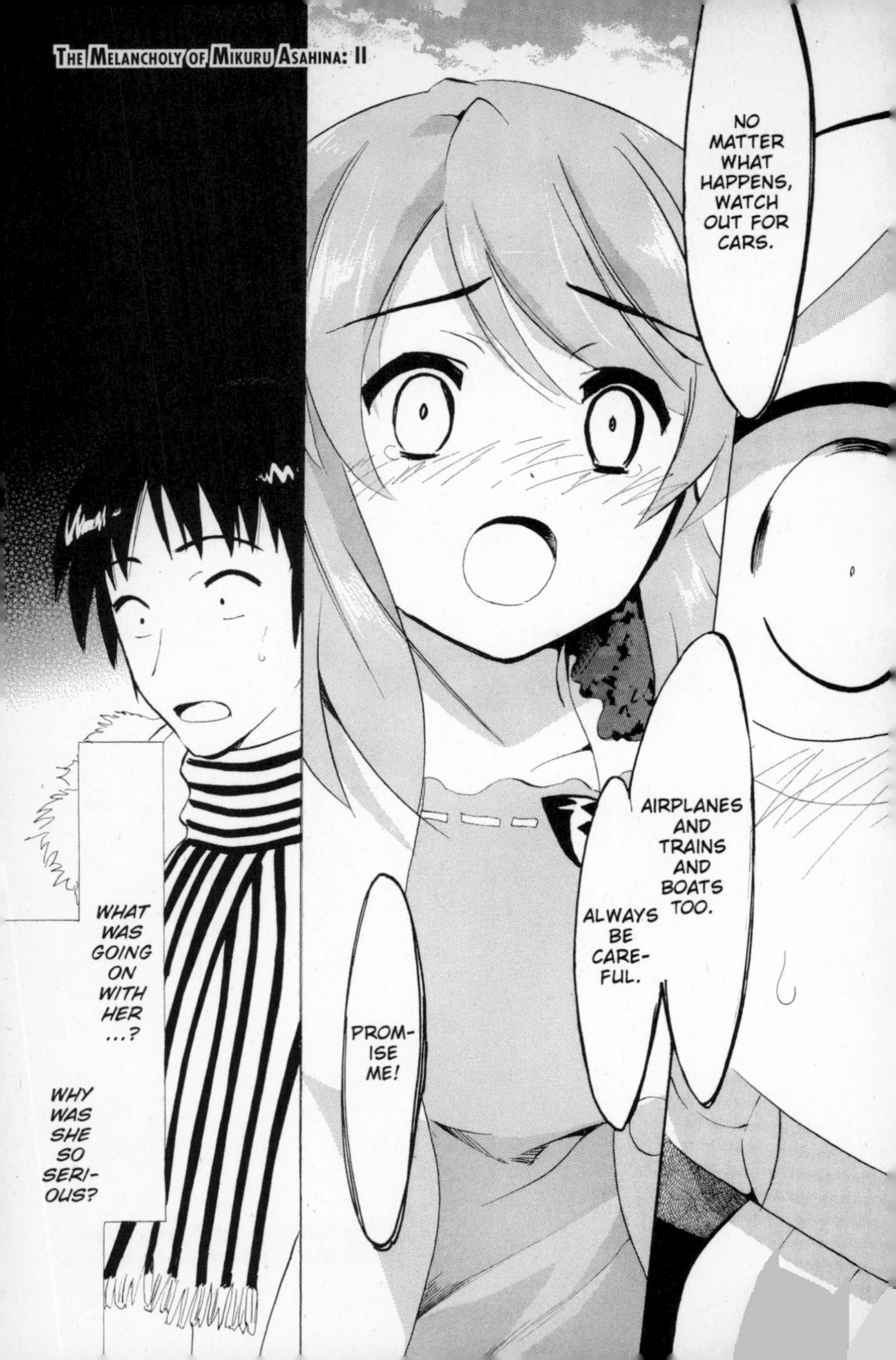
NO MATTER WHAT HAPPENS, WATCH OUT FOR CARS.
AIRPLANES AND TRAINS AND BOATS TOO.
ALWAYS BE CARE-FUL.
PROM-ISE ME!
WHAT WAS GOING ON WITH HER ...?
WHY WAS SHE SO SERI-OUS?

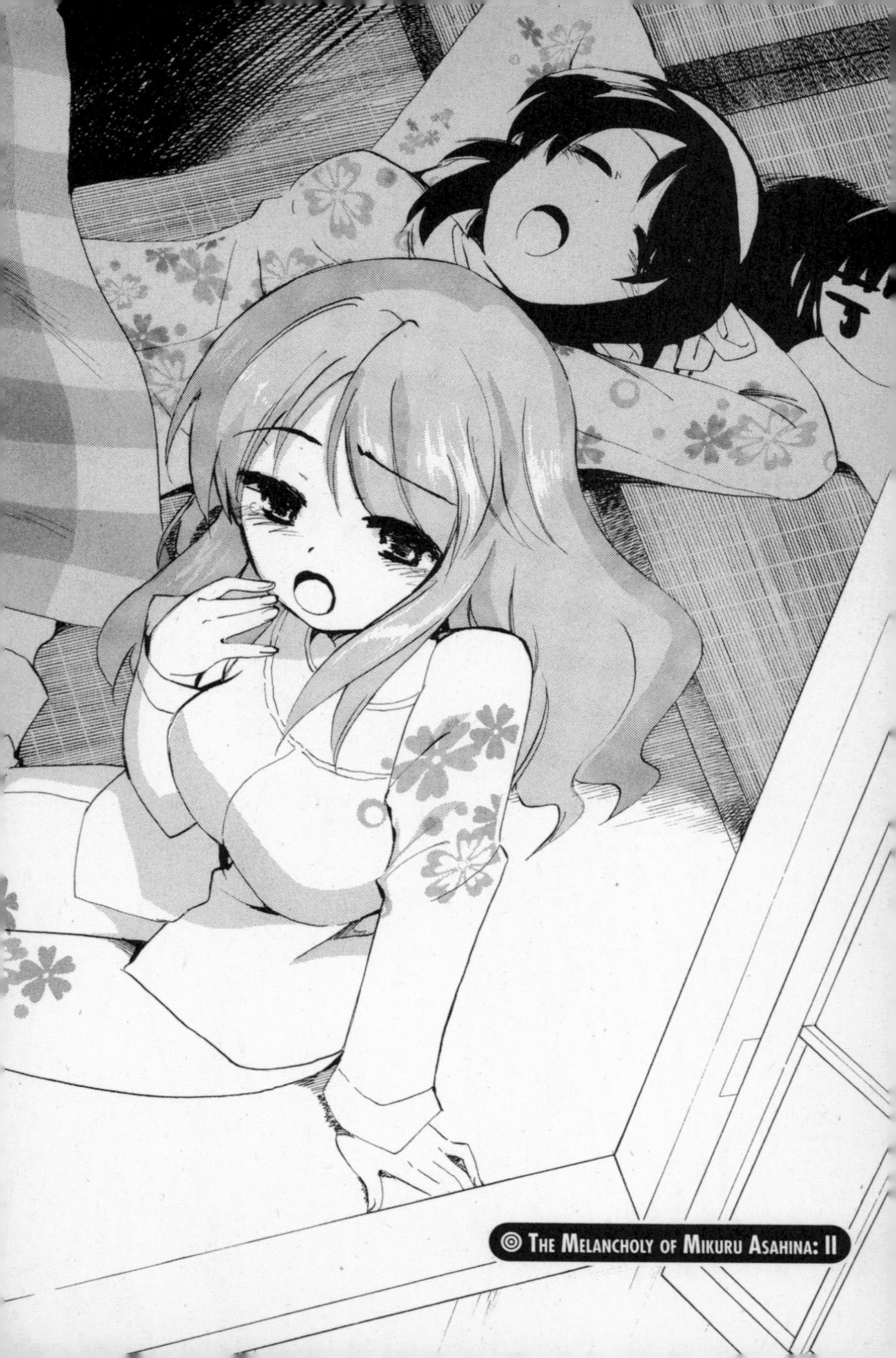
THE MELANCHOLY OF MIKURU ASAHINA: II

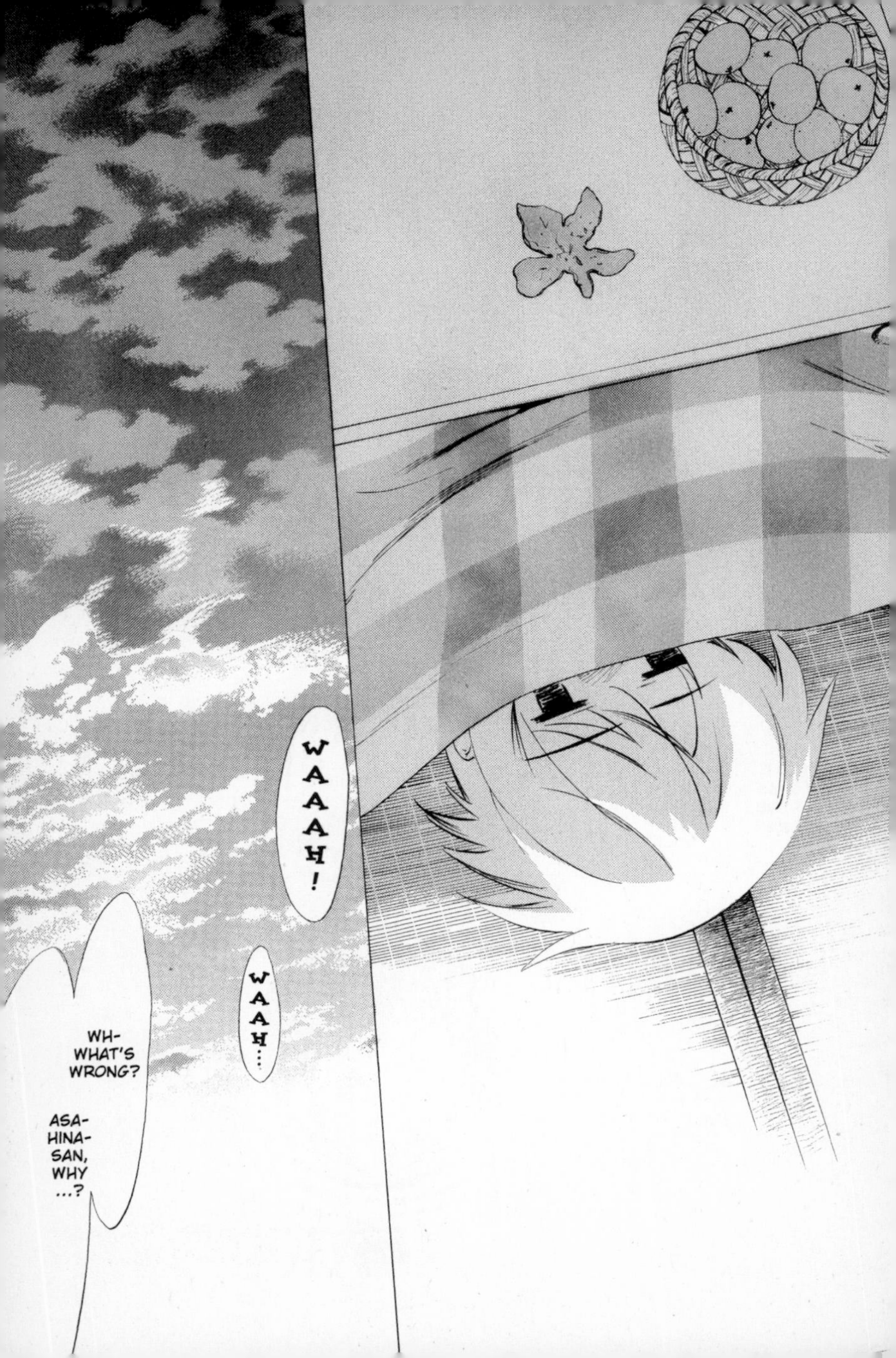
WAAAAH!
WAAAH...
WH-WHAT'S WRONG? ASA-HINA-SAN, WHY ...?

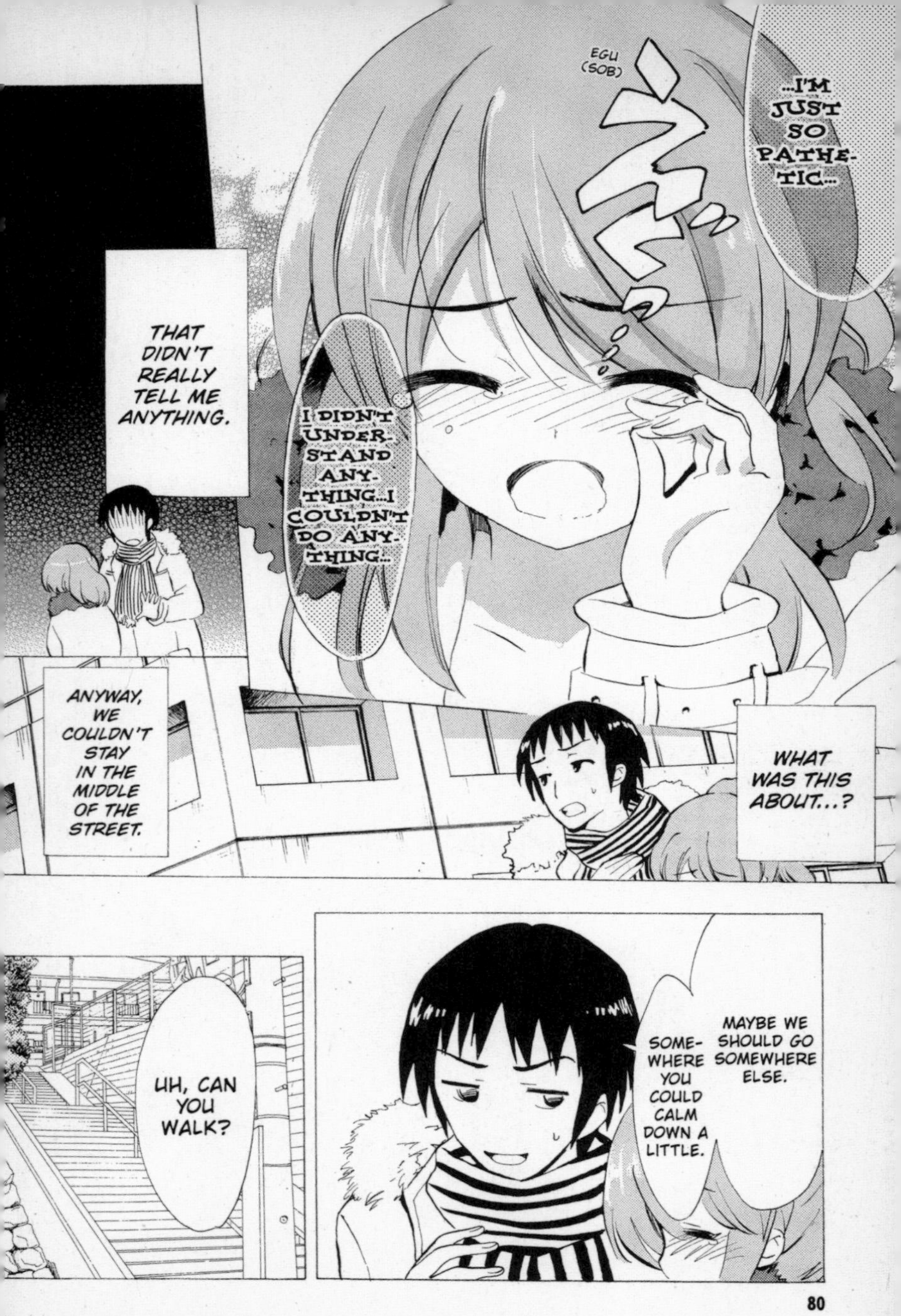
EGU (SOB)
...I'M JUST SO PATHETIC...
I DIDN'T UNDERSTAND ANYTHING...I COULDN'T DO ANYTHING...
THAT DIDN'T REALLY TELL ME ANYTHING.
WHAT WAS THIS ABOUT...?
ANYWAY, WE COULDN'T STAY IN THE MIDDLE OF THE STREET.
MAYBE WE SHOULD GO SOMEWHERE ELSE.
SOMEWHERE YOU COULD CALM DOWN A LITTLE.
UH, CAN YOU WALK?

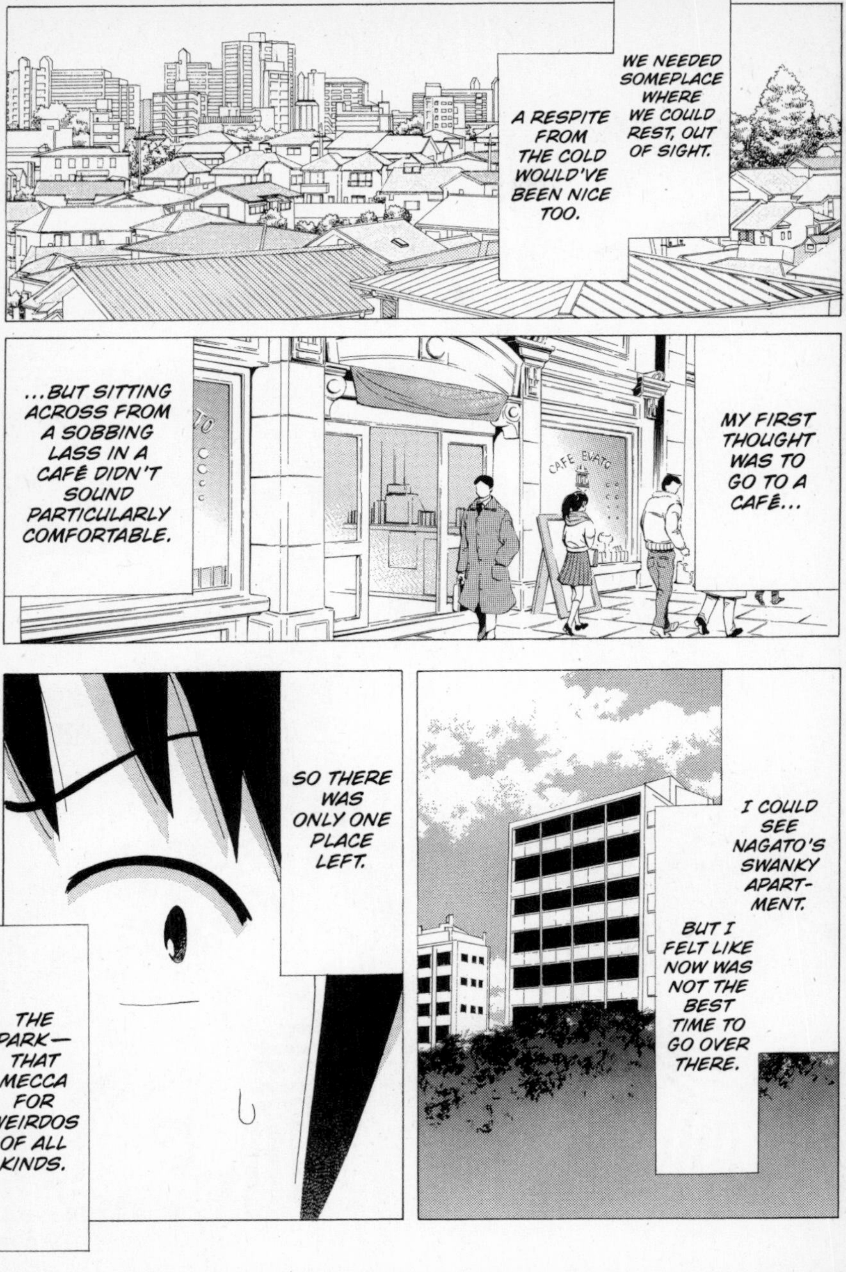
WE NEEDED SOMEPLACE WHERE WE COULD REST, OUT OF SIGHT.
A RESPITE FROM THE COLD WOULD'VE BEEN NICE TOO.
MY FIRST THOUGHT WAS TO GO TO A CAFÉ...
...BUT SITTING ACROSS FROM A SOBBING LASS IN A CAFÉ DIDN'T SOUND PARTICULARLY COMFORTABLE.
I COULD SEE NAGATO'S SWANKY APART-MENT.
BUT I FELT LIKE NOW WAS NOT THE BEST TIME TO GO OVER THERE.
SO THERE WAS ONLY ONE PLACE LEFT.
THE PARK—THAT MECCA FOR WEIRDOS OF ALL KINDS.

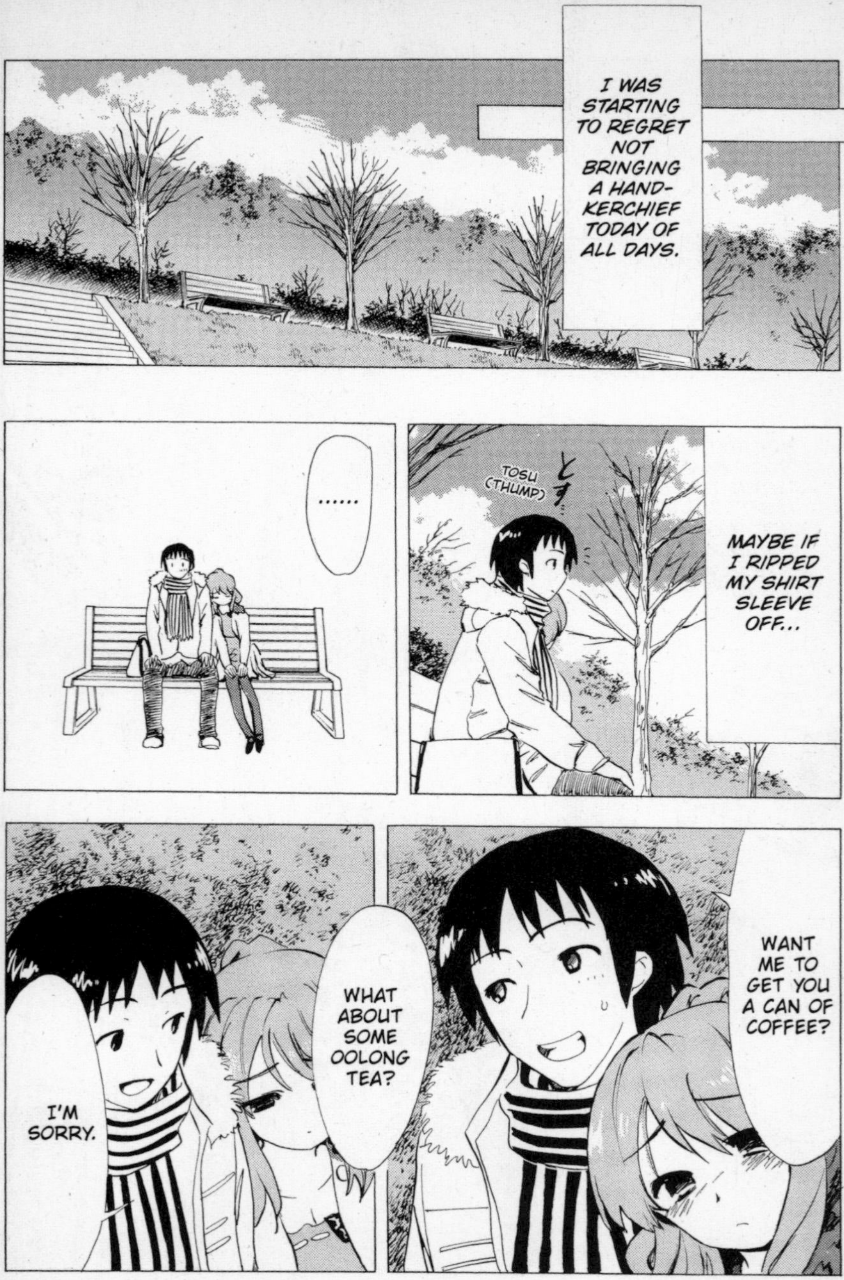
I WAS STARTING TO REGRET NOT BRINGING A HAND-KERCHIEF TODAY OF ALL DAYS.
とす
TOSU (THUMP)
MAYBE IF I RIPPED MY SHIRT SLEEVE OFF...
......
WANT ME TO GET YOU A CAN OF COFFEE?
WHAT ABOUT SOME OOLONG TEA?
I'M SORRY.

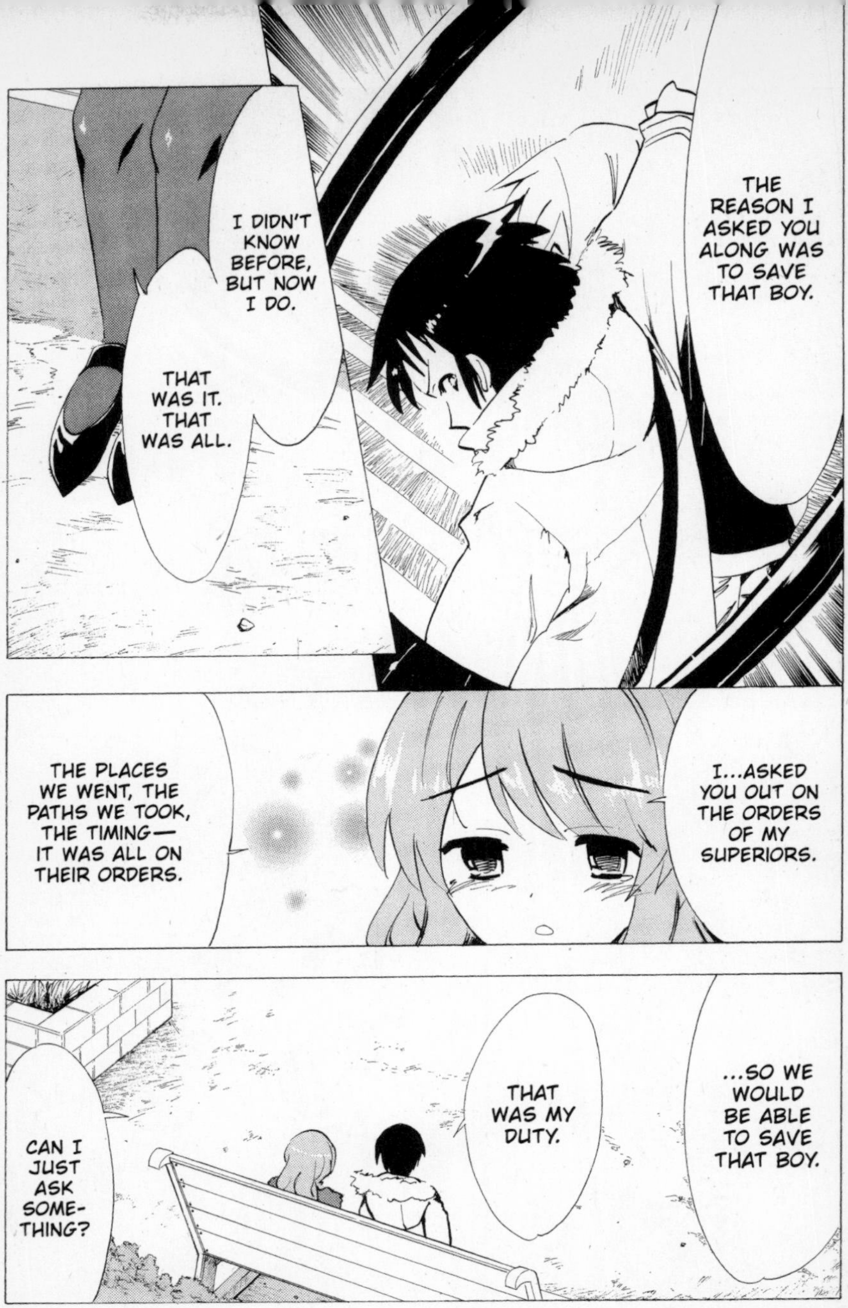
THE REASON I ASKED YOU ALONG WAS TO SAVE THAT BOY.
I DIDN'T KNOW BEFORE, BUT NOW I DO.
THAT WAS IT. THAT WAS ALL.
I...ASKED YOU OUT ON THE ORDERS OF MY SUPERIORS.
THE PLACES WE WENT, THE PATHS WE TOOK, THE TIMING— IT WAS ALL ON THEIR ORDERS.
...SO WE WOULD BE ABLE TO SAVE THAT BOY.
THAT WAS MY DUTY.
CAN I JUST ASK SOME-THING?

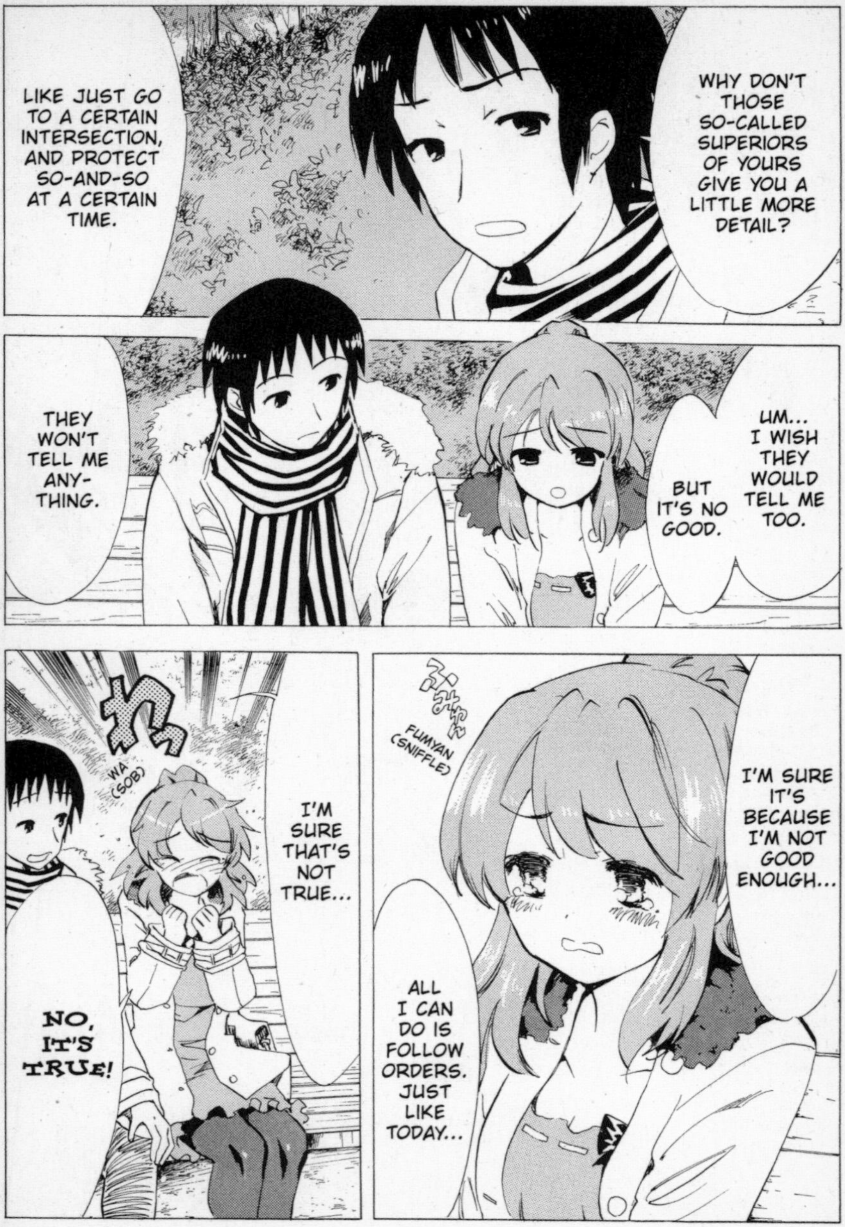
WHY DON'T THOSE SO-CALLED SUPERIORS OF YOURS GIVE YOU A LITTLE MORE DETAIL?
LIKE JUST GO TO A CERTAIN INTERSECTION, AND PROTECT SO-AND-SO AT A CERTAIN TIME.
UM... I WISH THEY WOULD TELL ME TOO.
BUT IT'S NO GOOD.
THEY WON'T TELL ME ANY-THING.
FUMYAN (SNIFFLE)
I'M SURE IT'S BECAUSE I'M NOT GOOD ENOUGH...
ALL I CAN DO IS FOLLOW ORDERS. JUST LIKE TODAY...
I'M SURE THAT'S NOT TRUE...
WA (SOB)
NO, IT'S TRUE!

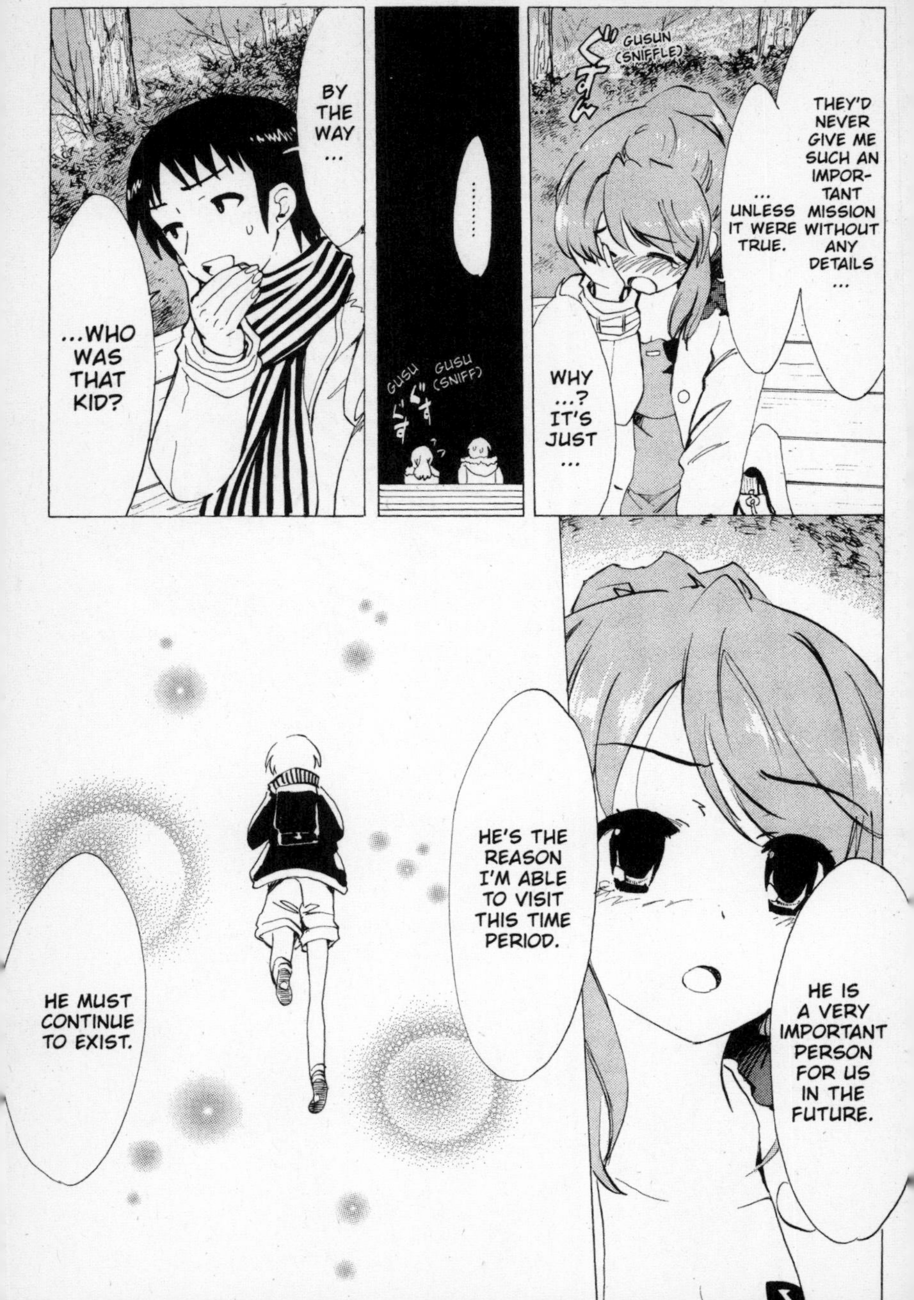

ぐすん
GUSUN (SNIFFLE)
THEY'D NEVER GIVE ME SUCH AN IMPOR-TANT MISSION WITHOUT ANY DETAILS ...
... UNLESS IT WERE TRUE.
WHY ...? IT'S JUST ...
......
ぐすぐす
GUSU GUSU (SNIFF)
BY THE WAY ...
...WHO WAS THAT KID?
HE IS A VERY IMPORTANT PERSON FOR US IN THE FUTURE.
HE'S THE REASON I'M ABLE TO VISIT THIS TIME PERIOD.
HE MUST CONTINUE TO EXIST.

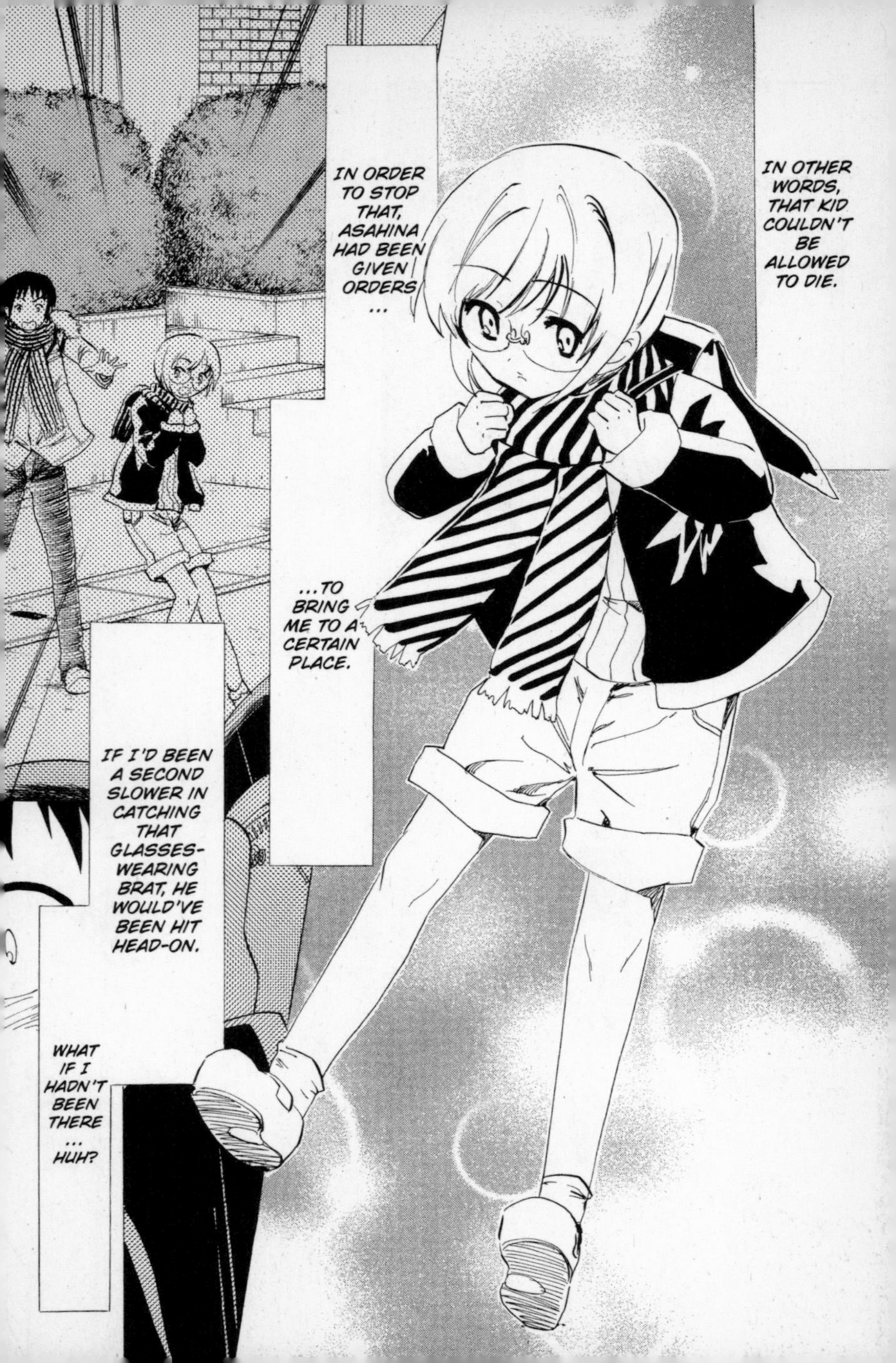
IN OTHER WORDS, THAT KID COULDN'T BE ALLOWED TO DIE.
IN ORDER TO STOP THAT, ASAHINA HAD BEEN GIVEN ORDERS...
...TO BRING ME TO A CERTAIN PLACE.
IF I'D BEEN A SECOND SLOWER IN CATCHING THAT GLASSES-WEARING BRAT, HE WOULD'VE BEEN HIT HEAD-ON.
WHAT IF I HADN'T BEEN THERE... HUH?

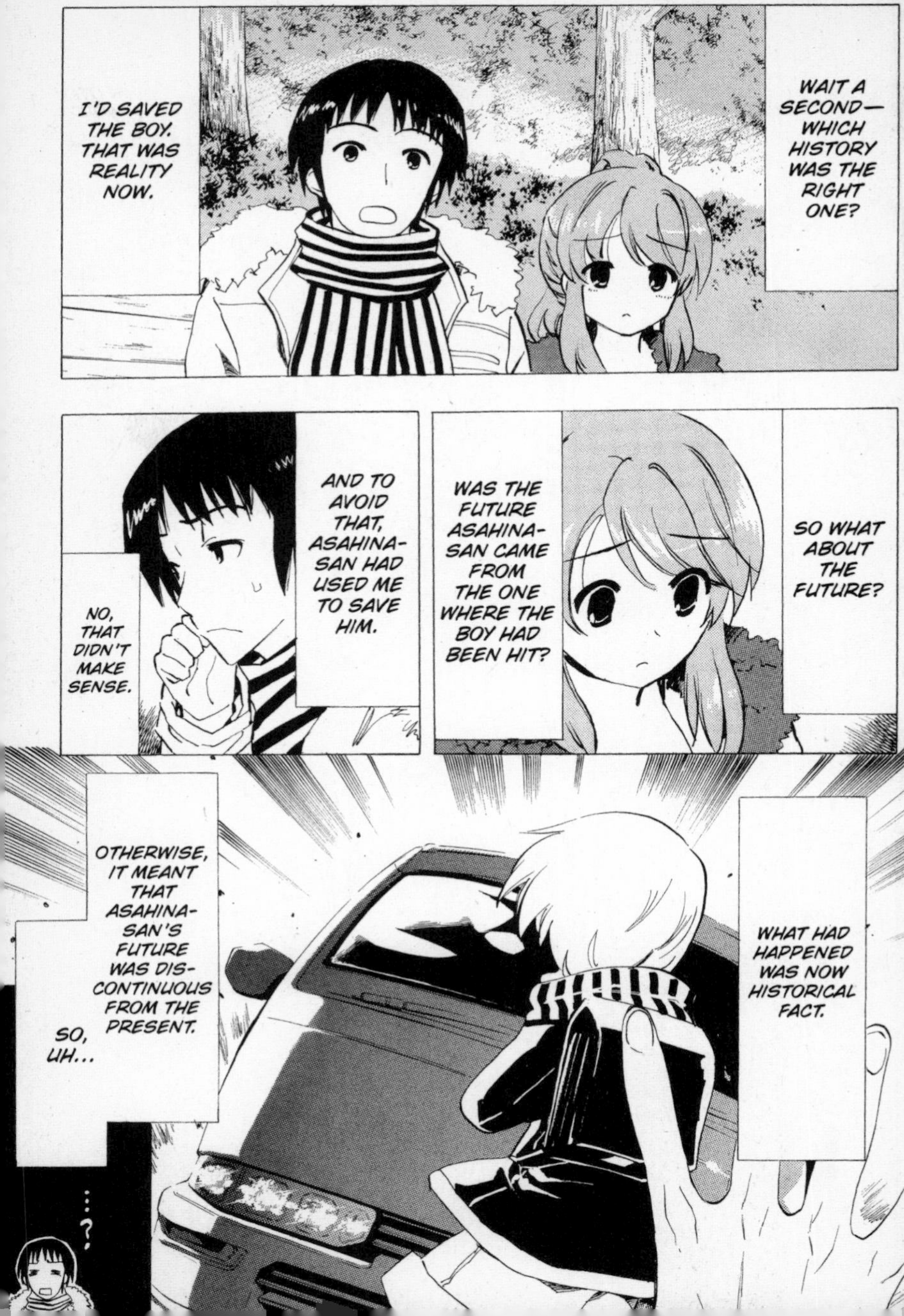
WAIT A SECOND—WHICH HISTORY WAS THE RIGHT ONE?
I'D SAVED THE BOY. THAT WAS REALITY NOW.
SO WHAT ABOUT THE FUTURE?
WAS THE FUTURE ASAHINA-SAN CAME FROM THE ONE WHERE THE BOY HAD BEEN HIT?
AND TO AVOID THAT, ASAHINA-SAN HAD USED ME TO SAVE HIM.
NO, THAT DIDN'T MAKE SENSE.
WHAT HAD HAPPENED WAS NOW HISTORICAL FACT.
OTHERWISE, IT MEANT THAT ASAHINA-SAN'S FUTURE WAS DIS-CONTINUOUS FROM THE PRESENT.
SO, UH...
...?

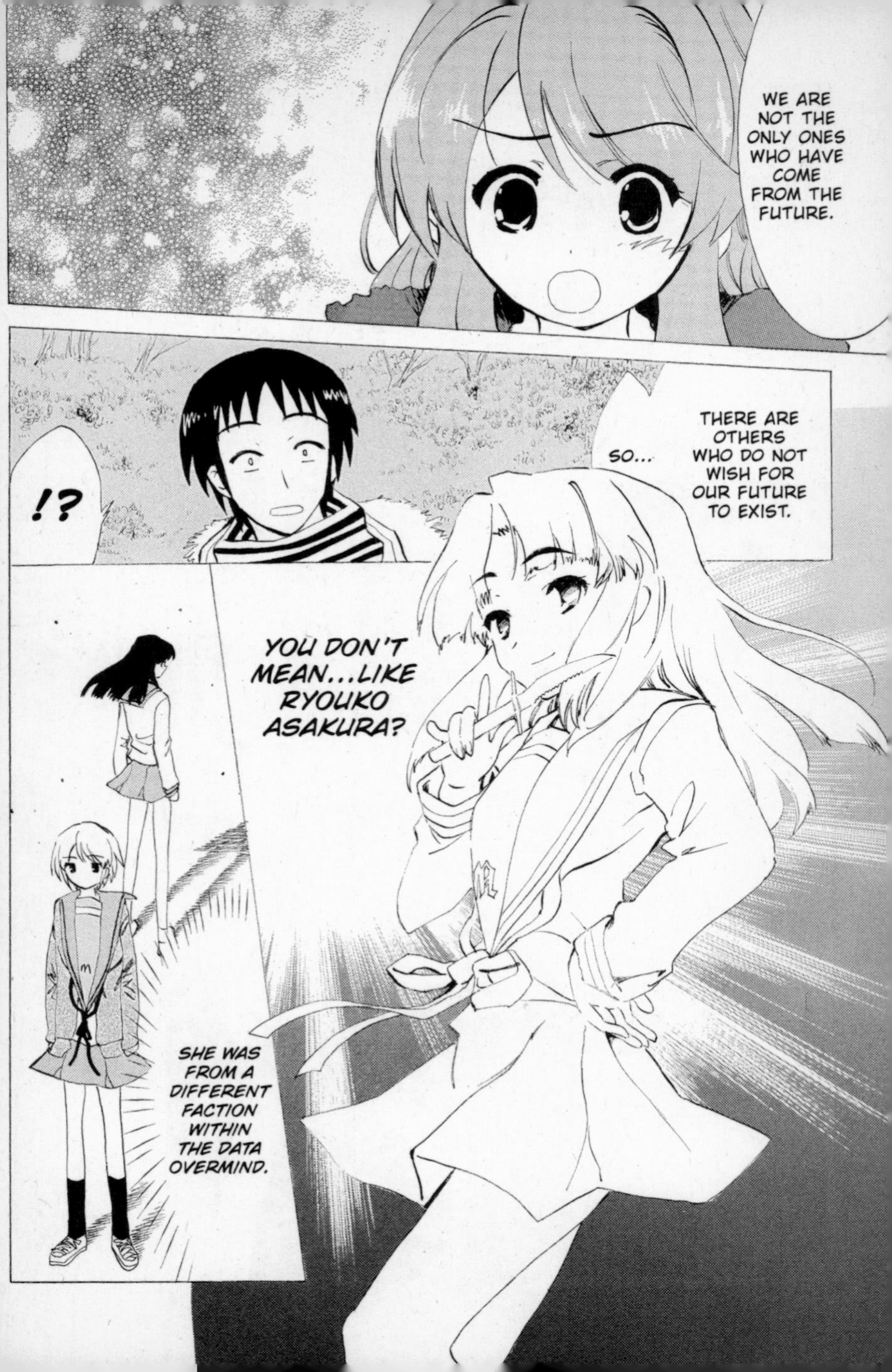

WE ARE NOT THE ONLY ONES WHO HAVE COME FROM THE FUTURE.
SO...
THERE ARE OTHERS WHO DO NOT WISH FOR OUR FUTURE TO EXIST.
!?
YOU DON'T MEAN...LIKE RYOUKO ASAKURA?
SHE WAS FROM A DIFFERENT FACTION WITHIN THE DATA OVERMIND.

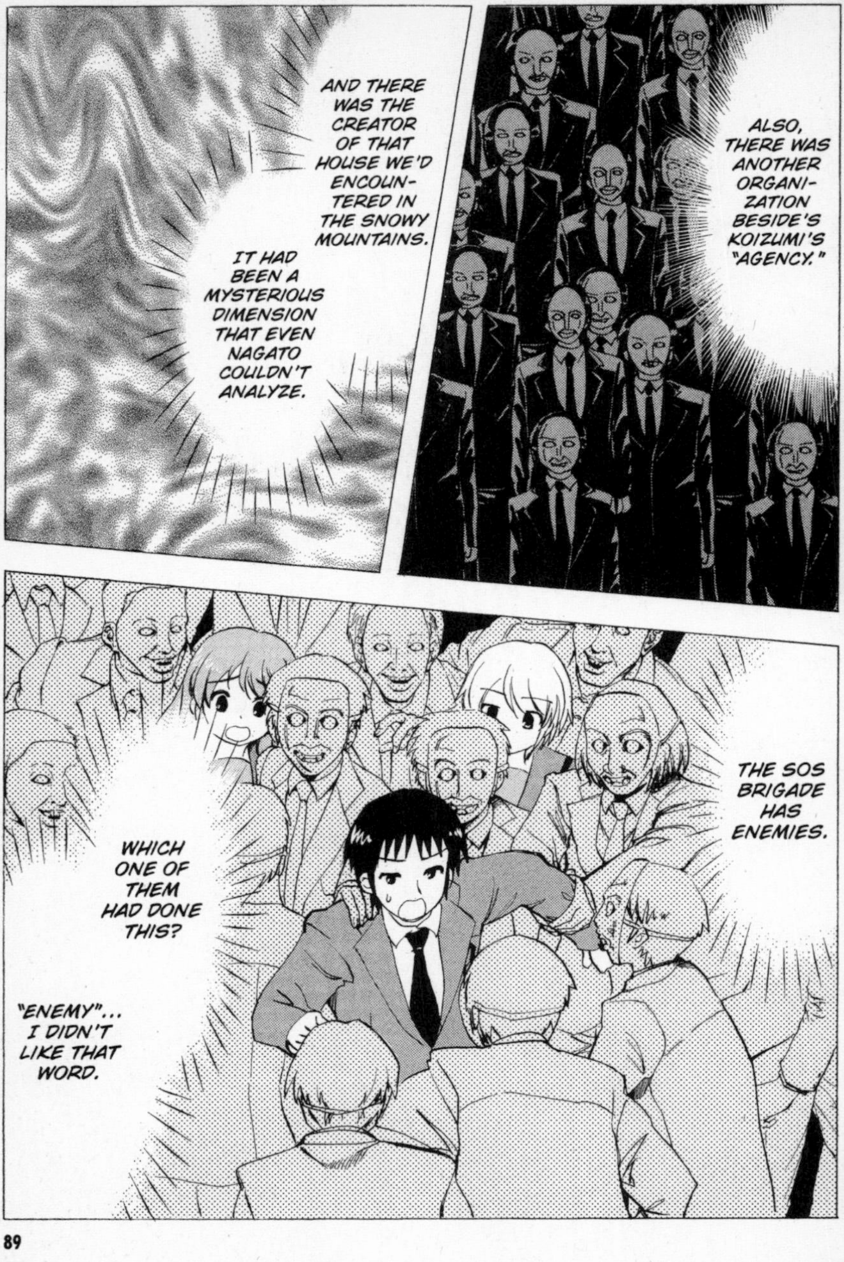
ALSO, THERE WAS ANOTHER ORGANI-ZATION BESIDE'S KOIZUMI'S "AGENCY."
AND THERE WAS THE CREATOR OF THAT HOUSE WE'D ENCOUN-TERED IN THE SNOWY MOUNTAINS.
IT HAD BEEN A MYSTERIOUS DIMENSION THAT EVEN NAGATO COULDN'T ANALYZE.
THE SOS BRIGADE HAS ENEMIES.
WHICH ONE OF THEM HAD DONE THIS?
"ENEMY"... I DIDN'T LIKE THAT WORD.

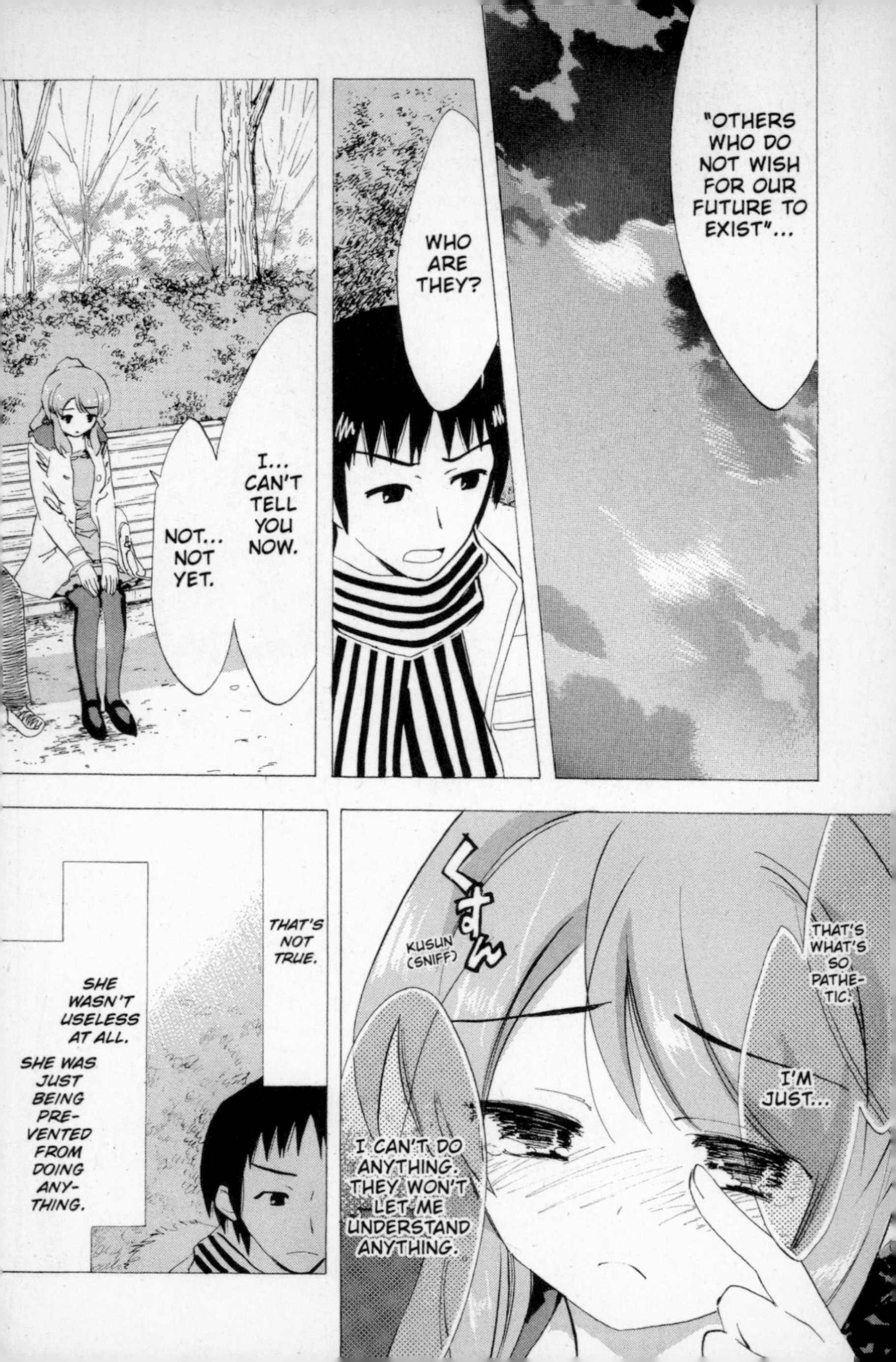
"OTHERS WHO DO NOT WISH FOR OUR FUTURE TO EXIST"...
WHO ARE THEY?
I... CAN'T TELL YOU NOW.
NOT... NOT YET.
THAT'S WHAT'S SO PATHETIC.
くすん
KUSUN (SNIFF)
I'M JUST...
I CAN'T DO ANYTHING. THEY WON'T LET ME UNDERSTAND ANYTHING.
THAT'S NOT TRUE.
SHE WASN'T USELESS AT ALL.
SHE WAS JUST BEING PRE-VENTED FROM DOING ANY-THING.

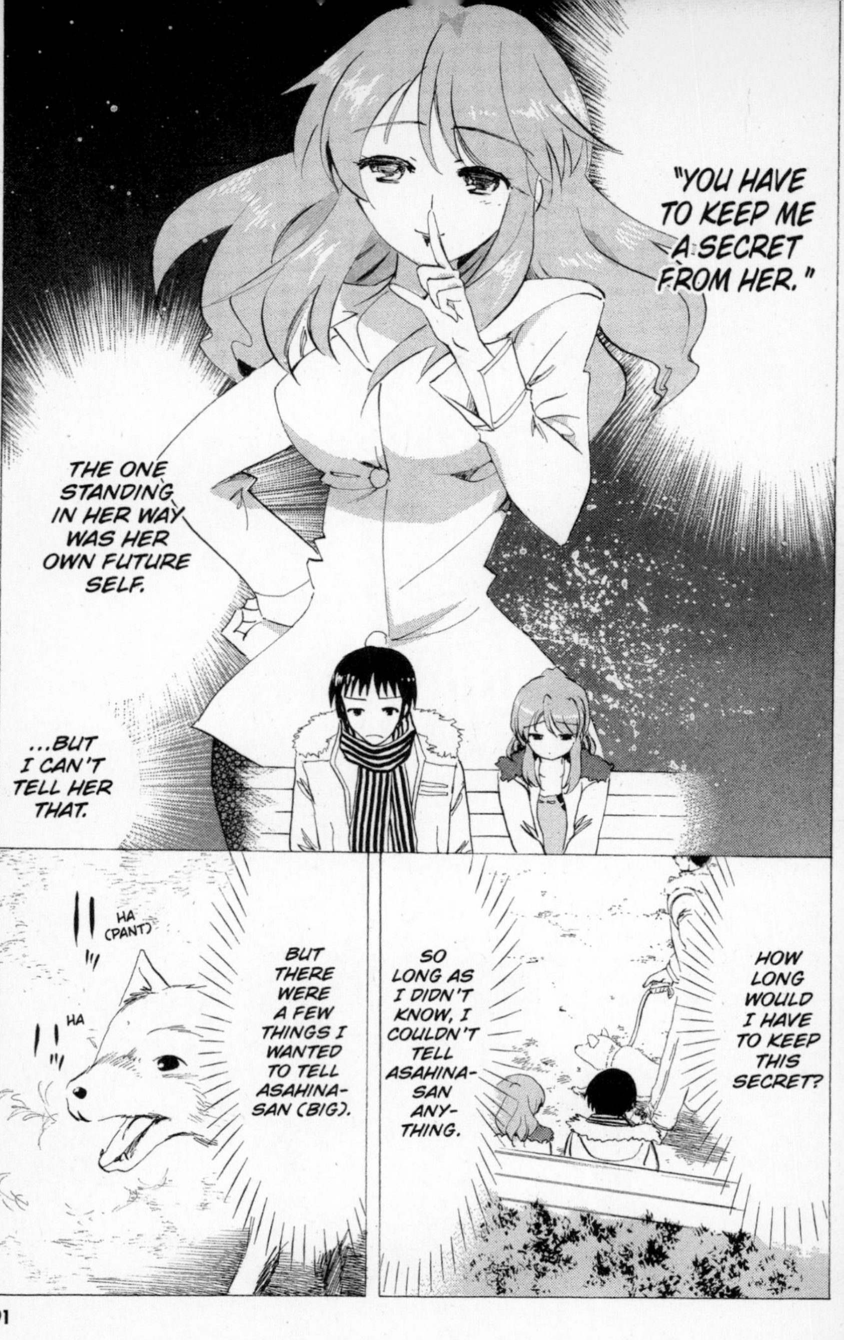
"YOU HAVE TO KEEP ME A SECRET FROM HER."
THE ONE STANDING IN HER WAY WAS HER OWN FUTURE SELF.
...BUT I CAN'T TELL HER THAT.
HOW LONG WOULD I HAVE TO KEEP THIS SECRET?
SO LONG AS I DIDN'T KNOW, I COULDN'T TELL ASAHINA-SAN ANYTHING.
BUT THERE WERE A FEW THINGS I WANTED TO TELL ASAHINA-SAN (BIG).
HA (PANT)
HA

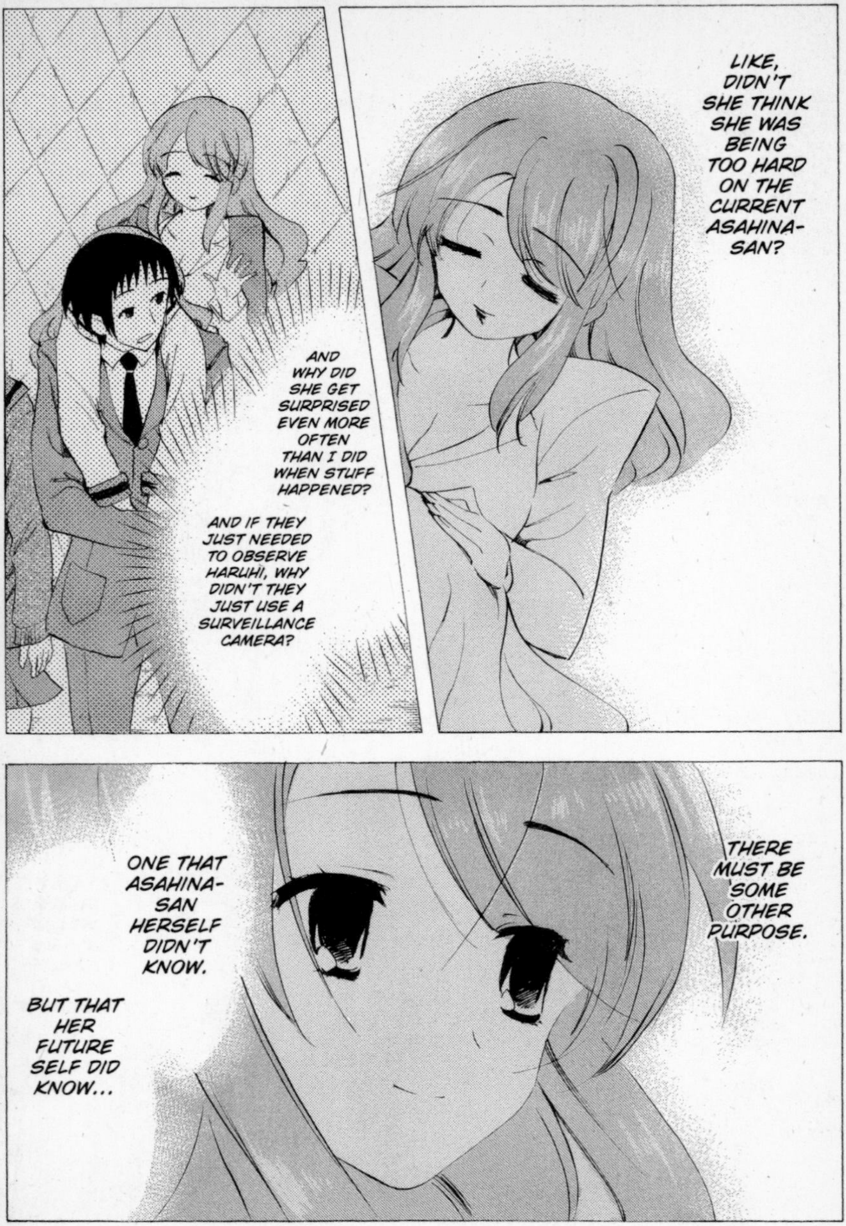
LIKE, DIDN'T SHE THINK SHE WAS BEING TOO HARD ON THE CURRENT ASAHINA-SAN?
AND WHY DID SHE GET SURPRISED EVEN MORE OFTEN THAN I DID WHEN STUFF HAPPENED?
AND IF THEY JUST NEEDED TO OBSERVE HARUHI, WHY DIDN'T THEY JUST USE A SURVEILLANCE CAMERA?
THERE MUST BE SOME OTHER PURPOSE.
ONE THAT ASAHINA-SAN HERSELF DIDN'T KNOW.
BUT THAT HER FUTURE SELF DID KNOW...

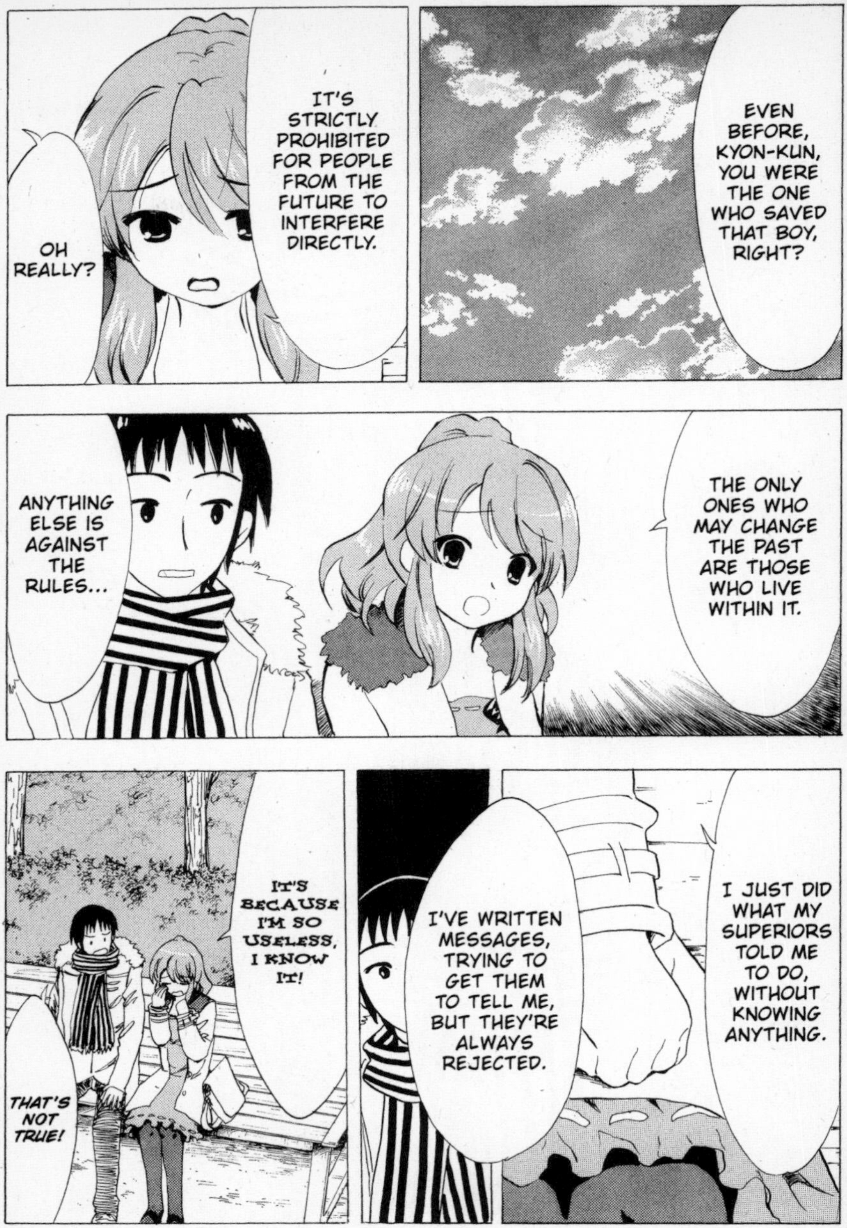
EVEN BEFORE, KYON-KUN, YOU WERE THE ONE WHO SAVED THAT BOY, RIGHT?
IT'S STRICTLY PROHIBITED FOR PEOPLE FROM THE FUTURE TO INTERFERE DIRECTLY.
OH REALLY?
THE ONLY ONES WHO MAY CHANGE THE PAST ARE THOSE WHO LIVE WITHIN IT.
ANYTHING ELSE IS AGAINST THE RULES...
I JUST DID WHAT MY SUPERIORS TOLD ME TO DO, WITHOUT KNOWING ANYTHING.
I'VE WRITTEN MESSAGES, TRYING TO GET THEM TO TELL ME, BUT THEY'RE ALWAYS REJECTED.
IT'S BECAUSE I'M SO USELESS, I KNOW IT!
THAT'S NOT TRUE!

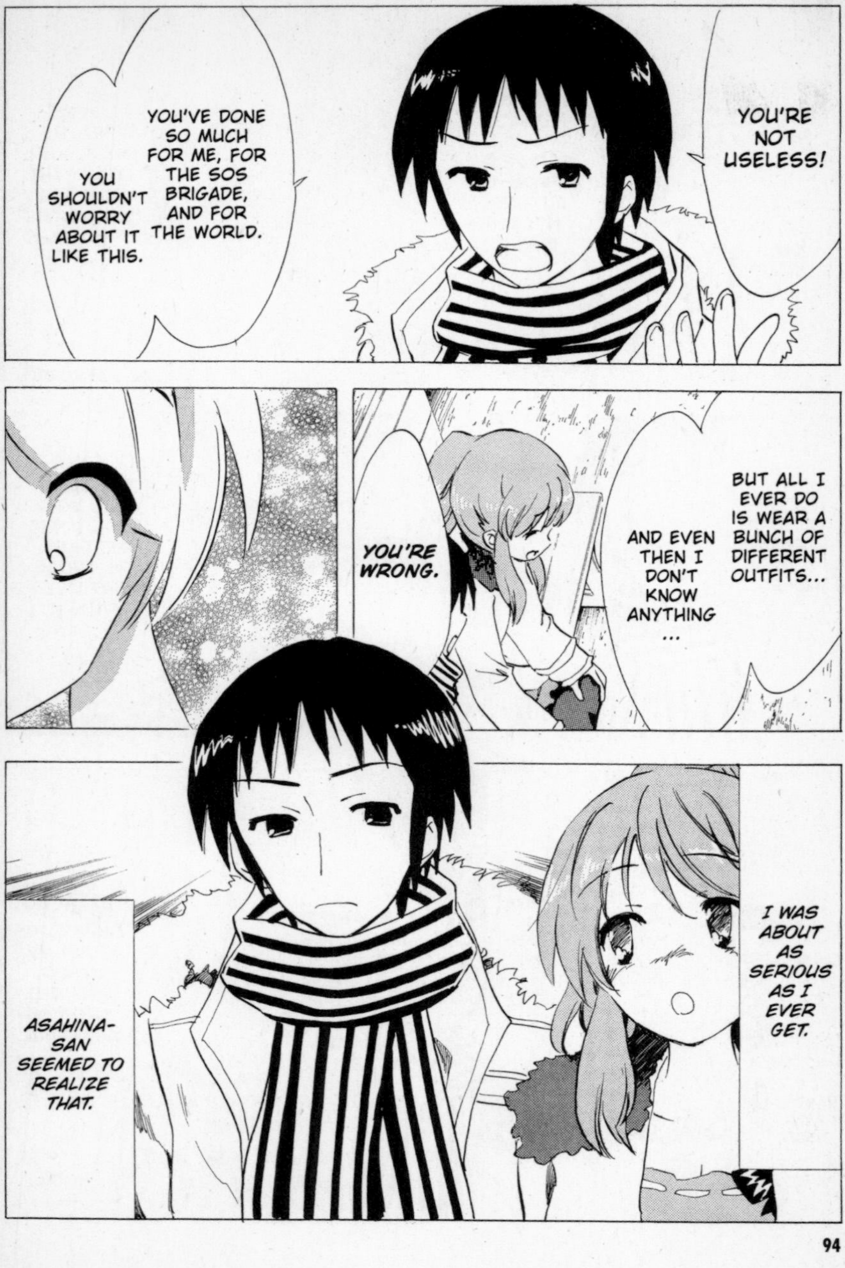
YOU'RE NOT USELESS!
YOU'VE DONE SO MUCH FOR ME, FOR THE SOS BRIGADE, AND FOR THE WORLD.
YOU SHOULDN'T WORRY ABOUT IT LIKE THIS.
BUT ALL I EVER DO IS WEAR A BUNCH OF DIFFERENT OUTFITS...
AND EVEN THEN I DON'T KNOW ANYTHING...
YOU'RE WRONG.
I WAS ABOUT AS SERIOUS AS I EVER GET.
ASAHINA-SAN SEEMED TO REALIZE THAT.

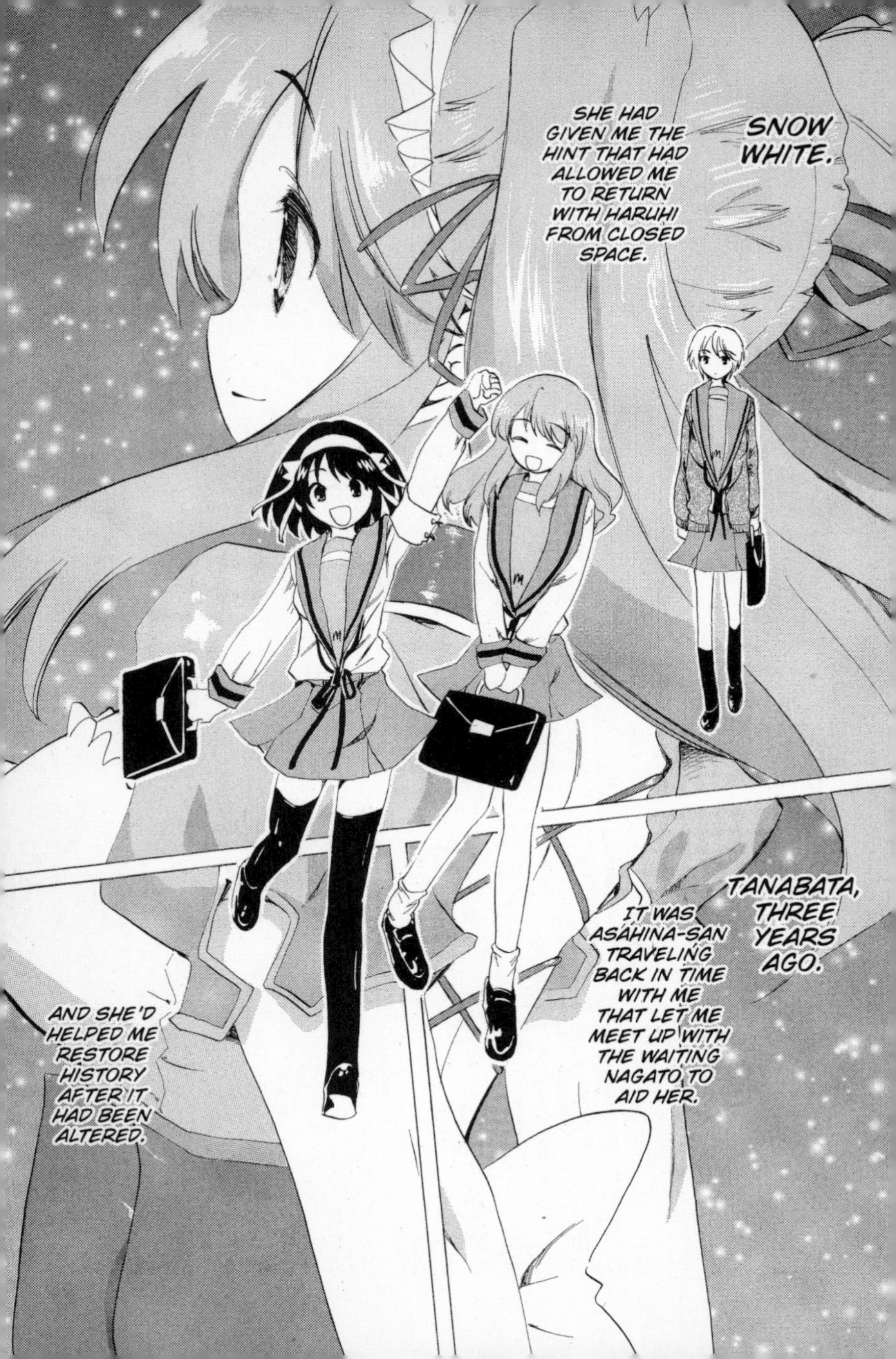
SNOW WHITE.
SHE HAD GIVEN ME THE HINT THAT HAD ALLOWED ME TO RETURN WITH HARUHI FROM CLOSED SPACE.
TANABATA, THREE YEARS AGO.
IT WAS ASAHINA-SAN TRAVELING BACK IN TIME WITH ME THAT LET ME MEET UP WITH THE WAITING NAGATO TO AID HER.
AND SHE'D HELPED ME RESTORE HISTORY AFTER IT HAD BEEN ALTERED.

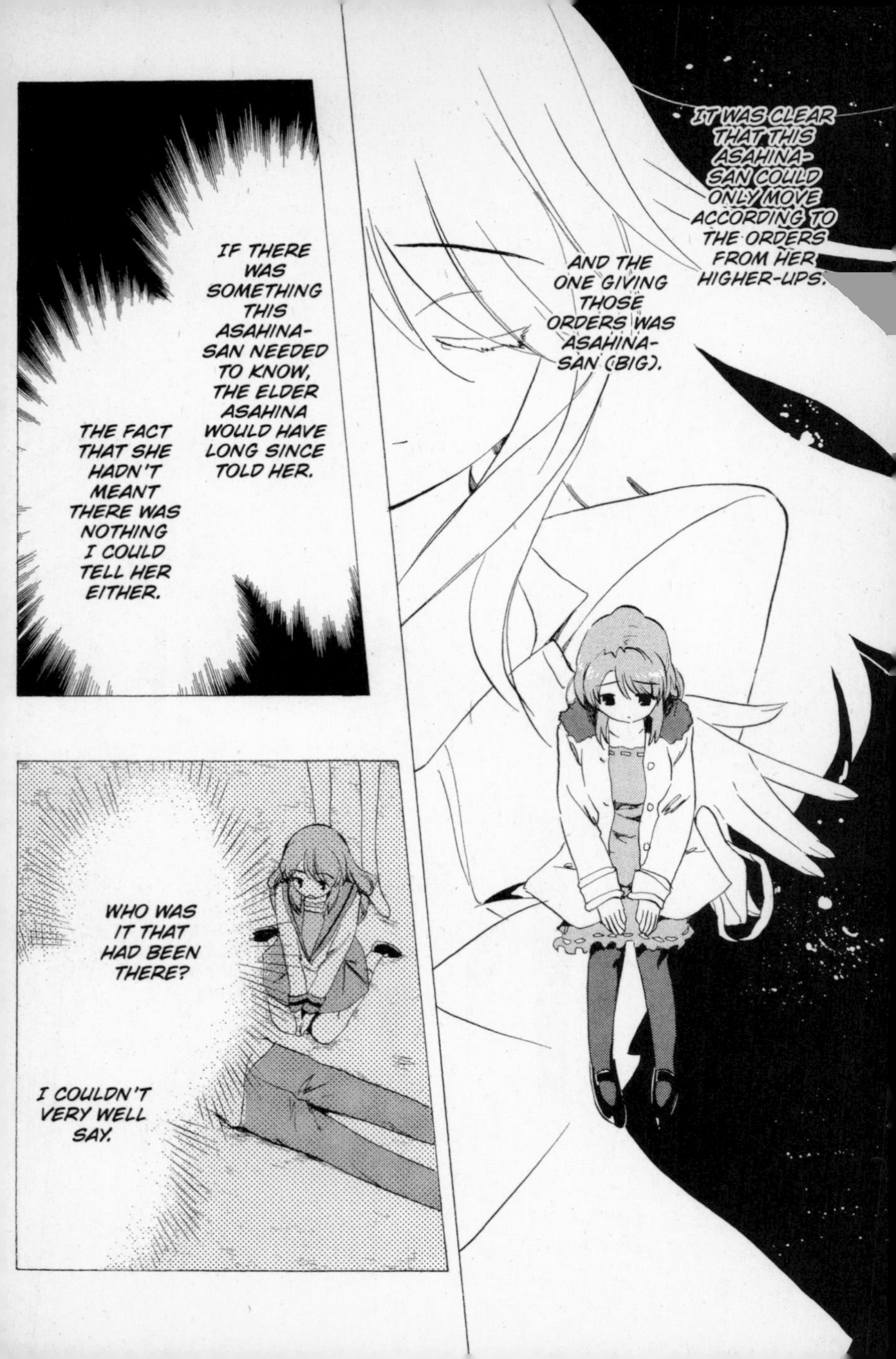
IT WAS CLEAR THAT THIS ASAHINA-SAN COULD ONLY MOVE ACCORDING TO THE ORDERS FROM HER HIGHER-UPS.
AND THE ONE GIVING THOSE ORDERS WAS ASAHINA-SAN (BIG).
IF THERE WAS SOMETHING THIS ASAHINA-SAN NEEDED TO KNOW, THE ELDER ASAHINA WOULD HAVE LONG SINCE TOLD HER.
THE FACT THAT SHE HADN'T MEANT THERE WAS NOTHING I COULD TELL HER EITHER.
WHO WAS IT THAT HAD BEEN THERE?
I COULDN'T VERY WELL SAY.

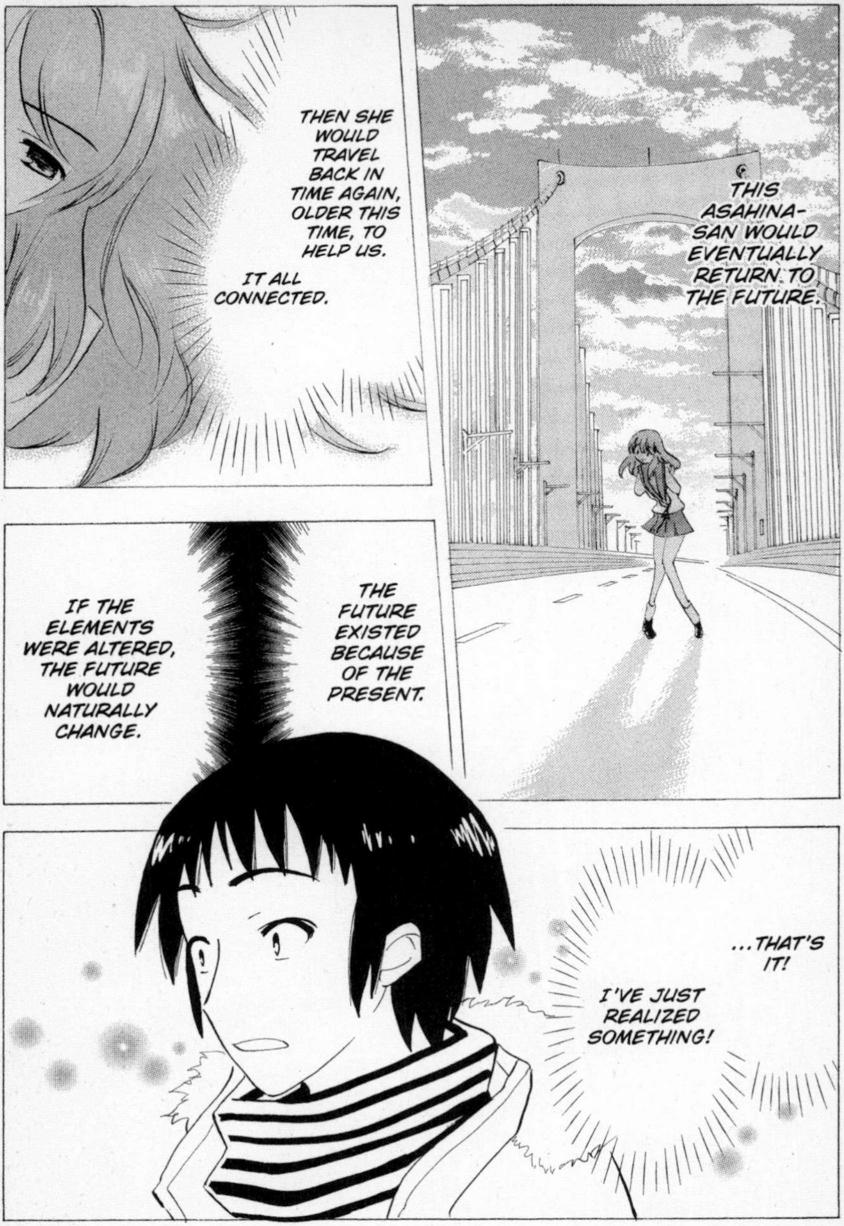
THIS ASAHINA-SAN WOULD EVENTUALLY RETURN TO THE FUTURE.
THEN SHE WOULD TRAVEL BACK IN TIME AGAIN, OLDER THIS TIME, TO HELP US.
IT ALL CONNECTED.
THE FUTURE EXISTED BECAUSE OF THE PRESENT.
IF THE ELEMENTS WERE ALTERED, THE FUTURE WOULD NATURALLY CHANGE.
...THAT'S IT!
I'VE JUST REALIZED SOMETHING!

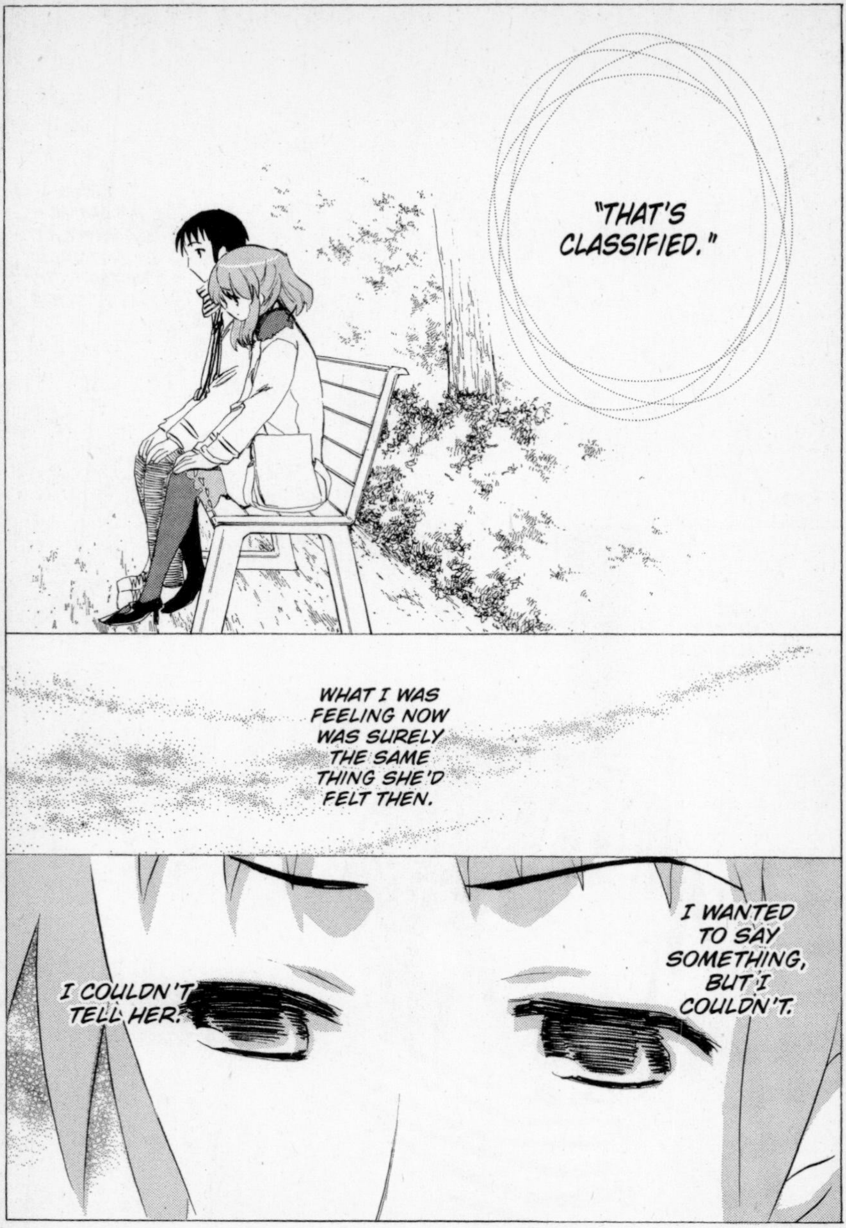
"THAT'S CLASSIFIED."
WHAT I WAS FEELING NOW WAS SURELY THE SAME THING SHE'D FELT THEN.
I WANTED TO SAY SOMETHING, BUT I COULDN'T.
I COULDN'T TELL HER.

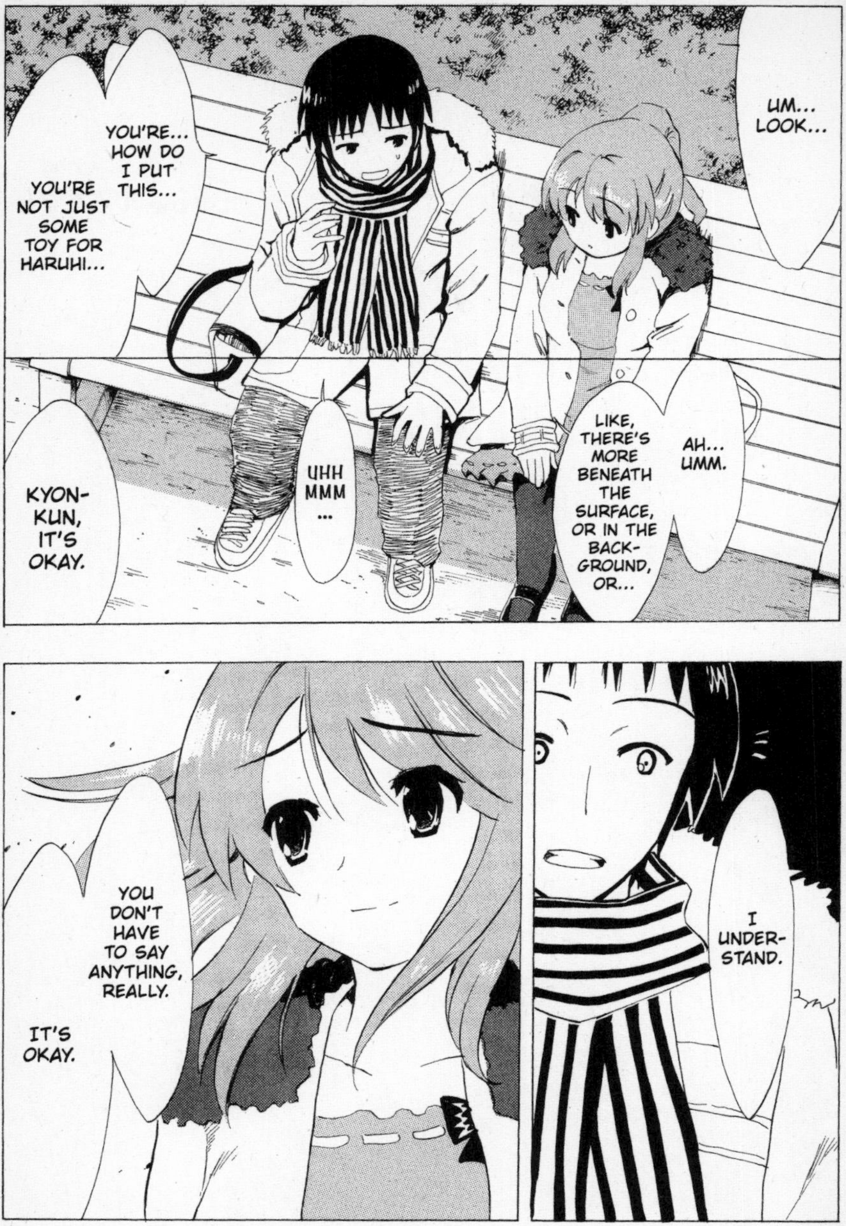
UM... LOOK...
YOU'RE... HOW DO I PUT THIS...
YOU'RE NOT JUST SOME TOY FOR HARUHI...
AH... UMM.
LIKE, THERE'S MORE BENEATH THE SURFACE, OR IN THE BACK-GROUND, OR...
UHH MMM ...
KYON-KUN, IT'S OKAY.
I UNDER-STAND.
YOU DON'T HAVE TO SAY ANYTHING, REALLY.
IT'S OKAY.

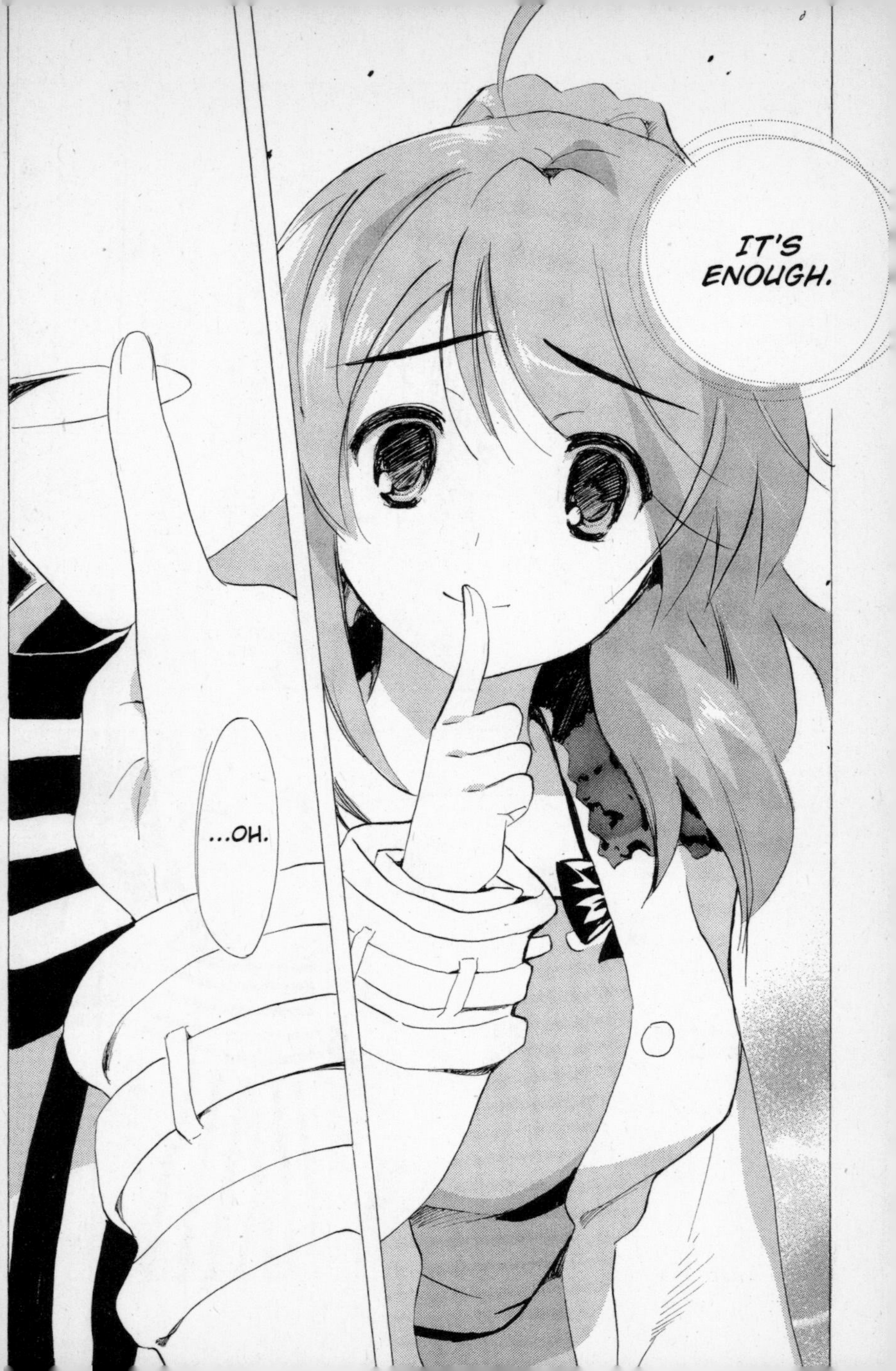
IT'S ENOUGH.
...OH.

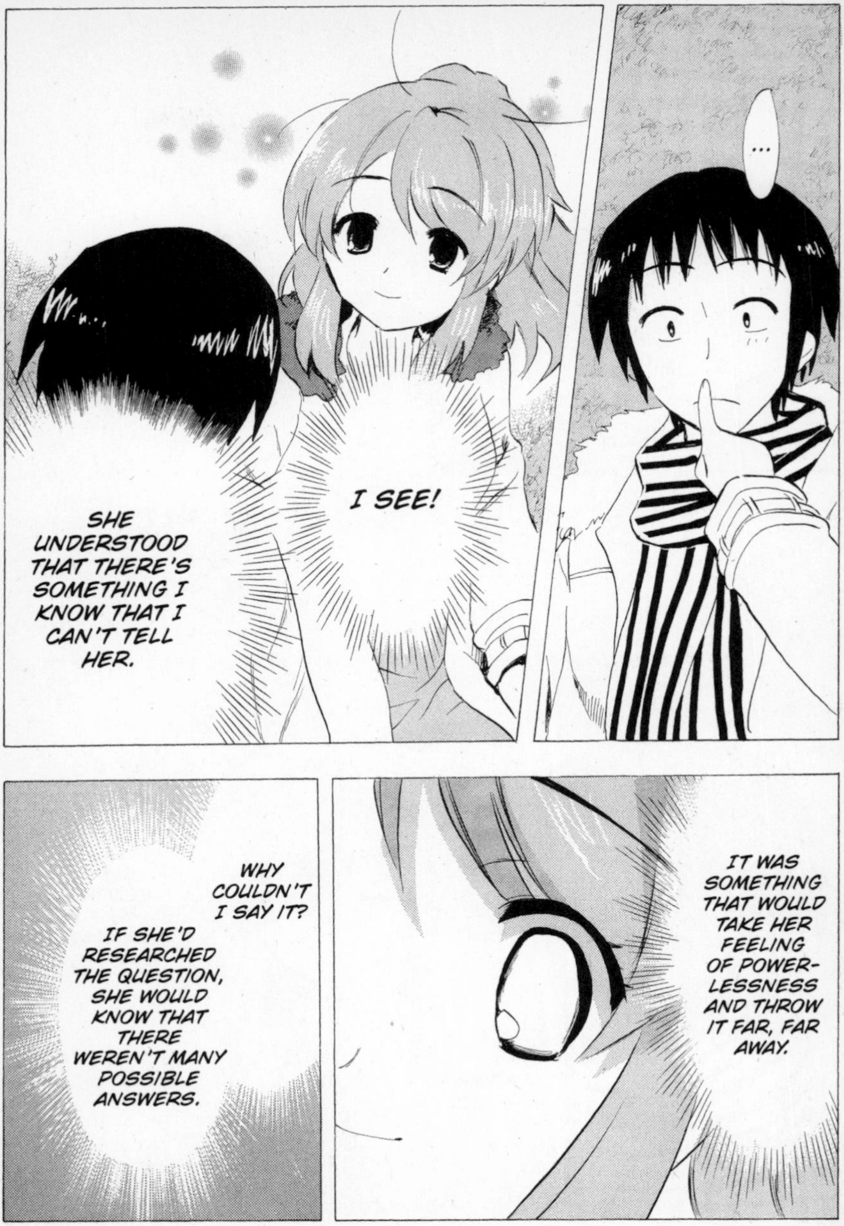
...
I SEE!
SHE UNDERSTOOD THAT THERE'S SOMETHING I KNOW THAT I CAN'T TELL HER.
IT WAS SOMETHING THAT WOULD TAKE HER FEELING OF POWER-LESSNESS AND THROW IT FAR, FAR AWAY.
WHY COULDN'T I SAY IT?
IF SHE'D RESEARCHED THE QUESTION, SHE WOULD KNOW THAT THERE WEREN'T MANY POSSIBLE ANSWERS.

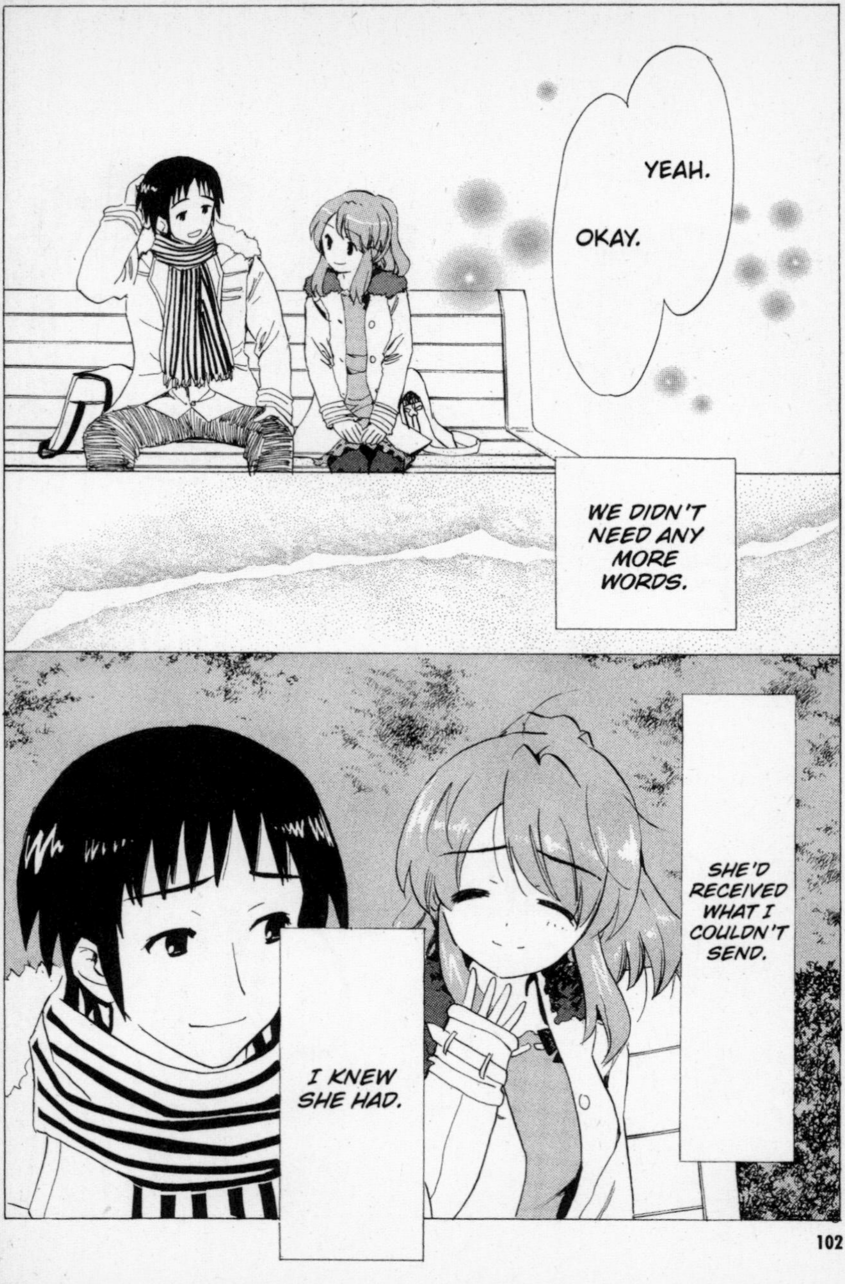
YEAH.
OKAY.
WE DIDN'T NEED ANY MORE WORDS.
SHE'D RECEIVED WHAT I COULDN'T SEND.
I KNEW SHE HAD.

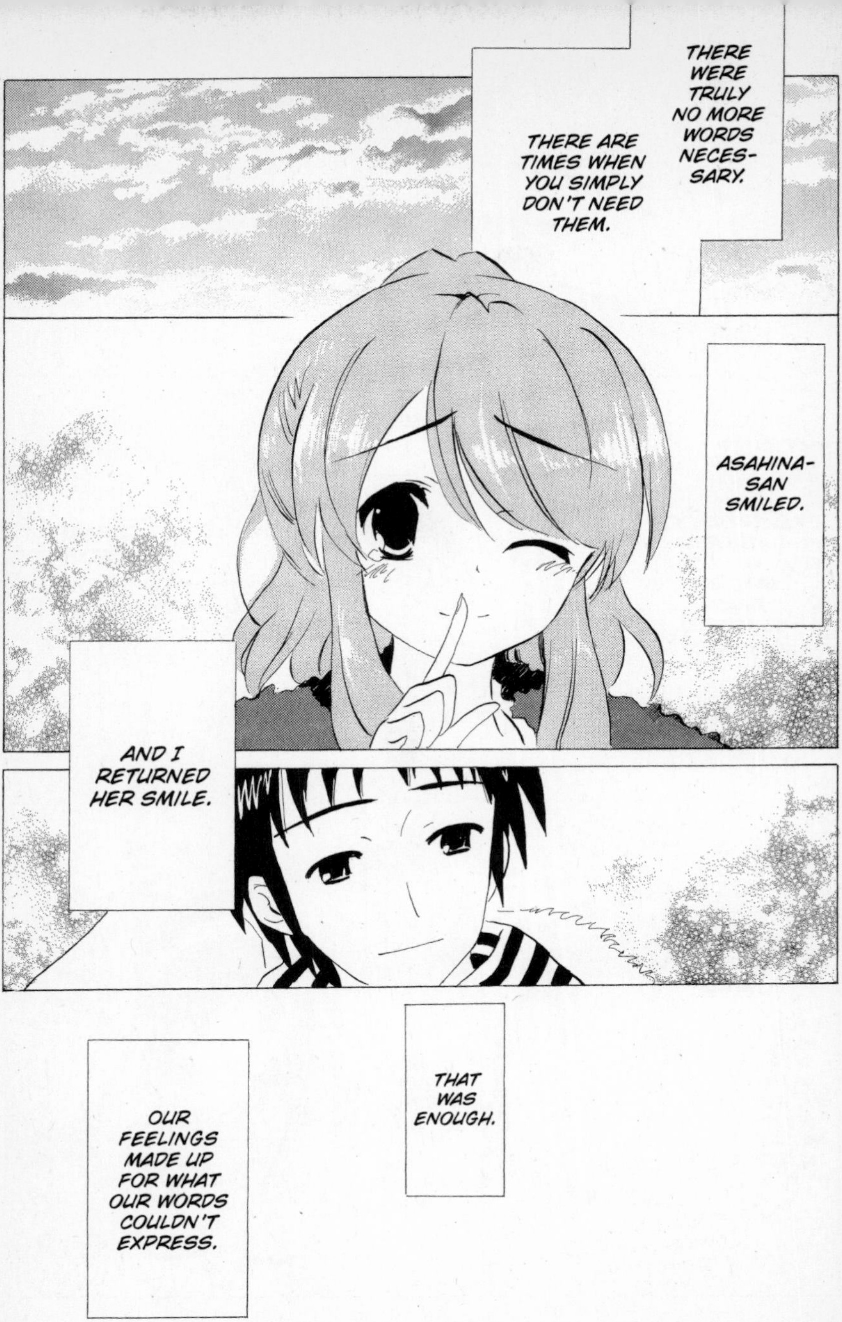
THERE WERE TRULY NO MORE WORDS NECES-SARY.
THERE ARE TIMES WHEN YOU SIMPLY DON'T NEED THEM.
ASAHINA-SAN SMILED.
AND I RETURNED HER SMILE.
THAT WAS ENOUGH.
OUR FEELINGS MADE UP FOR WHAT OUR WORDS COULDN'T EXPRESS.

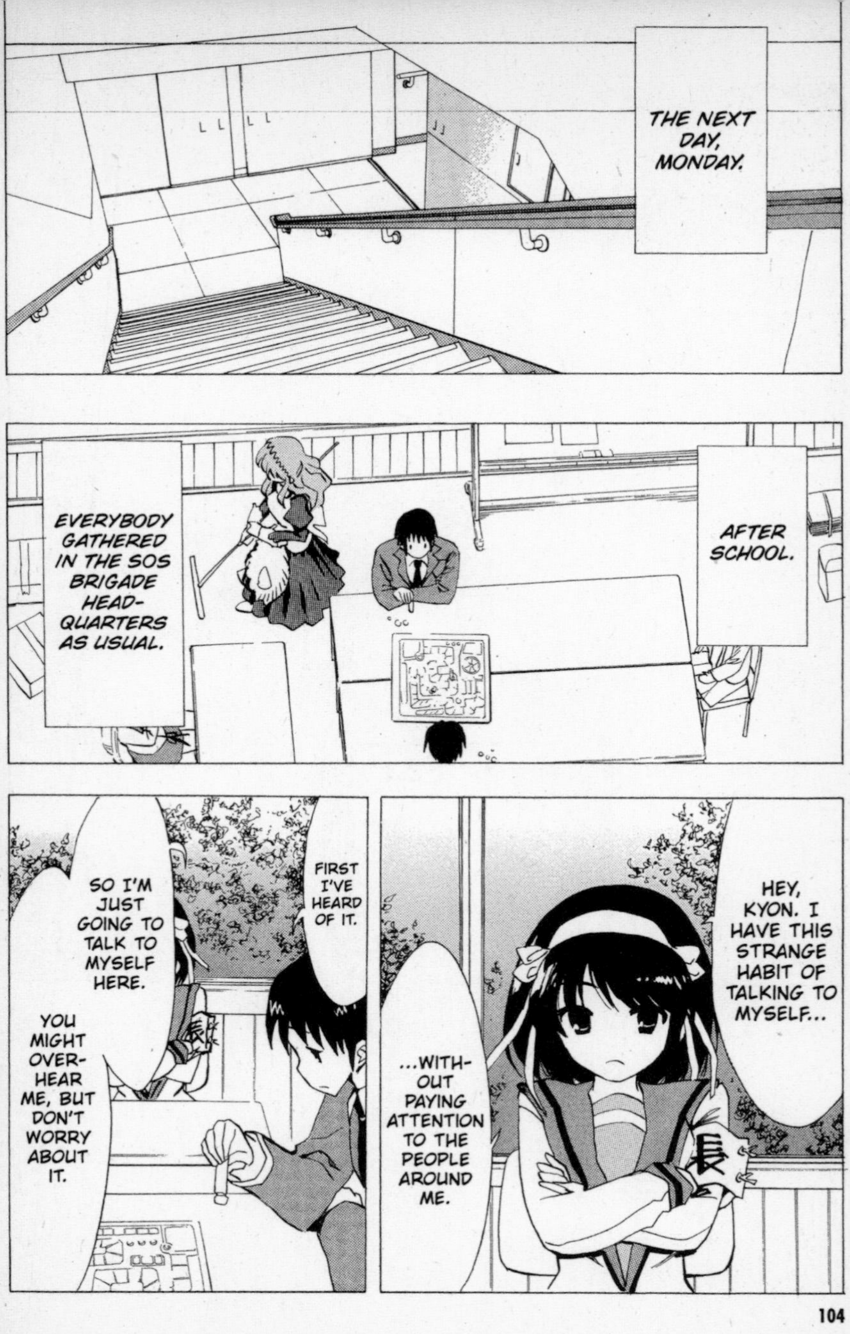
THE NEXT DAY, MONDAY.
AFTER SCHOOL.
EVERYBODY GATHERED IN THE SOS BRIGADE HEADQUARTERS AS USUAL.
HEY, KYON. I HAVE THIS STRANGE HABIT OF TALKING TO MYSELF...
...WITHOUT PAYING ATTENTION TO THE PEOPLE AROUND ME.
FIRST I'VE HEARD OF IT.
SO I'M JUST GOING TO TALK TO MYSELF HERE.
YOU MIGHT OVERHEAR ME, BUT DON'T WORRY ABOUT IT.

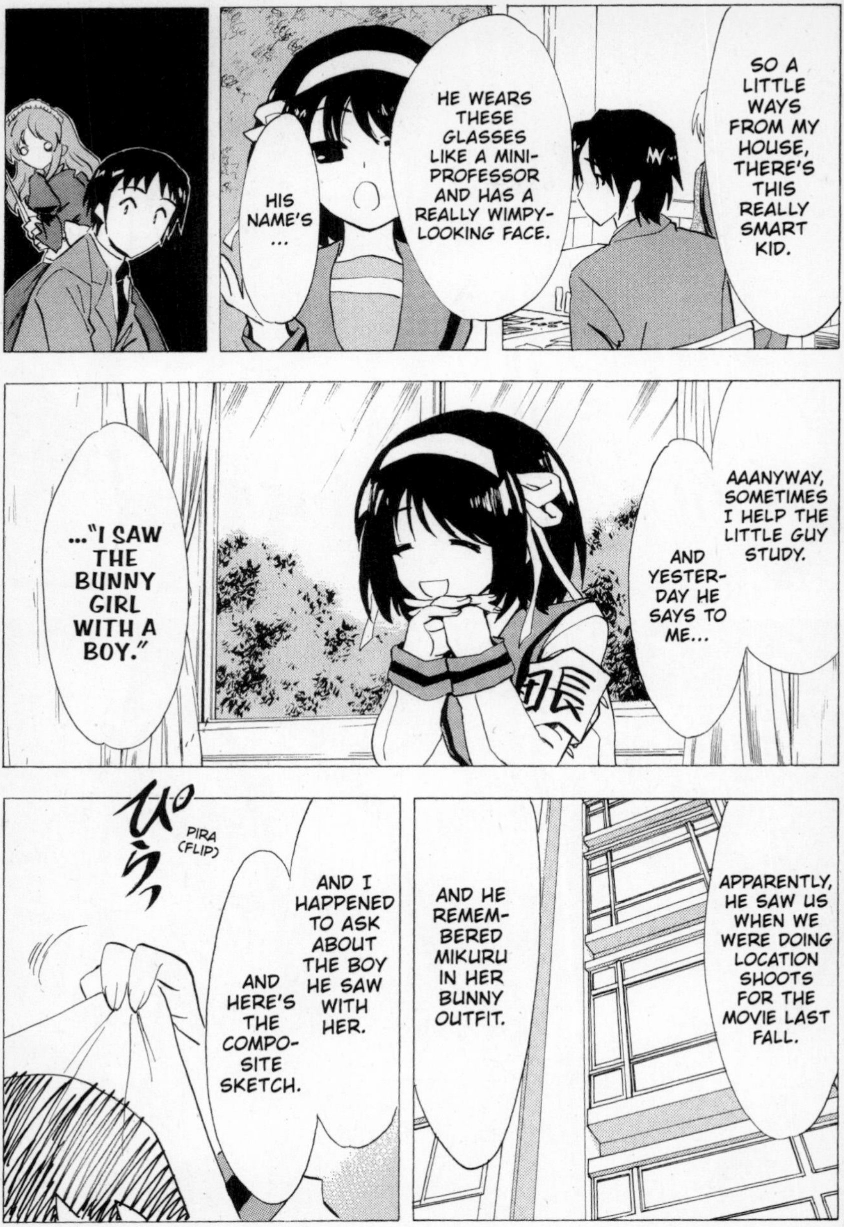

SO A LITTLE WAYS FROM MY HOUSE, THERE'S THIS REALLY SMART KID.
HE WEARS THESE GLASSES LIKE A MINI-PROFESSOR AND HAS A REALLY WIMPY-LOOKING FACE.
HIS NAME'S ...
AAANYWAY, SOMETIMES I HELP THE LITTLE GUY STUDY.
AND YESTER-DAY HE SAYS TO ME...
..."I SAW THE BUNNY GIRL WITH A BOY."
APPARENTLY, HE SAW US WHEN WE WERE DOING LOCATION SHOOTS FOR THE MOVIE LAST FALL.
AND HE REMEM-BERED MIKURU IN HER BUNNY OUTFIT.
AND I HAPPENED TO ASK ABOUT THE BOY HE SAW WITH HER.
ぴらっ
PIRA (FLIP)
AND HERE'S THE COMPO-SITE SKETCH.

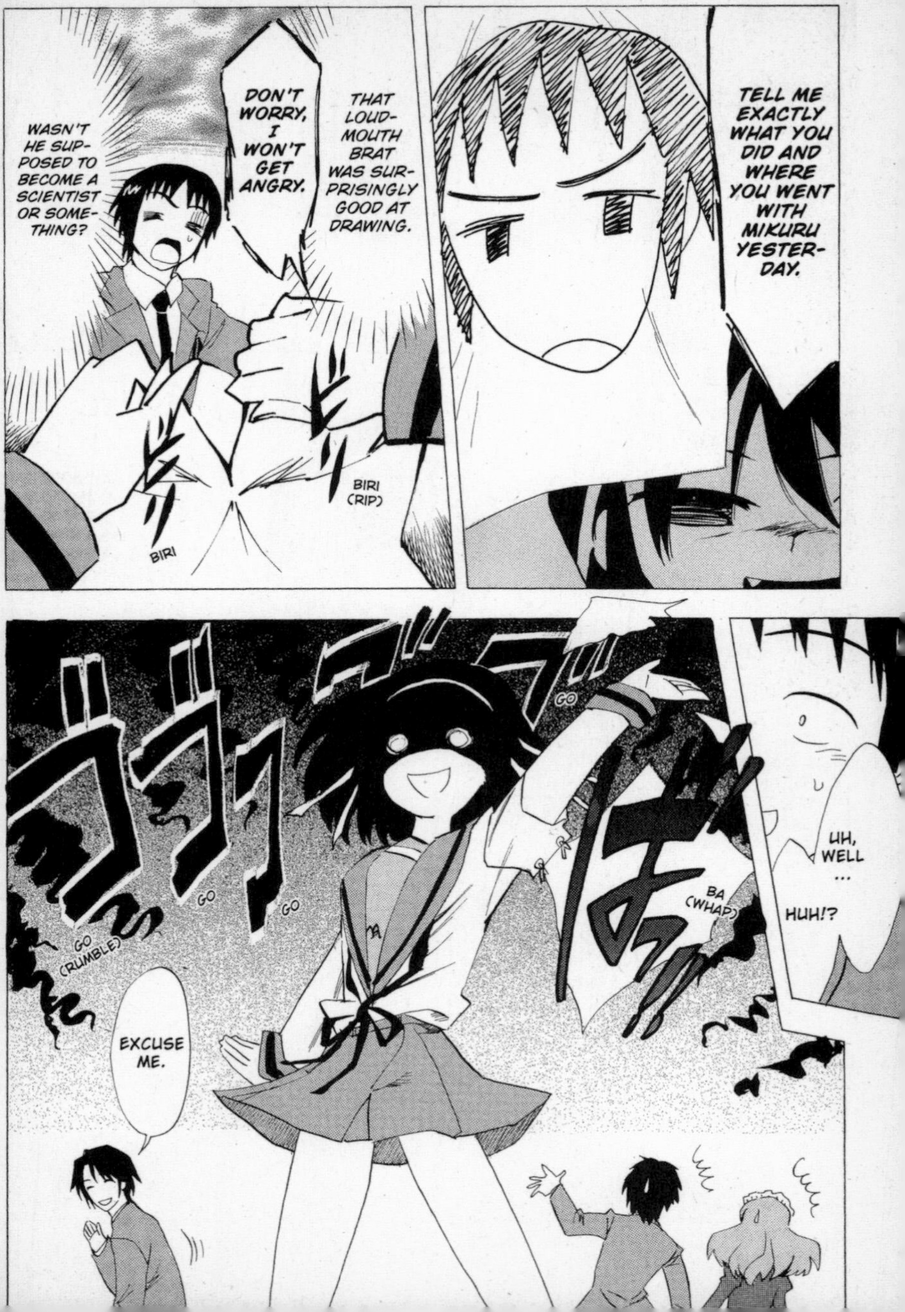
TELL ME EXACTLY WHAT YOU DID AND WHERE YOU WENT WITH MIKURU YESTERDAY.
THAT LOUD-MOUTH BRAT WAS SUR-PRISINGLY GOOD AT DRAWING.
DON'T WORRY, I WON'T GET ANGRY.
WASN'T HE SUP-POSED TO BECOME A SCIENTIST OR SOME-THING?
BIRI (RIP)
BIRI
UH, WELL ...
HUH!?
GO
BA (WHAP)
GO
GO
GO (RUMBLE)
EXCUSE ME.

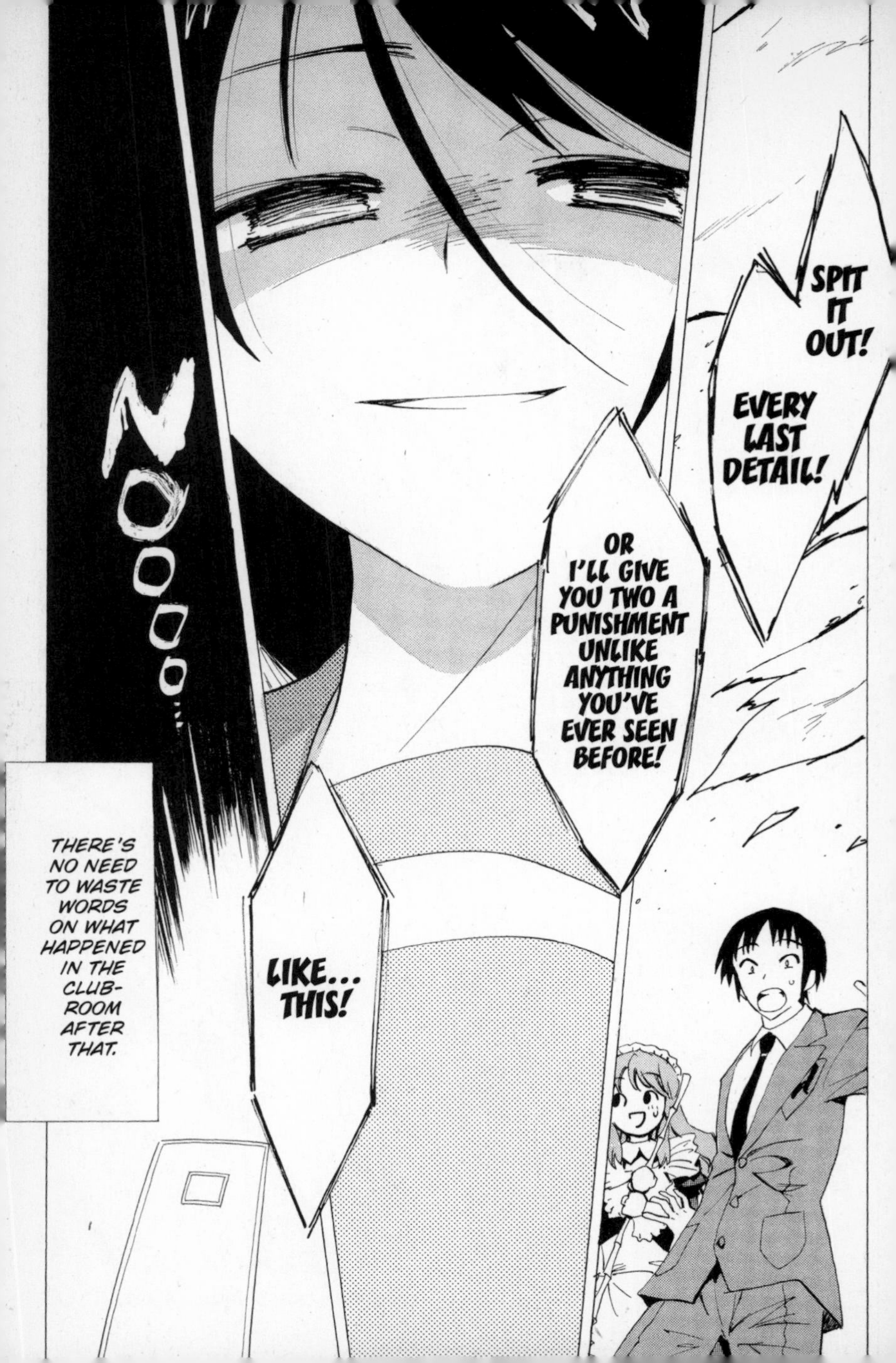
SPIT IT OUT!
EVERY LAST DETAIL!
OR I'LL GIVE YOU TWO A PUNISHMENT UNLIKE ANYTHING YOU'VE EVER SEEN BEFORE!
LIKE... THIS!
ZOOOO...
THERE'S NO NEED TO WASTE WORDS ON WHAT HAPPENED IN THE CLUB-ROOM AFTER THAT.

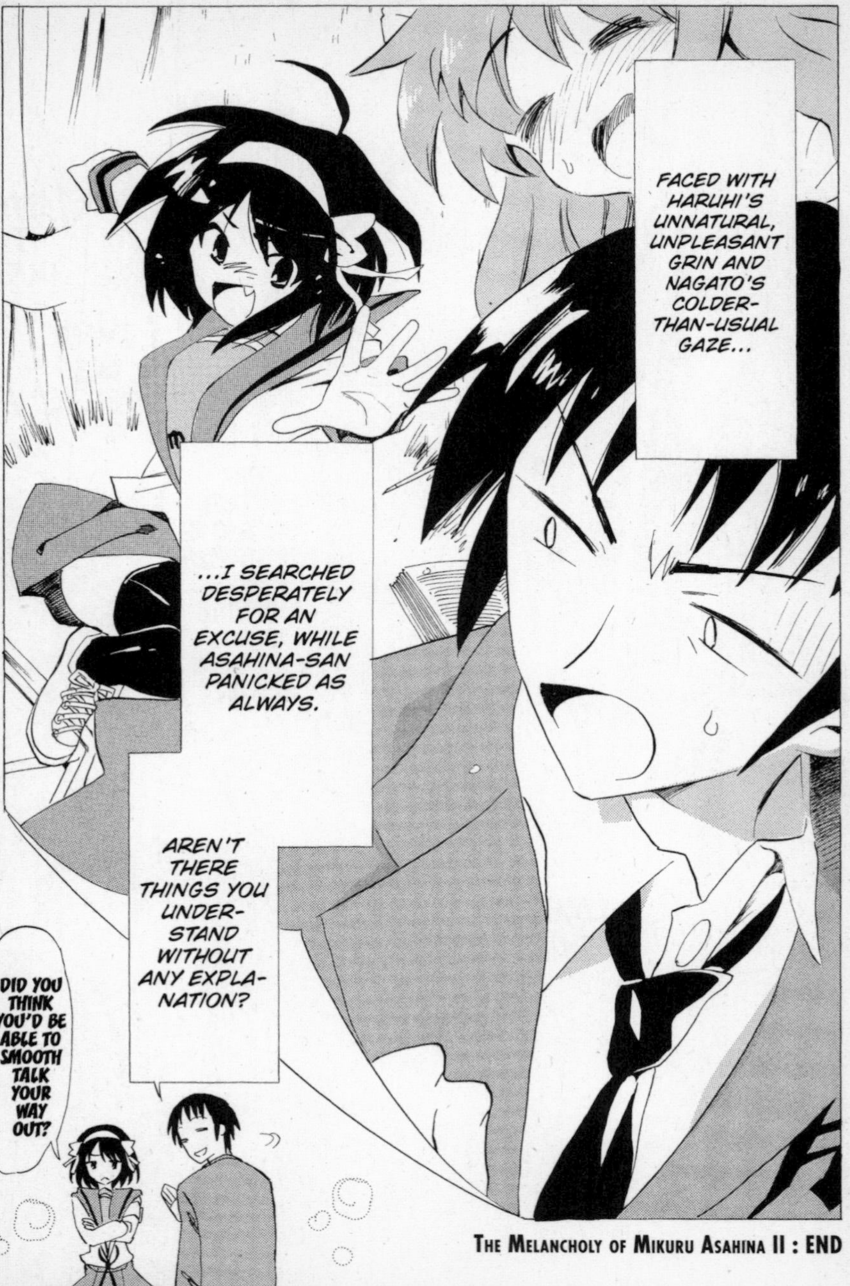

FACED WITH HARUHI'S UNNATURAL, UNPLEASANT GRIN AND NAGATO'S COLDER-THAN-USUAL GAZE...
...I SEARCHED DESPERATELY FOR AN EXCUSE, WHILE ASAHINA-SAN PANICKED AS ALWAYS.
AREN'T THERE THINGS YOU UNDER-STAND WITHOUT ANY EXPLA-NATION?
DID YOU THINK YOU'D BE ABLE TO SMOOTH TALK YOUR WAY OUT?

THE MELANCHOLY OF MIKURU ASAHINA II : END

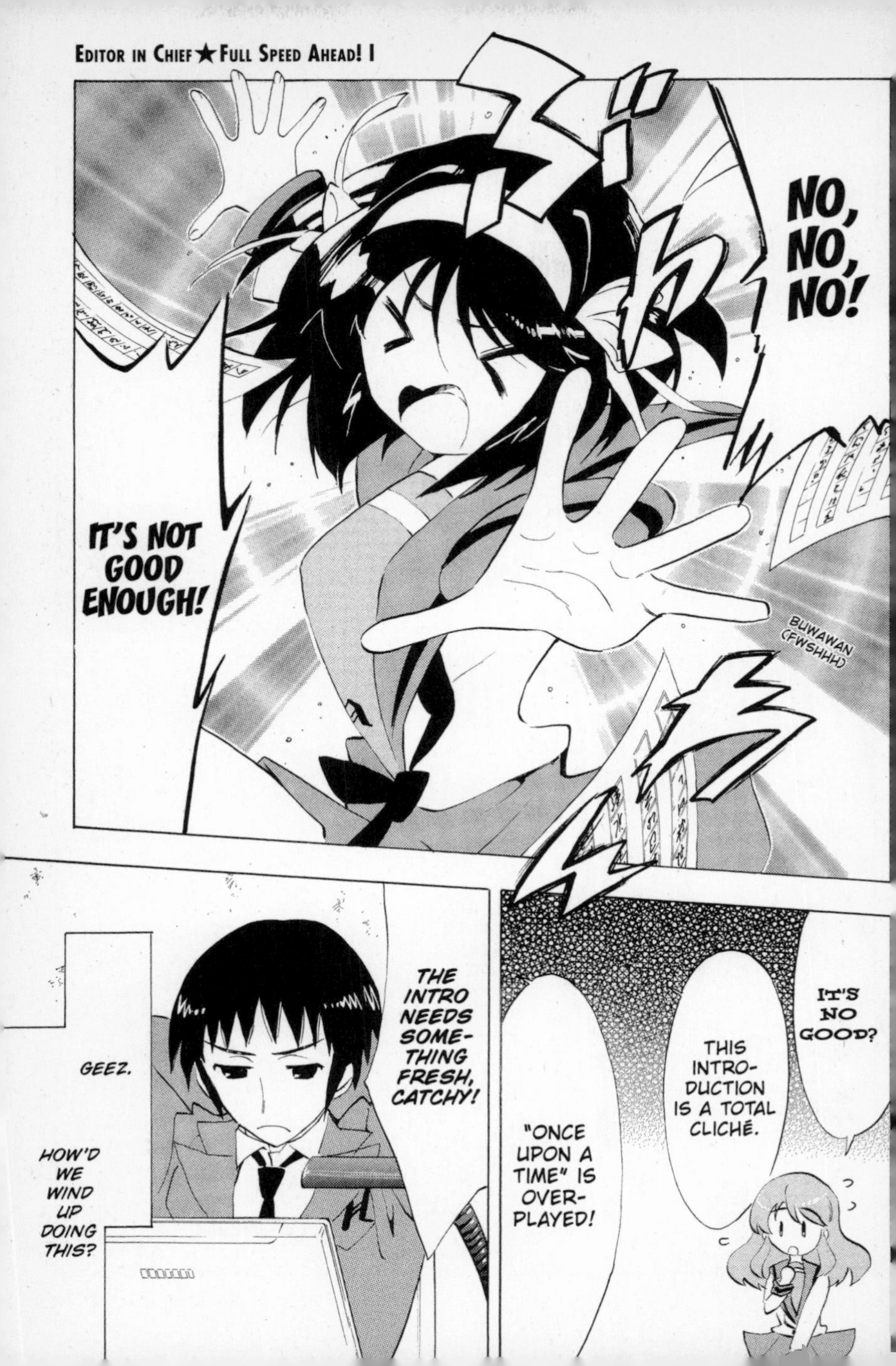
NO, NO, NO!
IT'S NOT GOOD ENOUGH!
BUWAWAN (FWSHHH)
IT'S NO GOOD?
THIS INTRO-DUCTION IS A TOTAL CLICHÉ.
"ONCE UPON A TIME" IS OVER-PLAYED!
THE INTRO NEEDS SOME-THING FRESH, CATCHY!
GEEZ.
HOW'D WE WIND UP DOING THIS?

ARMBAND: EDITOR IN CHIEF

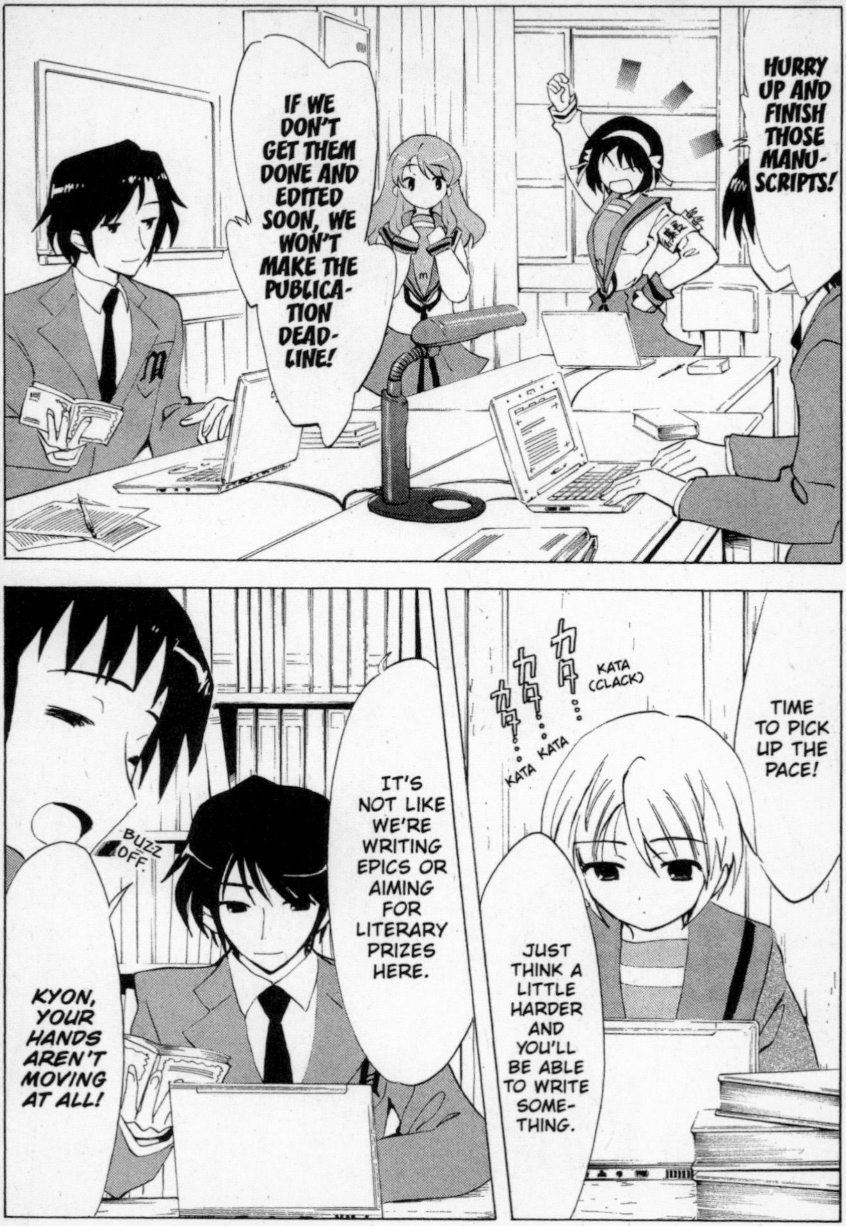
HURRY UP AND FINISH THOSE MANU-SCRIPTS!
IF WE DON'T GET THEM DONE AND EDITED SOON, WE WON'T MAKE THE PUBLICA-TION DEAD-LINE!
TIME TO PICK UP THE PACE!
KATA (CLACK)
KATA KATA
JUST THINK A LITTLE HARDER AND YOU'LL BE ABLE TO WRITE SOME-THING.
IT'S NOT LIKE WE'RE WRITING EPICS OR AIMING FOR LITERARY PRIZES HERE.
BUZZ OFF
KYON, YOUR HANDS AREN'T MOVING AT ALL!

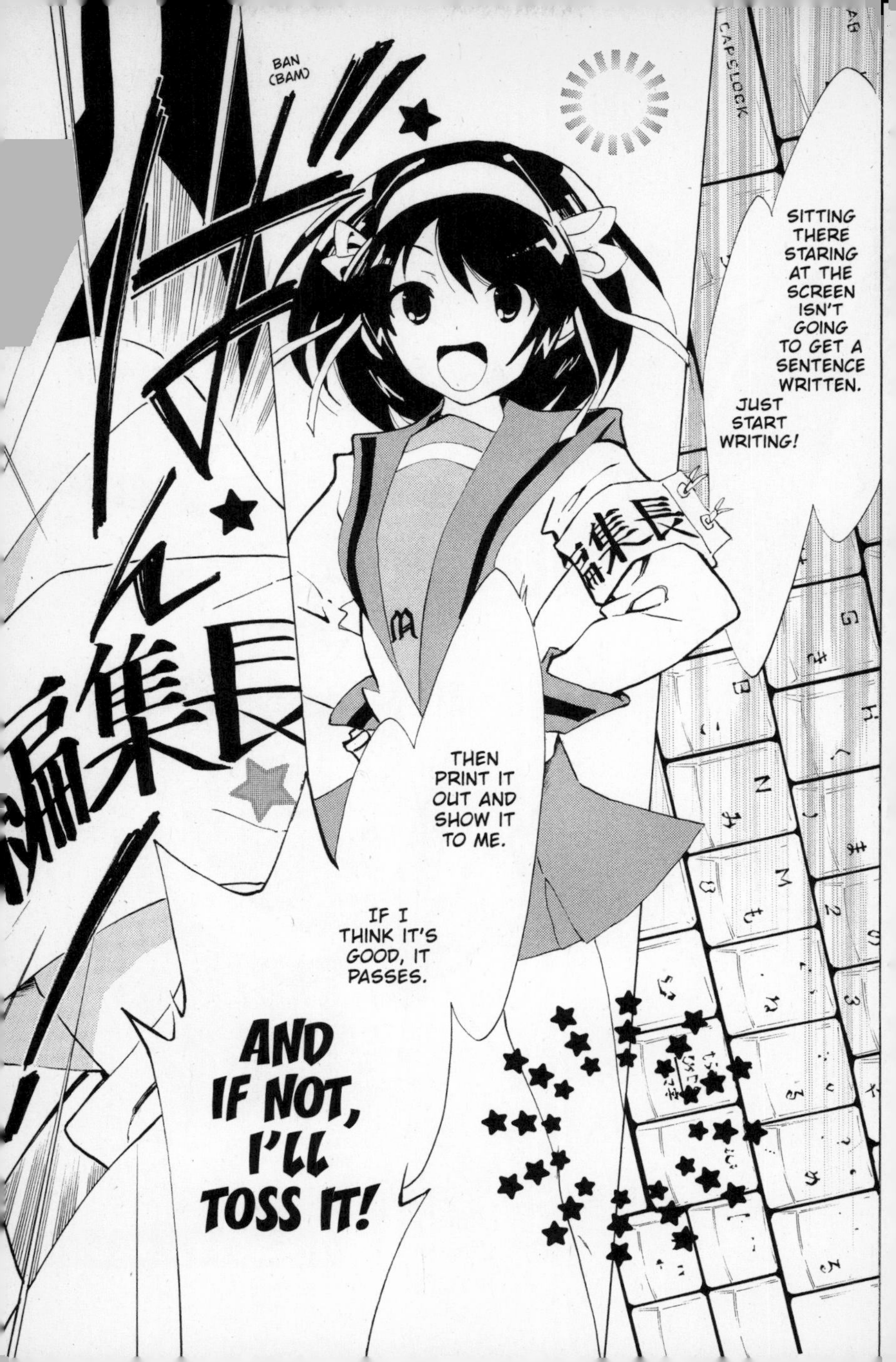
BAN (BAM)
SITTING THERE STARING AT THE SCREEN ISN'T GOING TO GET A SENTENCE WRITTEN.
JUST START WRITING!
THEN PRINT IT OUT AND SHOW IT TO ME.
IF I THINK IT'S GOOD, IT PASSES.
AND IF NOT, I'LL TOSS IT!
編集長
編集長

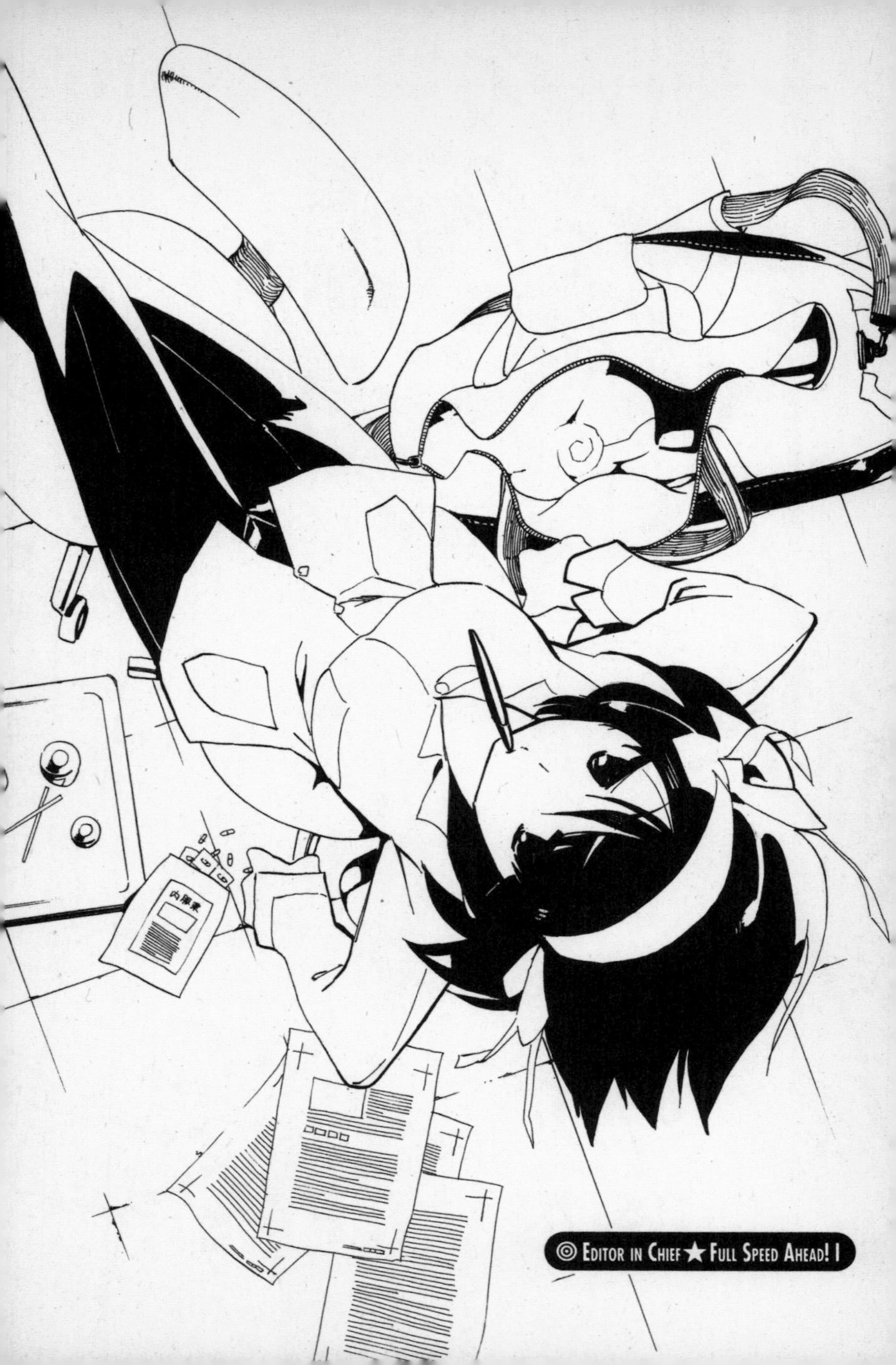
内服薬

◎ EDITOR IN CHIEF ★ FULL SPEED AHEAD! I

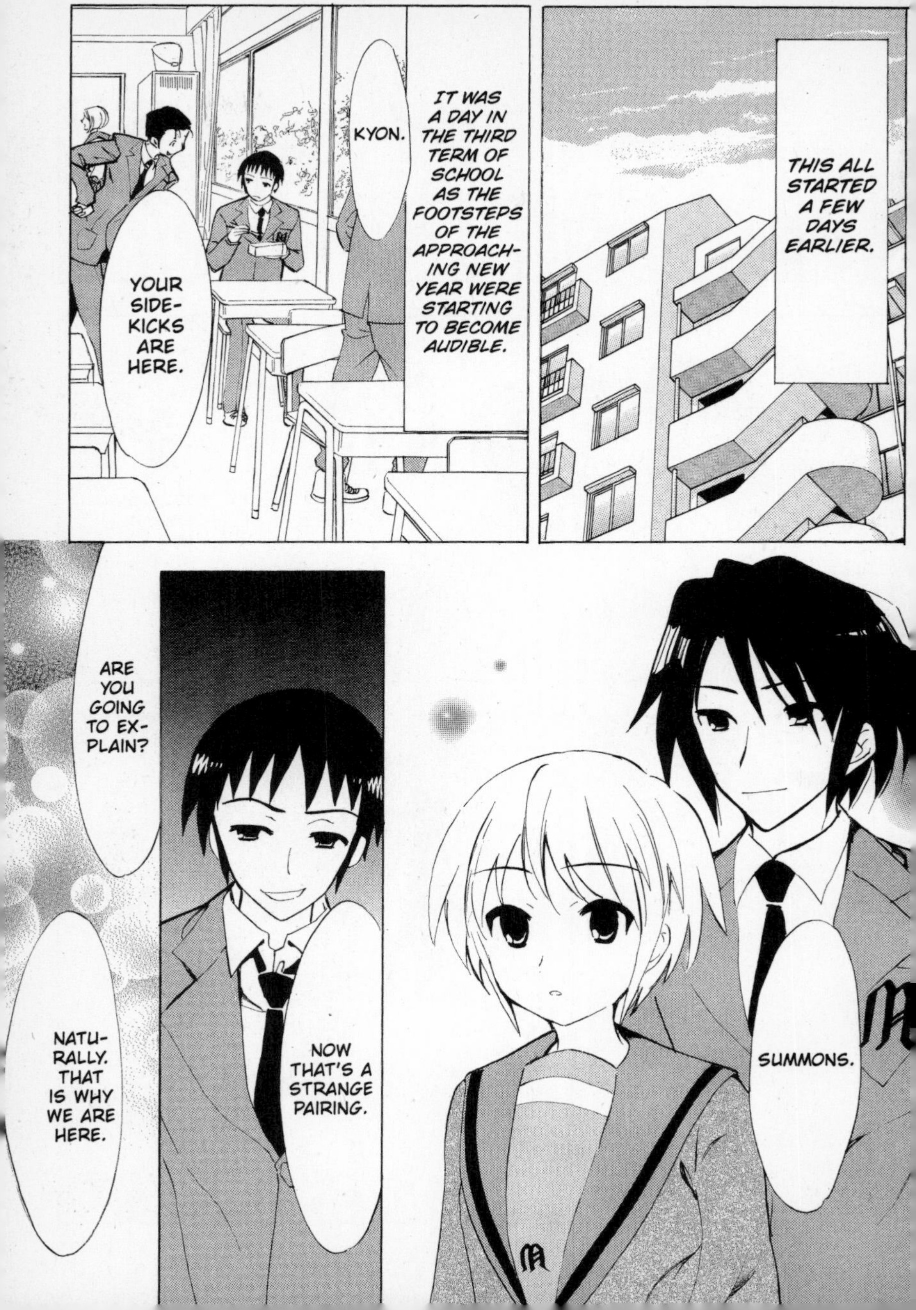
THIS ALL STARTED A FEW DAYS EARLIER.
IT WAS A DAY IN THE THIRD TERM OF SCHOOL AS THE FOOTSTEPS OF THE APPROACHING NEW YEAR WERE STARTING TO BECOME AUDIBLE.
KYON.
YOUR SIDEKICKS ARE HERE.
SUMMONS.
NOW THAT'S A STRANGE PAIRING.
ARE YOU GOING TO EXPLAIN?
NATURALLY. THAT IS WHY WE ARE HERE.

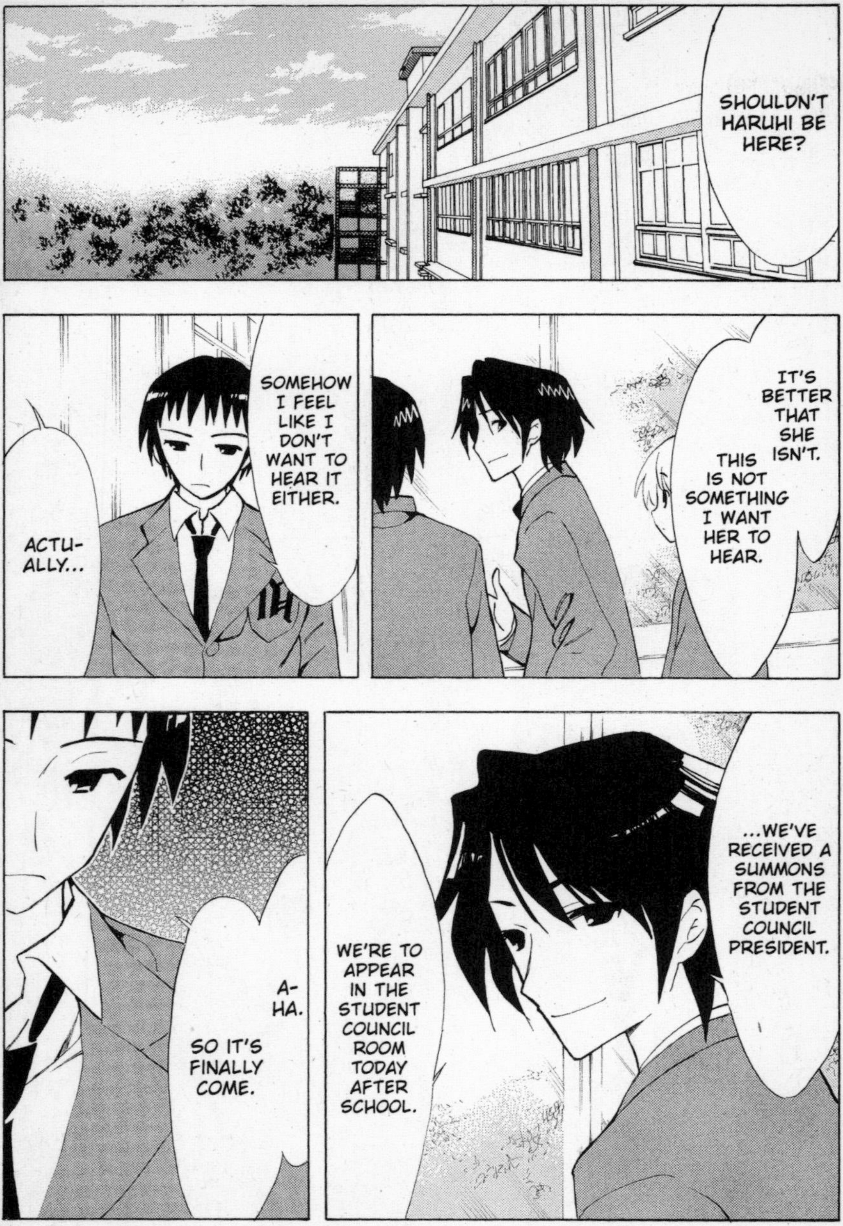
SHOULDN'T HARUHI BE HERE?
IT'S BETTER THAT SHE ISN'T.
THIS IS NOT SOMETHING I WANT HER TO HEAR.
SOMEHOW I FEEL LIKE I DON'T WANT TO HEAR IT EITHER.
ACTU-ALLY...
...WE'VE RECEIVED A SUMMONS FROM THE STUDENT COUNCIL PRESIDENT.
WE'RE TO APPEAR IN THE STUDENT COUNCIL ROOM TODAY AFTER SCHOOL.
A-HA.
SO IT'S FINALLY COME.

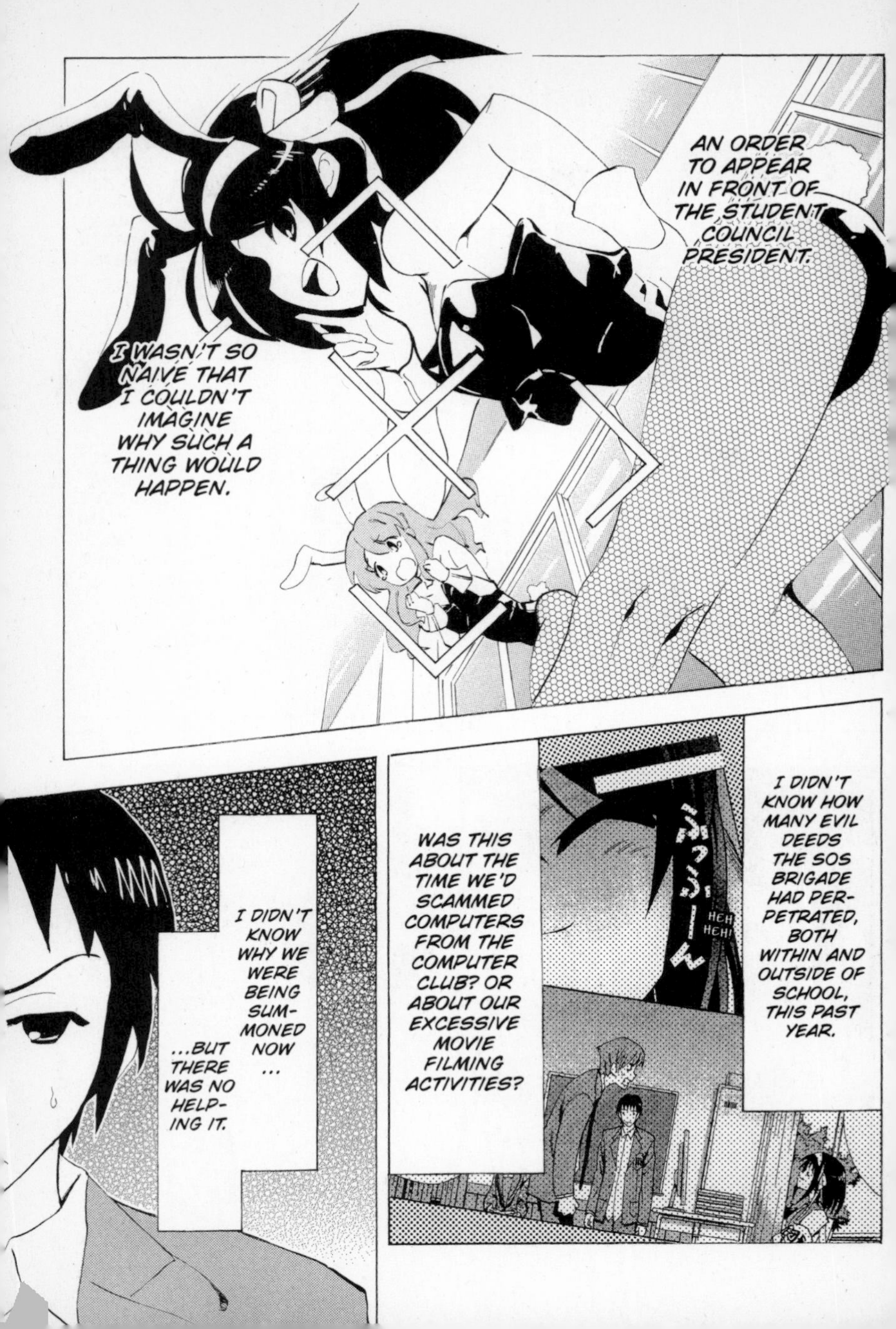
AN ORDER TO APPEAR IN FRONT OF THE STUDENT COUNCIL PRESIDENT.
I WASN'T SO NAIVE THAT I COULDN'T IMAGINE WHY SUCH A THING WOULD HAPPEN.
I DIDN'T KNOW HOW MANY EVIL DEEDS THE SOS BRIGADE HAD PERPETRATED, BOTH WITHIN AND OUTSIDE OF SCHOOL, THIS PAST YEAR.
HEH HEH!
WAS THIS ABOUT THE TIME WE'D SCAMMED COMPUTERS FROM THE COMPUTER CLUB? OR ABOUT OUR EXCESSIVE MOVIE FILMING ACTIVITIES?
I DIDN'T KNOW WHY WE WERE BEING SUMMONED NOW ...
...BUT THERE WAS NO HELPING IT.

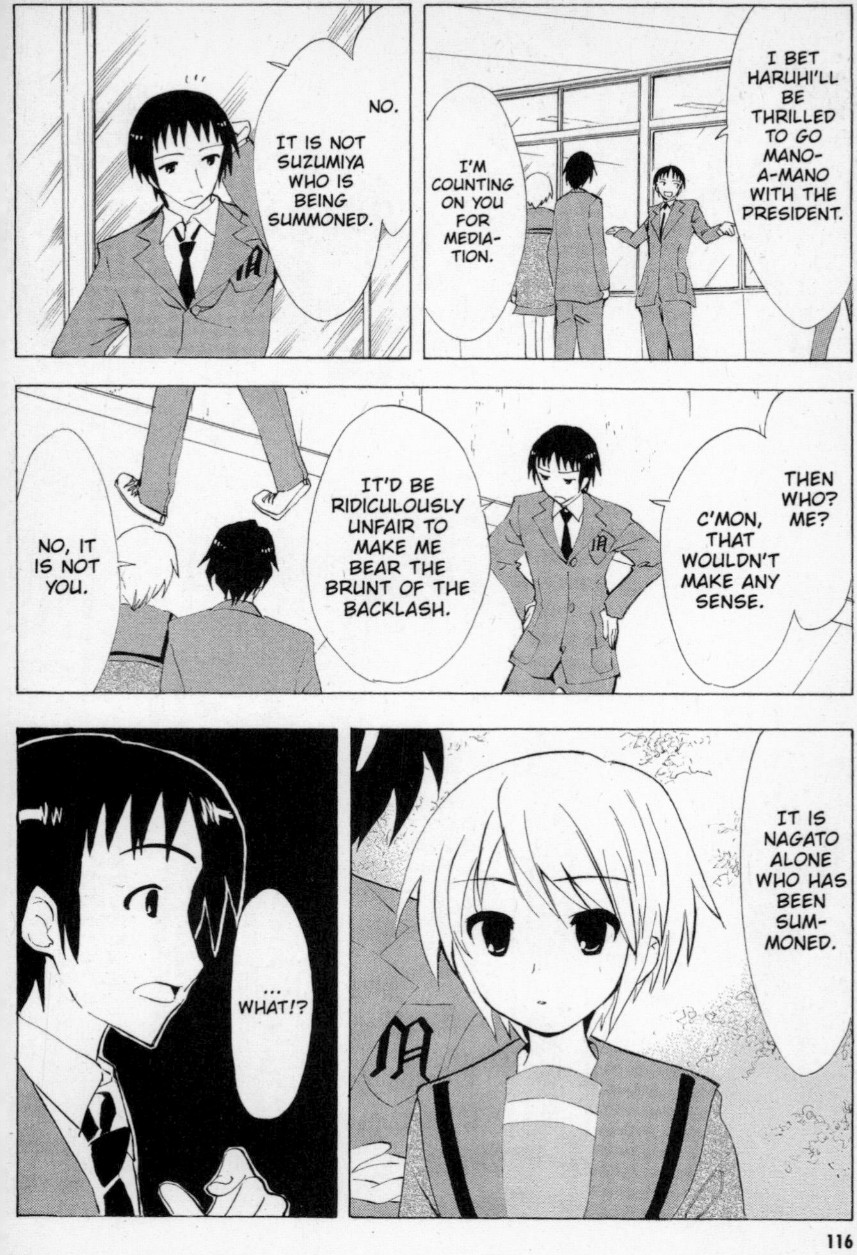
I BET HARUHI'LL BE THRILLED TO GO MANO-A-MANO WITH THE PRESIDENT.
I'M COUNTING ON YOU FOR MEDIATION.
NO.
IT IS NOT SUZUMIYA WHO IS BEING SUMMONED.
THEN WHO? ME?
C'MON, THAT WOULDN'T MAKE ANY SENSE.
IT'D BE RIDICULOUSLY UNFAIR TO MAKE ME BEAR THE BRUNT OF THE BACKLASH.
NO, IT IS NOT YOU.
IT IS NAGATO ALONE WHO HAS BEEN SUMMONED.
... WHAT!?

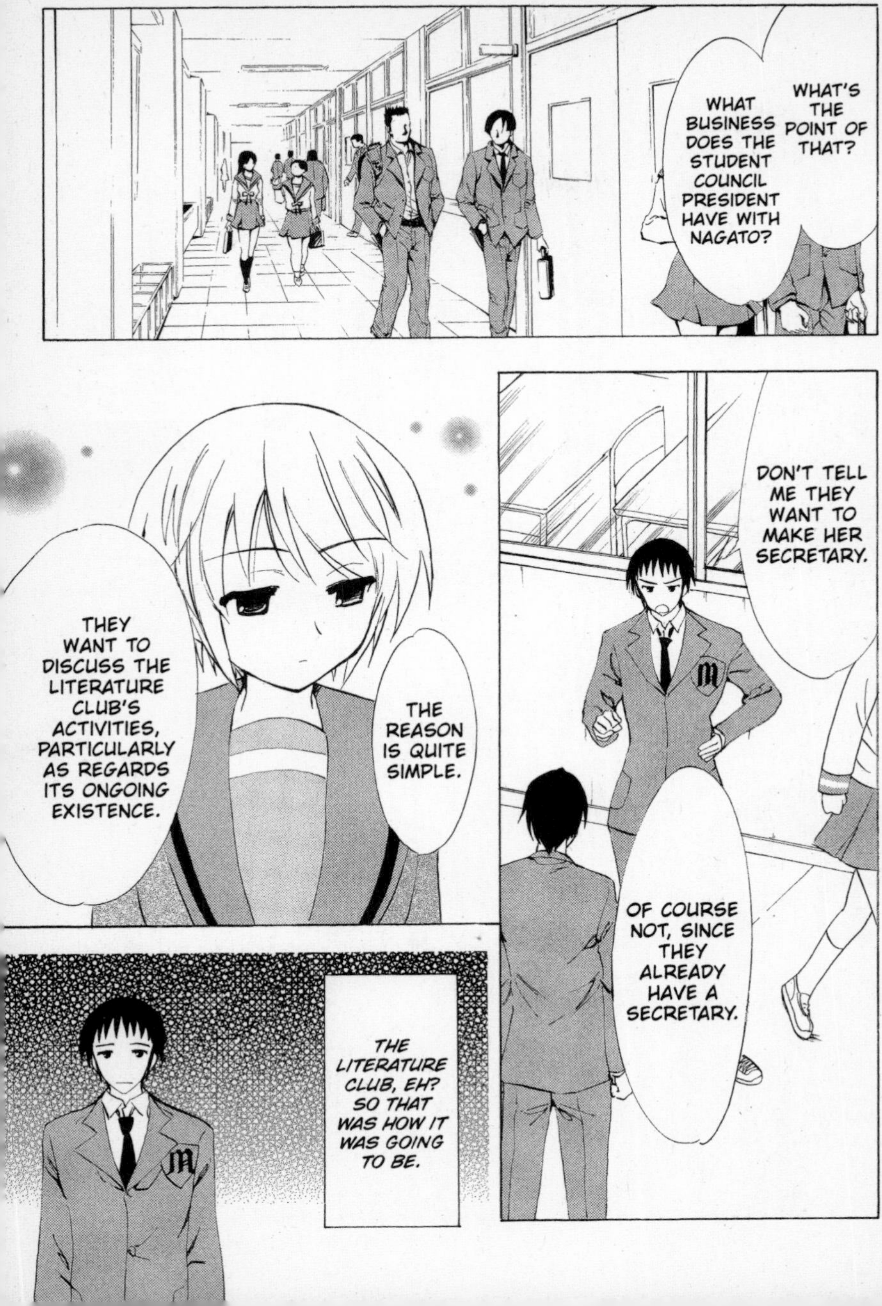
WHAT'S THE POINT OF THAT?
WHAT BUSINESS DOES THE STUDENT COUNCIL PRESIDENT HAVE WITH NAGATO?
DON'T TELL ME THEY WANT TO MAKE HER SECRETARY.
OF COURSE NOT, SINCE THEY ALREADY HAVE A SECRETARY.
THE REASON IS QUITE SIMPLE.
THEY WANT TO DISCUSS THE LITERATURE CLUB'S ACTIVITIES, PARTICULARLY AS REGARDS ITS ONGOING EXISTENCE.
THE LITERATURE CLUB, EH? SO THAT WAS HOW IT WAS GOING TO BE.

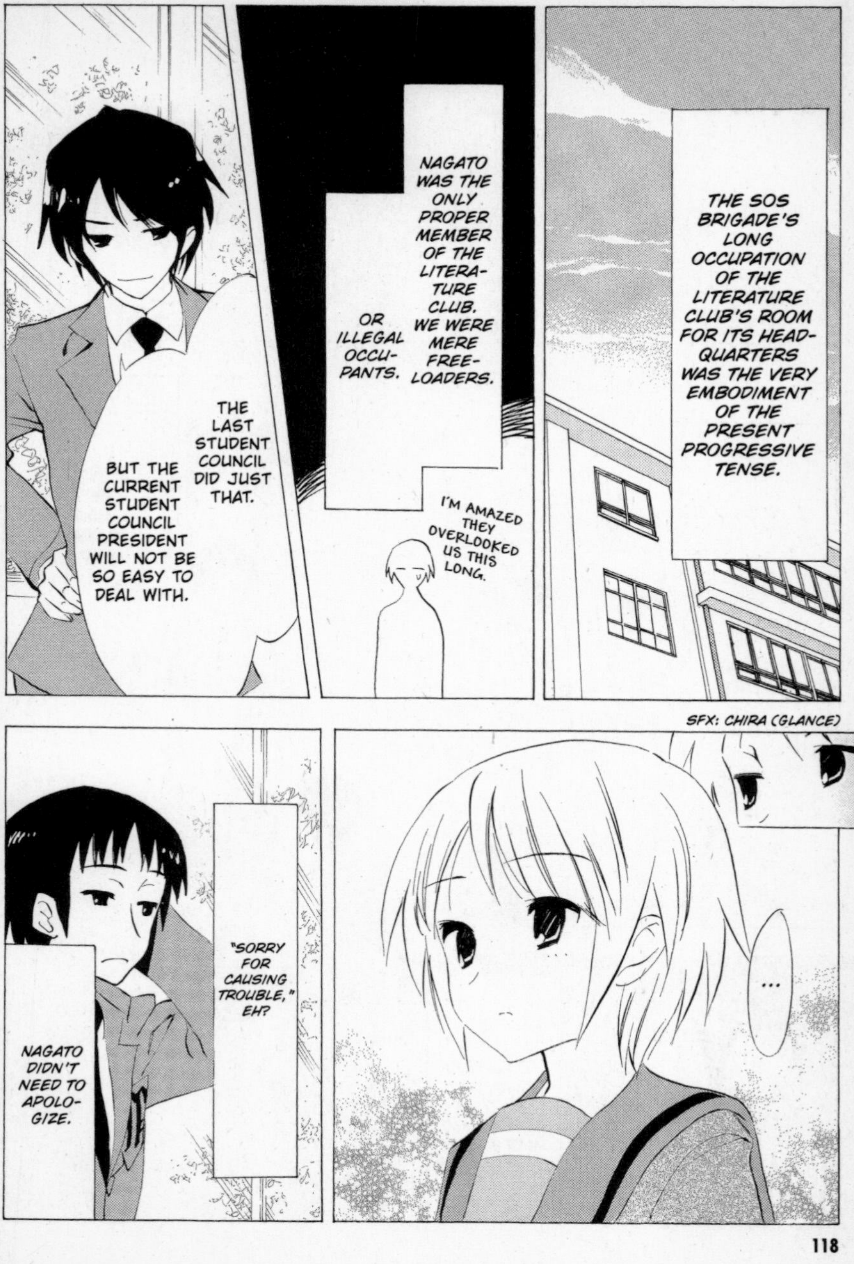
THE SOS BRIGADE'S LONG OCCUPATION OF THE LITERATURE CLUB'S ROOM FOR ITS HEADQUARTERS WAS THE VERY EMBODIMENT OF THE PRESENT PROGRESSIVE TENSE.
NAGATO WAS THE ONLY PROPER MEMBER OF THE LITERATURE CLUB. WE WERE MERE FREELOADERS.
OR ILLEGAL OCCUPANTS.
I'M AMAZED THEY OVERLOOKED US THIS LONG.
THE LAST STUDENT COUNCIL DID JUST THAT.
BUT THE CURRENT STUDENT COUNCIL PRESIDENT WILL NOT BE SO EASY TO DEAL WITH.
SFX: CHIRA (GLANCE)
...
"SORRY FOR CAUSING TROUBLE," EH?
NAGATO DIDN'T NEED TO APOLOGIZE.

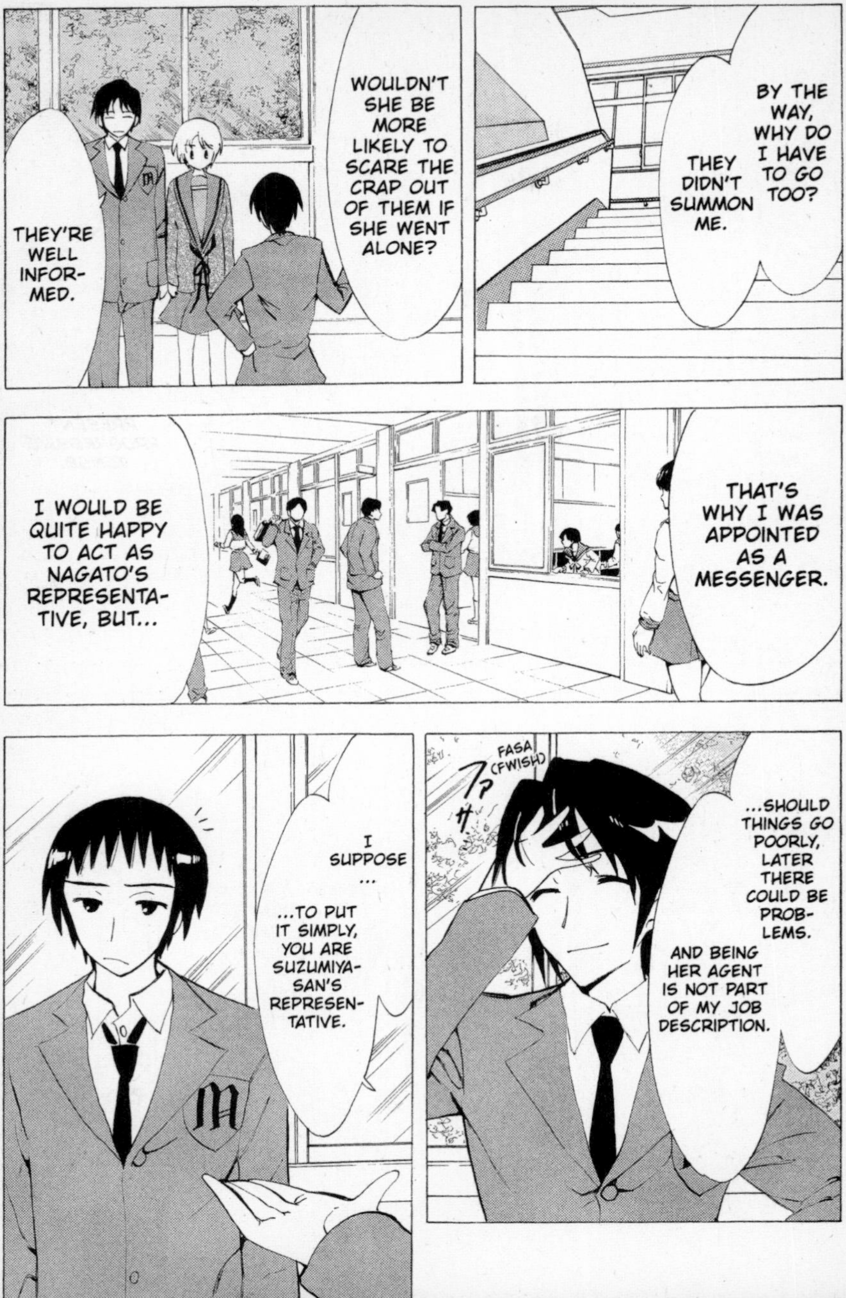
BY THE WAY, WHY DO I HAVE TO GO TOO?
THEY DIDN'T SUMMON ME.
WOULDN'T SHE BE MORE LIKELY TO SCARE THE CRAP OUT OF THEM IF SHE WENT ALONE?
THEY'RE WELL INFORMED.
THAT'S WHY I WAS APPOINTED AS A MESSENGER.
I WOULD BE QUITE HAPPY TO ACT AS NAGATO'S REPRESENTATIVE, BUT...
FASA (FWISH)
...SHOULD THINGS GO POORLY, LATER THERE COULD BE PROBLEMS.
AND BEING HER AGENT IS NOT PART OF MY JOB DESCRIPTION.
I SUPPOSE ...
...TO PUT IT SIMPLY, YOU ARE SUZUMIYA-SAN'S REPRESENTATIVE.

HARUHI: WHAT'D YOU SAY!? WE'LL NEVER LET YOU HAVE IT!!

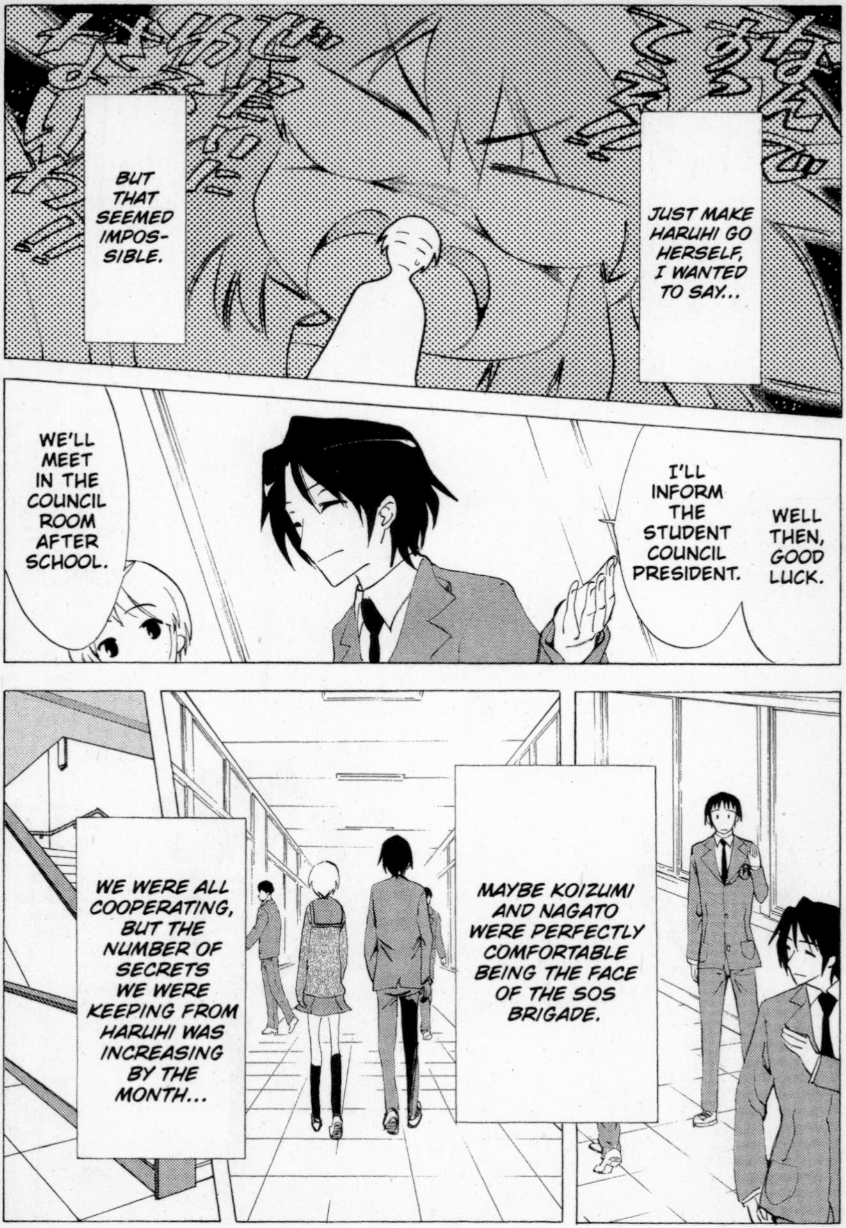
JUST MAKE HARUHI GO HERSELF, I WANTED TO SAY...
BUT THAT SEEMED IMPOSSIBLE.
WELL THEN, GOOD LUCK.
I'LL INFORM THE STUDENT COUNCIL PRESIDENT.
WE'LL MEET IN THE COUNCIL ROOM AFTER SCHOOL.
MAYBE KOIZUMI AND NAGATO WERE PERFECTLY COMFORTABLE BEING THE FACE OF THE SOS BRIGADE.
WE WERE ALL COOPERATING, BUT THE NUMBER OF SECRETS WE WERE KEEPING FROM HARUHI WAS INCREASING BY THE MONTH...

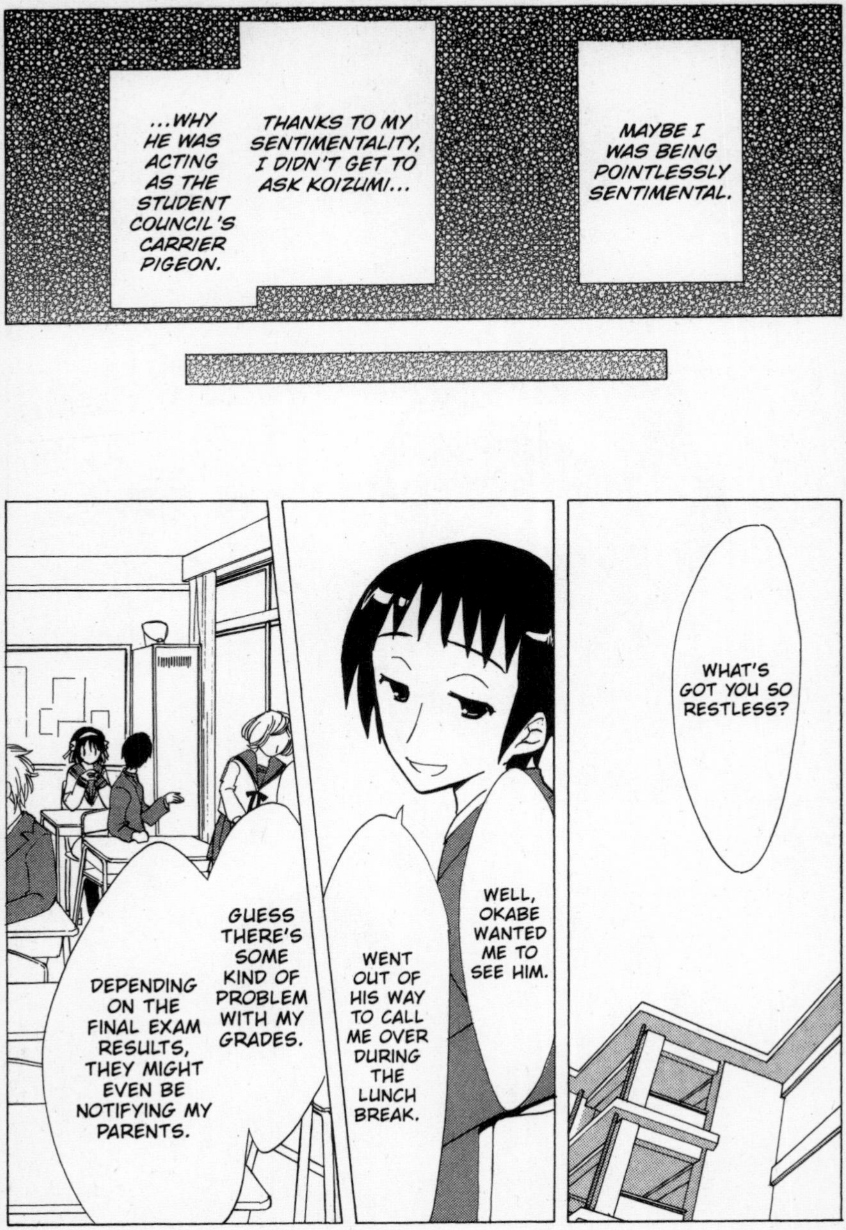
MAYBE I WAS BEING POINTLESSLY SENTIMENTAL.
THANKS TO MY SENTIMENTALITY, I DIDN'T GET TO ASK KOIZUMI...
...WHY HE WAS ACTING AS THE STUDENT COUNCIL'S CARRIER PIGEON.
WHAT'S GOT YOU SO RESTLESS?
WELL, OKABE WANTED ME TO SEE HIM.
WENT OUT OF HIS WAY TO CALL ME OVER DURING THE LUNCH BREAK.
GUESS THERE'S SOME KIND OF PROBLEM WITH MY GRADES.
DEPENDING ON THE FINAL EXAM RESULTS, THEY MIGHT EVEN BE NOTIFYING MY PARENTS.

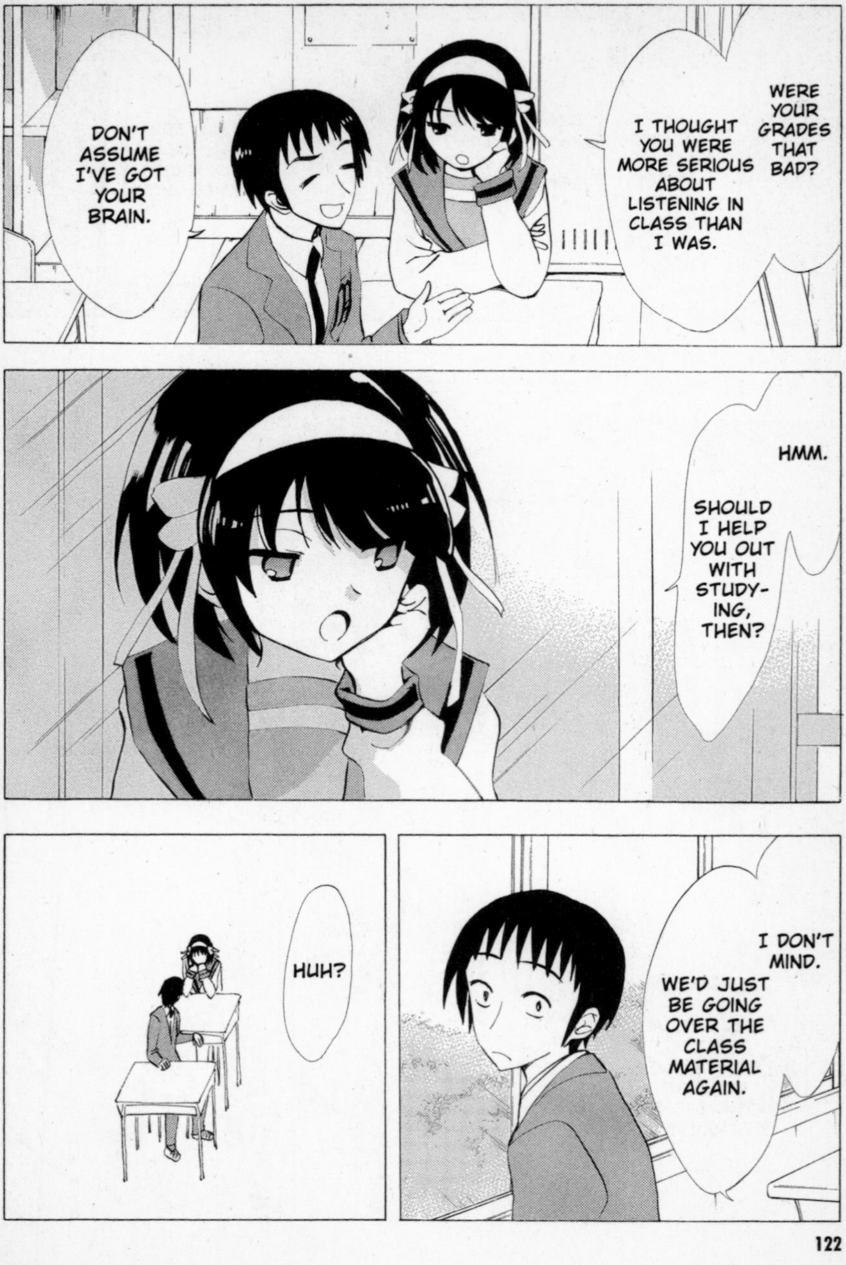
WERE YOUR GRADES THAT BAD?
I THOUGHT YOU WERE MORE SERIOUS ABOUT LISTENING IN CLASS THAN I WAS.
DON'T ASSUME I'VE GOT YOUR BRAIN.
HMM.
SHOULD I HELP YOU OUT WITH STUDYING, THEN?
I DON'T MIND.
WE'D JUST BE GOING OVER THE CLASS MATERIAL AGAIN.
HUH?

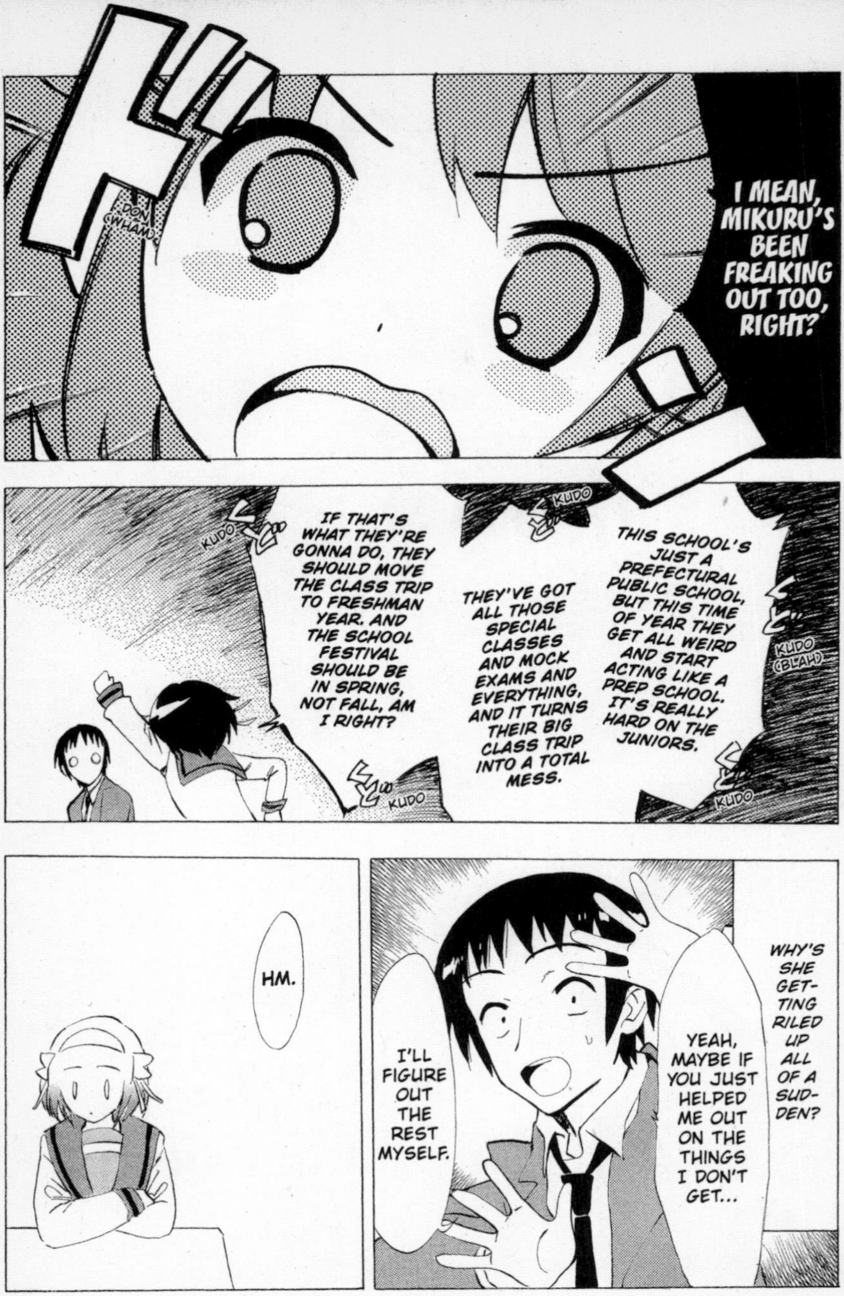
I MEAN, MIKURU'S BEEN FREAKING OUT TOO, RIGHT?
DON (WHAM)
KUDO (BLAH)
KUDO
THIS SCHOOL'S JUST A PREFECTURAL PUBLIC SCHOOL, BUT THIS TIME OF YEAR THEY GET ALL WEIRD AND START ACTING LIKE A PREP SCHOOL. IT'S REALLY HARD ON THE JUNIORS.
KUDO
THEY'VE GOT ALL THOSE SPECIAL CLASSES AND MOCK EXAMS AND EVERYTHING, AND IT TURNS THEIR BIG CLASS TRIP INTO A TOTAL MESS.
KUDO
IF THAT'S WHAT THEY'RE GONNA DO, THEY SHOULD MOVE THE CLASS TRIP TO FRESHMAN YEAR. AND THE SCHOOL FESTIVAL SHOULD BE IN SPRING, NOT FALL, AM I RIGHT?
KUDO
WHY'S SHE GET-TING RILED UP ALL OF A SUD-DEN?
YEAH, MAYBE IF YOU JUST HELPED ME OUT ON THE THINGS I DON'T GET...
I'LL FIGURE OUT THE REST MYSELF.
HM.

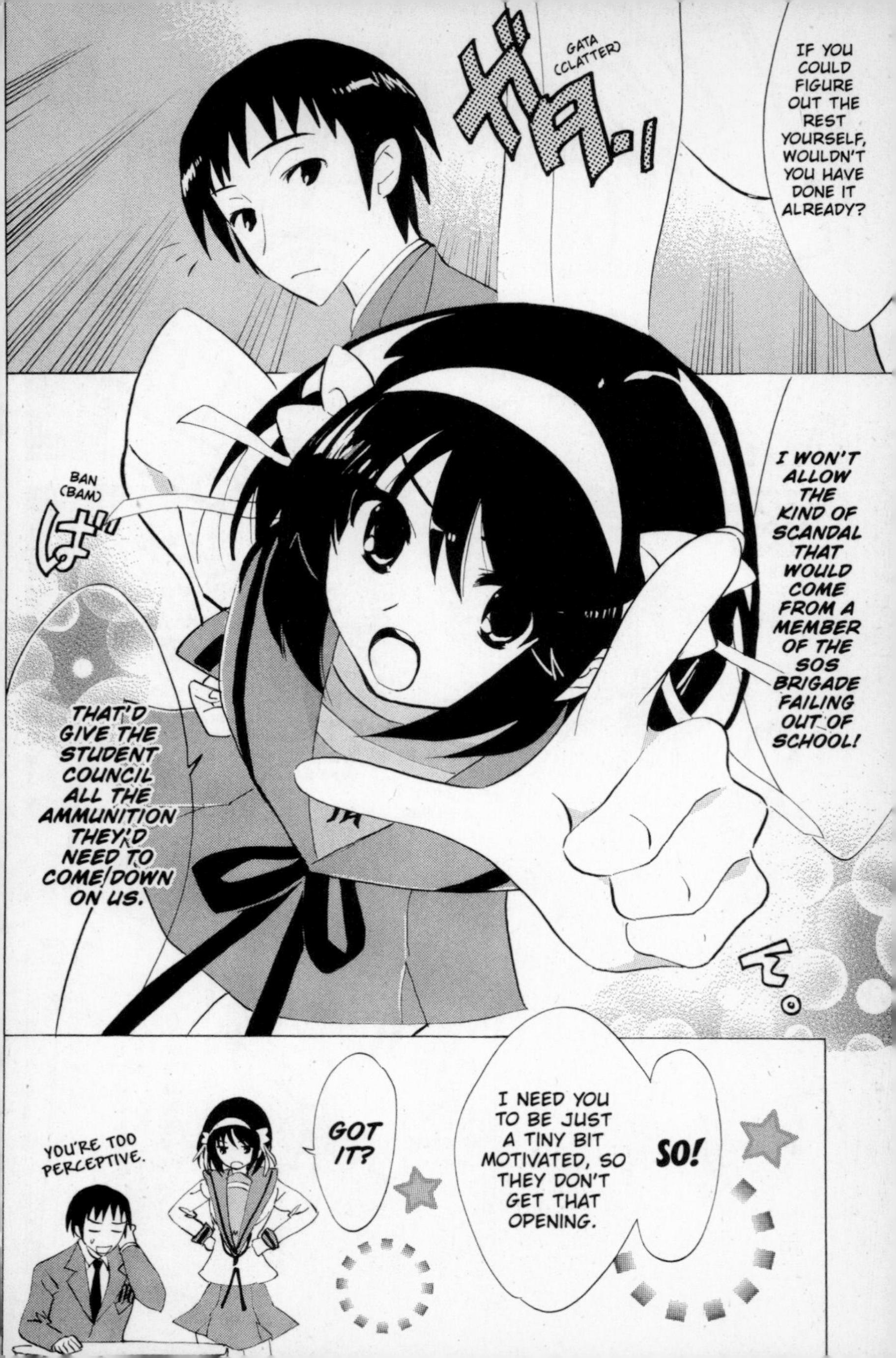
IF YOU COULD FIGURE OUT THE REST YOURSELF, WOULDN'T YOU HAVE DONE IT ALREADY?
GATA (CLATTER)
I WON'T ALLOW THE KIND OF SCANDAL THAT WOULD COME FROM A MEMBER OF THE SOS BRIGADE FAILING OUT OF SCHOOL!
BAN (BAM)
THAT'D GIVE THE STUDENT COUNCIL ALL THE AMMUNITION THEY'D NEED TO COME DOWN ON US.
SO!
I NEED YOU TO BE JUST A TINY BIT MOTIVATED, SO THEY DON'T GET THAT OPENING.
GOT IT?
YOU'RE TOO PERCEPTIVE.

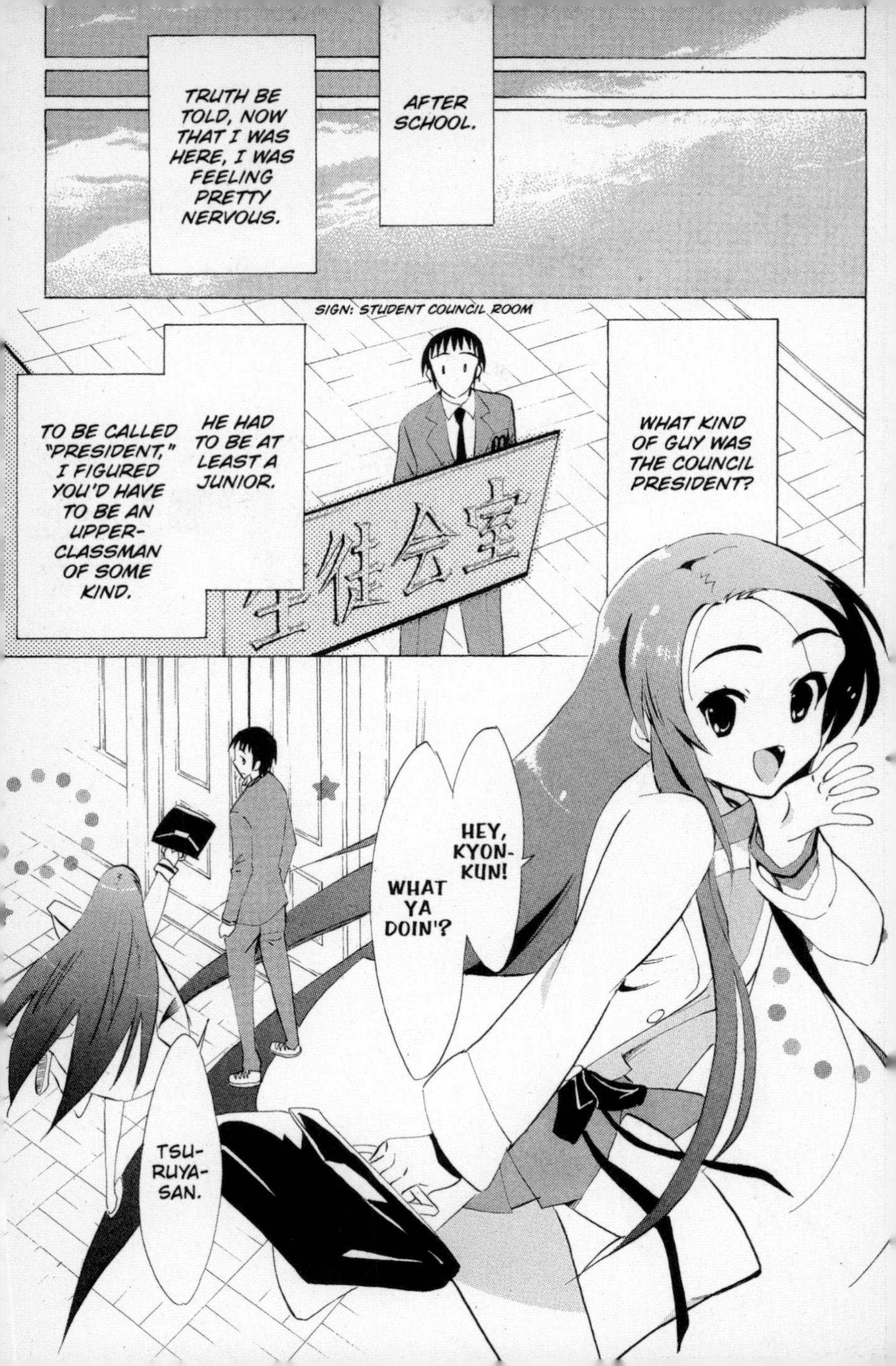
AFTER SCHOOL.
TRUTH BE TOLD, NOW THAT I WAS HERE, I WAS FEELING PRETTY NERVOUS.
WHAT KIND OF GUY WAS THE COUNCIL PRESIDENT?
SIGN: STUDENT COUNCIL ROOM
HE HAD TO BE AT LEAST A JUNIOR.
TO BE CALLED "PRESIDENT," I FIGURED YOU'D HAVE TO BE AN UPPER-CLASSMAN OF SOME KIND.
HEY, KYON-KUN!
WHAT YA DOIN'?
TSU-RUYA-SAN.

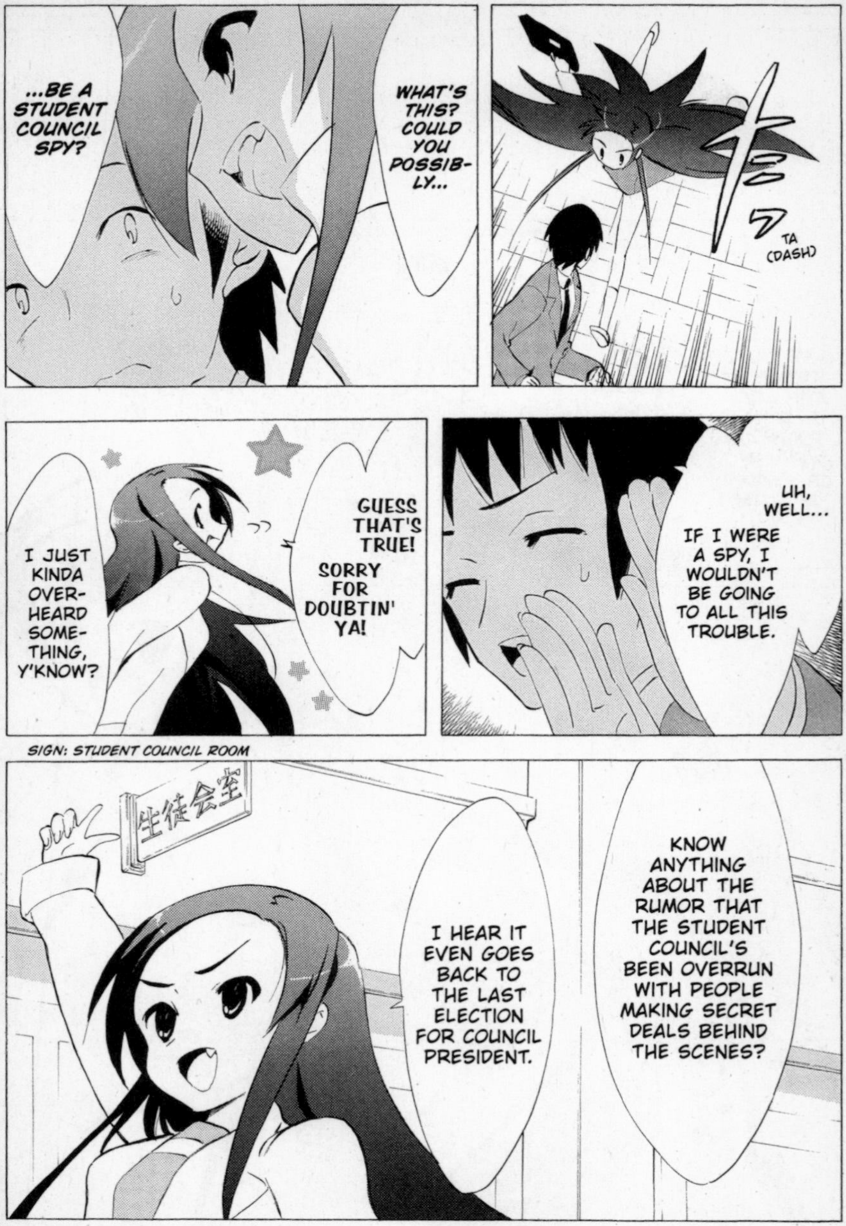
TA (DASH)
WHAT'S THIS? COULD YOU POSSIBLY...
...BE A STUDENT COUNCIL SPY?
UH, WELL...
IF I WERE A SPY, I WOULDN'T BE GOING TO ALL THIS TROUBLE.
GUESS THAT'S TRUE!
SORRY FOR DOUBTIN' YA!
I JUST KINDA OVERHEARD SOMETHING, Y'KNOW?
SIGN: STUDENT COUNCIL ROOM
生徒会室
KNOW ANYTHING ABOUT THE RUMOR THAT THE STUDENT COUNCIL'S BEEN OVERRUN WITH PEOPLE MAKING SECRET DEALS BEHIND THE SCENES?
I HEAR IT EVEN GOES BACK TO THE LAST ELECTION FOR COUNCIL PRESIDENT.

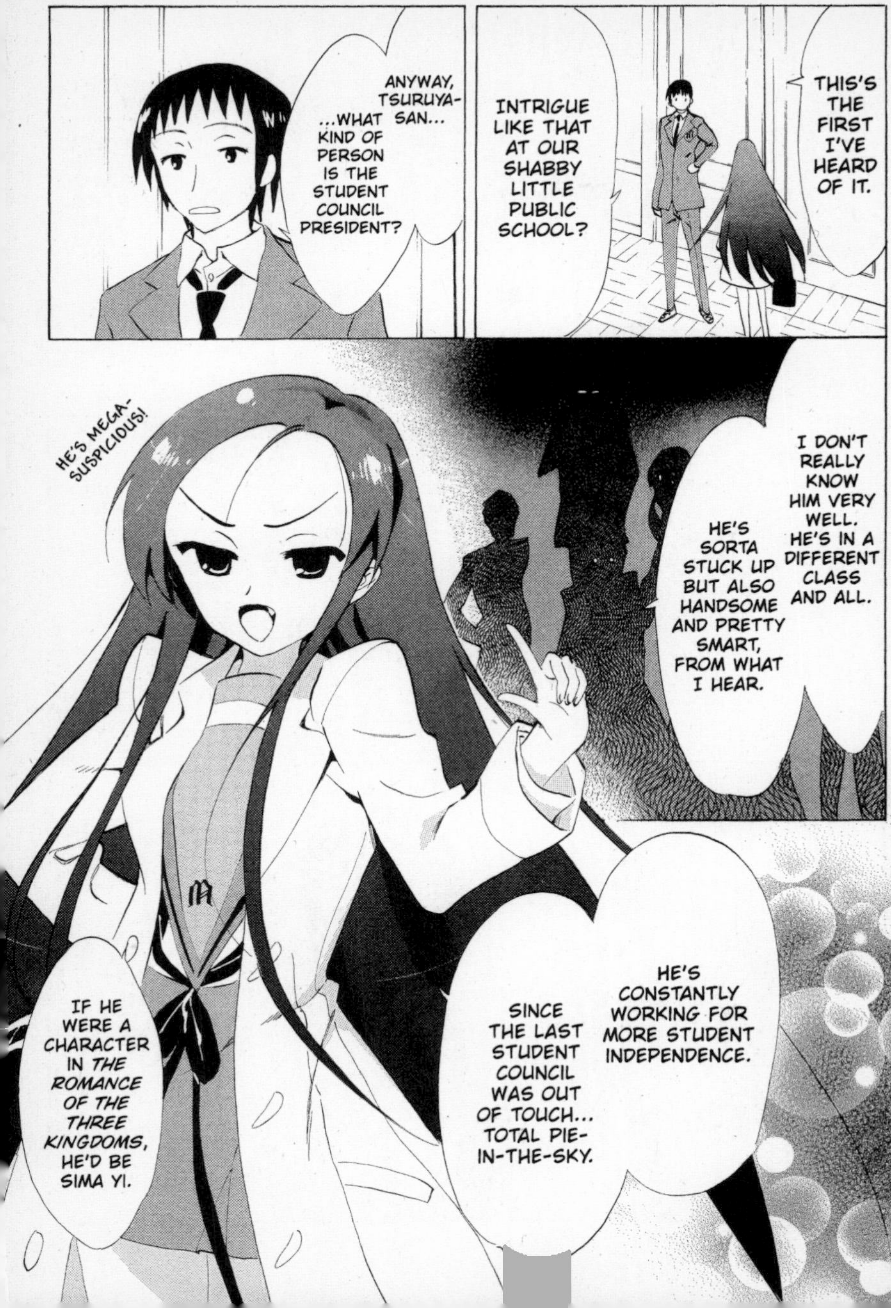
THIS'S THE FIRST I'VE HEARD OF IT.
INTRIGUE LIKE THAT AT OUR SHABBY LITTLE PUBLIC SCHOOL?
ANYWAY, TSURUYA-SAN... ...WHAT KIND OF PERSON IS THE STUDENT COUNCIL PRESIDENT?
I DON'T REALLY KNOW HIM VERY WELL. HE'S IN A DIFFERENT CLASS AND ALL.
HE'S SORTA STUCK UP BUT ALSO HANDSOME AND PRETTY SMART, FROM WHAT I HEAR.
HE'S MEGA-SUSPICIOUS!
HE'S CONSTANTLY WORKING FOR MORE STUDENT INDEPENDENCE.
SINCE THE LAST STUDENT COUNCIL WAS OUT OF TOUCH... TOTAL PIE-IN-THE-SKY.
IF HE WERE A CHARACTER IN *THE ROMANCE OF THE THREE KINGDOMS*, HE'D BE SIMA YI.

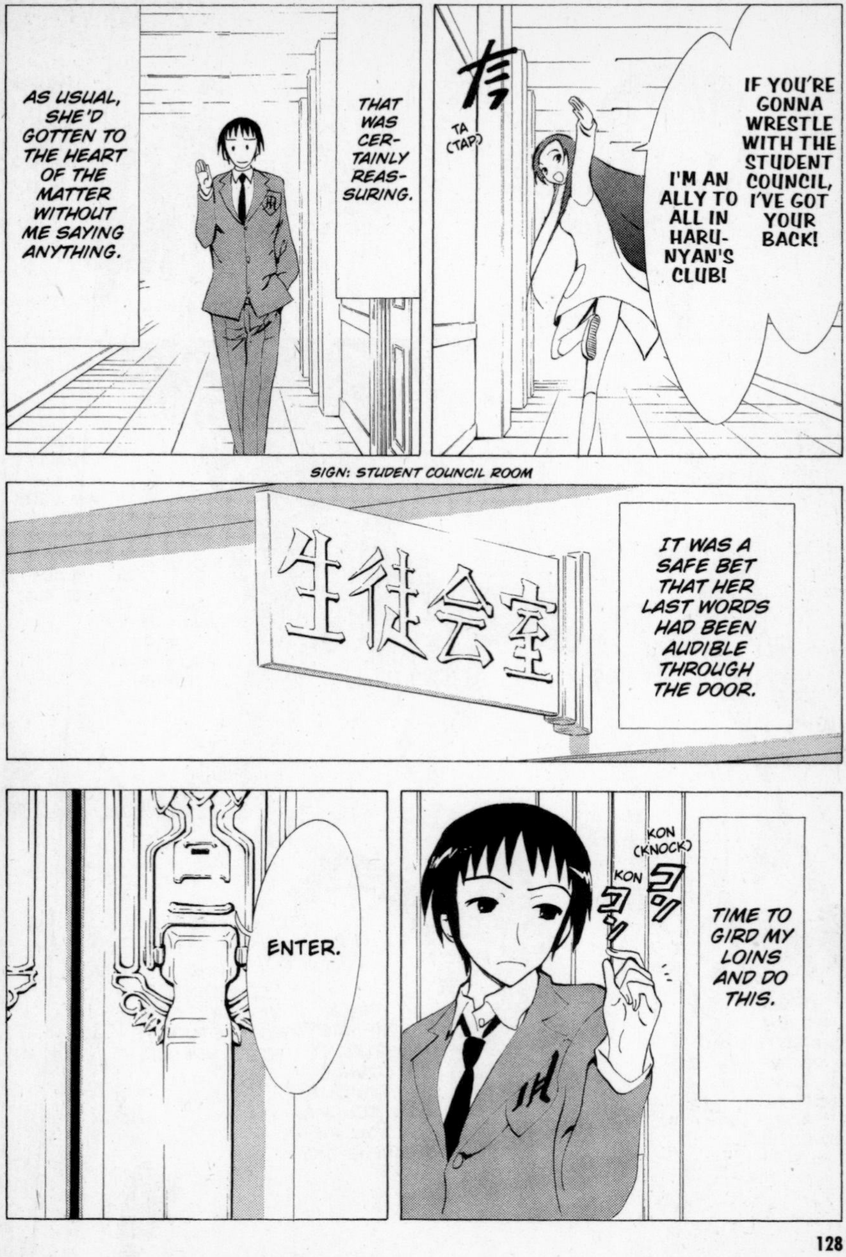
IF YOU'RE GONNA WRESTLE WITH THE STUDENT COUNCIL, I'VE GOT YOUR BACK!
I'M AN ALLY TO ALL IN HARU-NYAN'S CLUB!
TA (TAP)
THAT WAS CER-TAINLY REAS-SURING.
AS USUAL, SHE'D GOTTEN TO THE HEART OF THE MATTER WITHOUT ME SAYING ANYTHING.
SIGN: STUDENT COUNCIL ROOM
生徒会室
IT WAS A SAFE BET THAT HER LAST WORDS HAD BEEN AUDIBLE THROUGH THE DOOR.
TIME TO GIRD MY LOINS AND DO THIS.
KON (KNOCK)
KON
ENTER.

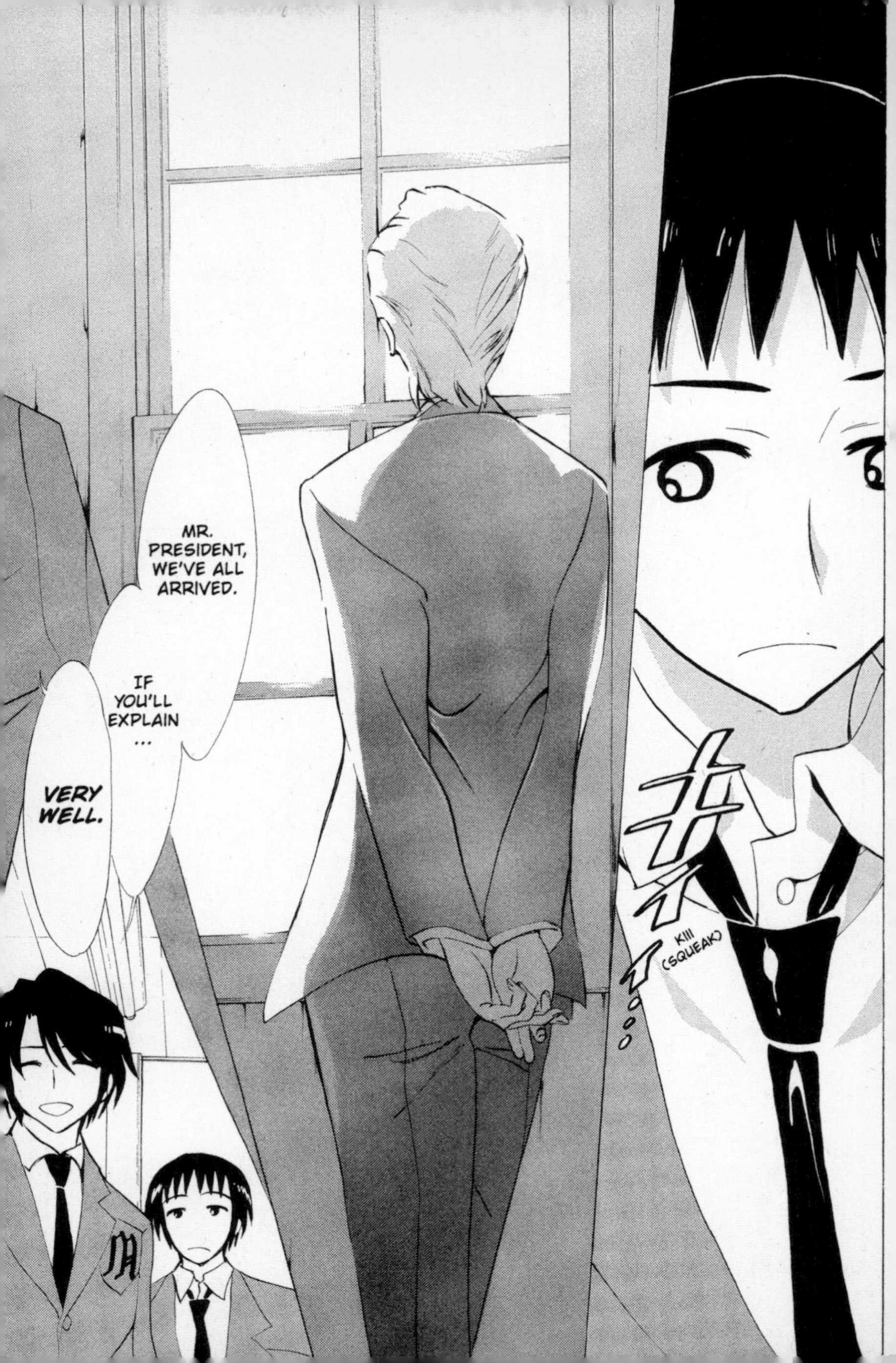
KIII (SQUEAK)
MR. PRESIDENT, WE'VE ALL ARRIVED.
IF YOU'LL EXPLAIN ...
VERY WELL.

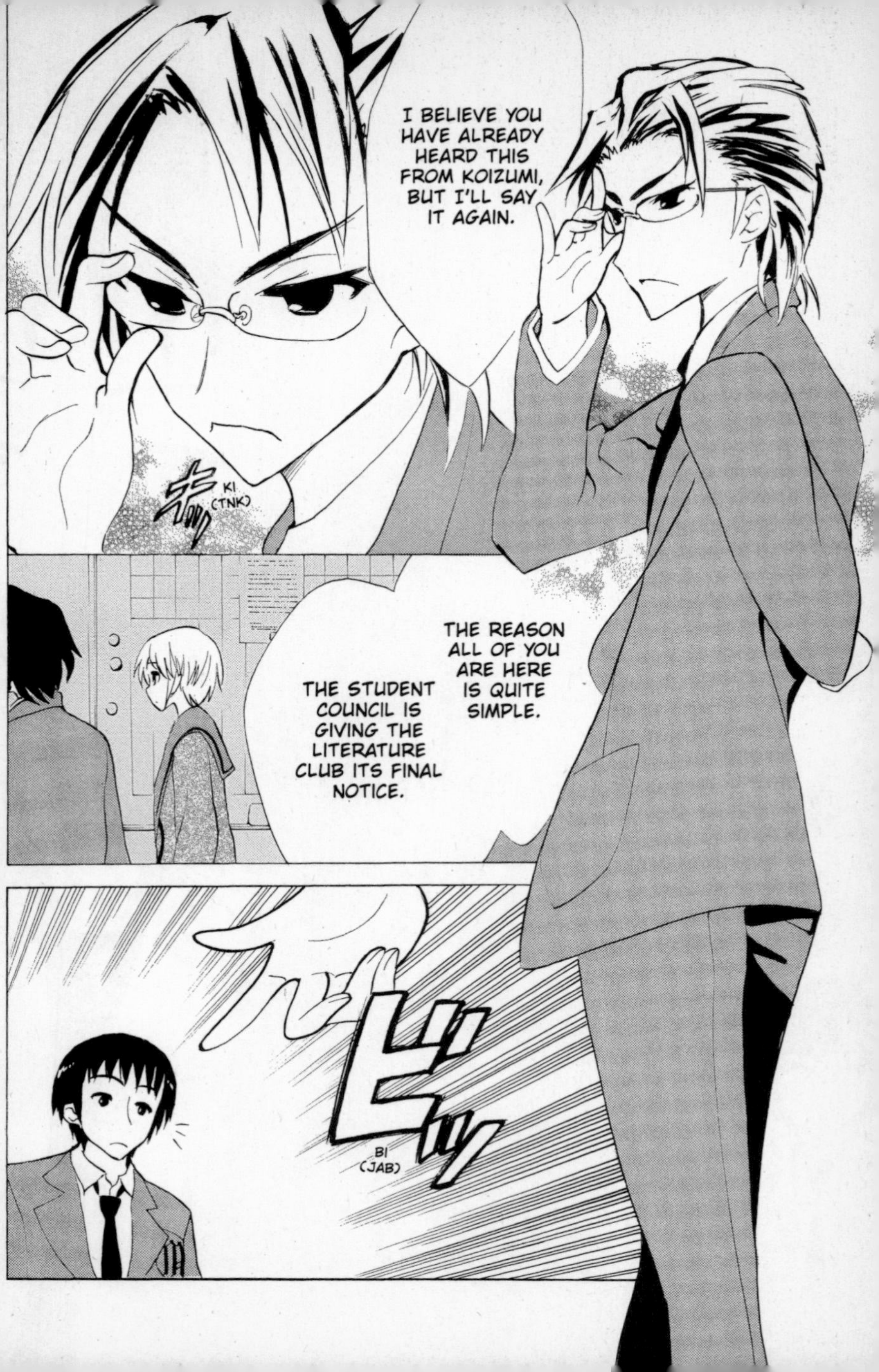
I BELIEVE YOU HAVE ALREADY HEARD THIS FROM KOIZUMI, BUT I'LL SAY IT AGAIN.
KI (TNK)
THE REASON ALL OF YOU ARE HERE IS QUITE SIMPLE.
THE STUDENT COUNCIL IS GIVING THE LITERATURE CLUB ITS FINAL NOTICE.
BI (JAB)

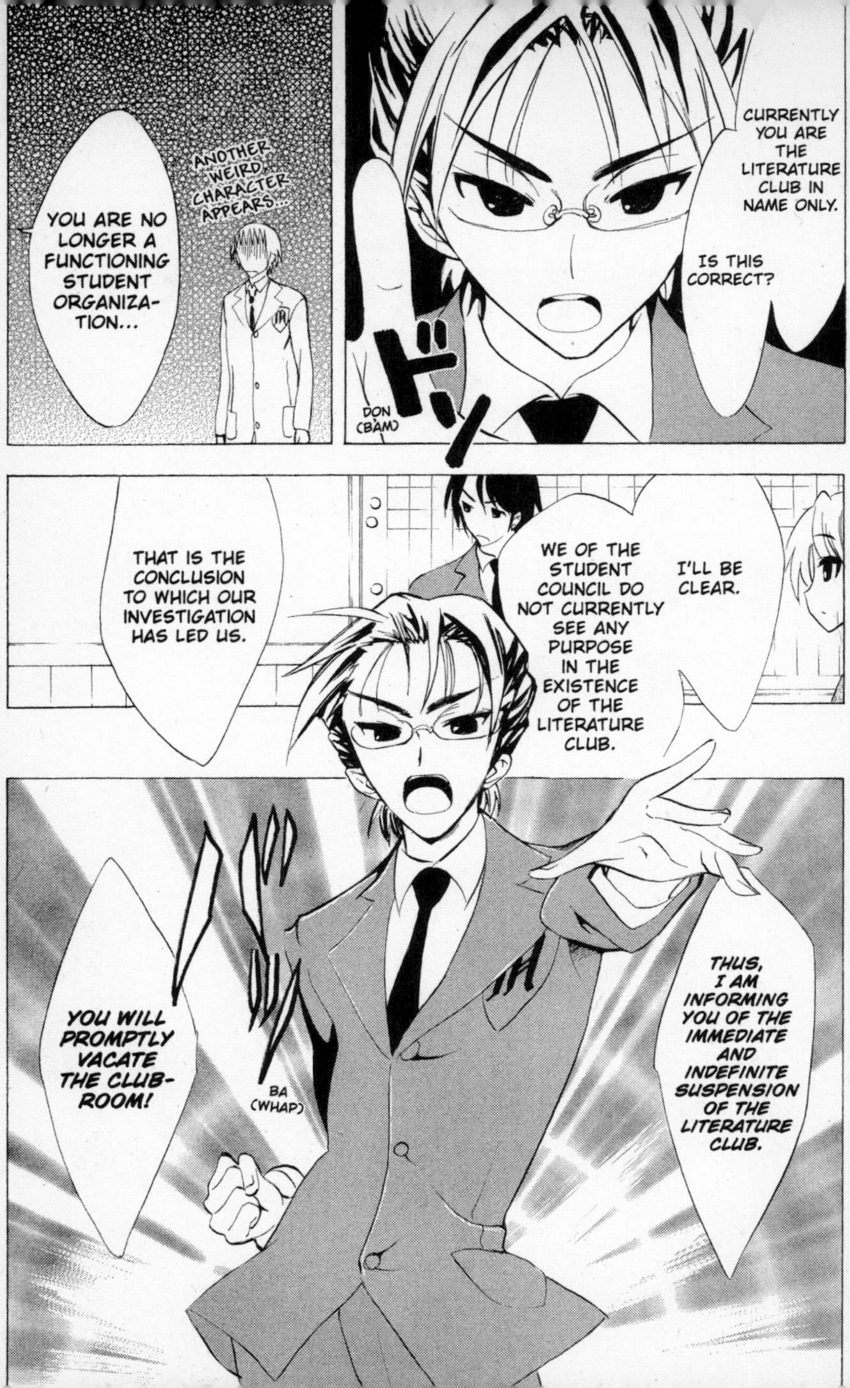
CURRENTLY YOU ARE THE LITERATURE CLUB IN NAME ONLY.
IS THIS CORRECT?
DON (BAM)
YOU ARE NO LONGER A FUNCTIONING STUDENT ORGANIZA-TION...
ANOTHER WEIRD CHARACTER APPEARS...
I'LL BE CLEAR.
WE OF THE STUDENT COUNCIL DO NOT CURRENTLY SEE ANY PURPOSE IN THE EXISTENCE OF THE LITERATURE CLUB.
THAT IS THE CONCLUSION TO WHICH OUR INVESTIGATION HAS LED US.
THUS, I AM INFORMING YOU OF THE IMMEDIATE AND INDEFINITE SUSPENSION OF THE LITERATURE CLUB.
BA (WHAP)
YOU WILL PROMPTLY VACATE THE CLUB-ROOM!

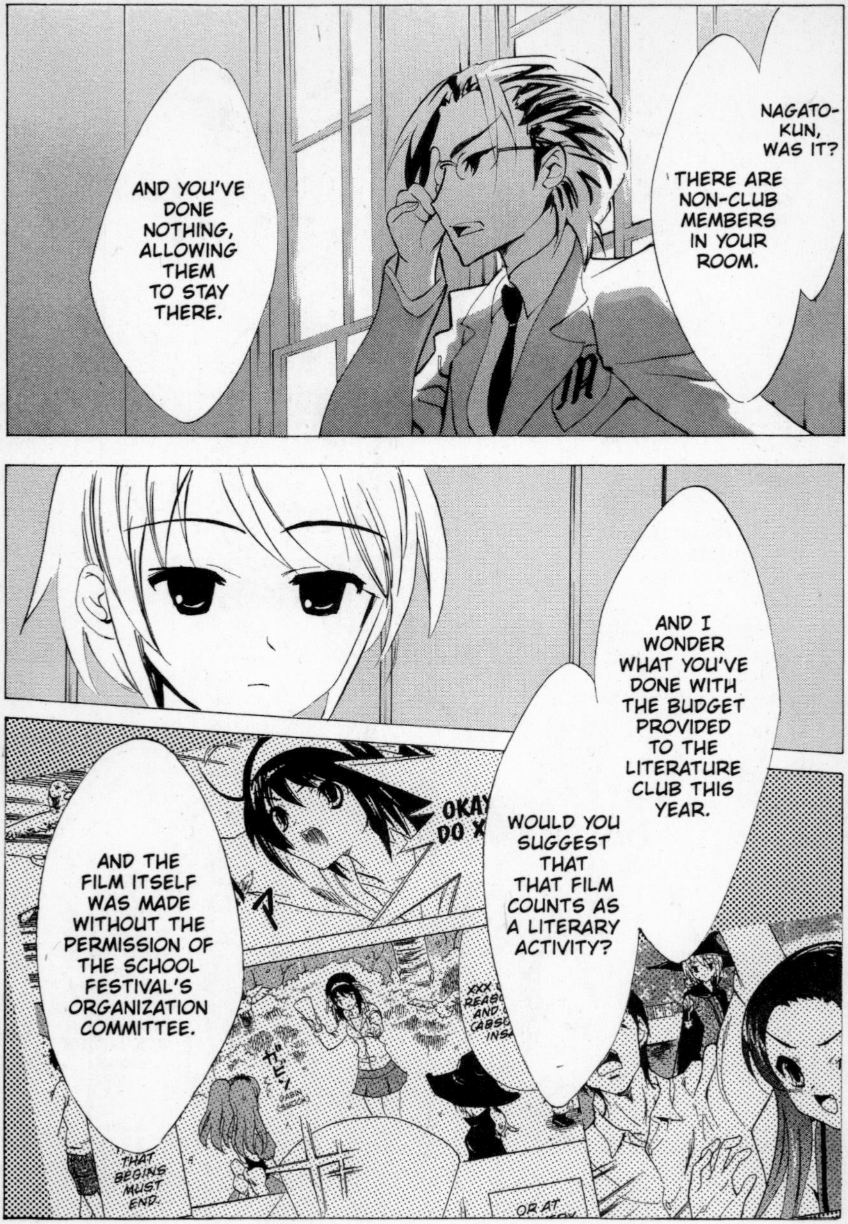
NAGATO-KUN, WAS IT?
THERE ARE NON-CLUB MEMBERS IN YOUR ROOM.
AND YOU'VE DONE NOTHING, ALLOWING THEM TO STAY THERE.
AND I WONDER WHAT YOU'VE DONE WITH THE BUDGET PROVIDED TO THE LITERATURE CLUB THIS YEAR.
WOULD YOU SUGGEST THAT THAT FILM COUNTS AS A LITERARY ACTIVITY?
AND THE FILM ITSELF WAS MADE WITHOUT THE PERMISSION OF THE SCHOOL FESTIVAL'S ORGANIZATION COMMITTEE.
THAT BEGINS MUST END.

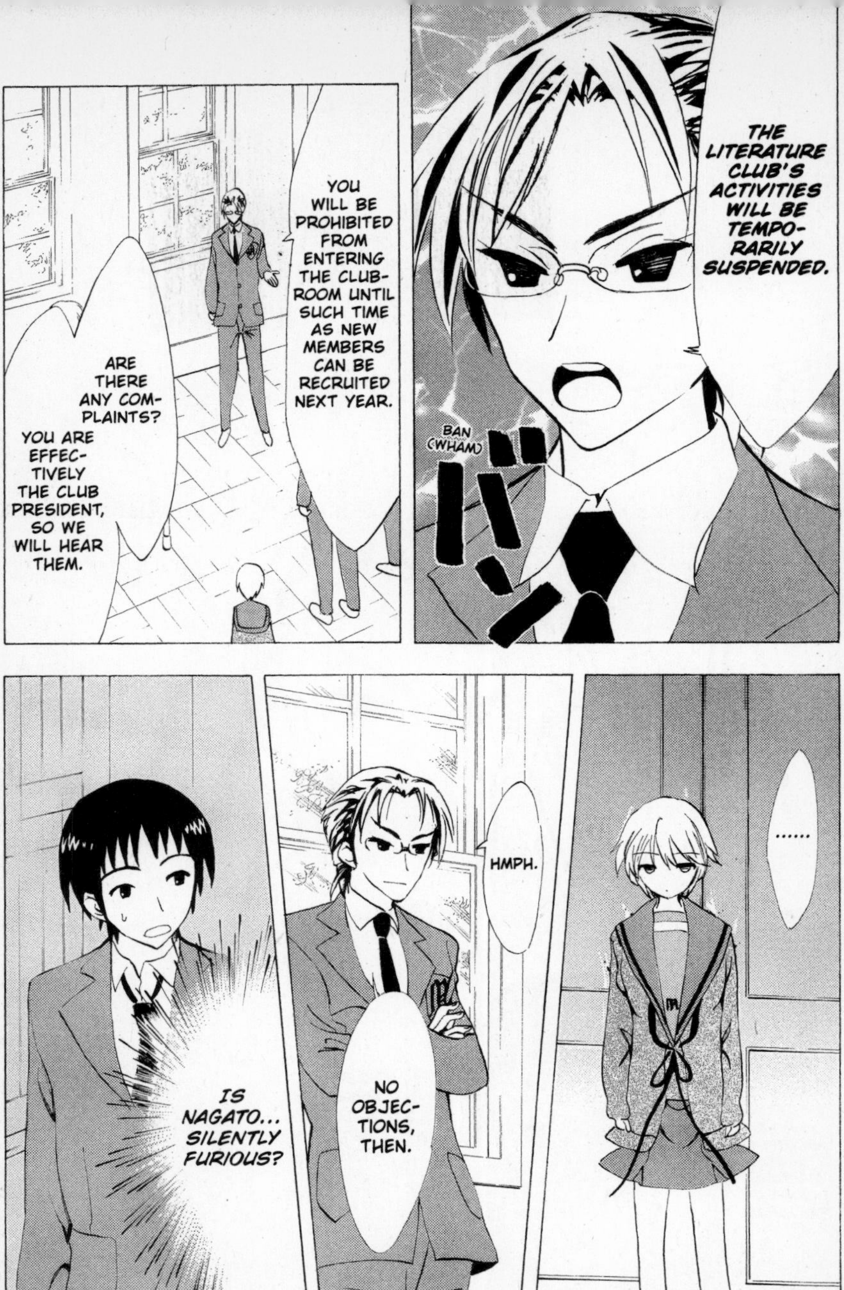
THE LITERATURE CLUB'S ACTIVITIES WILL BE TEMPORARILY SUSPENDED.
BAN (WHAM)
YOU WILL BE PROHIBITED FROM ENTERING THE CLUBROOM UNTIL SUCH TIME AS NEW MEMBERS CAN BE RECRUITED NEXT YEAR.
ARE THERE ANY COMPLAINTS?
YOU ARE EFFECTIVELY THE CLUB PRESIDENT, SO WE WILL HEAR THEM.
......
HMPH.
NO OBJECTIONS, THEN.
IS NAGATO... SILENTLY FURIOUS?

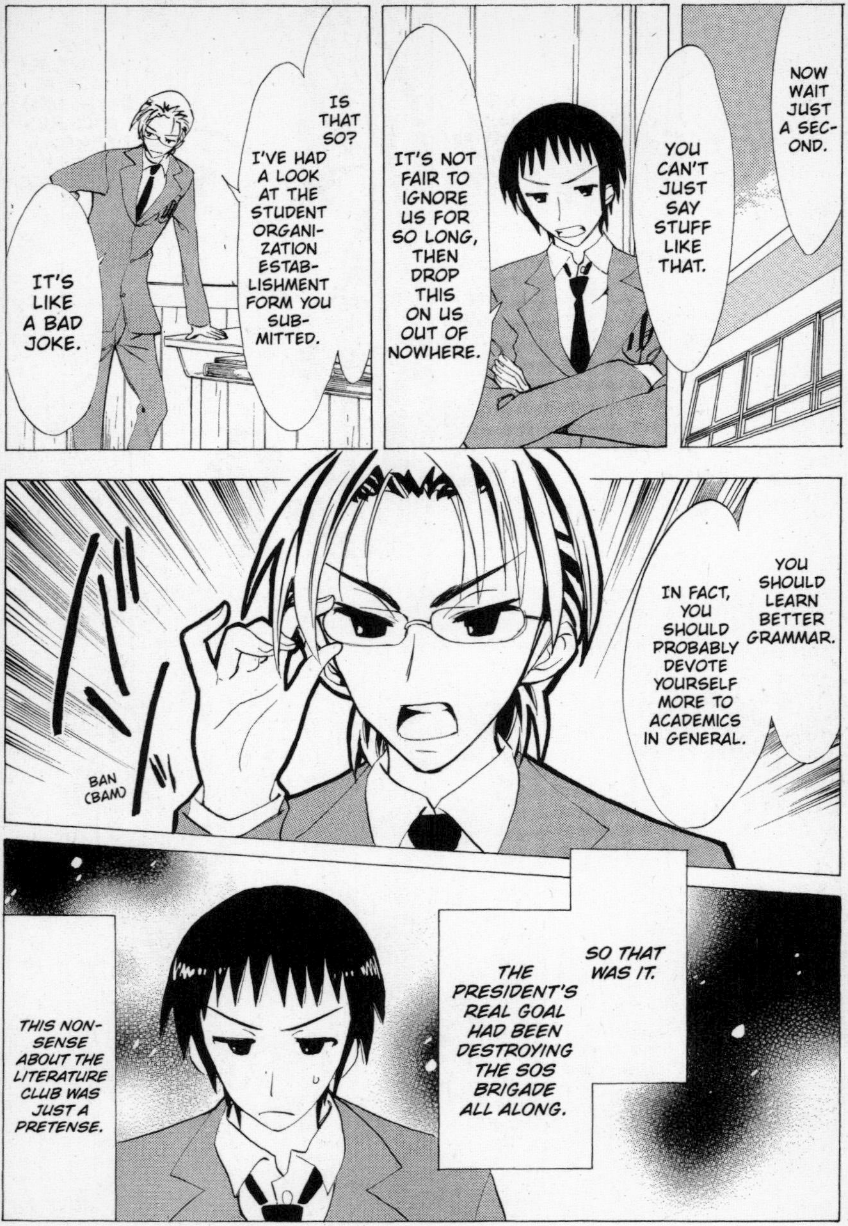
NOW WAIT JUST A SECOND.
YOU CAN'T JUST SAY STUFF LIKE THAT.
IT'S NOT FAIR TO IGNORE US FOR SO LONG, THEN DROP THIS ON US OUT OF NOWHERE.
IS THAT SO?
I'VE HAD A LOOK AT THE STUDENT ORGANIZATION ESTABLISHMENT FORM YOU SUBMITTED.
IT'S LIKE A BAD JOKE.
YOU SHOULD LEARN BETTER GRAMMAR.
IN FACT, YOU SHOULD PROBABLY DEVOTE YOURSELF MORE TO ACADEMICS IN GENERAL.
BAN (BAM)
SO THAT WAS IT.
THE PRESIDENT'S REAL GOAL HAD BEEN DESTROYING THE SOS BRIGADE ALL ALONG.
THIS NONSENSE ABOUT THE LITERATURE CLUB WAS JUST A PRETENSE.

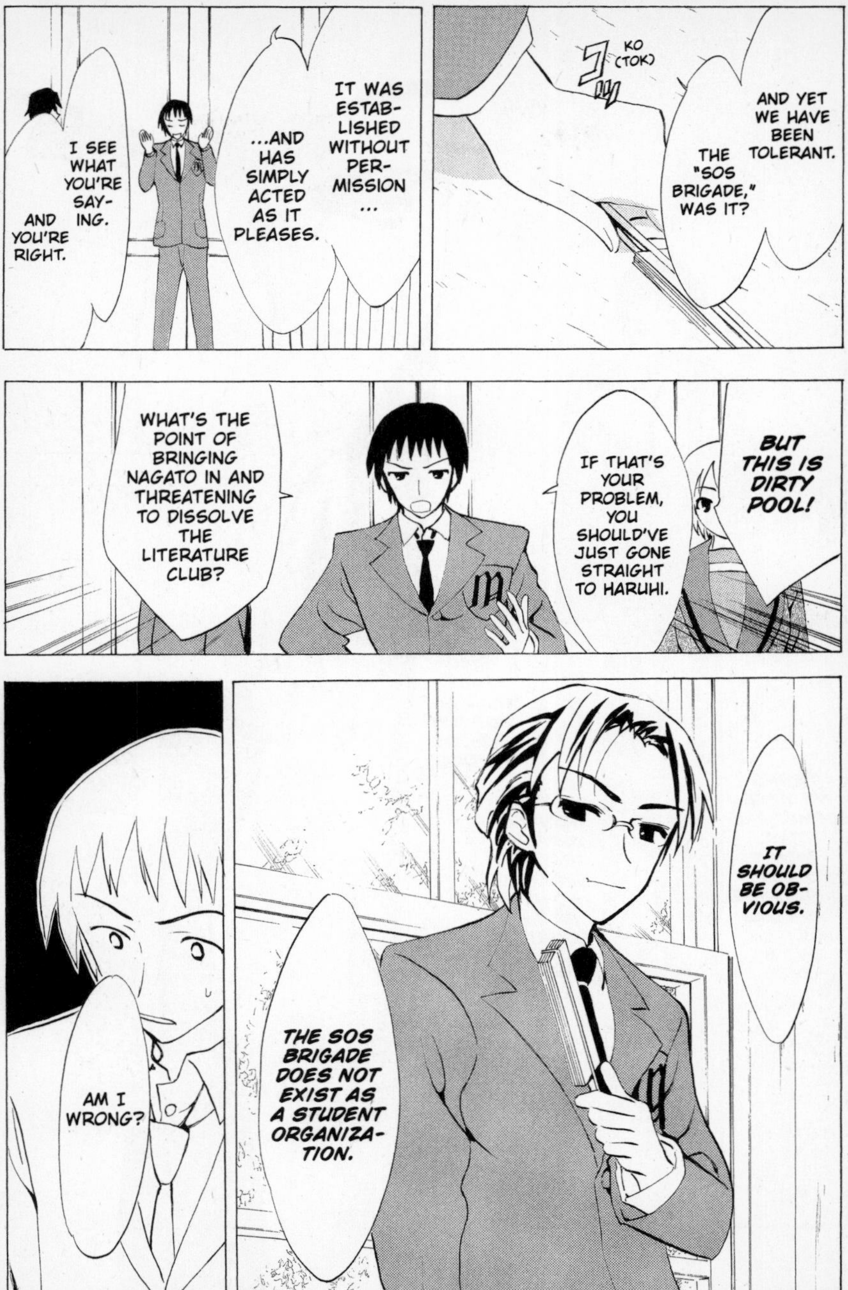
KO (TOK)
AND YET WE HAVE BEEN TOLERANT.
THE "SOS BRIGADE," WAS IT?
IT WAS ESTAB-LISHED WITHOUT PER-MISSION...
...AND HAS SIMPLY ACTED AS IT PLEASES.
I SEE WHAT YOU'RE SAY-ING.
AND YOU'RE RIGHT.
BUT THIS IS DIRTY POOL!
IF THAT'S YOUR PROBLEM, YOU SHOULD'VE JUST GONE STRAIGHT TO HARUHI.
WHAT'S THE POINT OF BRINGING NAGATO IN AND THREATENING TO DISSOLVE THE LITERATURE CLUB?
IT SHOULD BE OB-VIOUS.
THE SOS BRIGADE DOES NOT EXIST AS A STUDENT ORGANIZA-TION.
AM I WRONG?

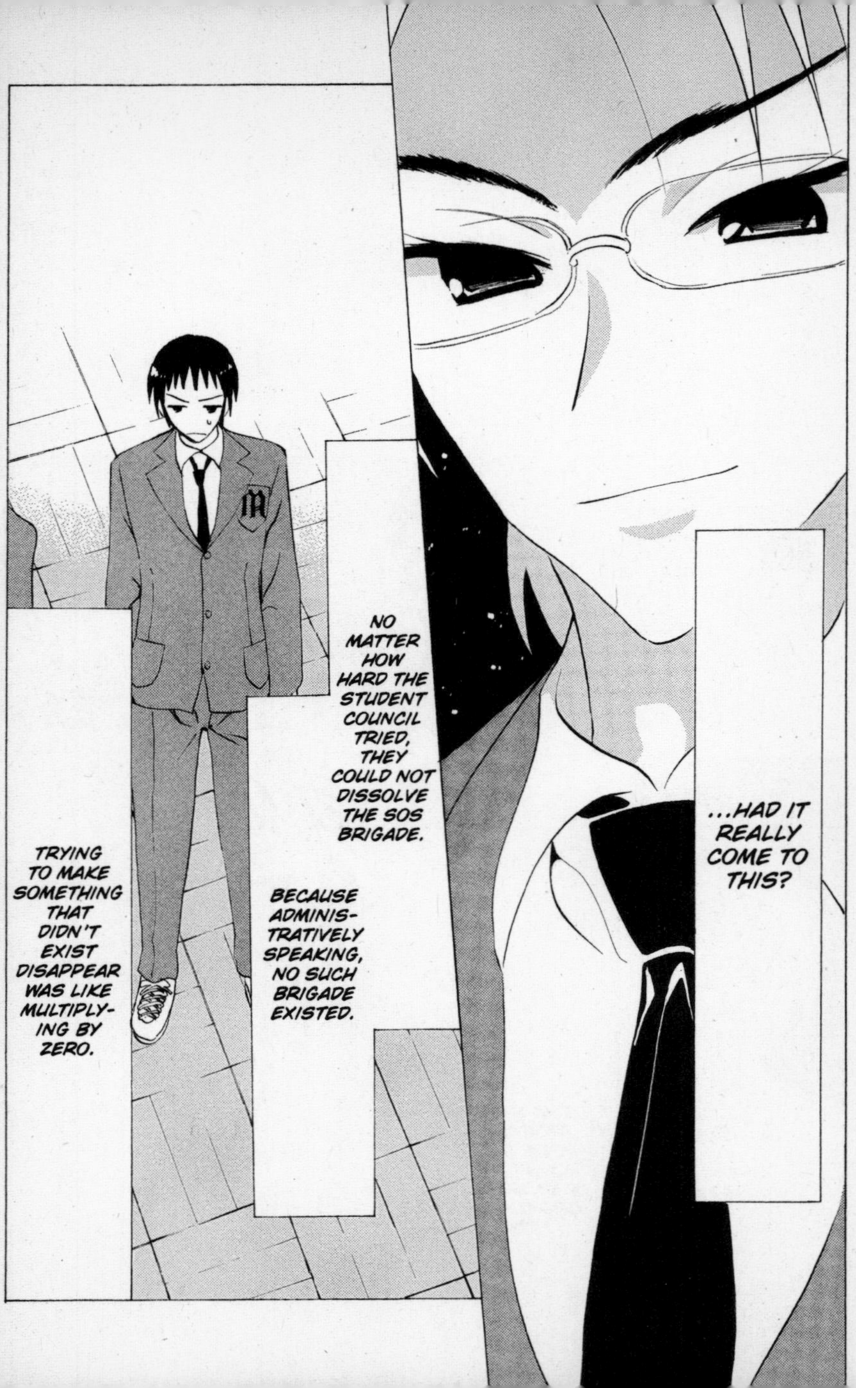
...HAD IT REALLY COME TO THIS?
NO MATTER HOW HARD THE STUDENT COUNCIL TRIED, THEY COULD NOT DISSOLVE THE SOS BRIGADE.
BECAUSE ADMINIS-TRATIVELY SPEAKING, NO SUCH BRIGADE EXISTED.
TRYING TO MAKE SOMETHING THAT DIDN'T EXIST DISAPPEAR WAS LIKE MULTIPLY-ING BY ZERO.

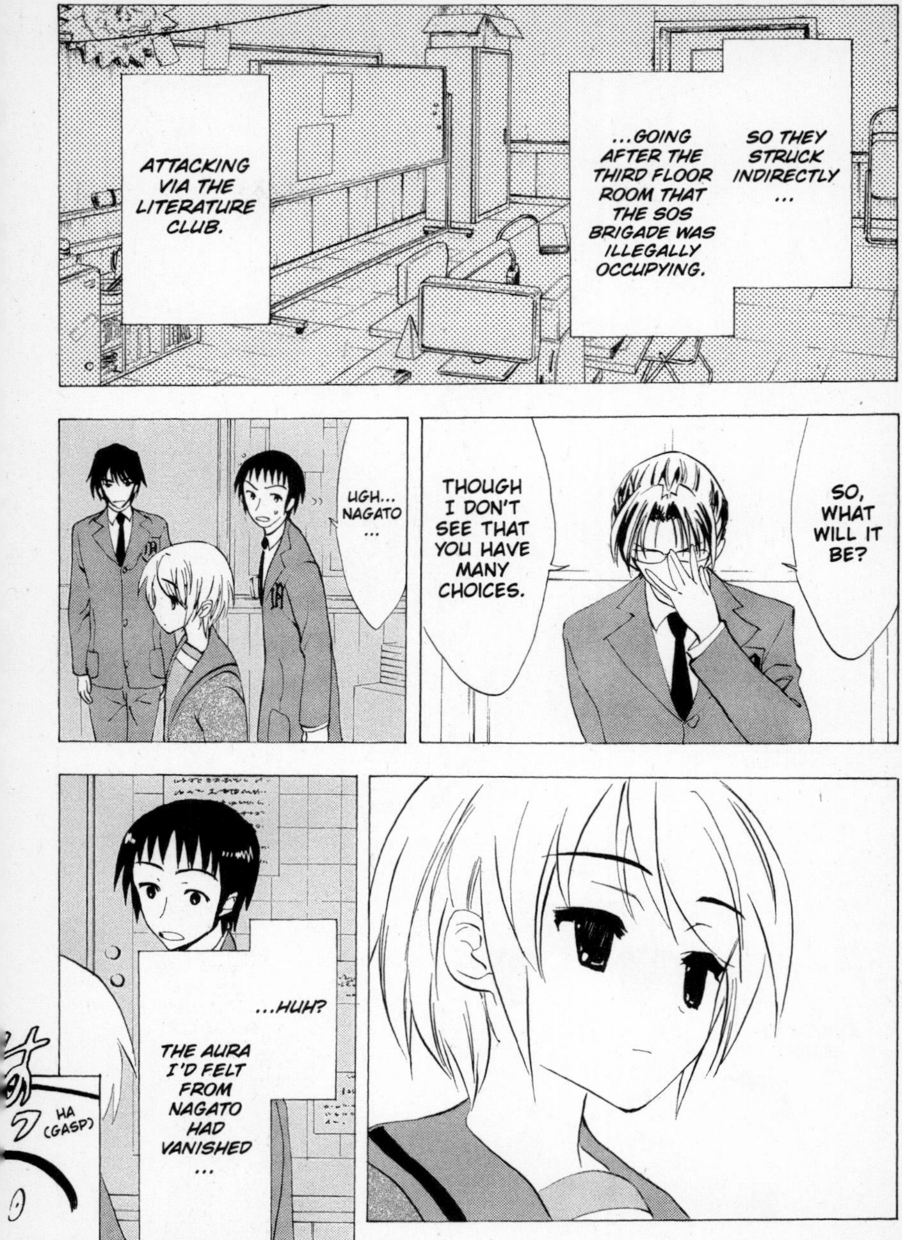
SO THEY STRUCK INDIRECTLY ...
...GOING AFTER THE THIRD FLOOR ROOM THAT THE SOS BRIGADE WAS ILLEGALLY OCCUPYING.
ATTACKING VIA THE LITERATURE CLUB.
SO, WHAT WILL IT BE?
THOUGH I DON'T SEE THAT YOU HAVE MANY CHOICES.
UGH... NAGATO ...
...HUH?
THE AURA I'D FELT FROM NAGATO HAD VANISHED ...
HA (GASP)

SIGN: SECRETARY

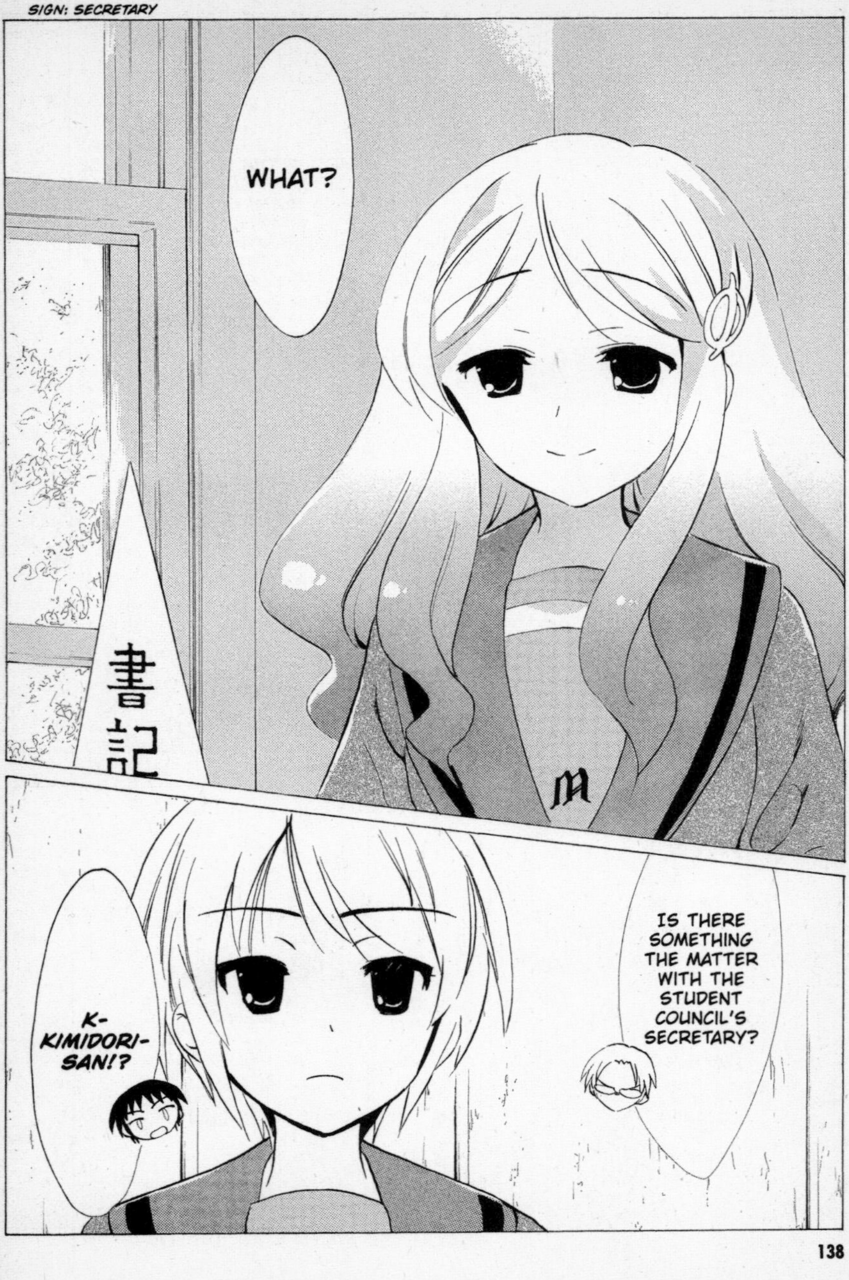
WHAT?
書記
IS THERE SOMETHING THE MATTER WITH THE STUDENT COUNCIL'S SECRETARY?
K-KIMIDORI-SAN!?

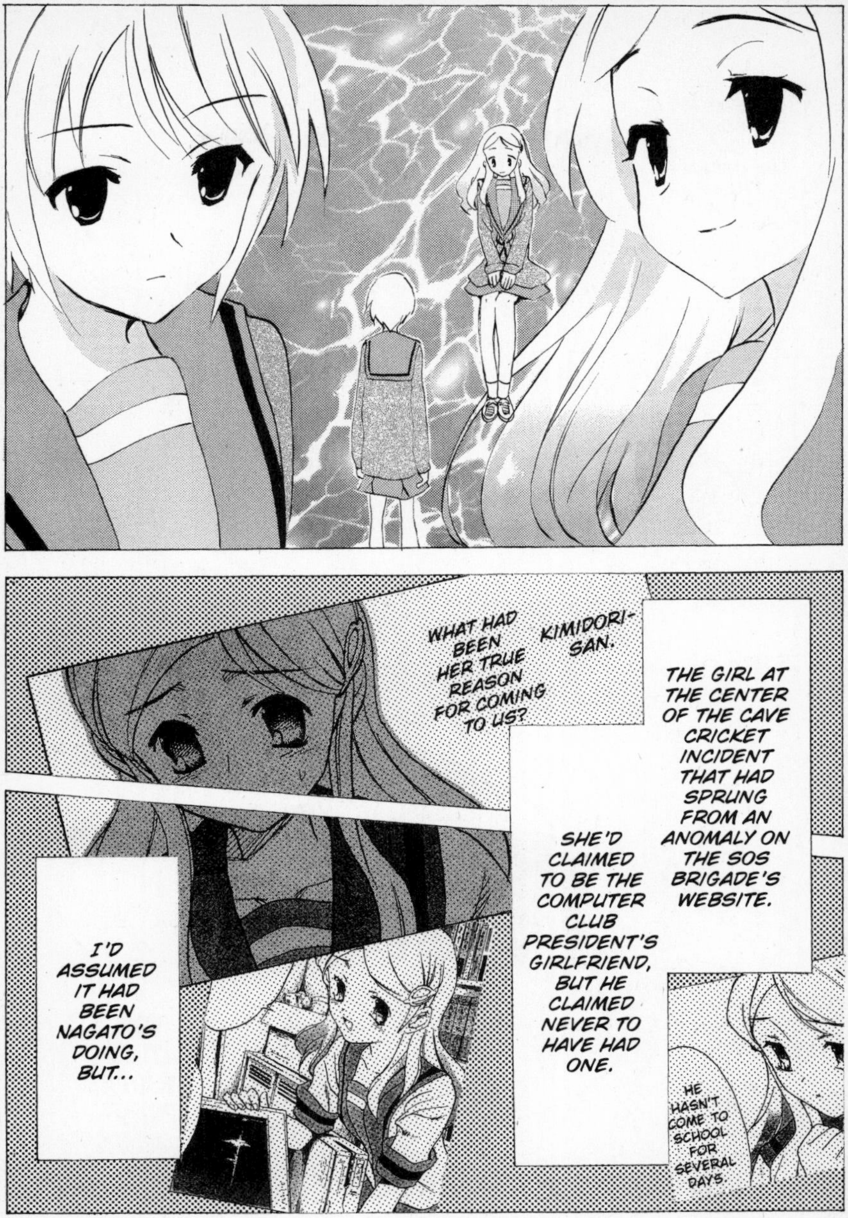
KIMIDORI-SAN.
WHAT HAD BEEN HER TRUE REASON FOR COMING TO US?
THE GIRL AT THE CENTER OF THE CAVE CRICKET INCIDENT THAT HAD SPRUNG FROM AN ANOMALY ON THE SOS BRIGADE'S WEBSITE.
SHE'D CLAIMED TO BE THE COMPUTER CLUB PRESIDENT'S GIRLFRIEND, BUT HE CLAIMED NEVER TO HAVE HAD ONE.
HE HASN'T COME TO SCHOOL FOR SEVERAL DAYS
I'D ASSUMED IT HAD BEEN NAGATO'S DOING, BUT...

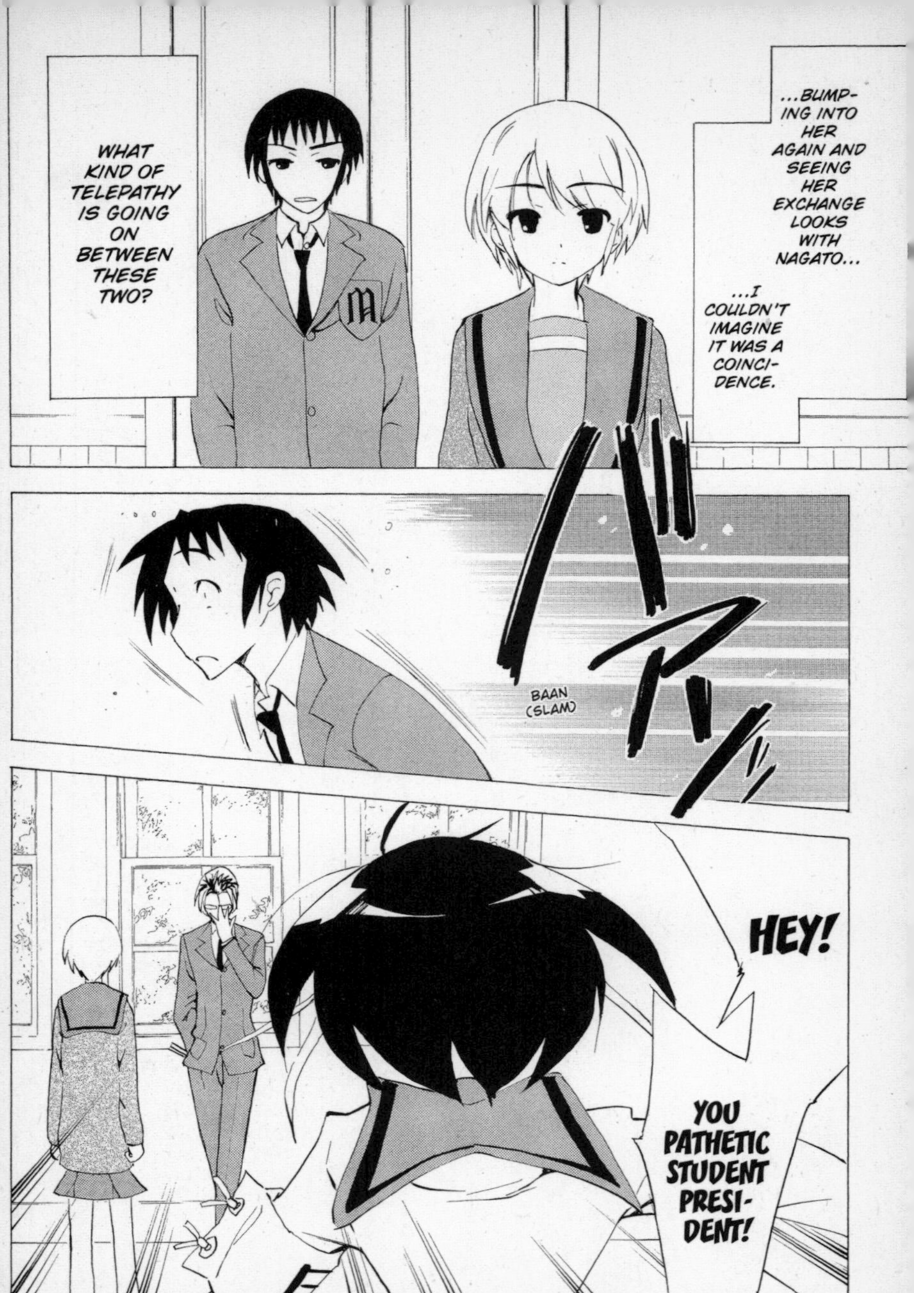
...BUMPING INTO HER AGAIN AND SEEING HER EXCHANGE LOOKS WITH NAGATO...
...I COULDN'T IMAGINE IT WAS A COINCIDENCE.
WHAT KIND OF TELEPATHY IS GOING ON BETWEEN THESE TWO?
BAAN (SLAM)
HEY!
YOU PATHETIC STUDENT PRESIDENT!

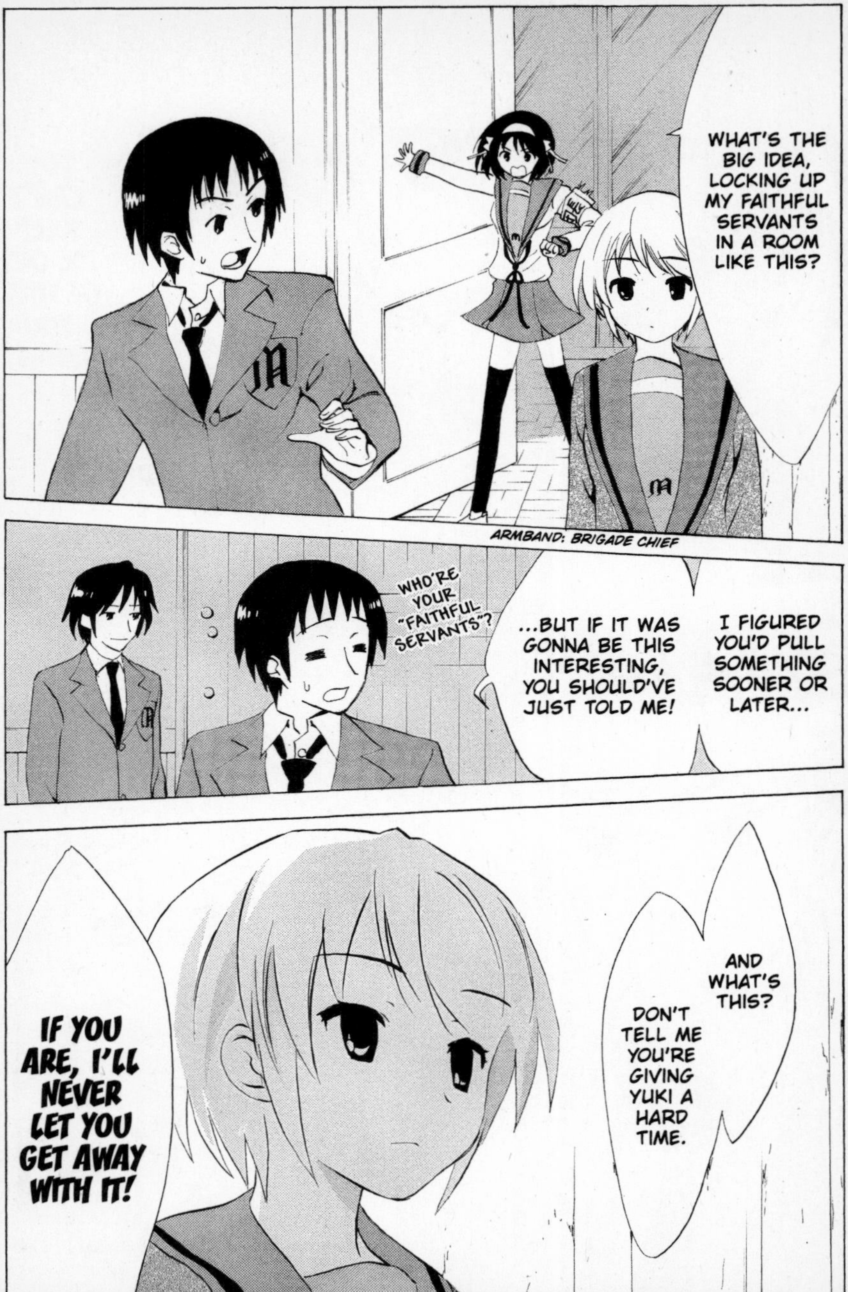
WHAT'S THE BIG IDEA, LOCKING UP MY FAITHFUL SERVANTS IN A ROOM LIKE THIS?
ARMBAND: BRIGADE CHIEF
I FIGURED YOU'D PULL SOMETHING SOONER OR LATER...
...BUT IF IT WAS GONNA BE THIS INTERESTING, YOU SHOULD'VE JUST TOLD ME!
WHO'RE YOUR "FAITHFUL SERVANTS"?
AND WHAT'S THIS?
DON'T TELL ME YOU'RE GIVING YUKI A HARD TIME.
IF YOU ARE, I'LL NEVER LET YOU GET AWAY WITH IT!

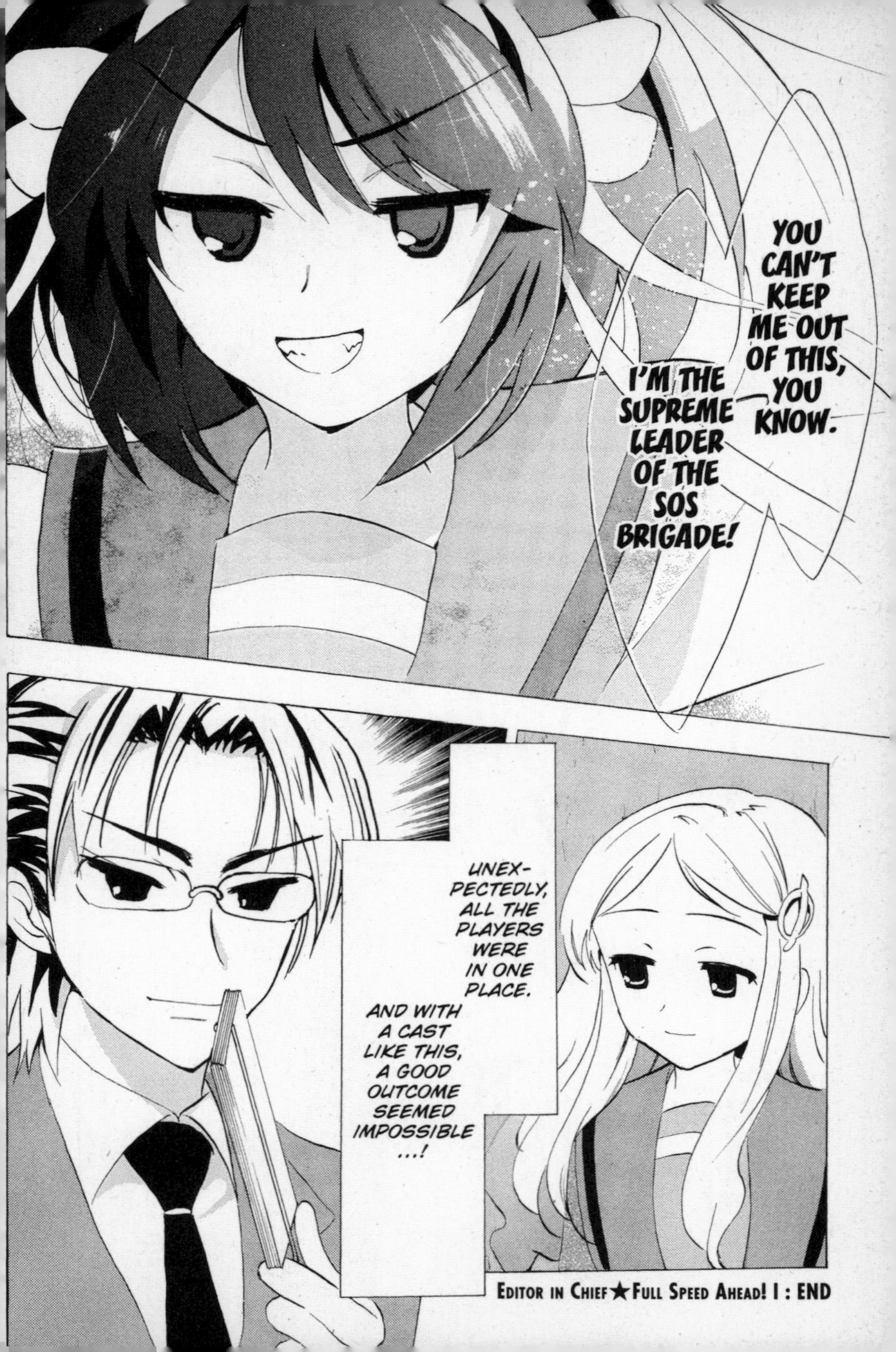
YOU CAN'T KEEP ME OUT OF THIS, YOU KNOW.
I'M THE SUPREME LEADER OF THE SOS BRIGADE!
UNEX-PECTEDLY, ALL THE PLAYERS WERE IN ONE PLACE.
AND WITH A CAST LIKE THIS, A GOOD OUTCOME SEEMED IMPOSSIBLE ...!

EDITOR IN CHIEF★FULL SPEED AHEAD! 1 : END

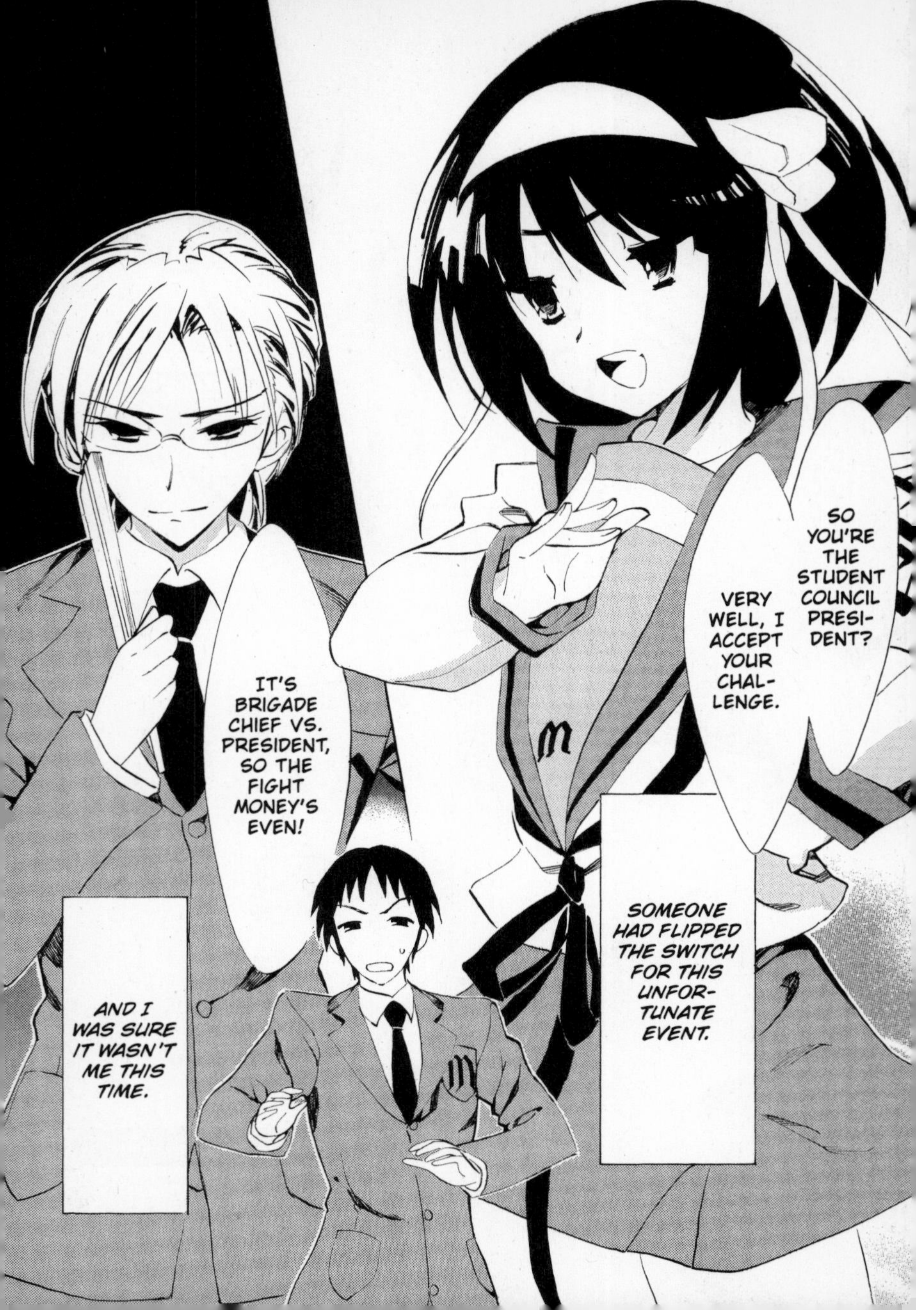
SO YOU'RE THE STUDENT COUNCIL PRESIDENT?
VERY WELL, I ACCEPT YOUR CHALLENGE.
IT'S BRIGADE CHIEF VS. PRESIDENT, SO THE FIGHT MONEY'S EVEN!
SOMEONE HAD FLIPPED THE SWITCH FOR THIS UNFORTUNATE EVENT.
AND I WAS SURE IT WASN'T ME THIS TIME.

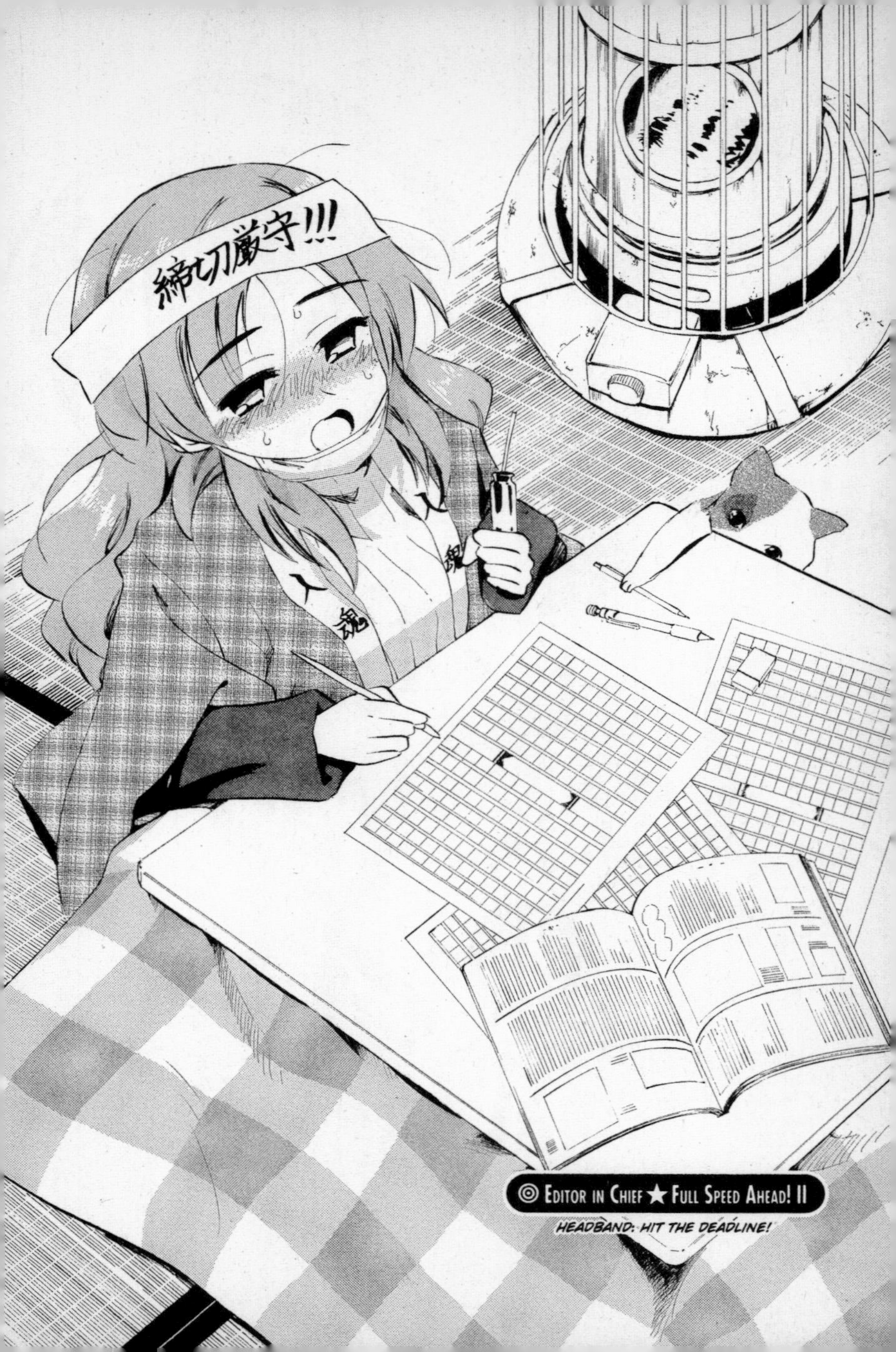
締切厳守!!!
魂
魂
◎ Editor in Chief ★ Full Speed Ahead! II
HEADBAND: HIT THE DEADLINE!

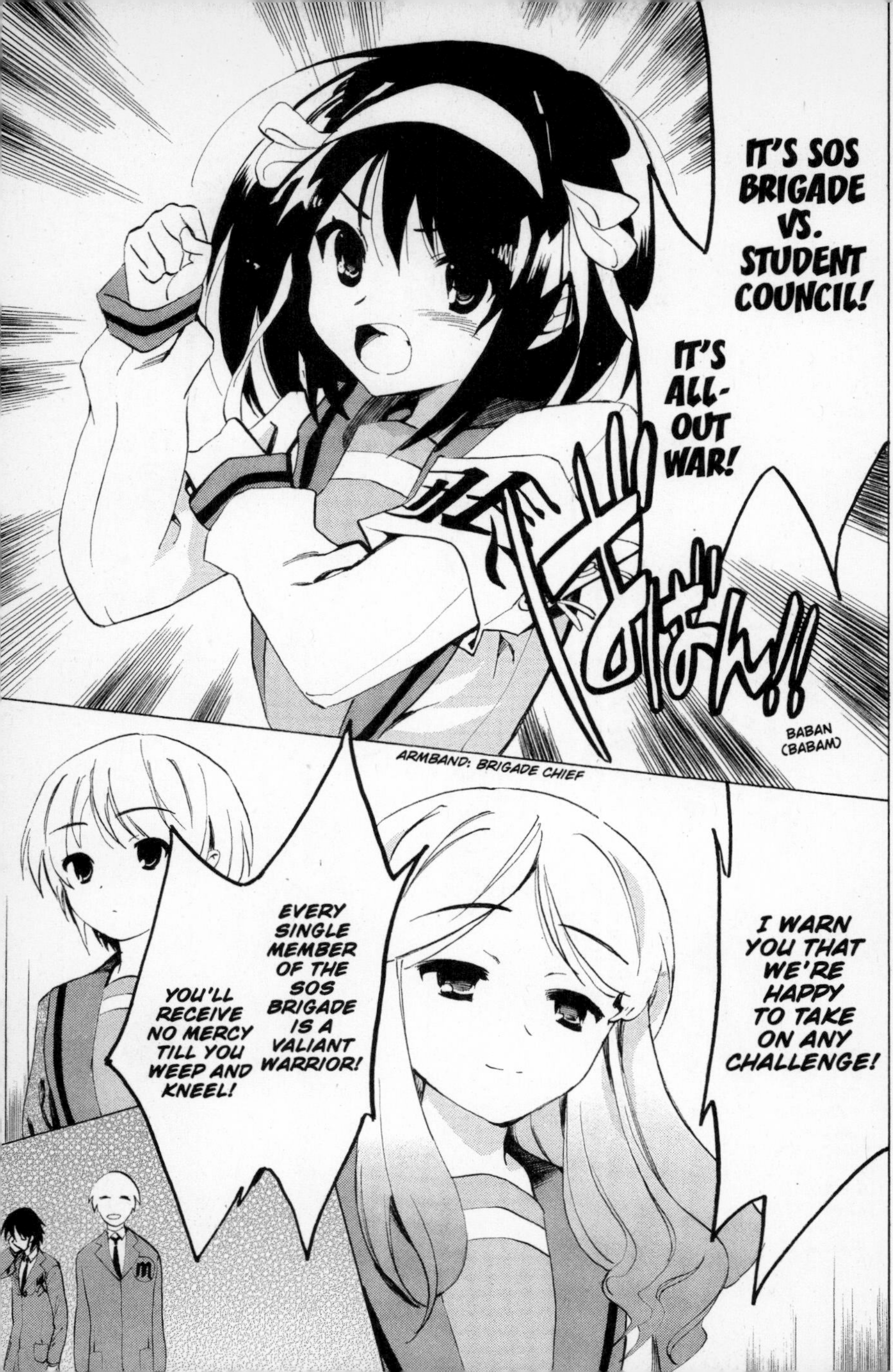
IT'S SOS BRIGADE VS. STUDENT COUNCIL!
IT'S ALL-OUT WAR!
ばばん!!
BABAN (BABAM)
ARMBAND: BRIGADE CHIEF
I WARN YOU THAT WE'RE HAPPY TO TAKE ON ANY CHALLENGE!
EVERY SINGLE MEMBER OF THE SOS BRIGADE IS A VALIANT WARRIOR!
YOU'LL RECEIVE NO MERCY TILL YOU WEEP AND KNEEL!

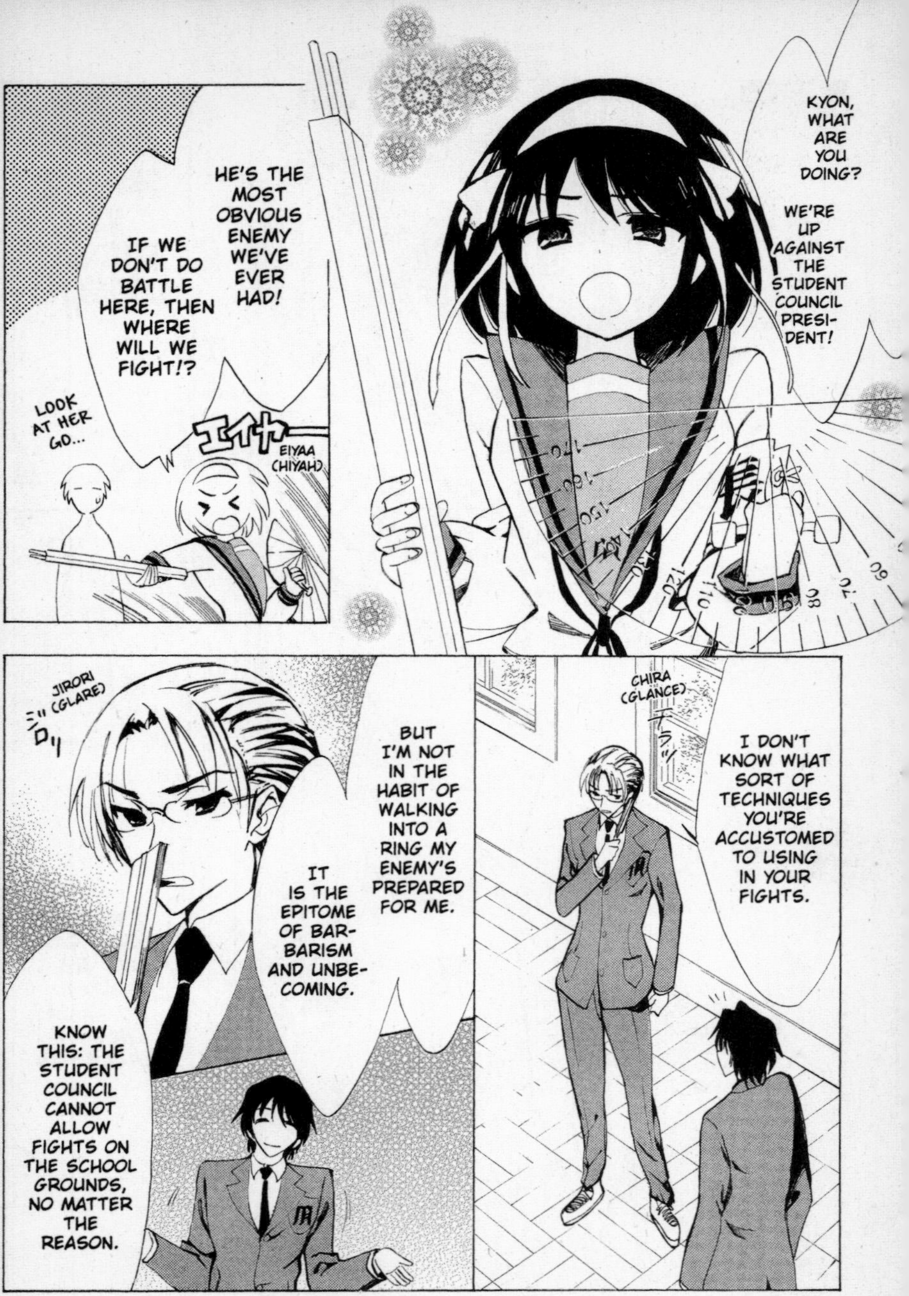
KYON, WHAT ARE YOU DOING?
WE'RE UP AGAINST THE STUDENT COUNCIL PRESIDENT!
HE'S THE MOST OBVIOUS ENEMY WE'VE EVER HAD!
IF WE DON'T DO BATTLE HERE, THEN WHERE WILL WE FIGHT!?
エイヤー
EIYAA (CHIYAH)
LOOK AT HER GO...
CHIRA (GLANCE)
チラッ
I DON'T KNOW WHAT SORT OF TECHNIQUES YOU'RE ACCUSTOMED TO USING IN YOUR FIGHTS.
JIRORI (GLARE)
ジロリ
BUT I'M NOT IN THE HABIT OF WALKING INTO A RING MY ENEMY'S PREPARED FOR ME.
IT IS THE EPITOME OF BAR-BARISM AND UNBE-COMING.
KNOW THIS: THE STUDENT COUNCIL CANNOT ALLOW FIGHTS ON THE SCHOOL GROUNDS, NO MATTER THE REASON.

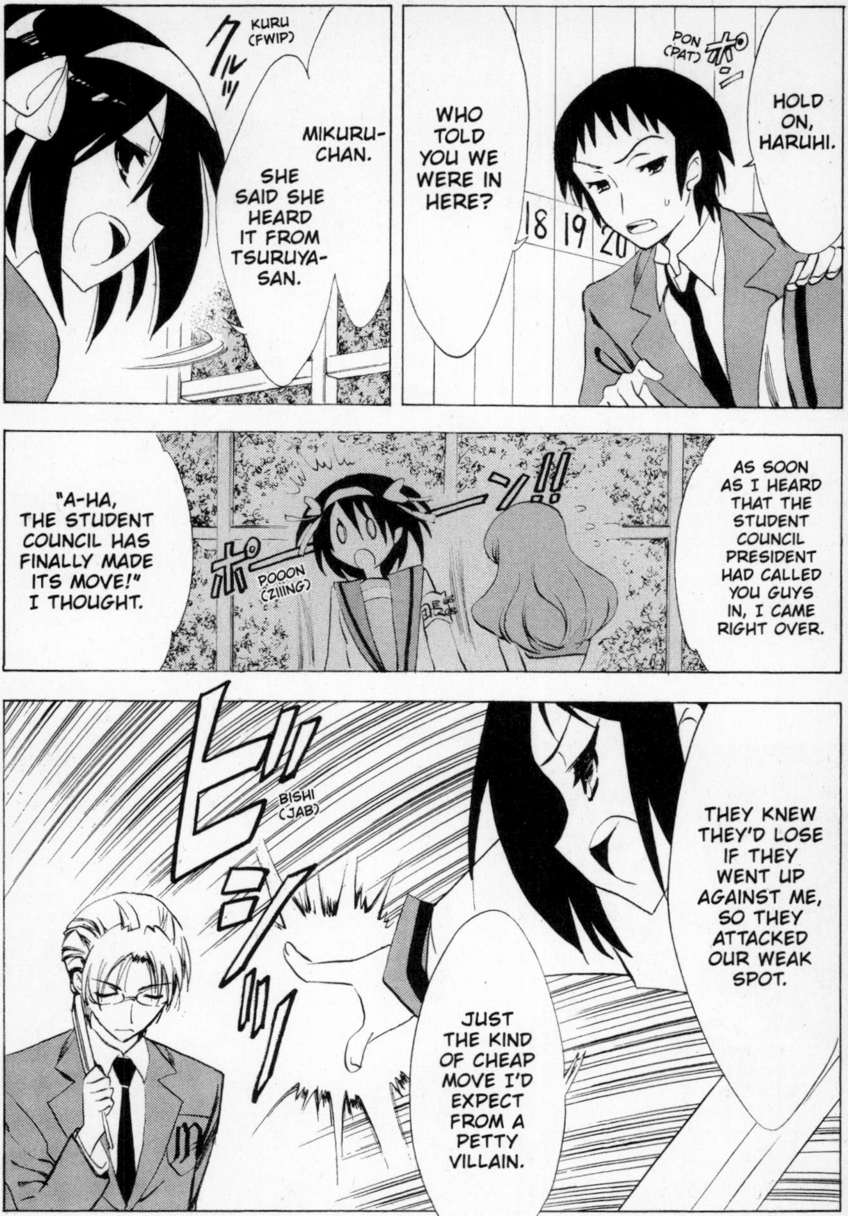

HOLD ON, HARUHI.
PON (PAT)
WHO TOLD YOU WE WERE IN HERE?
18 19 20
KURU (FWIP)
MIKURU-CHAN.
SHE SAID SHE HEARD IT FROM TSURUYA-SAN.
AS SOON AS I HEARD THAT THE STUDENT COUNCIL PRESIDENT HAD CALLED YOU GUYS IN, I CAME RIGHT OVER.
POOON (ZIIING)
"A-HA, THE STUDENT COUNCIL HAS FINALLY MADE ITS MOVE!" I THOUGHT.
THEY KNEW THEY'D LOSE IF THEY WENT UP AGAINST ME, SO THEY ATTACKED OUR WEAK SPOT.
BISHI (JAB)
JUST THE KIND OF CHEAP MOVE I'D EXPECT FROM A PETTY VILLAIN.

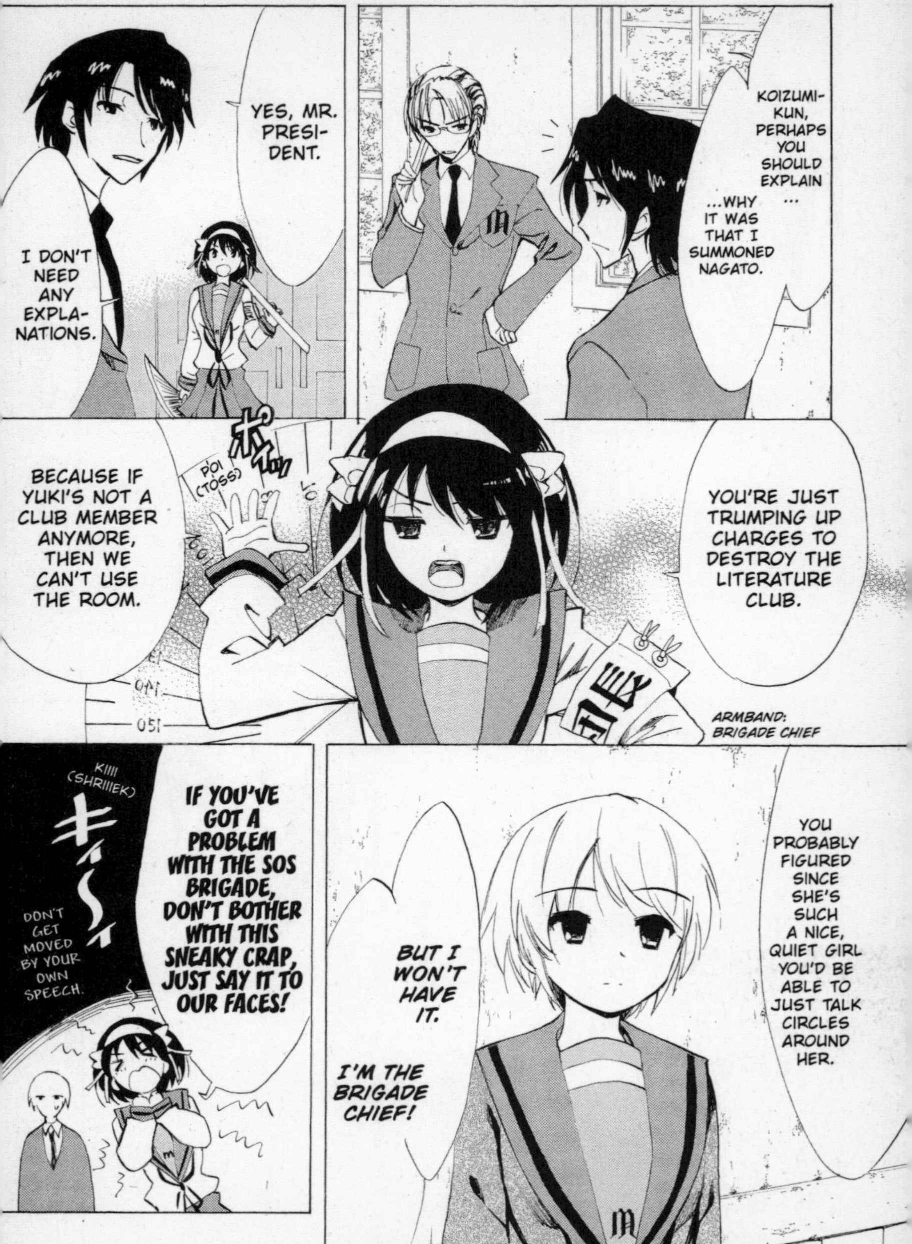
KOIZUMI-KUN, PERHAPS YOU SHOULD EXPLAIN ...
...WHY IT WAS THAT I SUMMONED NAGATO.
YES, MR. PRESIDENT.
I DON'T NEED ANY EXPLANATIONS.
YOU'RE JUST TRUMPING UP CHARGES TO DESTROY THE LITERATURE CLUB.
POI (TOSS)
BECAUSE IF YUKI'S NOT A CLUB MEMBER ANYMORE, THEN WE CAN'T USE THE ROOM.
ARMBAND: BRIGADE CHIEF
YOU PROBABLY FIGURED SINCE SHE'S SUCH A NICE, QUIET GIRL YOU'D BE ABLE TO JUST TALK CIRCLES AROUND HER.
BUT I WON'T HAVE IT.
I'M THE BRIGADE CHIEF!
KIIII (SHRIIIEK)
IF YOU'VE GOT A PROBLEM WITH THE SOS BRIGADE, DON'T BOTHER WITH THIS SNEAKY CRAP, JUST SAY IT TO OUR FACES!
DON'T GET MOVED BY YOUR OWN SPEECH.

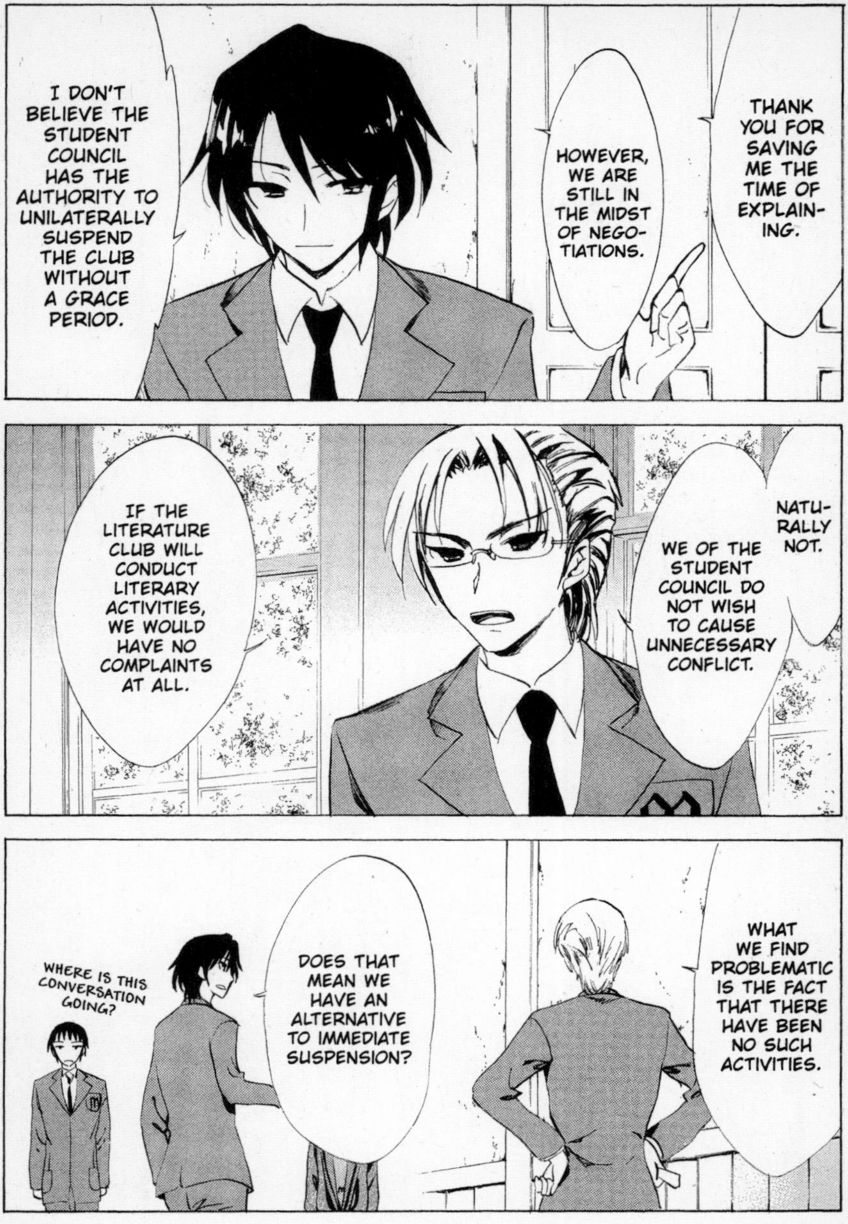
THANK YOU FOR SAVING ME THE TIME OF EXPLAINING.
HOWEVER, WE ARE STILL IN THE MIDST OF NEGOTIATIONS.
I DON'T BELIEVE THE STUDENT COUNCIL HAS THE AUTHORITY TO UNILATERALLY SUSPEND THE CLUB WITHOUT A GRACE PERIOD.
NATURALLY NOT.
WE OF THE STUDENT COUNCIL DO NOT WISH TO CAUSE UNNECESSARY CONFLICT.
IF THE LITERATURE CLUB WILL CONDUCT LITERARY ACTIVITIES, WE WOULD HAVE NO COMPLAINTS AT ALL.
WHAT WE FIND PROBLEMATIC IS THE FACT THAT THERE HAVE BEEN NO SUCH ACTIVITIES.
DOES THAT MEAN WE HAVE AN ALTERNATIVE TO IMMEDIATE SUSPENSION?
WHERE IS THIS CONVERSATION GOING?

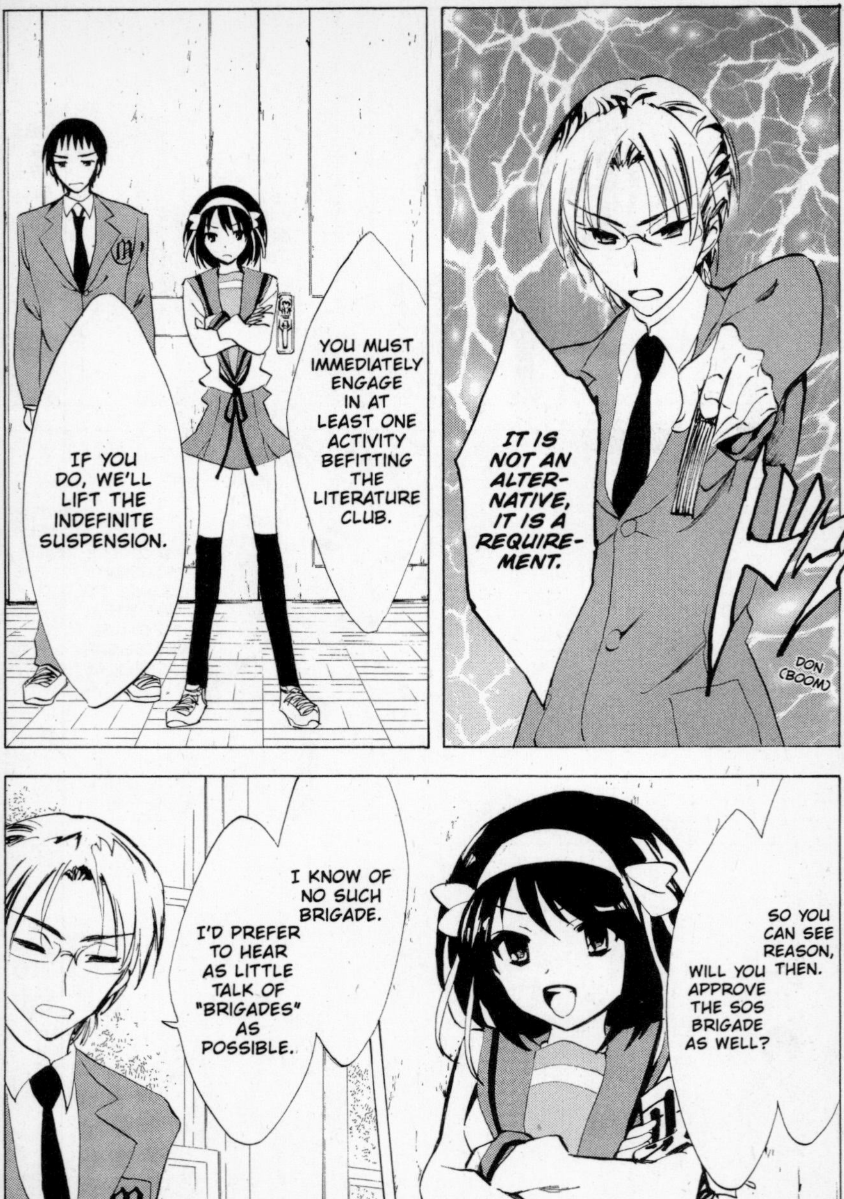
IT IS NOT AN ALTER-NATIVE, IT IS A REQUIRE-MENT.
DON (BOOM)
YOU MUST IMMEDIATELY ENGAGE IN AT LEAST ONE ACTIVITY BEFITTING THE LITERATURE CLUB.
IF YOU DO, WE'LL LIFT THE INDEFINITE SUSPENSION.
SO YOU CAN SEE REASON, THEN.
WILL YOU APPROVE THE SOS BRIGADE AS WELL?
I KNOW OF NO SUCH BRIGADE.
I'D PREFER TO HEAR AS LITTLE TALK OF "BRIGADES" AS POSSIBLE.

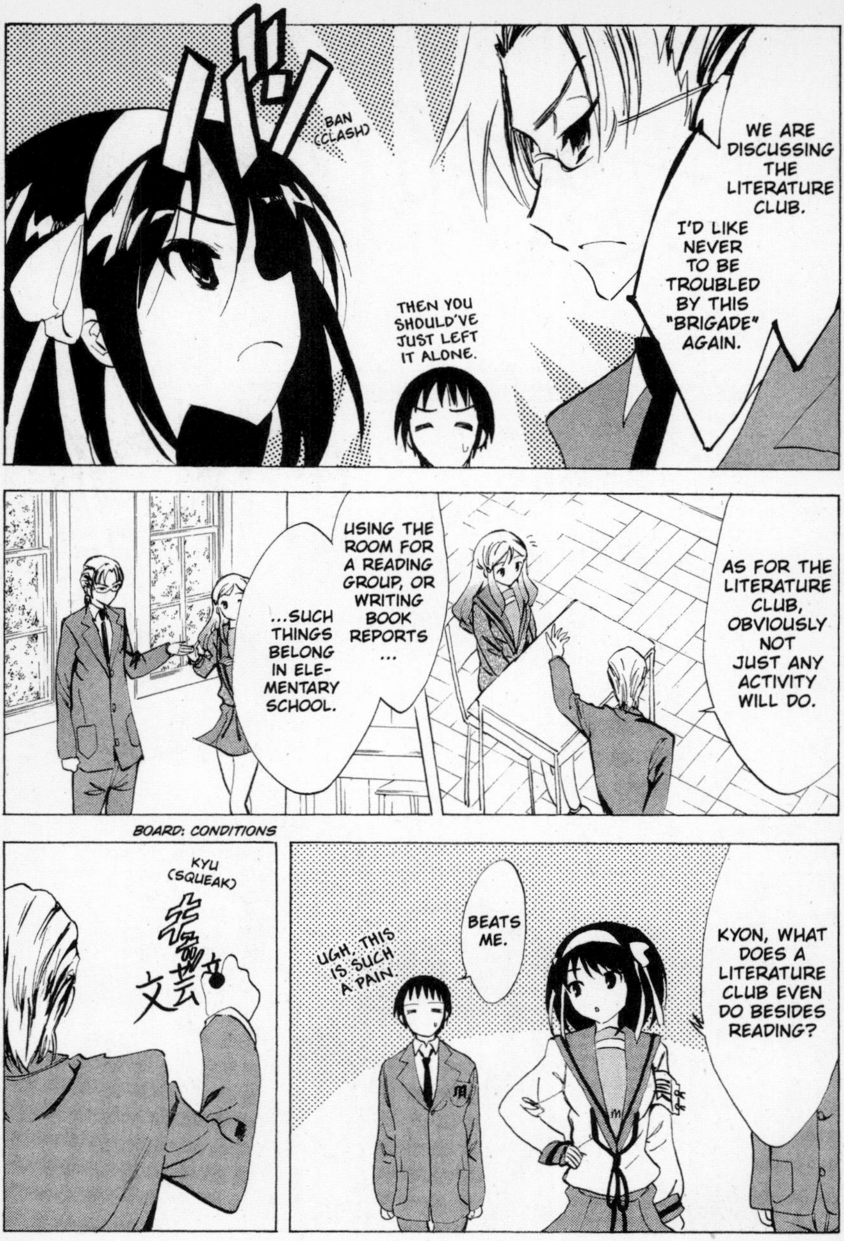
WE ARE DISCUSSING THE LITERATURE CLUB.
I'D LIKE NEVER TO BE TROUBLED BY THIS "BRIGADE" AGAIN.
BAN (CLASH)
THEN YOU SHOULD'VE JUST LEFT IT ALONE.
AS FOR THE LITERATURE CLUB, OBVIOUSLY NOT JUST ANY ACTIVITY WILL DO.
USING THE ROOM FOR A READING GROUP, OR WRITING BOOK REPORTS ...
...SUCH THINGS BELONG IN ELE-MENTARY SCHOOL.
KYON, WHAT DOES A LITERATURE CLUB EVEN DO BESIDES READING?
BEATS ME.
UGH, THIS IS SUCH A PAIN.
BOARD: CONDITIONS
KYU (SQUEAK)
文芸

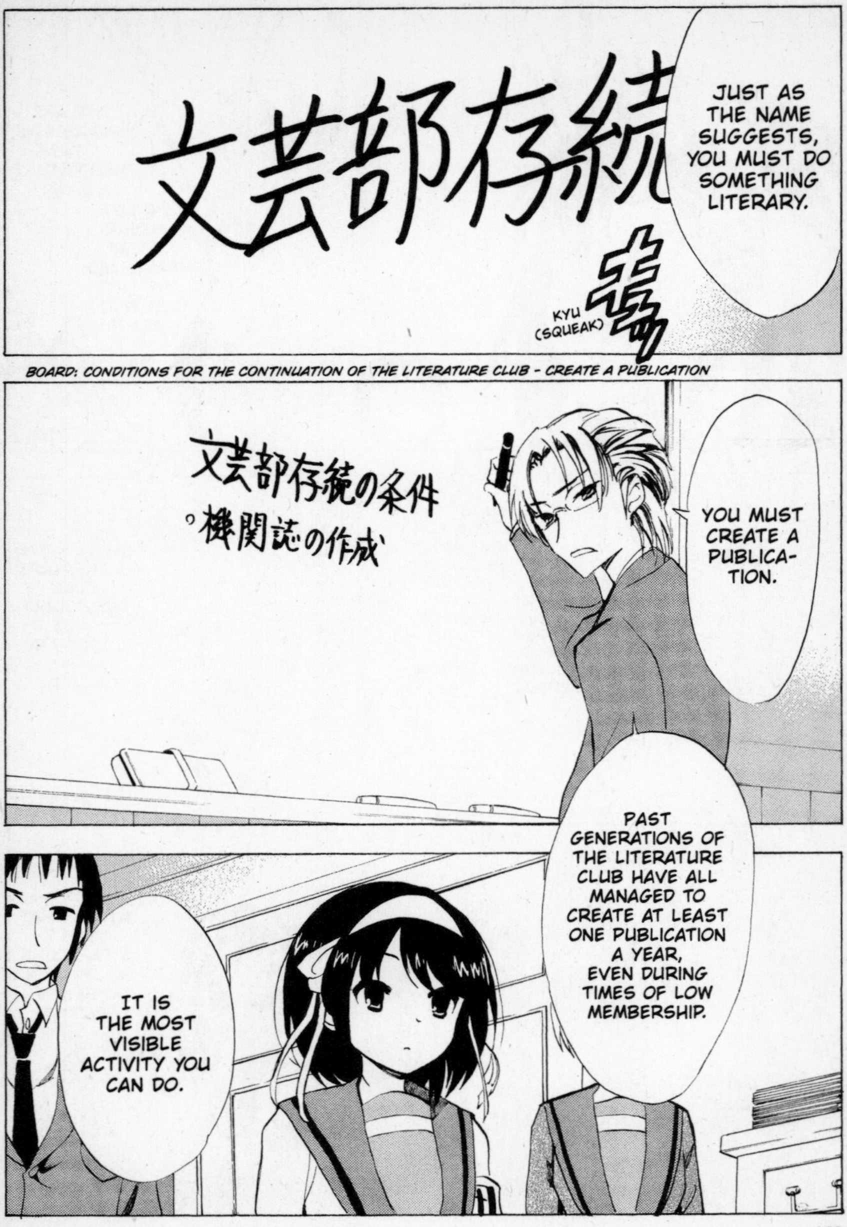
文芸部存続
JUST AS THE NAME SUGGESTS, YOU MUST DO SOMETHING LITERARY.
KYU (SQUEAK)
BOARD: CONDITIONS FOR THE CONTINUATION OF THE LITERATURE CLUB - CREATE A PUBLICATION
文芸部存続の条件
。機関誌の作成
YOU MUST CREATE A PUBLICA-TION.
PAST GENERATIONS OF THE LITERATURE CLUB HAVE ALL MANAGED TO CREATE AT LEAST ONE PUBLICATION A YEAR, EVEN DURING TIMES OF LOW MEMBERSHIP.
IT IS THE MOST VISIBLE ACTIVITY YOU CAN DO.

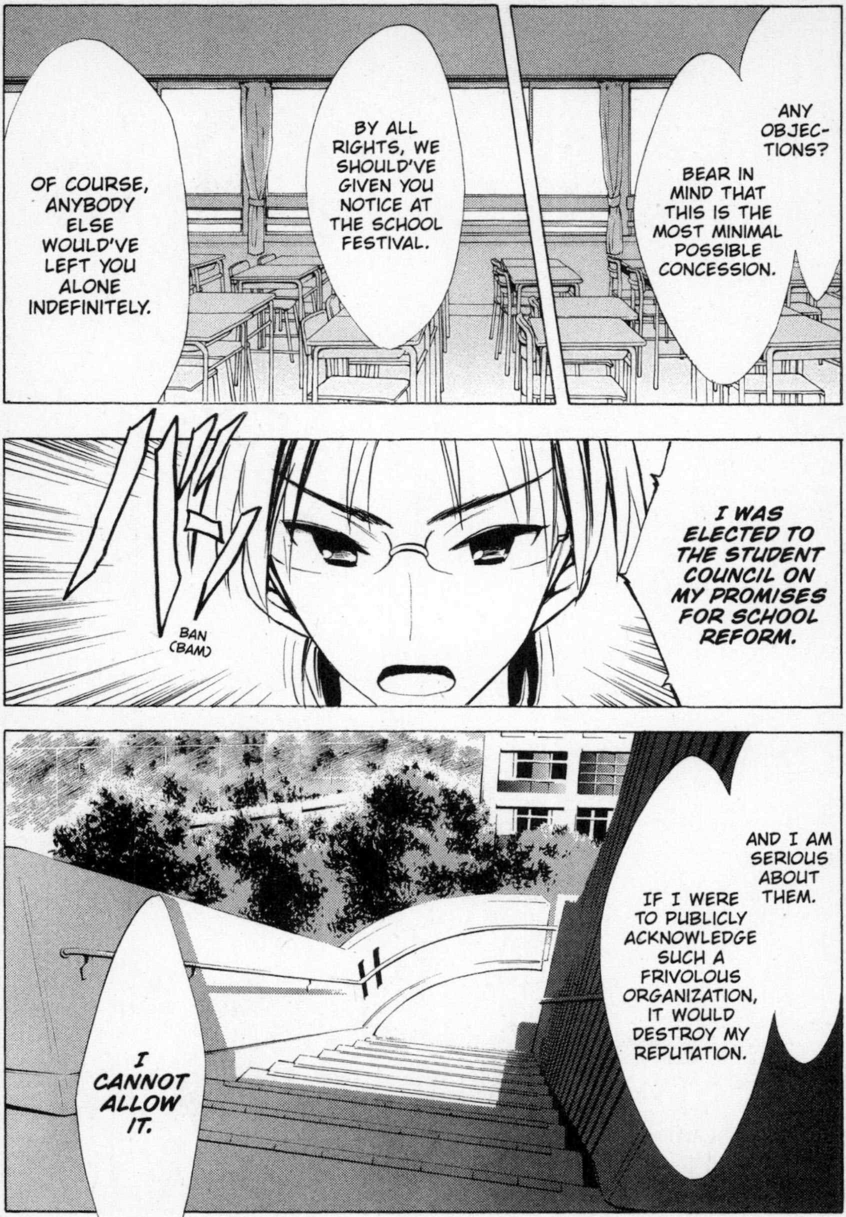

ANY OBJECTIONS?
BEAR IN MIND THAT THIS IS THE MOST MINIMAL POSSIBLE CONCESSION.
BY ALL RIGHTS, WE SHOULD'VE GIVEN YOU NOTICE AT THE SCHOOL FESTIVAL.
OF COURSE, ANYBODY ELSE WOULD'VE LEFT YOU ALONE INDEFINITELY.
I WAS ELECTED TO THE STUDENT COUNCIL ON MY PROMISES FOR SCHOOL REFORM.
BAN (BAM)
AND I AM SERIOUS ABOUT THEM.
IF I WERE TO PUBLICLY ACKNOWLEDGE SUCH A FRIVOLOUS ORGANIZATION, IT WOULD DESTROY MY REPUTATION.
I CANNOT ALLOW IT.

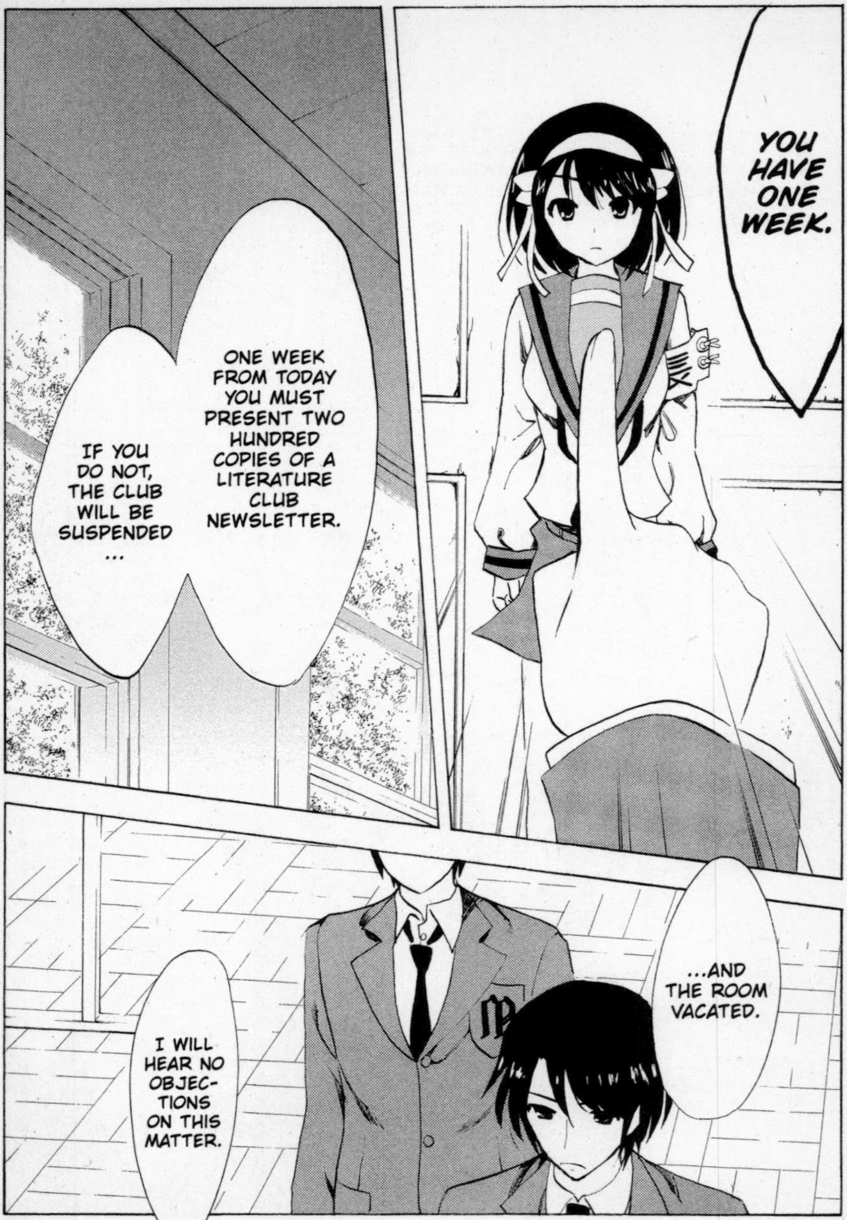
YOU HAVE ONE WEEK.
ONE WEEK FROM TODAY YOU MUST PRESENT TWO HUNDRED COPIES OF A LITERATURE CLUB NEWSLETTER.
IF YOU DO NOT, THE CLUB WILL BE SUSPENDED ...
...AND THE ROOM VACATED.
I WILL HEAR NO OBJEC- TIONS ON THIS MATTER.

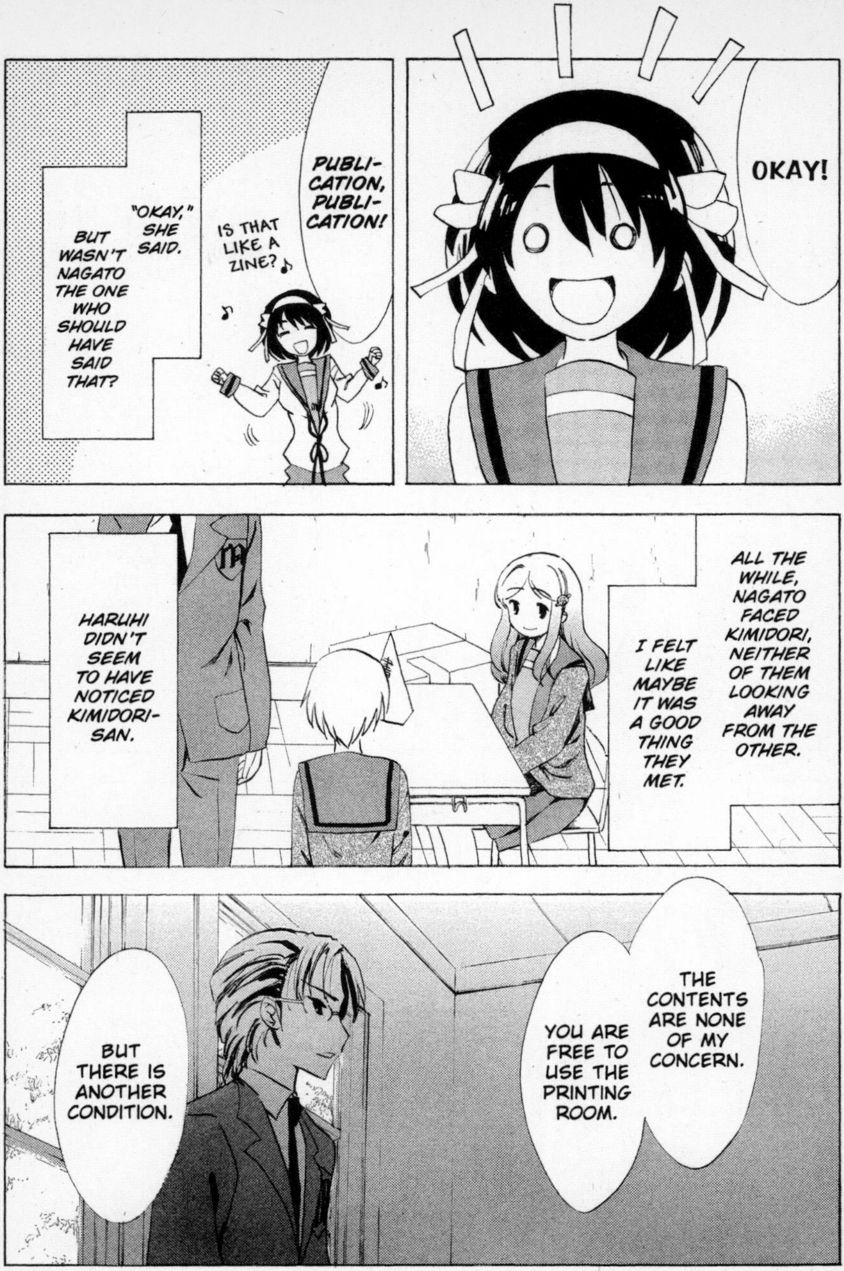
OKAY!
PUBLICATION, PUBLICATION!
IS THAT LIKE A ZINE? ♪
"OKAY," SHE SAID.
BUT WASN'T NAGATO THE ONE WHO SHOULD HAVE SAID THAT?
ALL THE WHILE, NAGATO FACED KIMIDORI, NEITHER OF THEM LOOKING AWAY FROM THE OTHER.
I FELT LIKE MAYBE IT WAS A GOOD THING THEY MET.
HARUHI DIDN'T SEEM TO HAVE NOTICED KIMIDORI-SAN.
THE CONTENTS ARE NONE OF MY CONCERN.
YOU ARE FREE TO USE THE PRINTING ROOM.
BUT THERE IS ANOTHER CONDITION.

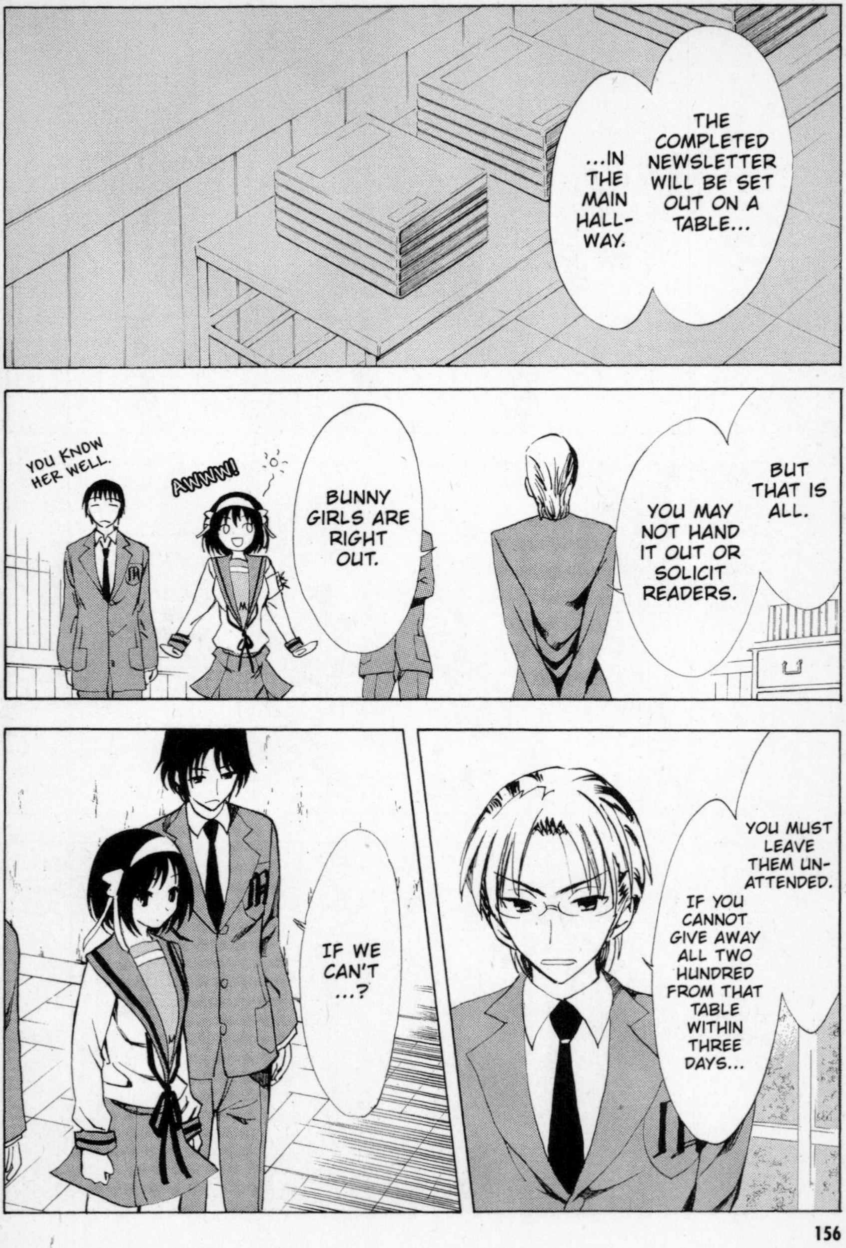
THE COMPLETED NEWSLETTER WILL BE SET OUT ON A TABLE...
...IN THE MAIN HALL-WAY.
BUT THAT IS ALL.
YOU MAY NOT HAND IT OUT OR SOLICIT READERS.
BUNNY GIRLS ARE RIGHT OUT.
AWWW!
YOU KNOW HER WELL.
YOU MUST LEAVE THEM UN-ATTENDED.
IF YOU CANNOT GIVE AWAY ALL TWO HUNDRED FROM THAT TABLE WITHIN THREE DAYS...
IF WE CAN'T ...?

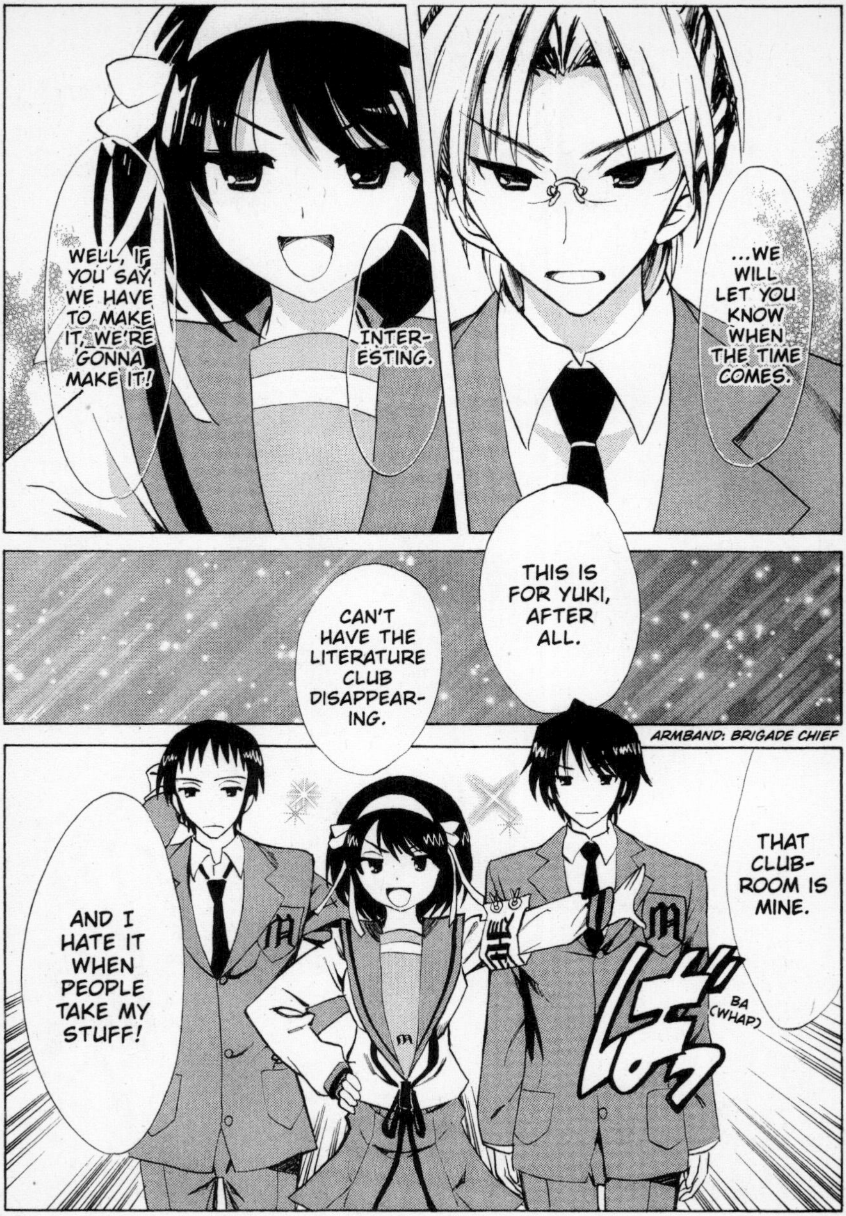
...WE WILL LET YOU KNOW WHEN THE TIME COMES.
INTER-ESTING.
WELL, IF YOU SAY WE HAVE TO MAKE IT, WE'RE GONNA MAKE IT!
THIS IS FOR YUKI, AFTER ALL.
CAN'T HAVE THE LITERATURE CLUB DISAPPEAR-ING.
ARMBAND: BRIGADE CHIEF
THAT CLUB-ROOM IS MINE.
BA (WHAP)
AND I HATE IT WHEN PEOPLE TAKE MY STUFF!

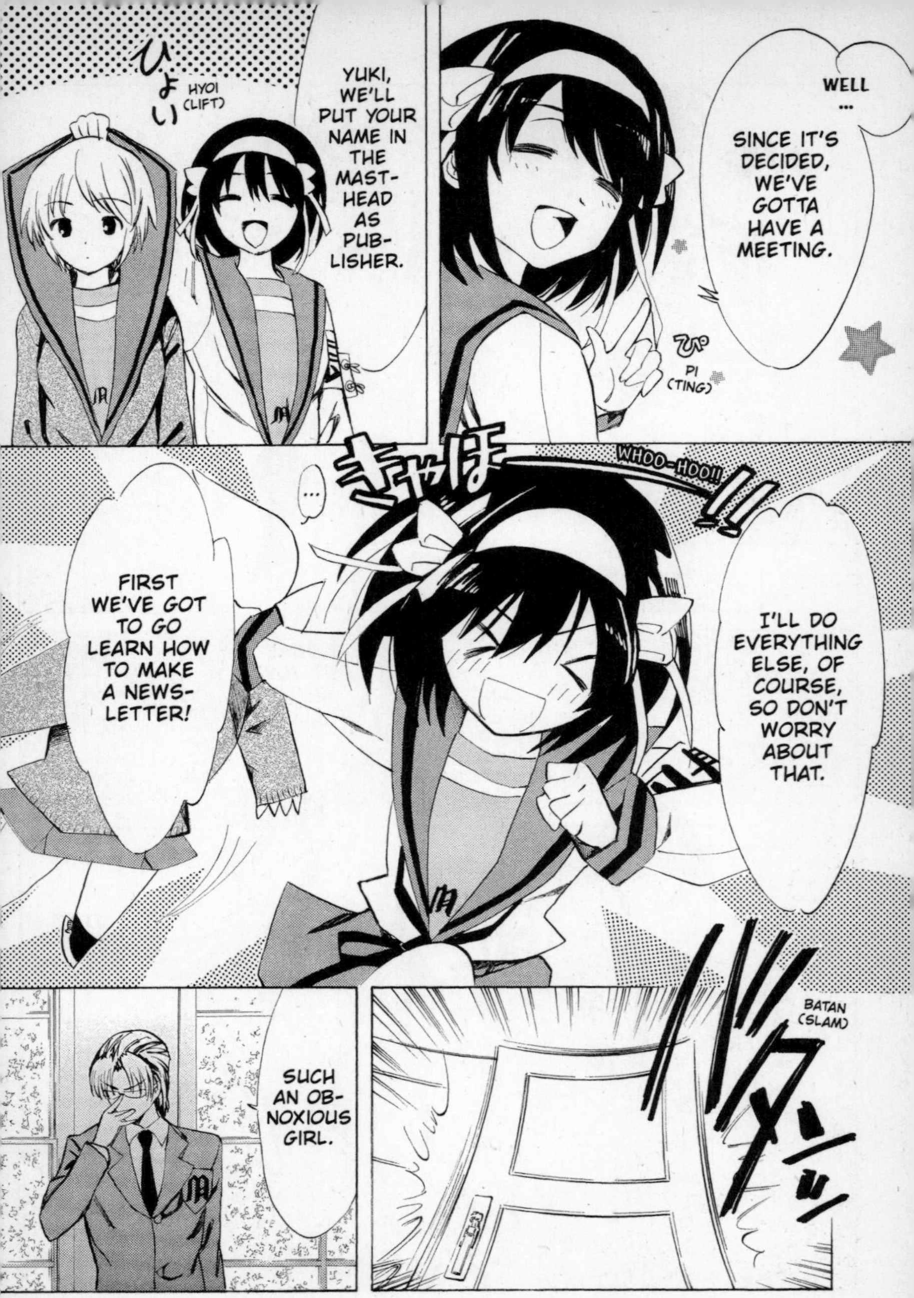
WELL ...
SINCE IT'S DECIDED, WE'VE GOTTA HAVE A MEETING.
ぴ
PI (TING)
YUKI, WE'LL PUT YOUR NAME IN THE MAST-HEAD AS PUB-LISHER.
ひょい
HYOI (LIFT)
きゃほ
WHOO-HOO!!
I'LL DO EVERYTHING ELSE, OF COURSE, SO DON'T WORRY ABOUT THAT.
...
FIRST WE'VE GOT TO GO LEARN HOW TO MAKE A NEWS-LETTER!
BATAN (SLAM)
SUCH AN OB-NOXIOUS GIRL.

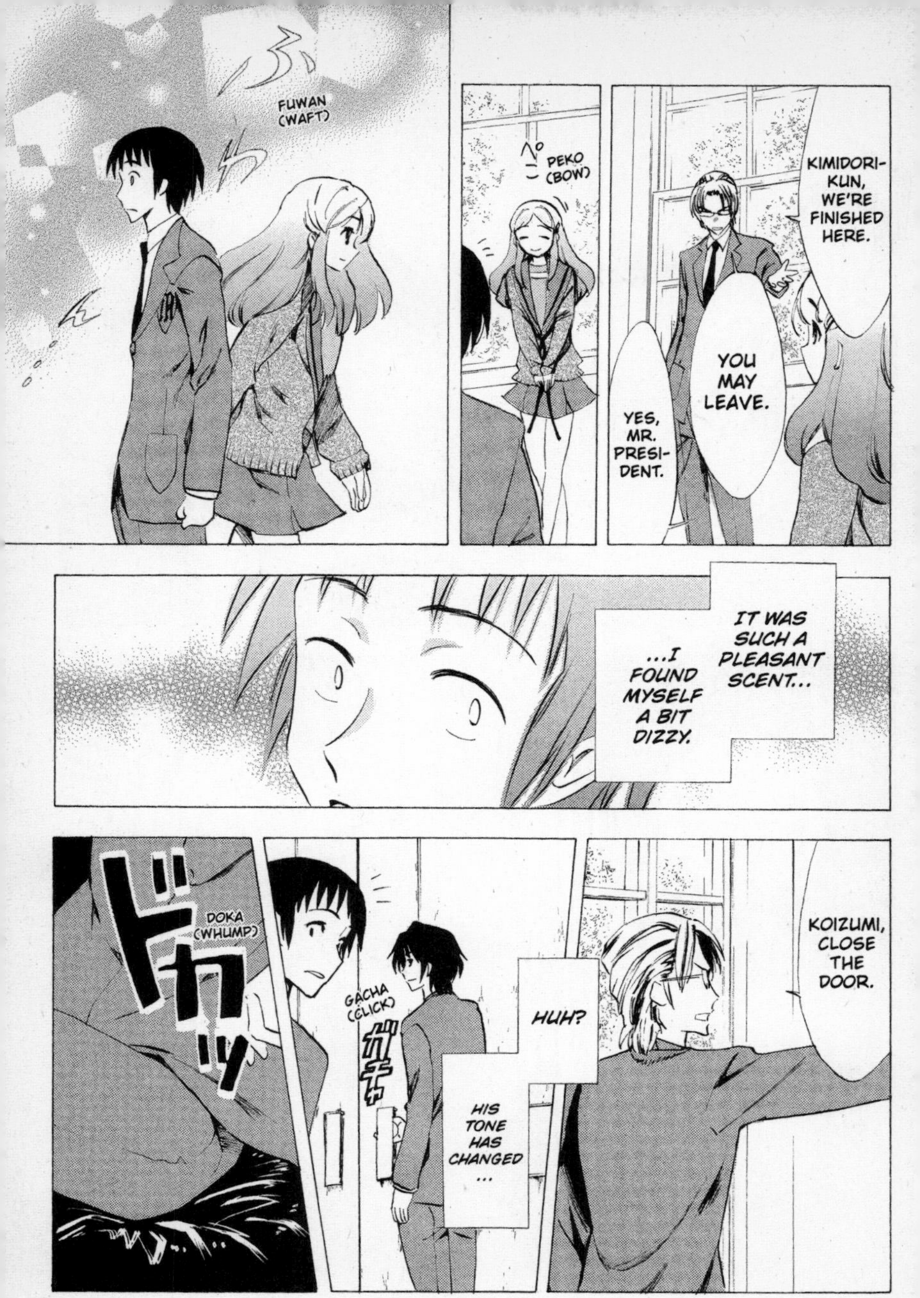
KIMIDORI-KUN, WE'RE FINISHED HERE.
YOU MAY LEAVE.
YES, MR. PRESIDENT.
PEKO (BOW)
FUWAN (WAFT)
IT WAS SUCH A PLEASANT SCENT...
...I FOUND MYSELF A BIT DIZZY.
KOIZUMI, CLOSE THE DOOR.
HUH?
HIS TONE HAS CHANGED...
GACHA (CLICK)
DOKA (WHUMP)

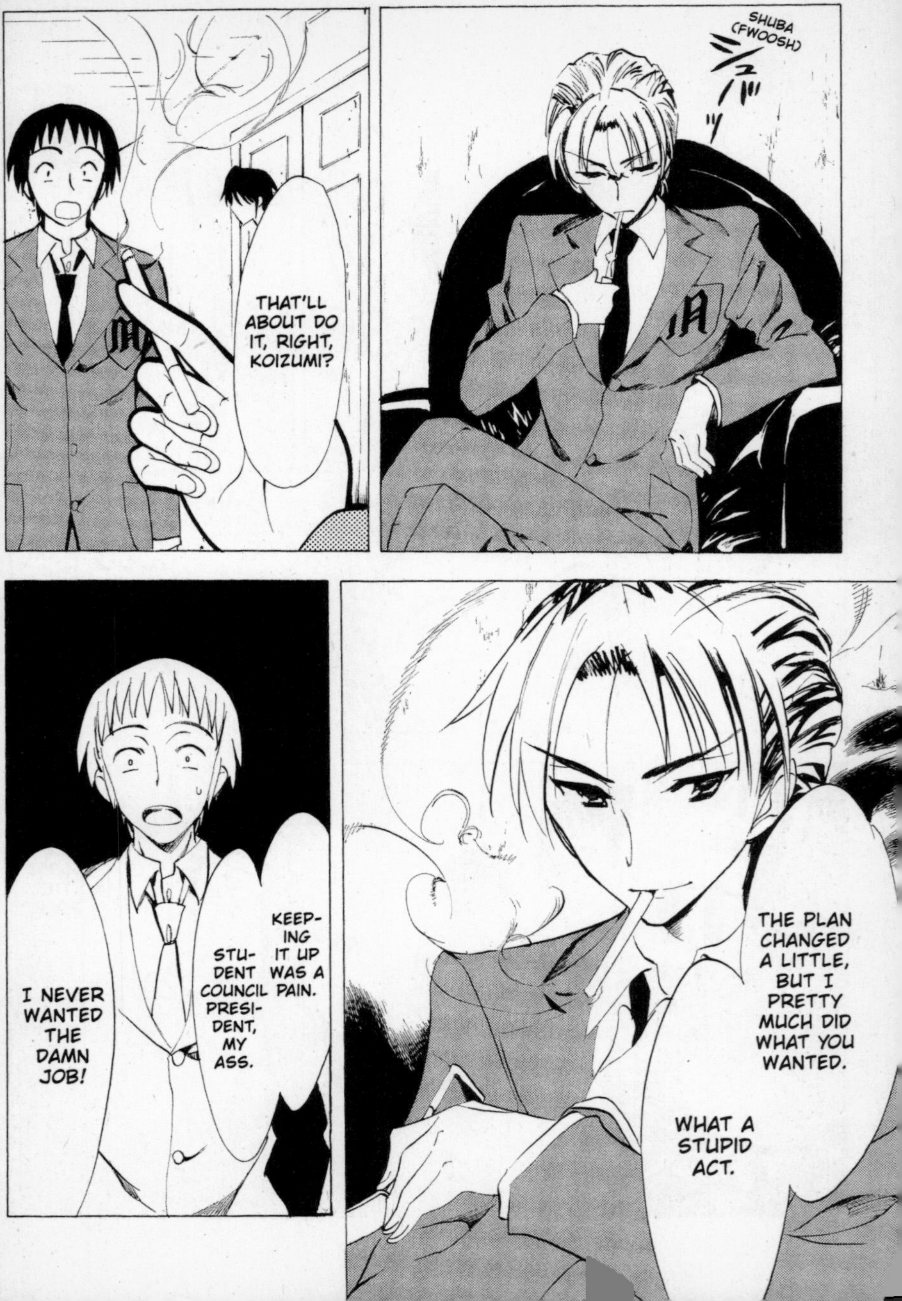
SHUBA (FWOOSH)
THAT'LL ABOUT DO IT, RIGHT, KOIZUMI?
THE PLAN CHANGED A LITTLE, BUT I PRETTY MUCH DID WHAT YOU WANTED.
WHAT A STUPID ACT.
KEEPING IT UP WAS A PAIN.
STUDENT COUNCIL PRESIDENT, MY ASS.
I NEVER WANTED THE DAMN JOB!

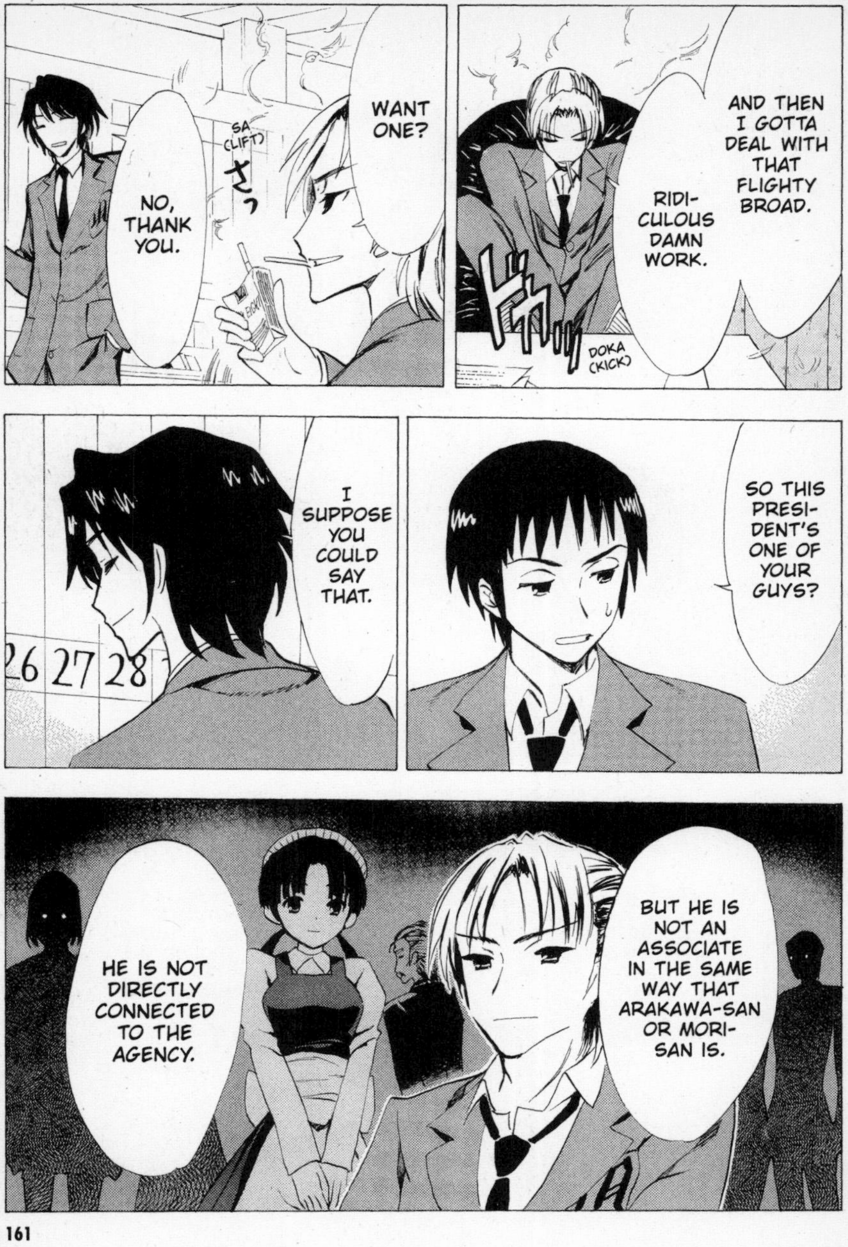
AND THEN I GOTTA DEAL WITH THAT FLIGHTY BROAD.
RIDICULOUS DAMN WORK.
ドカッ
DOKA (KICK)
WANT ONE?
SA (LIFT)
さっ
NO, THANK YOU.
SO THIS PRESIDENT'S ONE OF YOUR GUYS?
I SUPPOSE YOU COULD SAY THAT.
26 27 28
BUT HE IS NOT AN ASSOCIATE IN THE SAME WAY THAT ARAKAWA-SAN OR MORI-SAN IS.
HE IS NOT DIRECTLY CONNECTED TO THE AGENCY.

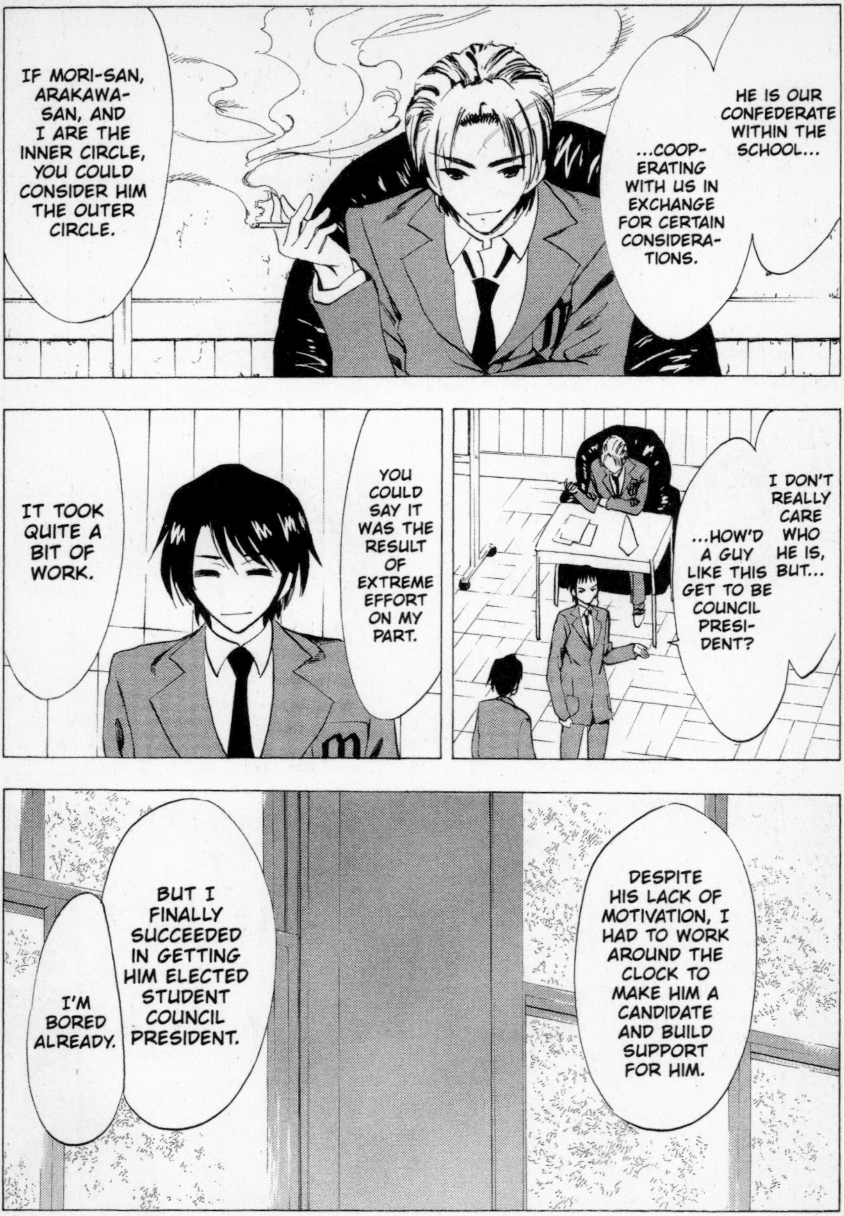
HE IS OUR CONFEDERATE WITHIN THE SCHOOL...
...COOPERATING WITH US IN EXCHANGE FOR CERTAIN CONSIDERATIONS.
IF MORI-SAN, ARAKAWA-SAN, AND I ARE THE INNER CIRCLE, YOU COULD CONSIDER HIM THE OUTER CIRCLE.
I DON'T REALLY CARE WHO HE IS, BUT...
...HOW'D A GUY LIKE THIS GET TO BE COUNCIL PRESIDENT?
YOU COULD SAY IT WAS THE RESULT OF EXTREME EFFORT ON MY PART.
IT TOOK QUITE A BIT OF WORK.
DESPITE HIS LACK OF MOTIVATION, I HAD TO WORK AROUND THE CLOCK TO MAKE HIM A CANDIDATE AND BUILD SUPPORT FOR HIM.
BUT I FINALLY SUCCEEDED IN GETTING HIM ELECTED STUDENT COUNCIL PRESIDENT.
I'M BORED ALREADY.

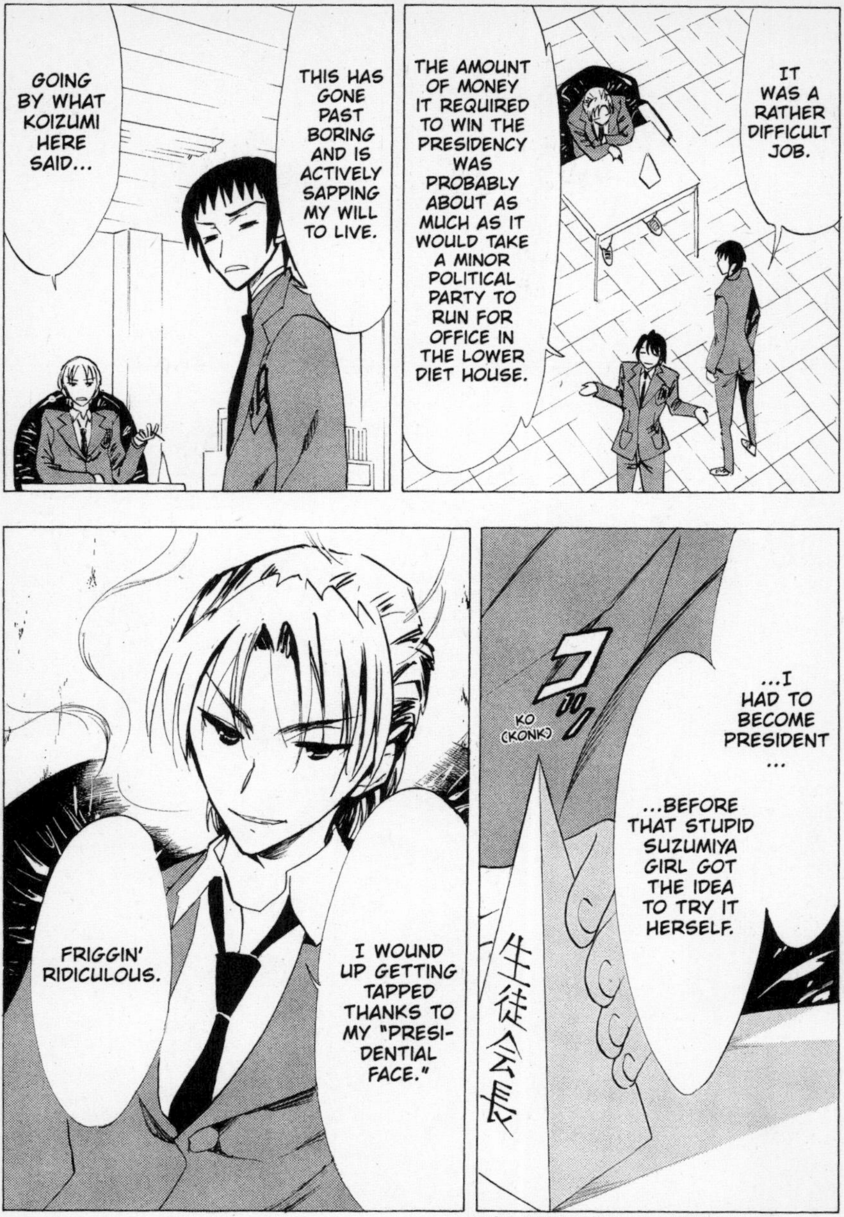
IT WAS A RATHER DIFFICULT JOB.
THE AMOUNT OF MONEY IT REQUIRED TO WIN THE PRESIDENCY WAS PROBABLY ABOUT AS MUCH AS IT WOULD TAKE A MINOR POLITICAL PARTY TO RUN FOR OFFICE IN THE LOWER DIET HOUSE.
THIS HAS GONE PAST BORING AND IS ACTIVELY SAPPING MY WILL TO LIVE.
GOING BY WHAT KOIZUMI HERE SAID...
...I HAD TO BECOME PRESIDENT...
KO (KONK)
...BEFORE THAT STUPID SUZUMIYA GIRL GOT THE IDEA TO TRY IT HERSELF.
生徒会長
I WOUND UP GETTING TAPPED THANKS TO MY "PRESIDENTIAL FACE."
FRIGGIN' RIDICULOUS.

SIGN: STUDENT COUNCIL PRESIDENT

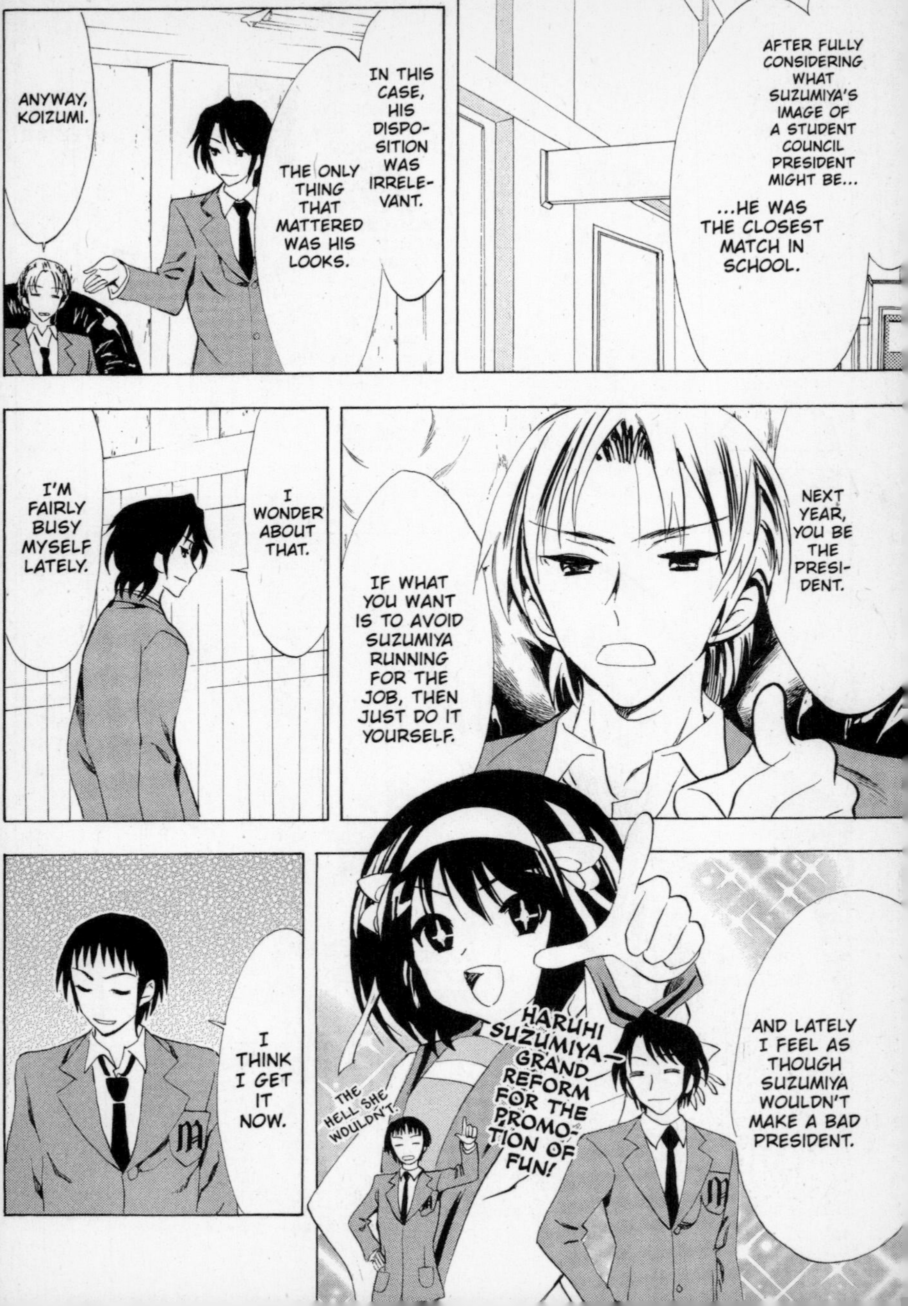
AFTER FULLY CONSIDERING WHAT SUZUMIYA'S IMAGE OF A STUDENT COUNCIL PRESIDENT MIGHT BE...
...HE WAS THE CLOSEST MATCH IN SCHOOL.
IN THIS CASE, HIS DISPOSITION WAS IRRELEVANT.
THE ONLY THING THAT MATTERED WAS HIS LOOKS.
ANYWAY, KOIZUMI.
NEXT YEAR, YOU BE THE PRESIDENT.
IF WHAT YOU WANT IS TO AVOID SUZUMIYA RUNNING FOR THE JOB, THEN JUST DO IT YOURSELF.
I WONDER ABOUT THAT.
I'M FAIRLY BUSY MYSELF LATELY.
AND LATELY I FEEL AS THOUGH SUZUMIYA WOULDN'T MAKE A BAD PRESIDENT.
HARUHI SUZUMIYA—GRAND REFORM FOR THE PROMOTION OF FUN!
THE HELL SHE WOULDN'T.
I THINK I GET IT NOW.

BOARD: CONDITIONS FOR THE CONTINUATION OF THE LITERATURE CLUB - CREATE A PUBLICATION - WITHIN ONE WEEK, PRINT TWO HUNDRED COPIES - LEAVE COPIES ON A TABLE IN THE MAIN HALLWAY

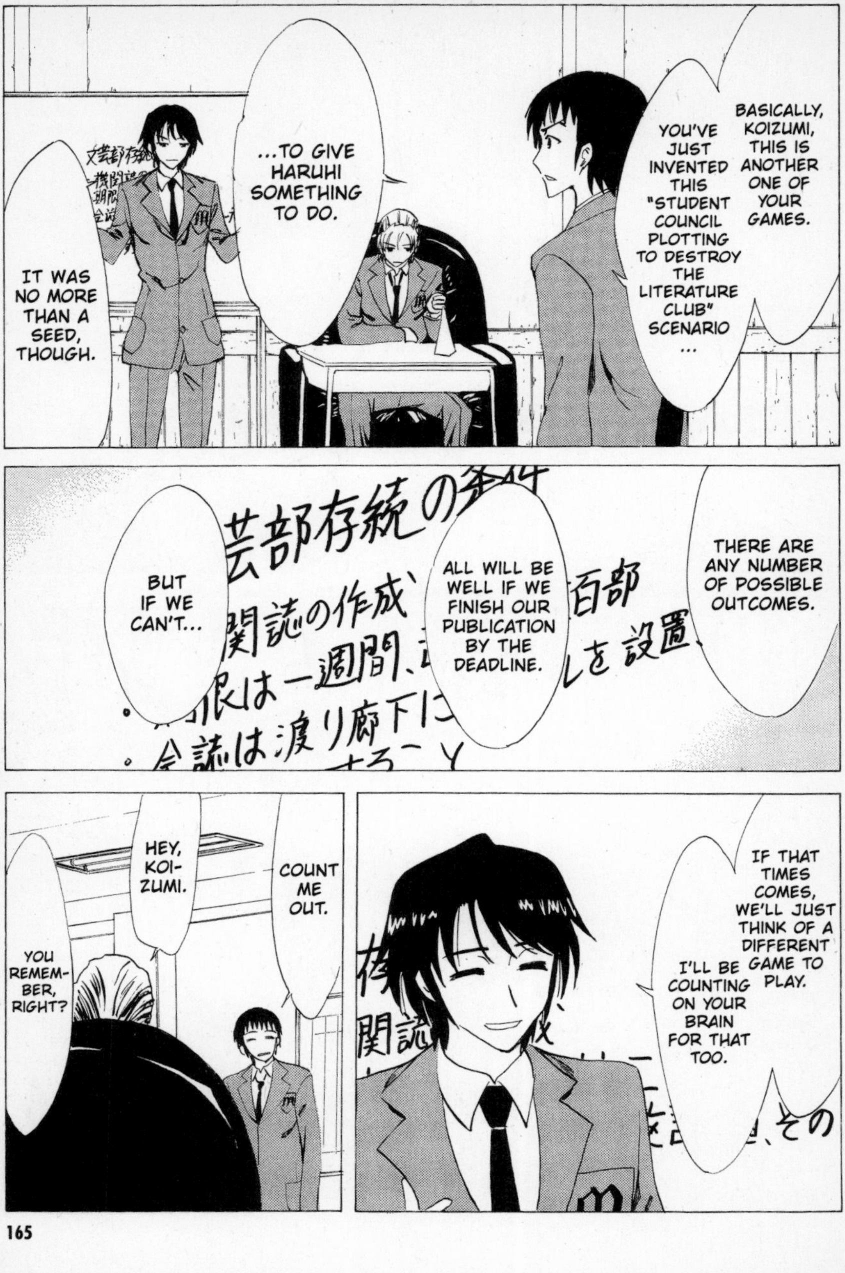
BASICALLY, KOIZUMI, THIS IS ANOTHER ONE OF YOUR GAMES.
YOU'VE JUST INVENTED THIS "STUDENT COUNCIL PLOTTING TO DESTROY THE LITERATURE CLUB" SCENARIO ...
...TO GIVE HARUHI SOMETHING TO DO.
IT WAS NO MORE THAN A SEED, THOUGH.
THERE ARE ANY NUMBER OF POSSIBLE OUTCOMES.
ALL WILL BE WELL IF WE FINISH OUR PUBLICATION BY THE DEADLINE.
BUT IF WE CAN'T...
IF THAT TIMES COMES, WE'LL JUST THINK OF A DIFFERENT GAME TO PLAY.
I'LL BE COUNTING ON YOUR BRAIN FOR THAT TOO.
COUNT ME OUT.
HEY, KOI-ZUMI.
YOU REMEMBER, RIGHT?

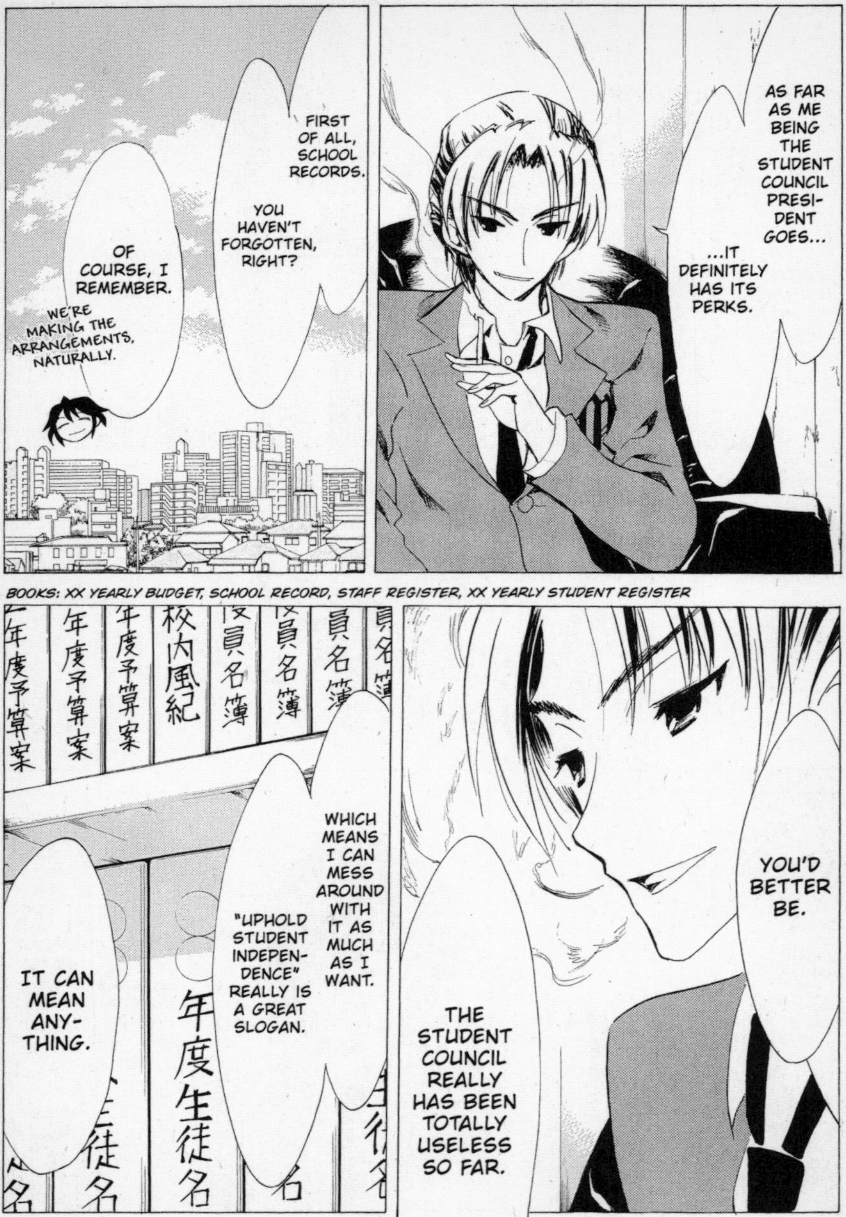
AS FAR AS ME BEING THE STUDENT COUNCIL PRESI-DENT GOES...
...IT DEFINITELY HAS ITS PERKS.
FIRST OF ALL, SCHOOL RECORDS.
YOU HAVEN'T FORGOTTEN, RIGHT?
OF COURSE, I REMEMBER.
WE'RE MAKING THE ARRANGEMENTS, NATURALLY.
BOOKS: XX YEARLY BUDGET, SCHOOL RECORD, STAFF REGISTER, XX YEARLY STUDENT REGISTER
YOU'D BETTER BE.
THE STUDENT COUNCIL REALLY HAS BEEN TOTALLY USELESS SO FAR.
WHICH MEANS I CAN MESS AROUND WITH IT AS MUCH AS I WANT.
"UPHOLD STUDENT INDEPEN-DENCE" REALLY IS A GREAT SLOGAN.
IT CAN MEAN ANY-THING.

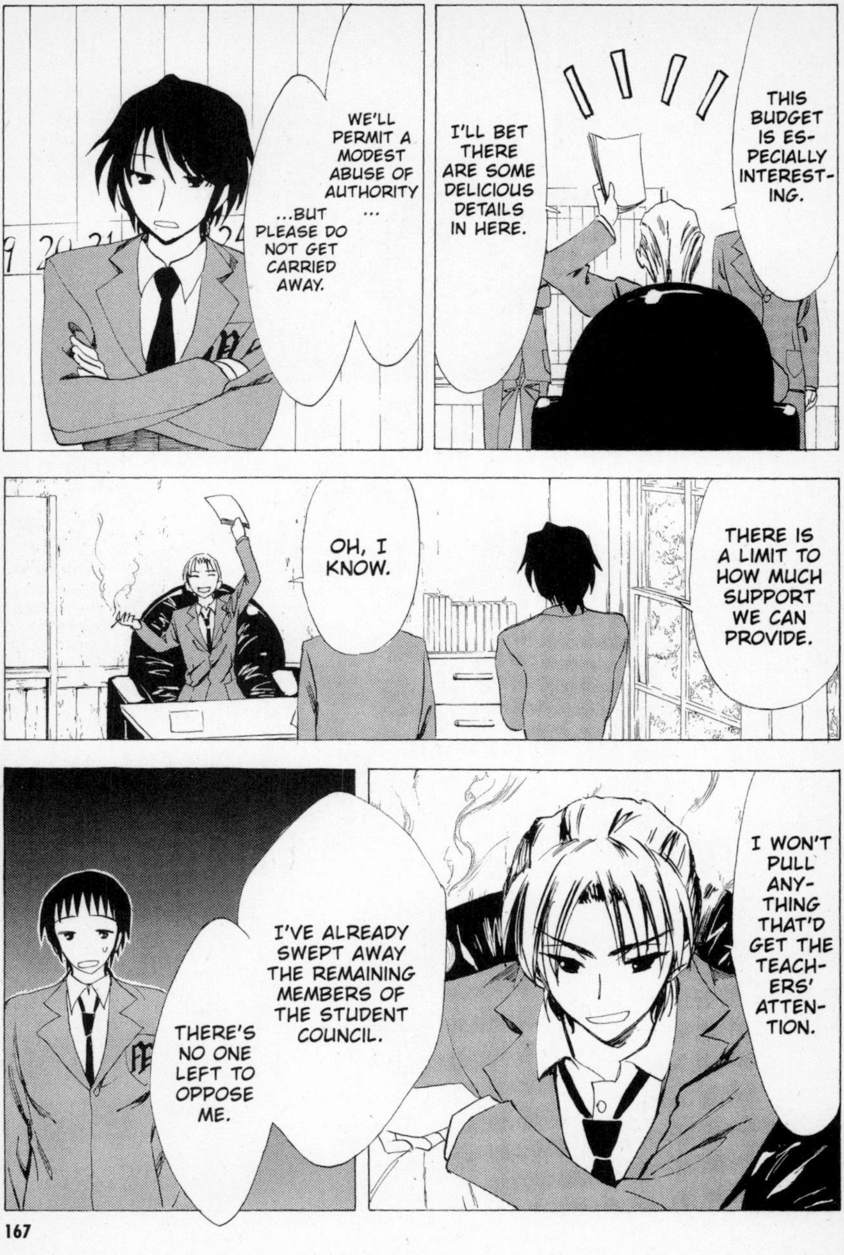
THIS BUDGET IS ES-PECIALLY INTEREST-ING.
I'LL BET THERE ARE SOME DELICIOUS DETAILS IN HERE.
WE'LL PERMIT A MODEST ABUSE OF AUTHORITY ...
...BUT PLEASE DO NOT GET CARRIED AWAY.
THERE IS A LIMIT TO HOW MUCH SUPPORT WE CAN PROVIDE.
OH, I KNOW.
I WON'T PULL ANY-THING THAT'D GET THE TEACH-ERS' ATTEN-TION.
I'VE ALREADY SWEPT AWAY THE REMAINING MEMBERS OF THE STUDENT COUNCIL.
THERE'S NO ONE LEFT TO OPPOSE ME.

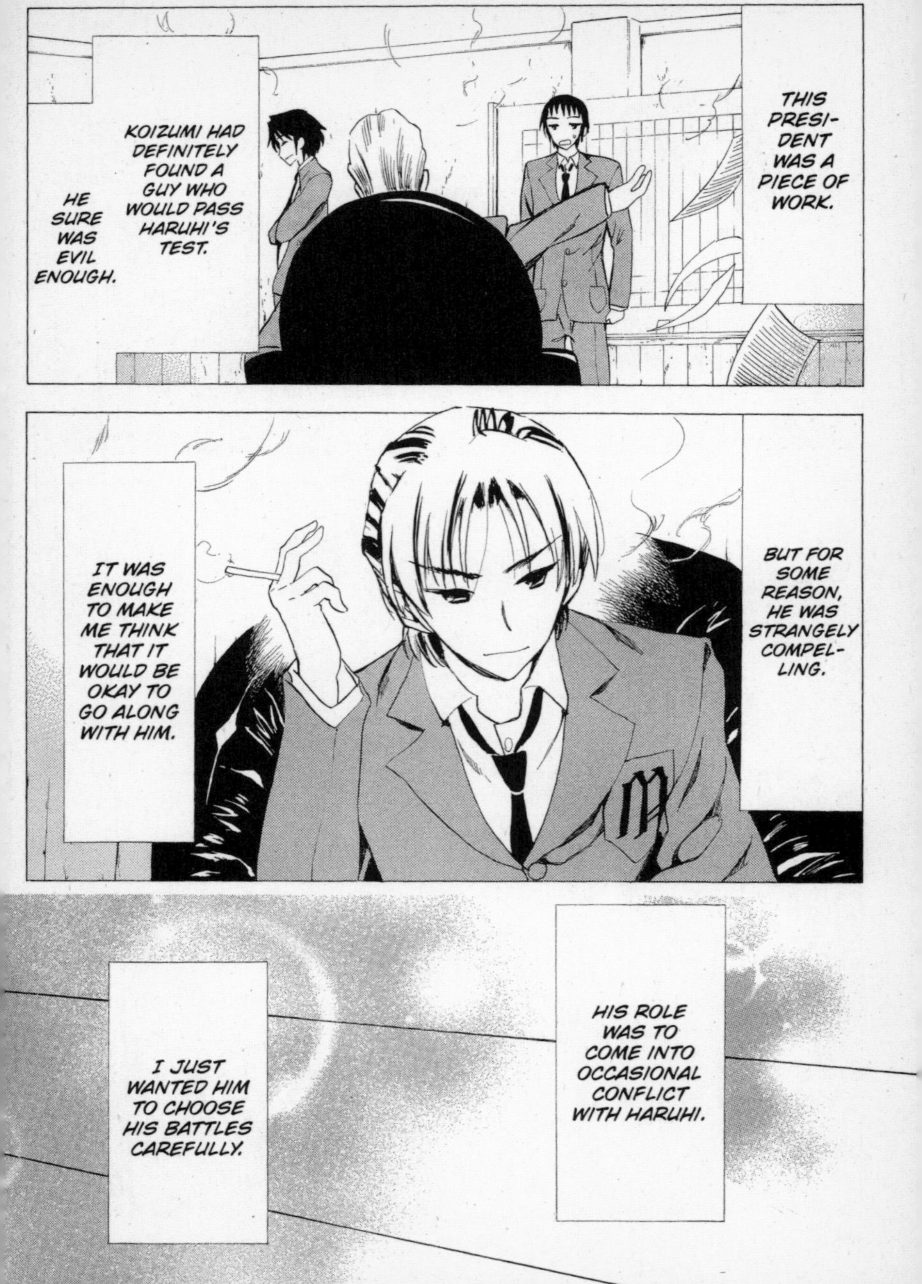
THIS PRESIDENT WAS A PIECE OF WORK.
KOIZUMI HAD DEFINITELY FOUND A GUY WHO WOULD PASS HARUHI'S TEST.
HE SURE WAS EVIL ENOUGH.
BUT FOR SOME REASON, HE WAS STRANGELY COMPELLING.
IT WAS ENOUGH TO MAKE ME THINK THAT IT WOULD BE OKAY TO GO ALONG WITH HIM.
HIS ROLE WAS TO COME INTO OCCASIONAL CONFLICT WITH HARUHI.
I JUST WANTED HIM TO CHOOSE HIS BATTLES CAREFULLY.

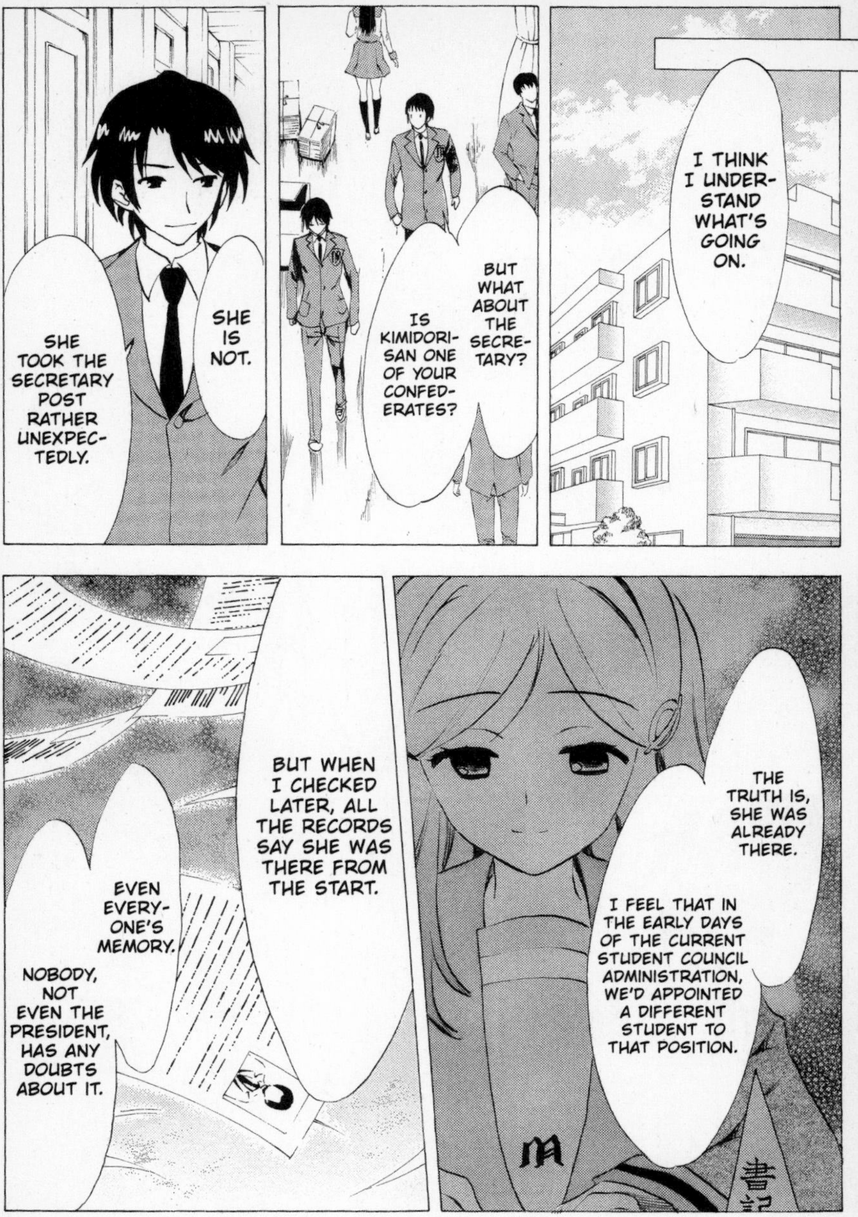
I THINK I UNDERSTAND WHAT'S GOING ON.
BUT WHAT ABOUT THE SECRETARY?
IS KIMIDORI-SAN ONE OF YOUR CONFEDERATES?
SHE IS NOT.
SHE TOOK THE SECRETARY POST RATHER UNEXPECTEDLY.
THE TRUTH IS, SHE WAS ALREADY THERE.
I FEEL THAT IN THE EARLY DAYS OF THE CURRENT STUDENT COUNCIL ADMINISTRATION, WE'D APPOINTED A DIFFERENT STUDENT TO THAT POSITION.
書記
BUT WHEN I CHECKED LATER, ALL THE RECORDS SAY SHE WAS THERE FROM THE START.
EVEN EVERYONE'S MEMORY.
NOBODY, NOT EVEN THE PRESIDENT, HAS ANY DOUBTS ABOUT IT.

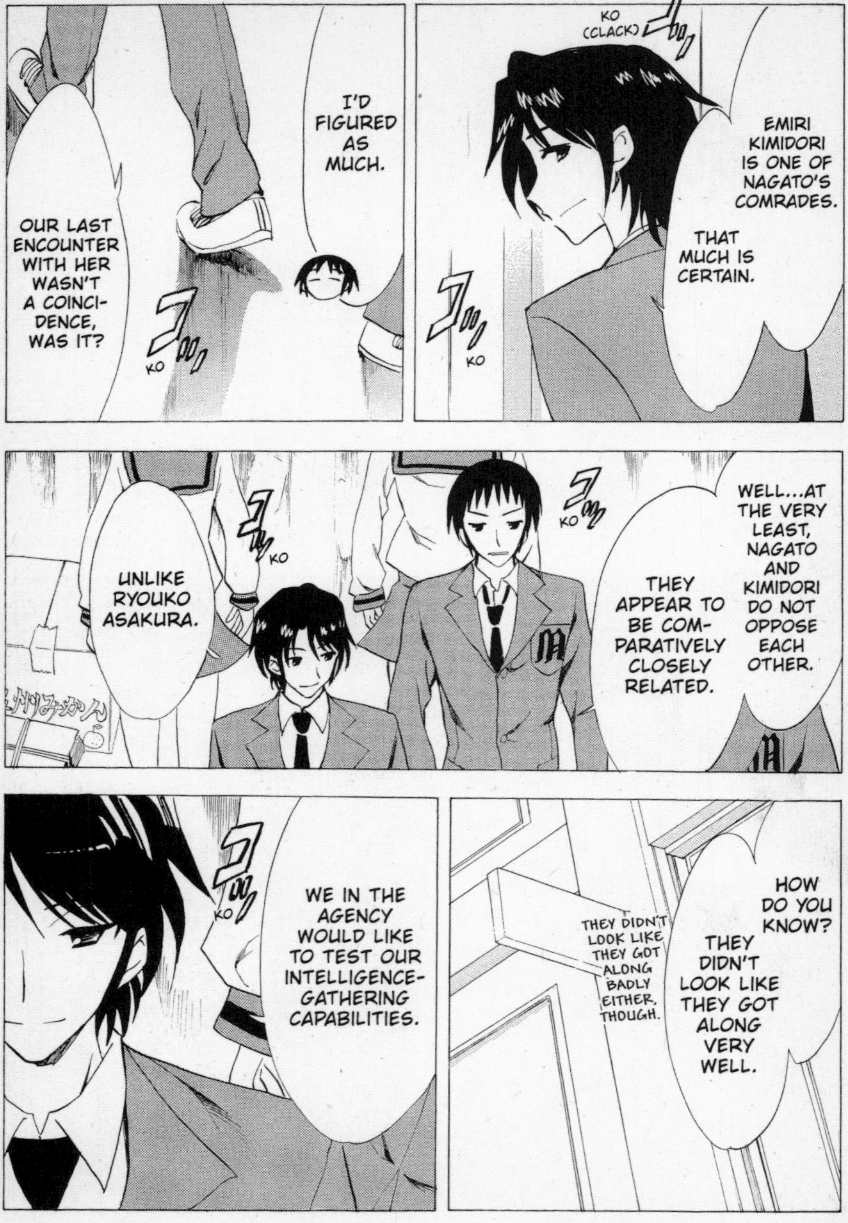
KO (CLACK)
EMIRI KIMIDORI IS ONE OF NAGATO'S COMRADES.
THAT MUCH IS CERTAIN.
KO
I'D FIGURED AS MUCH.
OUR LAST ENCOUNTER WITH HER WASN'T A COINCIDENCE, WAS IT?
KO
KO
WELL...AT THE VERY LEAST, NAGATO AND KIMIDORI DO NOT OPPOSE EACH OTHER.
THEY APPEAR TO BE COMPARATIVELY CLOSELY RELATED.
KO
UNLIKE RYOUKO ASAKURA.
HOW DO YOU KNOW?
THEY DIDN'T LOOK LIKE THEY GOT ALONG VERY WELL.
THEY DIDN'T LOOK LIKE THEY GOT ALONG BADLY EITHER, THOUGH.
KO
WE IN THE AGENCY WOULD LIKE TO TEST OUR INTELLIGENCE-GATHERING CAPABILITIES.

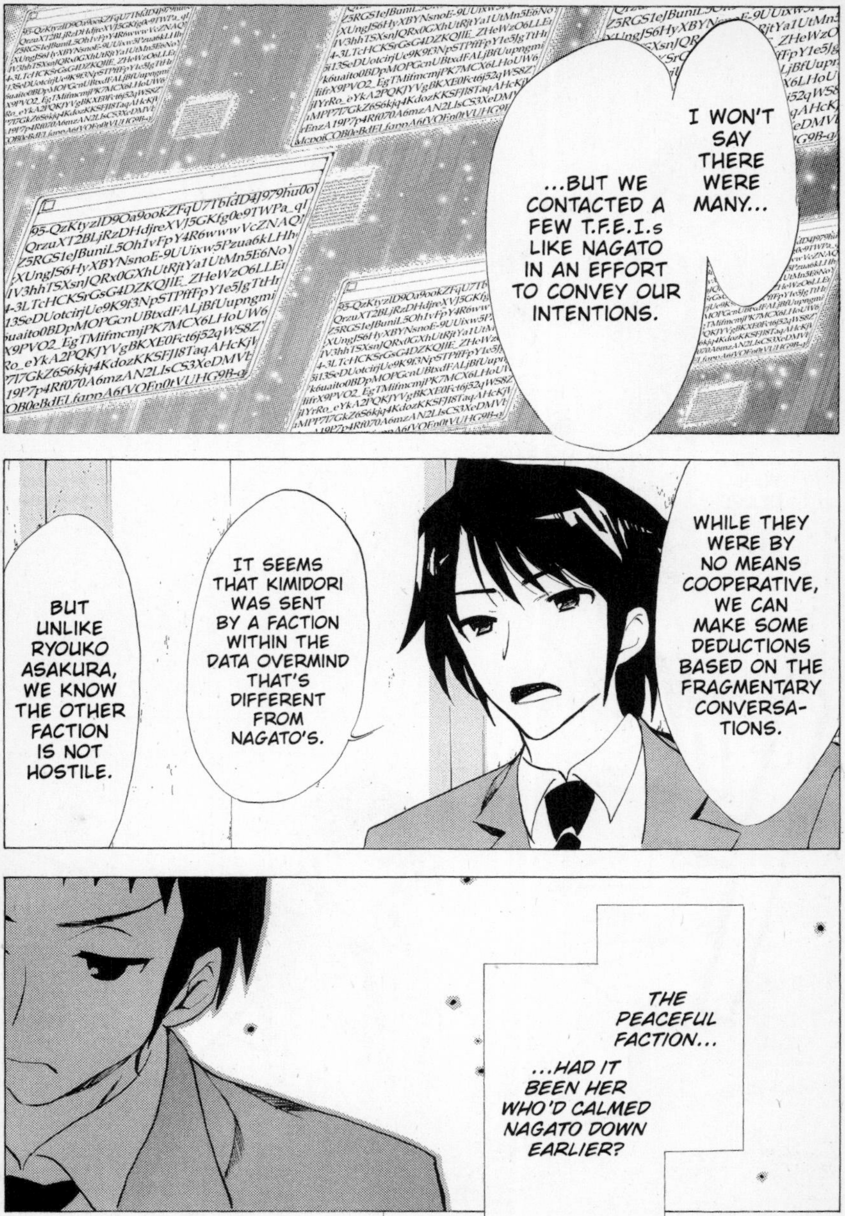
I WON'T SAY THERE WERE MANY...
...BUT WE CONTACTED A FEW T.F.E.I.s LIKE NAGATO IN AN EFFORT TO CONVEY OUR INTENTIONS.
WHILE THEY WERE BY NO MEANS COOPERATIVE, WE CAN MAKE SOME DEDUCTIONS BASED ON THE FRAGMENTARY CONVERSATIONS.
IT SEEMS THAT KIMIDORI WAS SENT BY A FACTION WITHIN THE DATA OVERMIND THAT'S DIFFERENT FROM NAGATO'S.
BUT UNLIKE RYOUKO ASAKURA, WE KNOW THE OTHER FACTION IS NOT HOSTILE.
THE PEACEFUL FACTION...
...HAD IT BEEN HER WHO'D CALMED NAGATO DOWN EARLIER?

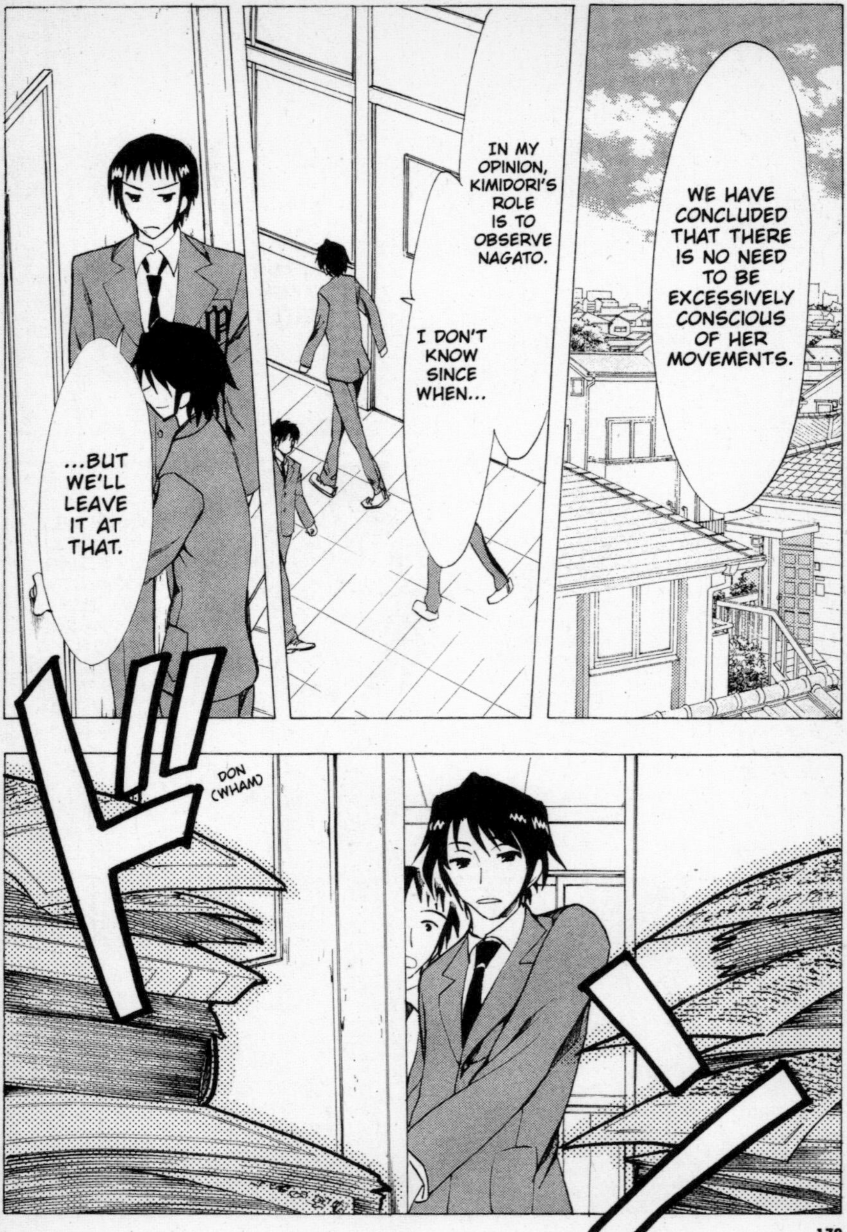
WE HAVE CONCLUDED THAT THERE IS NO NEED TO BE EXCESSIVELY CONSCIOUS OF HER MOVEMENTS.
IN MY OPINION, KIMIDORI'S ROLE IS TO OBSERVE NAGATO.
I DON'T KNOW SINCE WHEN...
...BUT WE'LL LEAVE IT AT THAT.
DON (WHAM)

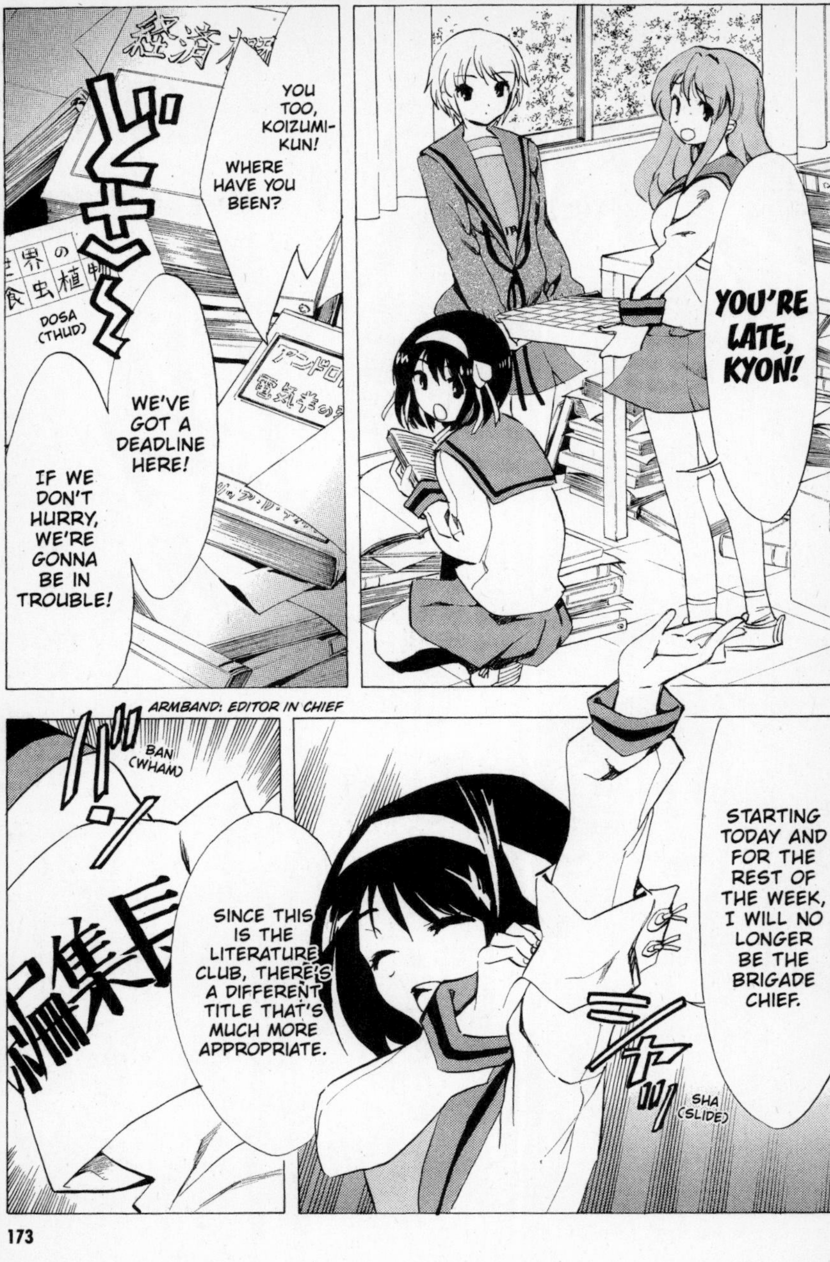
YOU'RE LATE, KYON!
YOU TOO, KOIZUMI-KUN!
WHERE HAVE YOU BEEN?
DOSA (THUD)
WE'VE GOT A DEADLINE HERE!
IF WE DON'T HURRY, WE'RE GONNA BE IN TROUBLE!
STARTING TODAY AND FOR THE REST OF THE WEEK, I WILL NO LONGER BE THE BRIGADE CHIEF.
SHA (SLIDE)
SINCE THIS IS THE LITERATURE CLUB, THERE'S A DIFFERENT TITLE THAT'S MUCH MORE APPROPRIATE.
ARMBAND: EDITOR IN CHIEF
BAN (WHAM)
編集長

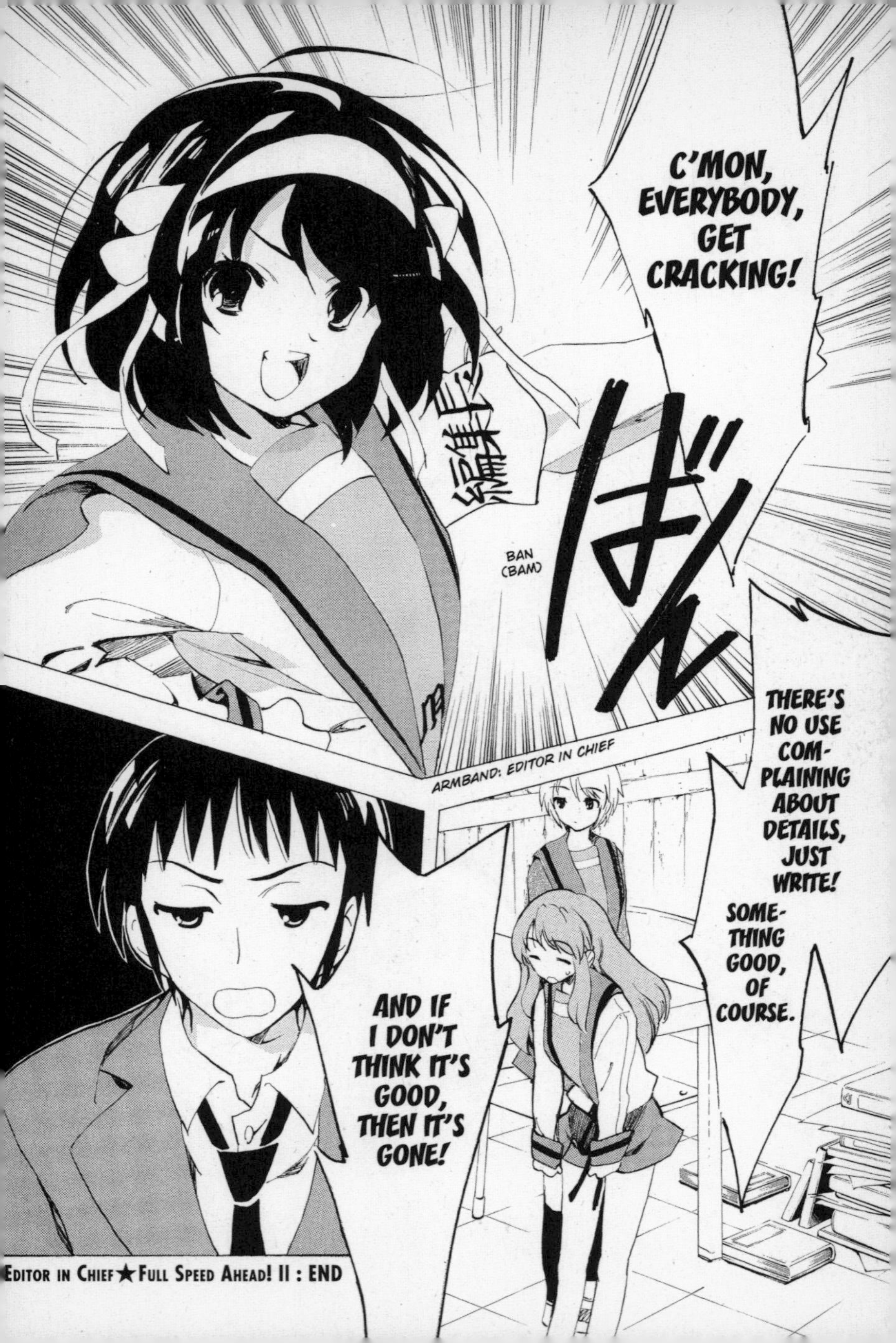
C'MON, EVERYBODY, GET CRACKING!
編集長
ばん
BAN (BAM)
ARMBAND: EDITOR IN CHIEF
THERE'S NO USE COM-PLAINING ABOUT DETAILS, JUST WRITE!
SOME-THING GOOD, OF COURSE.
AND IF I DON'T THINK IT'S GOOD, THEN IT'S GONE!

EDITOR IN CHIEF★FULL SPEED AHEAD! II : END

TO BE CONTINUED

UNDER HARUHI'S DIRECTION, EACH MEMBER DRAWS A RANDOM WRITING ASSIGNMENT...

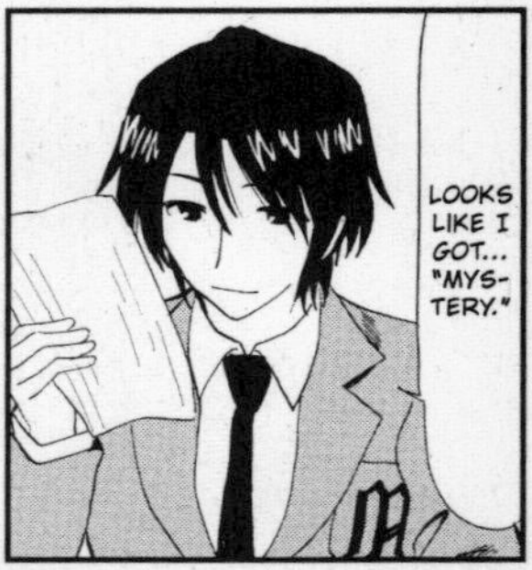
LOOKS LIKE I GOT... "MYSTERY."

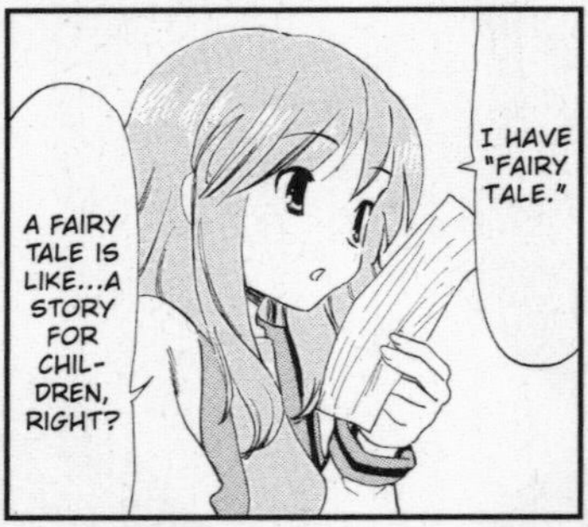
I HAVE "FAIRY TALE."
A FAIRY TALE IS LIKE...A STORY FOR CHILDREN, RIGHT?

PAPER: MYSTERY/HORROR

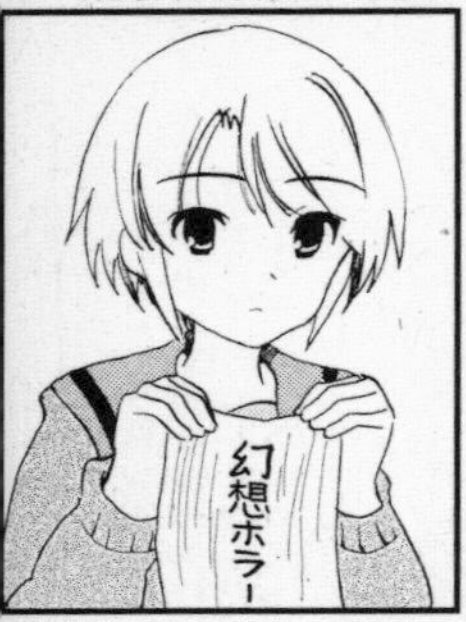
幻想ホラー

KYON'S GENRE TURNS OUT TO BE: "LOVE STORY" ...!!

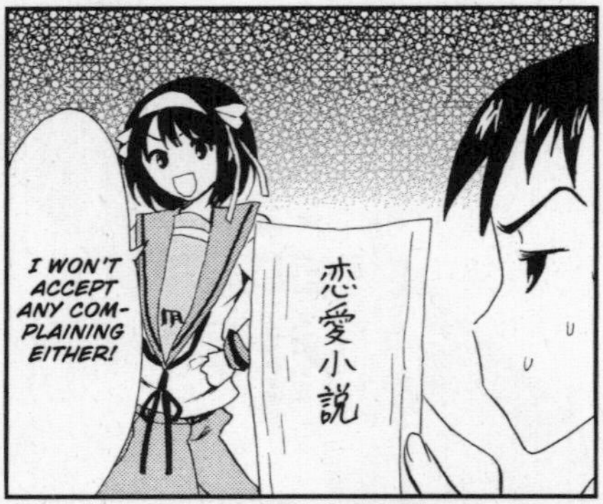
恋愛小説
I WON'T ACCEPT ANY COMPLAINING EITHER!

PAPER: LOVE STORY

AN AGONIZED KYON TURNS TO KOIZUMI FOR HELP AND BEGINS TO WRITE... HIS TRUE-LIFE EXPERIENCES!?

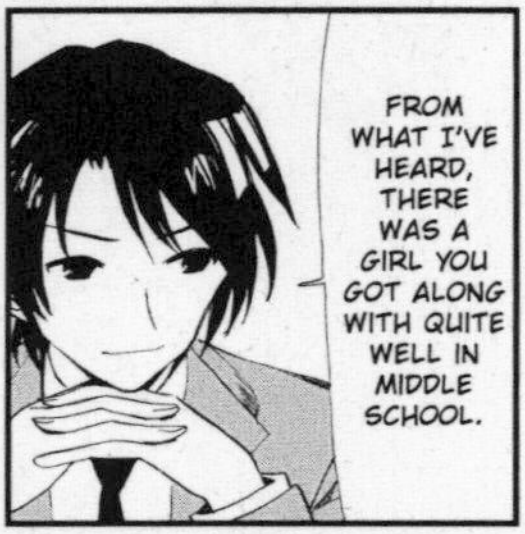
FROM WHAT I'VE HEARD, THERE WAS A GIRL YOU GOT ALONG WITH QUITE WELL IN MIDDLE SCHOOL.

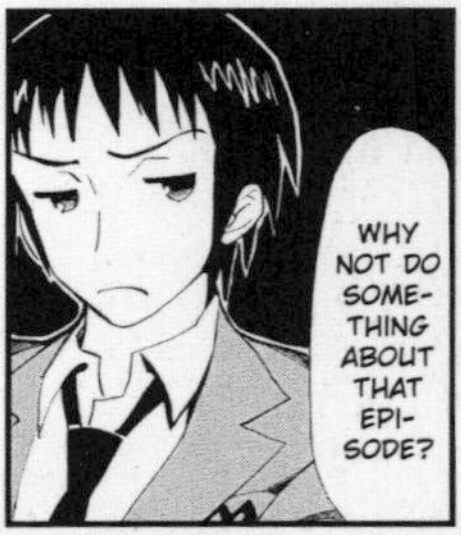
WHY NOT DO SOMETHING ABOUT THAT EPISODE?

AND MORE FROM "THE INDIGNATION OF HARUHI SUZUMIYA!"

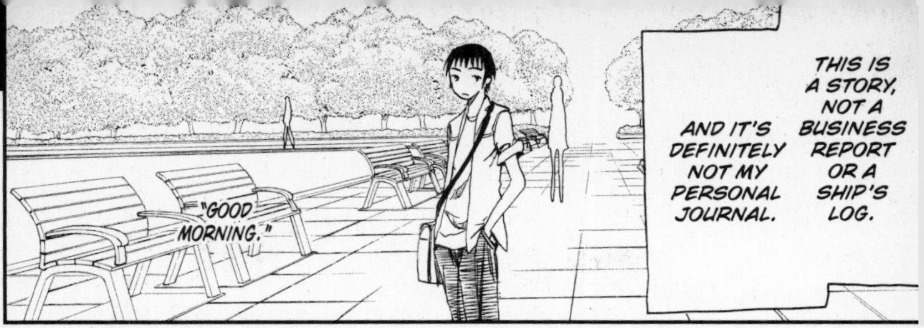
THIS IS A STORY, NOT A BUSINESS REPORT OR A SHIP'S LOG.
AND IT'S DEFINITELY NOT MY PERSONAL JOURNAL.
"GOOD MORNING."

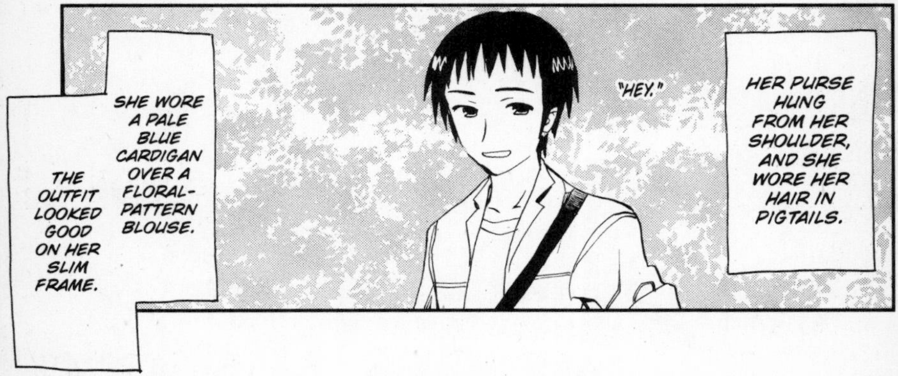
HER PURSE HUNG FROM HER SHOULDER, AND SHE WORE HER HAIR IN PIGTAILS.
"HEY."
SHE WORE A PALE BLUE CARDIGAN OVER A FLORAL-PATTERN BLOUSE.
THE OUTFIT LOOKED GOOD ON HER SLIM FRAME.

BUT THE UNUSUAL CONTENTS OF KYON'S STORY

SEND HARUHI INTO A RAGE!

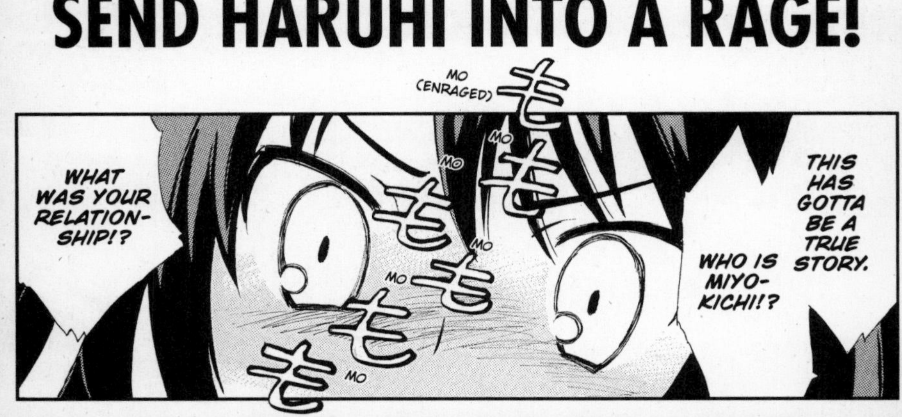
THIS HAS GOTTA BE A TRUE STORY.
WHO IS MIYO-KICHI!?
MO (ENRAGED)
MO
MO
MO
MO
MO
WHAT WAS YOUR RELATION-SHIP!?

NEXT VOLUME:

THE CONCLUSION OF "EDITOR IN CHIEF★FULL SPEED AHEAD!"

THE MELANCHOLY OF HARUHI SUZUMIYA

Original Story: Nagaru Tanigawa
Manga: Gaku Tsugano
Character Design: Noizi Ito

Translation: Paul Starr
Lettering: Alexis Eckerman

SUZUMIYA HARUHI NO YUUTSU Volume 12 © Nagaru TANIGAWA • Noizi ITO 2010 © Gaku TSUGANO 2010. First published in Japan in 2010 by KADOKAWA SHOTEN CO., LTD., Tokyo. English translation rights arranged with KADOKAWA SHOTEN CO., LTD., Tokyo through TUTTLE-MORI AGENCY, INC., Tokyo.

English translation © 2012 by Hachette Book Group, Inc.

Yen Press
Hachette Book Group
237 Park Avenue, New York, NY 10017

www.HachetteBookGroup.com
www.YenPress.com

Yen Press is an imprint of Hachette Book Group, Inc. The Yen Press name and logo are trademarks of Hachette Book Group, Inc.

First Yen Press Edition: May 2012

ISBN: 978-0-316-20946-5

10 9 8 7 6 5 4 3 2

BVG

Printed in the United States of America